Publication as Autobiography

Publication as Autobiography

Occasional and Forsaken Texts
— and Endangered Cinema Species

Scott MacDonald

Sticking Place Books
New York

© Sticking Place Books 2024

Scott MacDonald's website: www.scottmacdonaldcinema.com

A case laminate hardback of this book with color images is available (ISBN 978-1-942782-76-6)

Back cover image: *Shirley—Visions of Reality* © Gustav Deutsch
Photograph © Jerzy Palacz

Designed by Goran Tovilovic

www.stickingplacebooks.com

All rights reserved.
No part of this book may be reproduced, stored in or introduced into a retrieval system, or transmitted, in any form or by any means (electronic, mechanical, photocopying, recording or otherwise) without the written permission of the publishers, except in the case of brief quotations embodied in critical articles or reviews.

ISBN 978-1-942782-75-9

Contents

Foreword by David E. James   i
Introduction   vii

1. 1973   The Confusing Dialogue in Hemingway's "A Clean, Well-Lighted Place"   1
2. 1976   Another Consideration of Larry Gottheim's *Mouches Volante*   11
3. 1977   Repetition as Technique in the Short Stories of Erskine Caldwell   17
4. 1977   J. J. Murphy: In Progress   31
5. 1983   Letters from Scott MacDonald to Marjorie Keller   37
6. 1985   ALL HAN ZON DEK!: A Reading of Emmett Williams' *THE VOY AGE*   43
7. 1986   Frames of Mind: Recent Filmmaking in Central New York   57
8. 1988   Avant-Garde Film: Cinema as Discourse   67
9. 1989   Review of *From the Pole to the Equator* by Yervant Gianikian and Angela Ricci Lucchi   79
10. 1991   Process is Product, Product is Process: Peter Watkins' *The Journey*   87
11. 1994   Catalogue essay on Trinh T. Minh-ha   99
12. 2002   Fade In Fade Out: The Work of Filmmaker Robert Nelson   109
13. 2002   Professional Myopia: How Academe Is Failing Cinema   117
14. 2002   9/11, Critique, and Avant-Garde Film   127
15. 2003   Essay for Shiho Kano (and Taka Iimura: in memoriam)   135
16. 2005   Forward to the 2005 Edition of Amos Vogel's *Film as a Subversive Art* (1974)   143
17. 2014   Nomination to the National Film Registry for James Benning's *13 Lakes* (2004)   153
18. 2015   *My So-Called Life*—A Cineaste's Reading   159
19. 2015   Documenting Devotion: A Brief History of North American CineScenes   207
20. 2015   Essay for DVD release of Gustav Deutsch's *Shirley—Visions of Reality* (2013)   217
21. 2016   Peter Hutton: Hudson River Filmmaker   223
22. 2019   Patrick Clancy's Early Photoscrolls— and (some of) what came later   237

23.	2020	Robert Huot: The Painter as Filmmaker	261
24.	2021	40-Year Diptych	271
25.	2024	Geezer Story	275
26.	2024	*Entanglement*: Going Against the Clock	279
27.	2024	A New Form of Cine-Scholarship: An interview with video-essayist Max Tohline	291

Index 309

Foreword by David E. James

> *C'est ici un livre de bonne foi, lecteur.*
> Michel de Montaigne, *Essais*

Scott MacDonald's contributions to cinema, and especially to artisanal non-commodity cinema, are without compare. Though he has always kept the industrial film clearly in his sights, for more than fifty years he has worked tirelessly and with a uniquely open-minded generosity on behalf of what, following Maya Deren, we think of as film made for love rather than money: variously, avant-garde, experimental, and so on. The results encompass some ninety published essays and almost as many interviews with filmmakers (not all of which have been collected in his, at last count, twenty-two books) and an ongoing teaching career of more than half a century, mostly at liberal arts colleges in upstate New York rather than at research universities replete with graduate students, grants, and other forms of assistance. His scholarship has been additionally sustained by the many exhibitions he curated in museums and art galleries, his assiduous attendance at conferences and festivals (many of which he organized), along with countless hours of screenings as adjuncts to his classes, to which he invited a phylum of visiting filmmakers from all over the world. Re-reading or merely glancing over even a small selection of these texts, one realizes in wonder that his entire adult life has been lived within and for cinema.

Now, foregrounding the role of his writing in all these activities, another volume: *Publication as Autobiography*, a miscellany of occasional texts that appeared in out-of-the-way publications, plus one never-published piece. Altogether his most autobiographical collection, it looks back on a life lived writing about cinema. Excepting perhaps his analysis of concrete poetry and his own forays in that mode included here, the present collection doesn't reveal any major additions to or recantations from the principles, strategies and commitments formulated and elaborated over the immense corpus of his accomplishments. But the span of the composition of the texts from 1973 to 2024, along with the retrospective commentary with which MacDonald presently introduces them, reveal not so much the evolution and only very rarely the revision of earlier positions as the progressive widening of a lifetime's commitment that came very early and virtually fully-formed.

In spring of 1972, during his first year as a literature professor, MacDonald attended a screening of avant-garde films at SUNY Binghamton and soon after another at a summer film institute at Hampshire College.* Together the events turned out to be transformative and more than thirty years later, he revisited them in a crucial autobiographical essay describing how they revealed his life's work to him. A condensed *bildungsroman*, it begins with the sequence of his decisive

---

* The events are described below in both "Avant Garde Film: Cinema as Discourse" and "Entanglement: Going against the Clock—An Essay Intercut with a Conversation," but my discussion quotes from the fuller account in the 2005 essay "Film History and 'Film History'" in MacDonald's *Adventures of Perception* (California, 2009).

enthusiasms: first seeing *King Kong* in his childhood, then the European New Wave of the early 1960s, and later a presentation by Andrew Sarris of Buster Keaton's *The General*. This progress culminated in the two programs mentioned, primarily of then recent U.S. avant-garde films, especially structural films. He found both programs initially frustrating and exhausting, but to his surprise his engrossment in them soon culminated in a Damascene conversion that revealed the possibilities of his own career. Not only was he eventually enthralled by the films, but he realized that "whatever scholarly abilities I had might be of particular use to what seemed the underserved field of avant-garde film." Such epiphanies are common in the biographies of artists, less so of scholars. But MacDonald seems not to have looked back from the vocation of sharing the aesthetic and social richness of his own enlightenment in teaching and otherwise promoting such films; imperative was experiencing them "in a theater with other spectators," that is, in a social event where their import could be discussed by people together, in a community. He clarified his new path via a distinction between "*film history*"—the chronicle of all the films ever produced—and *film history*—the activity that understands these in the context of theatrical film viewing and (subsequently introduced) their other social realizations (what I designate as *cinema*).

A reference to literature illustrates the primacy of the latter over the former. During her lifetime Emily Dickinson published a handful of poems and died virtually unknown. Only the posthumous work of her friends and later the machinery of literary studies and popular enthusiasm secured her recognition as one of the most important of U.S. poets: her promotion, as it were, from "*literary history*" to *literary history*. Dickinson was an inspired analogy; her exclusion from the institutions of her time, her extreme, inflexible formal idiosyncrasies and innovations, and her all but exclusive concern with her own subjectivity together anticipated the conditions of the "poetic film," as the mid-century avant-garde film was often described. Newly conceptualized in socio-historical terms, the scholar's role then became the pro-active participation in the social institutions that once brought poems and now brings films to life in the public arena, especially radical, difficult, and controversial films. To these aesthetic and social communities, MacDonald immediately dedicated his life. One or two other scholars have played similarly multiple roles: the scholarship of Amos Vogel and P. Adams Sitney in the U.S., for example, and David Curtis in the U.K. also flowered in their lifetime involvement in the creation of alternative cinemas. But once MacDonald perceived his vocation, his road lay open and he committed himself to it unconditionally and productively. His role in the manifold institutions of cinema, in *film history*, has been as generative as that of any of the filmmakers he has so single-mindedly explored, interviewed, and otherwise supported: a unique life, well lived in cinema with unique generosity and consequence.

MacDonald's transition from a "literature person" to a "cinema person" ("Geezer Story") coincided with the late 1960's generational shift that saw literature professors creating new college film programs. These usually privileged the feature film, moving as MacDonald had, from Hollywood classics to European New Waves and thence to feminism and other identity politics and the mostly French theoretical systems imported to legitimize these. MacDonald was distinguished from these colleagues by his interest, not in narrative which commonly subtended their move from literature to the feature film, but in the non-narrative visual specificity of concrete poetry. When he did write about canonical novelists, as he did for his M.A. and Ph.D. degrees, he focused on experimental textual elements in them. The early essays reproduced here on Ernest Hemingway's idiosyncratic typological reproduction of dialogue and on Erskine Caldwell's use of verbal counterpoint (sandwiched as they are here between essays on structural filmmakers, Larry Gottheim and J. J. Murphy!) both emphasize formal elements in literature akin to Gottheim and Murphy's own materialist procedures in film. MacDonald could not have known at the time, but symptomatically these two filmmakers also introduced what would eventually mature into the fundamental social and intellectual dynamic of his work. His interest in fictional dialogue in Hemingway, he tells us, fed into his "decade-long fascination with conducting and editing dialogues with filmmakers," while in some of Caldwell's stories "heavy repetition causes conversations to take on symbolic implications." As his commitment to cinema expanded, the generative generic and epistemological foundation of his work became the *conversation*.

First, conversation is the basis of MacDonald's conception of the total structure of cinema. At the time of his intervention, the avant-garde was so marginal that only the proposal of its radical alterity to the industry could secure sympathetic consideration of its own specificity; the two modes of production were supposed to be entirely distinct, each unaffected by the other. In the introduction to his first collection of interviews, a leap of empathic projection led him to propose to the contrary that the filmmakers who interested him did not all accept that binarization; rather they perceived the dominant cinema "as a set of culturally conditioned and accepted approaches to cinema—a cultural text—to be analyzed from within the medium of film itself."* Rather than anticipating the commercial cinema, in certain respects, the avant-garde gnawed at its heels. The range of this newly-formulated dialogic cinema explored in that first collection consequently ranged from the degree zero of Hollis Frampton, whose films "owe almost nothing to the history of commercial film," to George Kuchar, for whose films the "conventions of the commercial movies provide a formal structure." Between them in "critical cinema," he introduced J. J. Murphy, John Waters and Bruce Conner, all having quite specific and various engagements with commercial film.

Gradually the scope of MacDonald's investigations widened. Initially he focused on his local up-state New York community, most of them within driving distance, then began interviewing filmmakers in North America at large, eventually approaching English (Peter Watkins), Austrian (Martin Arnold), Portuguese (Susana de Sousa Dias), Iranian (Shirin Neshat) and other foreign artists. In tandem with this expanded frame of reference, his initial focus on the U.S. avant-garde loosened, most crucially with his turn to avant-garde/

---

* *A Critical Cinema: Interviews with Independent Filmmakers* (Berkeley: University of Californian Press, 1988), 1.

documentary hybrids and, beginning with an interview with Todd Haynes, eventually to commercial filmmakers. As these revealed more and more interrelationships, the field of cinema began to resemble a global *parlement*, a conference of many discourses where with the help of sympathetic scholars, otherwise unrecognized filmmakers might have a voice, especially those excluded from other conversations.

MacDonald recapitulated his vision of the interactions and interdependencies among the various components of cinema in his own role in the interviews that form the core of his achievement. In each case he approaches his subject as neither a submissive subordinate nor a combative interrogator, but rather as a partner in the shared enterprise of elucidation and revelation. Each conversation is introduced by his succinct summary of the filmmaker's career to date and, given the difficulty of systematic study of the elusive, poorly distributed avant-garde film, he always reveals an astonishing command of the filmmaker's entire oeuvre. His own knowledge and forethought make each a shared composition that proves his "commitment not just to interviewing, but to a conception of an interview with an accomplished filmmaker as a work of literature."

MacDonald's conversations with his filmmakers recur in yet a third register as the conversation between MacDonald and his readers. Perhaps less so than fifty years ago, academically approved scholarship is still pseudo-scientific, masquerading as observation or analysis uncontaminated by the writer's subjectivity and personal history. Such a pose never seems never to have been a possibility or even an interest for him. Though he's hardly present in the essay on Hemingway, he does appear in the second essay reproduced here, his first on film: "As one grows more familiar with [Gottheim's] *Mouches Volantes*, certain patterns of relationship do become distinguishable."

From this point on, MacDonald's own consciousness and experience are the point of origin and the primary arbiter of his composition. Though over time he more readily admits a spiritual dimension in film, his criticism is less Anatole France's "adventures of his soul among masterpieces" so much as the adventures of his analytic intelligence and historical self-consciousness—in short, the wisdom—that his ongoing commitments accrue. Like the classic essayist, he begins from his own experience and his exposition moves via personal enunciation and personal anecdotes. In his accounts of his own itinerary around and through the issues under discussion, his own voice is familiarly straightforward, using a frankly Thoreauvian plain language that avoids both cliché and jargon. The terms of engagement, moreover, mobilize an entire phenomenology; the conversations are both spatially and temporally specific.

Among the most celebrated of MacDonald's contribution to cinema studies has been his insistence on the importance of the environment and of geography. During the "spatial turn" in the humanities and well before cinema studies' current ecological considerations, his essay "Towards an Ecocinema"* established the terms of this engagement. Almost twenty years earlier the essay reprinted here, "'Frames of Mind': Recent Filmmaking in Central New York," introduced his concern with his proximate environment, Central New York State, and the

---

* *ISLE: Interdisciplinary Studies in Literature and Environment*, 11.2 (Summer 2004), 107-132.

interplay between local geography and local institutions that characterized the work of a dozen major filmmaker, all then internationally known even as they were locally obscure. Later, this essay's historical and theoretical innovations matured: on the one hand, into his own documentations of cinema studies at SUNY Binghamton (*Binghamton Babylon: Voices from the Cinema Department, 1967-1977*) and several other institutions where the avant-garde and especially the avant-doc flourished, and, on the other, his own magisterial and seminal overview of cinema and geography, *The Garden in the Machine: A Field Guide to Independent Films about Place* (Berkeley: University of California Press, 2001). But just as *Publication as Autobiography* underscores how MacDonald's essays have been underwritten by the places in which he lived, so the sequence of them illuminates the historical developments in cinema and cinema studies over the half-century of his intervention in them.

Several of these have been crucial to his own work. "Avant-Garde Film: Cinema as Discourse," for example, debates the importance of the academy to the avant-garde despite its marginality there, while "Professional Myopia: How Academe is Failing Cinema" addresses the greatest crisis in avant-garde cinema during his involvement: the demise of 16mm film. But apart from the widespread deterioration of almost all extant 16mm films and the loss of certain classic works that later technologies could not reproduce (Anthony McCall's *Line Describing a Cone* is one he often cites), digital technologies have not proven as categorically deleterious to independent filmmaking as the first appearances of VHS/DVD initially portended. Indeed, over the past twenty years they have sustained a previously unimaginable ecumenicity in independent moving image production: a global digital avant-garde that has enfranchised many people who previously had no role in cinema except consumption.

And in at least one case new possibilities have emerged that radically enhance the cultural communities that have inspired MacDonald for so long. As introduced in the conversation with Max Tohline, the *video essay* now appears as a new avant-garde with radically amplified utopian possibilities. As a video-essayist, the scholar can at last converse with films and with filmmakers in a new mode that transcends the division between them. And you can be sure that Scott is already at work in this new field, one whose possibilities retroactively seem to have always been implicit in his vision: a conversation undertaken in good faith.

Born in Laxton, England, David E. James has spent most of his adult life in Los Angeles. His most recent books are *Rock 'N' Film: Cinema's Dance with Popular Music* and *Power Misses II: Cinema, Asian and Modern*.

Introduction

When Paul Cronin asked if I would consider putting together a collection of my writings that had never been published or that had been published in catalogues or periodicals that even most cineastes would probably not be able to find, I was resistant. I wondered who, if anyone, would be likely to read such a book. My writing has been mostly interviews and articles about independent filmmakers and filmmaking: early on, what had come to be called "avant-garde film," and later, a range of avant-garde and documentary film with some forays into feature entertainments. My mission as a film writer has always been focused on helping accomplished, but under-appreciated films and filmmakers find their way to the audiences they deserve. As I thought about Cronin's suggestion, I realized that taking on this new project might contribute to my earlier efforts—and decided that such a book could be worth a try.

As I examined my vita and my files to see which essays might make sense to include in the book I was beginning to imagine, I found only two essays that had not been published: one that had been rejected and that I'd given up on; and the other, a chapter for a prospective book edited by a scholar who had not, at least so far, seen that project through. I did find any number of "occasional" essays, written for art shows, film retrospectives, and other one-time events that had generated catalogues that were now available only to those who'd attended or had known about those events. I also read, for the first time in decades, some of my earliest attempts to write publishable essays about literature and avant-garde film, often for fledgling journals that, in some cases, lasted for a few issues and could now be found only with difficulty. If these essays were limited, they did evoke a certain period, the 1970s-1980s, and at least one person's discovery of films that were simultaneously works of cinematic art and critiques of film history itself. I also realized that certain of my earliest publications—not about film but about literary accomplishments—probably had some input into the kinds of writing about independent film I've been doing for going on fifty years.

In the end, since the essays that seemed worth including in this new book spanned my decades of teaching and writing about cinema, I decided that organizing this book chronologically might provide some coherence and, perhaps, some insight into the emergence, beginning during the 1970s, of what was a new academic undertaking: the field of cinema studies, now cinema and media studies. My contributions to this field are obviously one thread in what would become the extensive weave of this history, but the contributions of others are, in many instances, evoked and contextualized by the essays collected

Some personal background might be useful. Before I became a "film person," I was, much to my parents' disappointment, a DePauw University English major. During my high school years, in the wake of Sputnik, mathematics had seemed both more important and more practical to my parents, and more exciting and more fun to my high-school self. My time away from home (this was an era well before cell phones, even before inexpensive long-distance phone conversations) helped me understand that for me the literary arts were more important, maybe even more practical. Cinema would come later, though even then, I was interested enough in films that I often walked alone to the two local movie theaters in Greencastle, Indiana. I remember loving *The Magnificent Seven* (1960) and being outraged by *8½* (1963).

I have a vivid memory of being part of a small group of English majors standing outside a classroom building in 1963 or 1964 with a professor (Clem Williams, I believe, who taught a memorable two-semester course in the British novel), who said something like, "I think it would be interesting to have a course in the movies." We students burst out laughing at the absurdity of such a notion—as if cinema could be taken seriously the way we took Milton, Wordsworth, Byron, Browning, and Jane Austen, George Eliot, and Thomas Hardy. And James Joyce!

In graduate school at the University of Florida (1964-1970), I expanded my understanding of English literature and was excited to be able to take American literature more seriously. As an undergraduate, I had seen, with few exceptions, only limited respect for American literature; great literature in English was *British* literature. At Florida, I took courses on Edmund Spenser *and* Emily Dickinson, in pre-Shakespearian drama, in British eighteenth-century poetry, *and* modern American fiction—and I wrote my M.A. and Ph.D. theses on Ernest Hemingway.

Simultaneously, however, like so many in my generation, I was increasingly fascinated with the many new kinds of film that were becoming available: feature narrative films from Europe, India, Japan, many of them demonstrating alternatives to traditional Hollywood genre filmmaking and in some cases influencing a new era of American feature filmmaking. And I was seeing new forms of documentary made possible by sync-sound shooting, plus a few "experimental" forms of filmmaking (that I was slow to embrace). When the Humanities chair at Florida asked who might be willing to teach a course in film—students were apparently demanding such a course—I volunteered.

Ironically, partly because I'd taught that one class in "film appreciation" during my final year as a graduate student, I was able to secure a job at what was then Utica College of Syracuse University (now Utica University) by agreeing to teach courses in modern American literature, first-year expository writing, along with a course in film history. As a tenure-track faculty person, I was immediately faced with two challenges. By 1971, American academe had become a publish-or-perish world. My first publications were essays based on chapters of my dissertation, "Narrative Perspective in the Short Stories of Ernest Hemingway" (University of Florida, 1970), one of which is included in this collection: "The Confusing Dialogue in Hemingway's 'A Clean, Well-Lighted Place': A Final Word?" That the text of what had become perhaps Hemingway's most canonical short story had been changed (without Hemingway's approval; he died in 1961) because some academics assumed Hemingway didn't know the "rule" that indenting during conversational dialogue meant a new speaker was now speaking seemed appalling to me, so appalling that I visited the office of the Scribner's editor to complain—only to be told that young scholars needed to have common sense! I trusted Hemingway more than the academics who'd corrected him, which may have had something to do with the kinds of cinema scholarship I would come to do.

The second, more difficult challenge was that I was teaching film history in what was essentially a brand-new field, with no formal training. Given limited access to much of cinema history—this is before videotape, DVDs, Blu-rays, even before retrospectives devoted to cinema history— I struggled. I had begun to use Andrew Sarris' *The American Cinema: Directors and Directions: 1929-1968* (New York: Dutton, 1968) as my guide to American films and was attending the "foreign films" that, in the early 1970s were sometimes showing in theaters. And when I discovered, mostly by accident, that Central New York State was where a good many "independent filmmakers" were living, working, and teaching, I found my way to them, and soon realized that my scholarly efforts could perhaps be of service to these filmmakers and their work, much of which I found brilliant and fascinating. When my first interviews and short essays about lesser-known cinematic accomplishments found outlets in the new cinema journals that were popping up, I was excited to think that my work could make a difference in the general awareness of this work.

Even when I began to focus my writing on cinema, I didn't entirely leave literature behind. Suddenly, my literary background seemed valuable in ways I couldn't have foreseen. My experience writing about Hemingway helped me gradually develop my writing chops; and more specifically, my fascination with Hemingway's focus on dialogue as action in his stories and novels—a focus evident also in the writings of Henry James, Stephen Crane, Gertrude Stein, Erskine Caldwell, Richard Wright and other writers I'd studied and was teaching—helped me become serious about crafting publishable conversations with filmmakers.

Further, since I was now from rural Central New York, a newcomer often traveling to New York City to interview filmmakers far more sophisticated than I felt, my experiences studying eighteenth-century literature at Florida provided a useful, if tongue-in-cheek metaphor. When I was in graduate school, Truman Capote's *In Cold Blood* (1966) was being discussed as a non-fiction novel. One engaging Florida professor suggested that James Boswell's *The Life of Samuel Johnson* (1791) could be understood as the first nonfiction novel. In his biography of Johnson, Boswell makes himself a character from the sticks of Scotland, and Johnson, the brilliant London sophisticate. I thought maybe I could function as a Boswell to my interview subjects' Samuel Johnsons!

The essays and other writings in *Publication as Autobiography* are organized chronologically according to the year when each was first published. Each chapter begins with a brief introduction that explains why I've included the piece and provides a bit of context, both historical and personal. Successive chapters implicitly reference the evolution of my general interests, my particular fascinations, and my approaches as an interviewer/writer, as well as the evolving nature of my prose. Re-reading the essays allowed me to recognize that much has changed for me over the years, but also that much has not.

As I worked through the writings I've assembled for *Publication as Autobiography*, at least one central theme became increasingly obvious. Many of the films and the film experiences I've enjoyed and admired, and have taught and written about, have become increasingly threatened by recent cultural and technological changes: most obviously, by the gradual, then relentless disappearance of what, for more than fifty years, was the fundamental apparatus for both classroom screenings and the public presentation avant-garde film: 16mm projection. Of course, new methods of preserving and retrieving film have also developed, as well as new and exciting kinds of "avant-garde" production—along with less naïve assumptions about the possible longevity of much of the cinema I have been committed to.

The concluding chapters of this collection—a visual poem ("40-year Diptych"); a bit of semi-flash nonfiction, "Geezer Story"; "*Entanglement*: Going against the Clock," a recent essay on my first interviewee, Larry Gottheim; and an extended interview with media scholar, video-essayist, Max Tohline—are meant to suggest that *Publication as Autobiography* is, for me, less a conclusion, a kind of summing-up, than a background for new considerations of what audiovisual media can be and do. When I wrote my essay on Hemingway's "A Clean, Well-lighted Place," fifty years ago, then my earliest essays on film, I could not have imagined that I would be writing about cinema and interviewing media-makers in my eighty-second year. Becoming an old man has been a surprise; it seems to have happened so fast! And it has become for me surprisingly full of unexpected excitements—both new ways of thinking about older interests and fascinations with new projects and new kinds of media creativity.

In the end, I decided to leave the original essays themselves pretty much as they were, with only minor changes to make the pieces a bit more readable for a contemporary audience. In the digital era, for example, paragraphing has generally shortened: a page-long paragraph now seems excessive. I've corrected spelling and minor snafus in punctuation—indications of specific changes are evident in various chapter introductions. Here and there, I've added a [bracketed] comment to correct what has become an obvious oversight or mistake, and a few times I've changed a word when it's clear that the current meaning of the word is so different from what it originally meant that to leave things as they were would be to undermine both my earlier and current understanding. Terminology for the world(s) of cinema that have been the subjects of my essays has always been a challenge. I hope that my use of "independent film," "avant-garde film," "experimental film," and "video essay" does not cause frustration or confusion; in particular instances, one or another term has seemed slightly more accurate and relevant than the others.

In "Sophistication," the penultimate story in Sherwood Anderson's 1919 book, *Winesburg, Ohio*, Anderson's narrator says of protagonist George Willard, "There is a time in the life of every boy where he for the first time takes a backward view of life. Perhaps that is the moment when he crosses the line into manhood." Of course, I passed into something like adulthood long ago, and I am fully aware that a different "line" awaits me down the road. As a result, I've been especially grateful for this opportunity to take a backward look at my publishing life. As a young person, I was lucky (and fortunate and privileged) enough to be able to find a passion that, for more than fifty years, has provided both occupation and pleasure. I'm well beyond conventional retirement age, fundamentally because I cannot imagine giving up the pleasures of teaching and writing about cinema. Growing old, I've recognized that my immersion in these pleasures has become as much of who I am, as fully a part of my autobiography, as my ongoing attempts to be a loving and effective parent, spouse, relative, neighbor, friend, and colleague.

I hope at least some readers will find this collection of interest, and that making these writings available will contribute to a broader recognition of remarkable cinematic accomplishments and to younger audiences' awareness of the achievements of film artists whose names they don't recognize and whose work they may never have heard of.

Many thanks to David LaRocca for his editing; to David James for his very kind forward; and to Mona Dunn for her assistance with the book's imagery. I am deeply grateful for a generous subvention from Hamilton College's Dean of Faculty office (special thanks to Dean Penny Yee). Thanks also to Hamilton colleagues Yvonne Schick, Bret Olsen, and Benjamin Widiss. And, as always, heartfelt thanks to Patricia Reichgott O'Connor for a half-century of support.

STUDIES IN AMERICAN FICTION

Department of English   Northeastern University
Volume 1   Spring 1973   Number 1

Contents

Articles

David L. Carson, "Ralph Ellison Twenty Years After" — 1

James F. Smith, Jr., "A Stereotyped Archetype: E. E. Cummings' Jean Le Negre" — 24

J. Donald Crowley, "The Design Of Hawthorne's *Twice-Told Tales*" — 35

Ruth Sullivan and Stewart Smith, "Narrative Stance in Kate Chopin's *The Awakening*" — 62

James Nagel, "An Annotated Bibliography of Selected Recent Books on American Fiction" — 76

Notes

Scott MacDonald, "The Confusing Dialogue in Hemingway's 'A Clean, Well-Lighted Place': A Final Word?" — 93

Randall H. Waldron, "Prefiguration in 'The Beast in the Jungle'" — 101

John B. Rosenman, "A Note on William Faulkner's *As I Lay Dying*" — 104

John Stark, "'The Cassock' Chapter in *Moby-Dick* and the Theme of Literary Creativity" — 105

1973

The Confusing Dialogue in Hemingway's "A Clean, Well-Lighted Place": A Final Word?

I've begun this collection with my second published essay, "The Confusing Dialogue in Hemingway's 'A Clean, Well-Lighted Place': A Final Word?" because, looking back, I can see that my early interest in fictional dialogue ultimately fed into my decades-long fascination with conducting and editing dialogues with filmmakers. Further, just as I've long been fascinated with those filmmakers who have been willing to question traditional cinematic conventions and to experiment with the nature of cinema, I admired Hemingway because he was willing to experiment with the nature of written fiction and nonfiction. This essay was originally instigated because a canonical Hemingway story had been altered, not because Hemingway wanted it changed, but because certain literary critics convinced Hemingway's publisher that the story needed to conform to a particular literary "rule." Since various "corrected" versions of "A Clean, Well-Lighted Place" remain in circulation, along with Hemingway's version, this essay seems as relevant now as it felt in 1973—and if not directly about cinema, important for my subsequent writing about films that, over the decades, many viewers and critics have tended to find "against the rules" of filmmaking.

* * *

In his generally sensible, but somewhat precipitant article, "Is Hemingway's Well-Lighted Place Really Clean Now?" Charles E. May shows how the long critical debate about the confusing dialogue in Hemingway's "A Clean, Well-Lighted Place" resulted in Charles Scribner's Sons changing the text of the story.[1] Until recently "A Clean, Well-Lighted Place" was printed so that near the end of the long exchange which has caused so much confusion, the younger waiter says, "His niece looks after him," and the older waiter responds, "I know. You said she cut him down." In the last few years, however, the passage has been printed so that the younger waiter says, "His niece looks after him. You said she cut him down," and the older waiter responds, "I know."

Clearly this is a crucial difference. By changing the identity of the waiter who knows about the attempted suicide, Scribner's has altered much of the story. One would expect that a change of this magnitude in one of the most highly respected and widely read of twentieth-century short stories would be based either on a request by Hemingway himself or on evidence from a manuscript of the story. Unfortunately, neither was the case. As May points out, the change was apparently a result of the critical article "Tidying Up Hemingway's Clean Well-Lighted Place" in which John V. Hagopian concluded that modifying the text was the only way of satisfactorily solving the difficulties caused by the dialogue.[2]

Hagopian recognized that to assume the passage was correct as originally published, it is necessary to suppose that in two instances during the exchange between the two waiters, Hemingway ignores conventional dialogue expectations and has a single speaker say two consecutive indented lines of dialogue. Hagopian refused to accept this possibility, he said, because it was not the simplest solution to the problem, because he felt there was no supporting evidence in the text, and because of his contention that nowhere else in Hemingway's fiction is such a device used even occasionally. As May suggests, however, Hagopian's arguments simply don't hold water. The contention that a change in the text is the simplest way to solve the problem of the confusing passage is clearly ridiculous. Obviously, to alter a text and develop a wholly new interpretation of a story is more complicated than to suppose that Hemingway failed to follow normal conventions in a passage of dialogue. May also points up the weakness of Hagopian's contention that there is nothing in the text itself to support the suggestion that in two instances a single speaker says two consecutive indented lines. A careful look at the text shows that it is quite possible that the younger waiter says, "He's drunk now" and then, after a pause, continues with the next indented line, "He's drunk every night"; and that later in the same passage the older waiter says, "He must be eighty years old" and then after a pause continues, "Anyway I should say he was eighty."[3] The one important weakness in May's article is his failure to prove that, despite what Hagopian says, Hemingway does ignore normal dialogue conventions in other works.

May cites a passage from *A Farewell to Arms* in which he believes that Hemingway has a character speak several consecutive indented lines. In the passage Rinaldi and Henry are discussing Catherine Barkley:

> "I will send her. Your lovely cool goddess. English goddess. My God what would a man do with a woman like that except worship her? What else is an Englishwoman good for?"
> "You are an ignorant foul-mouthed dago."
> "A what?"
> "An ignorant wop."
> "Wop. You are a frozen-faced...wop."
> "You are ignorant. Stupid." I saw that word pricked him and kept on.
> "Uninformed. Inexperienced, stupid from inexperience."[4]

May apparently feels that Henry says "An ignorant wop" and both the following statements. While it may not be impossible to read the passage in this way, May's interpretation is strained and un-necessary. There is nothing in the text which indicates that Rinaldi does not say, "Wop. You are a frozen-faced... wop." In fact, the repetition of the single word "Wop" and the pause indicated by the ellipsis suggests the Italian's difficulty in coming to grips with Henry's American slang. Further, the use of "frozen-faced" seems to be Rinaldi's mocking prediction of what will happen to Frederic Henry as a result of being in contact with a "cool" Englishwoman. The passage, in other words, is best read in the conventional manner.

Though May fails to support his belief that Hemingway ignores normal dialogue conventions, this contention can and should be substantiated. If enough critics can be made aware of the weakness of Hagopian's arguments, it may be possible to convince Scribner's that their revision of "A Clean, Well-Lighted Place" was a mistake.

As has been mentioned, Hagopian's arguments are based to a significant extent on his contention that "nowhere else in *The Short Stories of Ernest Hemingway*... is there an instance of a reflective pause between two lines of dialogue by the same speaker without some indication of the fact..."⁵ While Hagopian indicates that the lack of such instances is not an absolute test, it is crucial to his reasoning. His article even lists a series of passages from the stories in which a single speaker speaks twice in succession, but in which intervening lines of description and the repetition of nouns or pronouns act as clear signals of what Hemingway is doing, passages such as this one from "The Killers":

> "Maybe it was just a bluff."
> "No. It ain't just a bluff."
> Ole Andreson rolled over toward the wall.
> "The only thing is," he said, talking toward the wall, "I just can't make up my mind to go out. I been in here all day."

and this one from "Now I Lay Me":

> "I think it's all bull, myself," he said. "I just heard it somewhere. You know how you hear things."
> We were both quiet and I listened to the silk-worms.
> "You hear those damn silk-worms?' he asked.⁶

Hagopian's implication is that in all cases Hemingway either abides by standard procedure or supplies these indications that he is not doing so. The fact is, however, that Hemingway *does* deviate from standard procedure without supplying explicit clues to the reader.

Passages in which Hemingway ignores normal dialogue conventions by indenting two consecutive speeches by a single speaker occur frequently enough and obviously enough in both the stories and the novels that one wonders how Hagopian was ever able to make his original assertion. In "The Three-Day Blow," for example, Nick Adams is talking about G. K. Chesterton with Bill:

> "That's right," said Nick. "I guess he's a better guy than Walpole."
> "Oh, he's a better guy, all right," Bill said.
> "But Walpole's a better writer."
> "I don't know," Nick said. "Chesterton's a classic."⁷

It is obvious from the context that Bill says Chesterton is a better guy and then emphasizes in the succeeding, indented line that Walpole is the better writer. And it is clear that Hemingway supplies no explicit clue in the story that he is disregarding normal conventions for writing dialogue.

A similar instance occurs in "The Gambler, the Nun, and the Radio." As Mr. Frazer sits talking with the Mexican "friends" of Cayetano, the Mexican who does not drink asks him:

> "How many tubes has the radio."
> "Seven."
> "Very beautiful," he said. "What does it cost?"

> "I don't know… It is rented."
> "You gentlemen are friends of Cayetano?"
> "No," said the big one. "We are friends of he who wounded him."⁸

It is obvious that Mr. Frazer says, "I don't know… It is rented," and then asks if the men are Cayetano's friends. As is true in "The Three-Day Blow," it is clear in "The Gambler, the Nun, and the Radio" who is saying what, but the reader's knowledge results from his understanding of the characters and their situations, not from specific indications in the text. In each of the above instances Hemingway's disregard of normal dialogue conventions functions to create a reflective pause. Bill's second, indented statement indicates his brief hesitation before qualifying his agreement with Nick. The indenting of Mr. Frazer's second comment emphasizes the difficulty the American is having making conversation with the Mexicans.

Passages of dialogue in which Hemingway indents lines of dialogue without changing speakers are also found in various novels. Near the end of *For Whom the Bell Tolls*, for example, as Robert Jordan lies wounded, he talks with Pablo about what he and his band should do:

> "Does it hurt much?" Pablo asked. He was bending close over Robert Jordan.
> "No. I think the nerve is crushed. Listen. Get along. I am mucked, see? I will talk to the girl for a moment. When I say to take her, take her. She will want to stay. I will only speak to her for a moment,"
> "Clearly, there is not much time," Pablo said.
> "Clearly."
> "I think you would do better in the Republic," Robert Jordan said.
> "Nay. I am for Gredos."
> "Use thy head."
> "Talk to her now," Pablo said. "There is little time. I am sorry thou hast this, *Ingles*."⁹

It is obvious from the context that Jordan responds, "Clearly" and then in the next line advises Pablo against going to Gredos. The indenting of the second statement indicates a short pause during which Jordan presumably decides to try to convince Pablo to escape to the Republic. Another instance, one in a passage of dialogue as long as the confusing passage in "A Clean, Well-Lighted Place" and with as few identifications of speaker, occurs earlier in *For Whom the Bell Tolls*. As Robert Jordan talks with El Sordo, the Spaniard asks Jordan if he likes the whiskey he has been served:

> "Very much," said Robert Jordan. "It's very good whiskey."
> "Am contented," Sordo grinned. "Was bringing tonight with information."
> "What information?"
> "Much troop movement."

"Where?"
"Segovia. Planes you saw."
"Yes."
"Bad, eh?"
"Bad."
"Troop movement?"
"Much between Villacastin and Segovia. On Valladolid road. Much between Villacastin and San Rafael. Much. Much."
"What do you think?"
"We prepare something?"
"Possibly."
"They know. Prepare too."
"It is possible."
"Why not blow bridge tonight?"
"Orders."
"Whose orders?"
"General Staff."
"So."[10]

It is clear that Jordan says, "Bad" and then in the next line asks, "Troop movement?" Again, the use of two consecutive indented lines seems to indicate a pause, in this case a pause in which Jordan and El Sordo contemplate the danger indicated by the increased troop movement and the presence of the planes.

Similar instances in which normal dialogue conventions are ignored occur in *The Sun Also Rises*. Near the end of Book II, for example, Jake Barnes returns from a walk with Brett, and, having promised her to look after Mike, goes by the Scotchman's room:

Mike lay on the bed looking like a death mask of himself. He opened his eyes and looked at me.
"Hello, Jake," he said very slowly. "I'm getting a lit tle sleep. I've want ed a lit tle sleep for a long time."
"Let me cover you over."
"No, I'm quite warm."
"Don't go. I have n't got ten to sleep yet."
"You'll sleep, Mike. Don't worry, boy."[11]

It is evident from the context that Mike tells Jake, "No, I'm quite warm," and then in the following line asks Jake not to leave. The indenting of Mike's second statement seems to indicate a pause during which Jake begins moving toward the door in the hope that Mike has fallen asleep. It is even possible that normal dialogue conventions are ignored again on the same page of *The Sun Also Rises* within a few lines of the last example. When Jake leaves Mike, he goes to his room:

Bill was in my room reading the paper.
"See Mike?"
"Yes."

"Let's go and eat."

"I won't eat downstairs with that German head-waiter. He was damned snotty when I was getting Mike upstairs."

"He was snotty to us, too."

It seems clear that Bill begins this exchange by asking Jake if he has seen Mike. When Jake and Brett arrive at the hotel, the German head-waiter tells them that Mike and Bill have gone up to their rooms, and it is likely that Jake would assume that Bill has seen Mike. The opening question thus makes most sense if Bill asks it. Since the reader knows that Jake was with Brett when Bill and Mike went to their rooms, it is clear that Bill must say the fourth line of the exchange. It follows then that either Jake responds, "Yes" and then says, "Let's go and eat," or that Bill says, "Let's go and eat" and then says that he won't eat downstairs. Of course, if Bill asks the opening question, the exchange can be read in conventional fashion, but it does seem possible that for the second time in less than a page Hemingway ignores conventional rules without supplying the reader with any signals that he is doing so.

Other passages in Hemingway's work during which a single character speaks two indented lines in succession can be found. There are two instances in "The Battler," for example.[12] It should be clear from the examples which have been discussed, however, that Hemingway ignores normal dialogue conventions with enough regularity to show that Hagopian's arguments are based to a significant degree on incomplete investigation.

The existence of passages in Hemingway's fiction in which Hemingway clearly ignores dialogue conventions, of course, does not prove that he ignores the conventions in "A Clean, Well-Lighted Place." At the same time, these instances do indicate that Hagopian should have given a good deal more consideration to this possibility than he was willing to give. Literary conventions, after all, are not laws. They are assessments of what authors have done, not of what they must do. It is true that most authors have consistently indented during passages of dialogue in order to indicate that a new speaker is speaking, but this is far from saying either that all writers always adhere to this way of doing things, or that all writers should always adhere to this way of doing things. The fact that at one point the original text of "A Clean, Well-Lighted Place" clearly indicates that the younger waiter is the one who knows about the attempted suicide must override any interpretation based on the assumption that Hemingway's dialogue must be conventional.[13]

Even if one were to agree that the interpretation Hagopian derives from the altered text is a fully consistent one, the conclusion would not be changed, for Hagopian's interpretation is surely no more consistent with the text as a whole than is the traditional interpretation. Surely, a consistent interpretation based on a significant change in an author's text cannot, and must not, override a consistent interpretation based on the assumption that an author disregards certain conventional rules, especially when they are rules which the same author has clearly broken in other places.

There is no doubt that Hemingway's disregard of convention in "A Clean, Well-Lighted Place" is misleading, far too misleading to be effective. The fact remains, however, that the problems which the story creates can and should be solved without recourse to alterations in Hemingway's text. It is highly unfortunate that the long critical discussion about the confusing dialogue resulted in a change in the way Scribner's prints the story, a change which Charles Scribner, Jr. admits was made, not on the basis of manuscript evidence or at the suggestion of Hemingway himself, but solely on the basis of the advice of critics and "common sense."[14] It might be common sense to alter the way a passage of dialogue was printed if the change eliminated confusion and caused no significant modification in the meaning of the text. But that is not the case here. The alteration in the dialogue of "A Clean, Well-Lighted Place" changes the meaning of the text significantly and, as a result, cannot help but create more confusion than it was meant to solve. Those readers who are introduced to the story through the "corrected" version will be forced to develop an interpretation of the two waiters—and of much of the rest of the story—which is very different from what is called for by Hemingway's original text. One can only hope that concerned scholars will be able to prevail upon Scribner's to reverse the recent policy and once again print the story Hemingway wrote and saw through numerous printings.

"The Confusing Dialogue in Hemingway's 'A Clean, Well-Lighted Place': A Final Word?" was published in *Studies in American Fiction* 1, no.1 (Spring 1973): 93-101.

---

1 Charles E. May, "Is Hemingway's 'Well-Lighted Place' Really Clean Now?" *SSF,* 8 (1971), 326-30.
2 John V. Hagopian, "Tidying Up Hemingway's Clean Well-Lighted Place," *SSF,* 2 (1964), 140-46. Only two alternatives had been suggested. One was Joseph F. Gabriel's contention that the confusing dialogue is an attempt by Hemingway to purposely confuse the reader and thus place him in the same existential position as the characters. See "The Logic of Confusion in Hemingway's 'A Clean, Well-Lighted Place,'" *CE,* 22 (May 1961), 539-46. The other was Otto Reinert's suggestion that Hemingway ignores conventional dialogue expectations and twice during the long exchange between the two waiters has a single waiter say two consecutive indented lines of dialogue. See "Hemingway's Waiters Once More," *CE,* 20 (May, 1959), 417-18. Hagopian correctly demonstrated why Gabriel's interpretation was over-ingenious. As is shown in the present discussion, however, Hagopian's reasons for dismissing Reinert's sensible suggestions were poorly thought out.
3 This is made all-the-more clear by the fact that the second of these instances is actually easier to understand if one does not attempt to alternate speakers. Were the reader to suppose that "He must be eighty years old" and "Anyway I should say he was eighty" are spoken by two different waiters, it would be difficult to understand the purpose of "Anyway" in the second sentence. As Reinert explains, the second sentence seems to indicate an admission of subjectivity on the part of the speaker of the previous line; it seems to be an attempt to disqualify after a pause, "the objective certainty of 'He must be eighty years old'" (Reinert, 418). While it is not impossible to read the two lines as though they were spoken by two different speakers, the feeling of continuity which is created by the use of "Anyway" makes it at least as acceptable to read the lines as spoken by the older waiter.
4 Ernest Hemingway, *A Farewell to Arms* (New York: Scribner's, 1967), 69.
5 Hagopian, 141.
6 Ernest Hemingway, *The Short Stories of Ernest Hemingway* (New York: Scribner's, 1953), 287.
7 *The Short Stories of Ernest Hemingway,* 119.
8 *The Short Stories of Ernest Hemingway,* 476.
9 Ernest Hemingway, *For Whom the Bell Tolls* (New York: Scribner's, 1940), 462.
10 *For Whom the Bell Tolls,* 143.
11 Ernest Hemingway, *The Sun Also Rises* (New York: Scribner's, 1954), 210.
12 One of these instances occurs as Ad is speaking angrily to Nick: "'How the hell do you get that way?' came out from under the cap sharply at Nick." Ad then says the following indented statement: "Who the hell do you think you are? You're a snotty bastard. You come in here where nobody asks you and eat a man's food and when he asks to borrow a knife you get snotty"

(*The Short Stories of Ernest Hemingway*, 135). The other example occurs at the end of the story when Bugs says the long paragraph which ends, "'Would you like to take some of that ham and some bread with you? No? You better take a sandwich,' all this in a low, smooth, polite nigger voice," and then says the next indented line, "Good. Well, good-bye, Mister Adams. Good-bye and good luck!" (*The Short Stories of Ernest Hemingway*, 138). There are additional examples in other works, too. It is likely, for example, that near the beginning of Book II of *The Sun Also Rises*, Brett says both, "Might" and the next indented statement, "I needed that" (*The Sun Also Rises*, 83).

13 As all critics have agreed, it is clear that at one point in the original text the younger waiter says, "His niece looks after him," and the older waiter replies, "I know. You said she cut him down." The question about these lines has never been how they should be read, but only if they are correct as they are printed, for if they are correct then it is clear that Hemingway does ignore dialogue conventions in "A Clean, Well-Lighted Place."

14 Information in a letter to the author from Charles Scribner, Jr., April 5, 1971.

Gottheim family members at window in *Mouches Volantes* (1976). Courtesy of Larry Gottheim.

1976

Another Consideration of Larry Gottheim's
Mouches Volantes: an attempt to continue an investigation begun in Ideolects by Raymond Foery's review

Looking back, it seems apparent to me why the first independent filmmaker I was powerfully drawn to was Larry Gottheim. I was transforming from a literature teacher/scholar to a cinema teacher/scholar and Gottheim himself had made much the same transition. He had studied comparative literature with René Wellek at Yale where he earned a Ph.D. in Comparative Literature and had taught at Northwestern before joining the faculty at what was then called SUNY Binghamton (now Binghamton University), where he taught literature and, by the end of the 1960s, had established what became an influential cinema department—my *Binghamton Babylon: Voices from the Cinema Department 1967-1977 (a nonfiction novel)* (SUNY Press, 2015) is a history of that project.

There was something about the calculated craft of Gottheim's films that felt related to the fiction I had studied and written about as a graduate student. Indeed, the world of experimental filmmaking that Gottheim's work led me into seemed, from the beginning, analogous to what I had understood and still understand as the experimental literature of the writers I loved and taught during my early decades as a college professor: Gertrude Stein, Sherwood Anderson, Hemingway, e. e. cummings, Faulkner, Richard Wright... Also, writing about Gottheim was a way of building on the work of a previous critic (Raymond Foery), as my essay on Hemingway's dialogue in "A Clean, Well-Lighted Place" built on Charles E. May's essay—a young scholar's attempt to become part of a scholarly community.

* * *

While it is too early to write confidently or conclusively about the recently completed *Mouches Volantes*, even limited study shows that the new work is comparable to *Horizons* (1973) in scope and complexity and that Gottheim is continuing to develop areas his earlier films are concerned with. More fully than any previous film, for example, Gottheim organizes *Mouches Volantes* so as to draw the viewer's attention to his own limitations, particular those perceptual and analytical limitations which create life's essential ambiguities and insecurities. A multitude of relationships is developed between widely varying footage Gottheim shot in earlier years and a repeated soundtrack made up of excerpts from Angelina Johnson's recorded reminiscences about her blues-singer husband Blind Willie Johnson. The film is constructed so that relationships between visuals and between visuals and sounds are frequently so subtle and evanescent that one is never quite sure he has seen and heard correctly. That Gottheim means to create this effect is obvious from his choice of title: "Mouches Volantes" refers to a phenomenon of the eye described by von Helmholz in statements included in Gottheim's program notes for the film:

> MOVING OBJECTS in the vitreous humor, commonly called "flying gnats" (Mouches Volantes or muscae volitantes). Sometimes these look like strings of pearls or groups of circles with bright nuclei... That these motions are real and not simply apparent is easily proved by holding the head erect and looking towards the sky through a window pane, and at the

same time noting some fixed mark on the glass; then as a rule the entoptical appearances will be seen to move slowly downwards, across the field of view… In making such observations there is a strong temptation to try to look at one of the "gnats" that is near the point of fixation so as to see it better; which makes it seem to fly away without ever being overtaken.

As one grows more familiar with *Mouches Volantes*, certain patterns of relationship do become distinguishable. For one thing, Gottheim develops relationships among visuals which involve both the activities and objects photographed and various qualities of the photography. In a majority of shots, Gottheim uses footage of his family taken at a variety of times in his past. We see his children playing in the snow and at the beach, his wife tending bees, and his family getting together with the Gottheim grandparents. In all instances, Gottheim's own experimentation with filmmaking is evident; as he photographed his family, he was exploring the qualities of telephoto shooting, the effects of refocusing with a shot, the possibilities of changing exposure during shooting, and a variety of other aspects of film technology. The film thus creates a record of the development of Gottheim's family and of the growth of the filmmaker-father who has become the family's chronicler.

Another kind of relationship developed in the visuals is created by Gottheim's choice and organization of the footage so that certain motifs become evident. The most important of these motifs is suggested by the title. Nearly all of the shots in the film reveal patterns of particles, patterns created by falling snow and rain, by the clouds of bees surrounding Debbie Gottheim as she tends the hives, by the interstices in the netting she wears and by the cells of the honeycomb, by the tiny flower petals floating in a pond, by granules of beach sand, by the bubbles of the foam on the waves, and by other aspects of Gottheim's imagery. As is true in so much of Gottheim's work, no distinction is made in visual importance between patterns in the "subject matter" and patterns created while photographing or during development. The viewer is frequently aware of the patterns made by the various grains of black-and-white and color film stocks Gottheim uses, by the tiny circles created when light reflects on the lens, and by the sprinkles of light made by dust in the emulsion. Ultimately, the consistent use of such patterns tends to emphasize the essential atomic or molecular nature of all reality and to suggest that whatever human beings do, whether it involves family activities or artistic endeavors or some other area, they do within the context of the laws of matter. The fact that the first and last "images" the viewer sees in the film are the flecks made by the particles suggests the most important of these laws—the fact that all human activity exists between the inevitable formation and destruction of our material nature, between dust and dust.

In many ways the most interesting level of *Mouches Volantes* is Gottheim's experimentation with sounds, specifically with the potential relationships of sounds and visuals. The significance of Gottheim's concern with this area is evident in the general organization of visuals and sounds during the film. Gottheim uses seven groups of shots, each group divided from the others by sections of dark leader. The groups are organized 1, 2, 3, 4, 5, 6, 7, 7, 6, 5, 4, 3, 2, 1. The four-and-a-half minutes of excerpts from Angelina Johnson's reminiscences are placed in juxtaposition with the groups of visuals so that the groups of shots alternate between silence and sound. Angelina Johnson's comments are heard first with group 2 of the visuals and subsequently matched with groups 3, 6, 7 (the second repetition of this group), 5, 3, 1, that is, so that by the end of the film her narrative has been heard with all the groups.

At first, the juxtaposition of sounds and visuals is somewhat jolting because of the obvious differences between the black woman's reminiscences and the white family's activities. But it is Gottheim's talent and his joy—"My mind loves bringing things together"—to develop a multitude of relationships between these two aspects of the film. Perhaps the most general level of similarity between the soundtrack and the visuals is that both are attempts to capture the past (Angelina Johnson talks about old times; Gottheim uses footage taken in earlier years) and that both involve the passing generations (Angelina Johnson describes aspects of Willie Johnson's childhood she has found out about from Johnson's father and later tells of Willie's death; Gottheim includes shots of his wife and children and many shots taken during visits with the Gottheim grandparents.)

Other sound-visual relationships are more specific. Gottheim has clearly studied the different effects of beginning Angelina Johnson's comments at different moments within each group of shots and has chosen the moment he feels is most productive. In a great many instances the sense of a spoken comment will seem to match activities taking place in the visuals. When Angelina tells of how Willie at five years of age told his father he "wanted to be a beacher, talkin' about a preacher," we see shots of a beach with the Gottheim children playing; when she describes conversations between her and Willie, we see conversations between Debbie and the children and at times the spoken words seem to match their lips. Generally, the details of Angelina Johnson's articulation seem to match subtle visual movements: gestures by people, motions of the waves, motions of the camera, changes from one shot to another, and so forth. Even the sounds on the soundtrack other than Angelina Johnson's voice—mechanical taps and a rushing sound evident whenever the tape of her voice is on, for example—are matched to visual events. The rushing sound often corresponds to the surf in the visuals, and the taps match exactly the flashes of imagery with which the final group of shots begins. The more one examines *Mouches Volantes*, the more aware he becomes that Gottheim has orchestrated the entire film so that a constant counterpoint of sounds and visual movements is created. Even our intermittent difficulty in understanding Angela Johnson, either because of distortions on the soundtrack or because of differences in dialect, often unites the soundtrack with the visuals, for Gottheim includes many shots in which we can't quite distinguish details.

Mouches Volantes clearly reemphasizes the importance of expanding our perceptions and intensifying our concentration on the world around us—a theme developed in *Horizons* and earlier films. Further, it reaffirms the persistent Gottheim theme that the recognition of the material limitations of life can be a catalyst for the creation and appreciation of beauty. Angelina Johnson's narrative about her creative husband is far more than a simple memory; she is presenting her listener with a creative rendition of a story which is moving not only in its facts but because of the immense subtlety and suggestibility of her voice. Similarly, Gottheim uses creative footage taken years ago and develops a context which gives the footage tremendous meaning. In contrast to earlier films, however, *Mouches Volantes* adds a social dimension to Gottheim's vision. The film demonstrates the idea that regardless of race, regardless of age, regardless of the details of our lives, we are formed of the same basic matter and have the same potential for engaging in experiences—love, procreation, art—which enable us to transcend our limitations, at least momentarily. Further, Gottheim structures the film so that the viewer has an opportunity to actively develop his ability to experience this fundamental unity. To the extent the viewer really listens to Angelina Johnson, growing to know her story and its meanings more fully with each repetition, to the extent he concentrates on the visuals and examines the subtle web of relationships Gottheim creates between them and the soundtrack, the more fully he realizes that beneath the apparent differences which seem to divide him from others are realities which can unite him with all mankind.

"Another Consideration of Larry Gottheim's Mouches Volantes: an attempt to continue an investigation begun in *Ideolects* by Raymond Foery's review" was published in *Ideolects* 1, no. 2 (August-November 1976), 3-5. Managing editor for this issue of *Ideolects* was Lee Krugman; the issue includes brief essays by David M. Cohen, Mick Eaton, Raymond Foery, Marshall Grossman, Nick Penkovsky, David Tafler, and brief letters from Bette Gordon, John Hanhardt, and J. Hoberman.

In 2023, Re:Voir published an updated DVD set of Gottheim's "Elective Affinities" series—*Horizons* (1973), *Mouches Volantes* (1976), *Four Shadows* (1978), *Tree of Knowledge* (1981). These and other Gottheim films are available both as 16mm prints and on DVD from Canyon Cinema (canyoncinema.com), and as digital files, from Light Cone (Paris). Gottheim's review of his filmmaking career and his thoughts on his films are available in his book *The Red Thread: Larry Gottheim and His Films* (New York: Film-Makers' Cooperative/Eyewash, 2024).

Erskine Caldwell, photographed by Margaret Bourke-White.
Courtesy Erskine Caldwell.

1977

Repetition as Technique in the Short Stories of Erskine Caldwell

As a relatively young person coming of professional age during the 1960s/early '70s, I wanted my scholarship to matter in ways beyond my personal professional security. As much as I enjoyed writing about Hemingway, I didn't feel that what I published could matter to anyone except other young scholars working to achieve tenure and promotion. I was sure that nothing I wrote could have mattered to Hemingway even if he had lived to see it; when he was alive, he seemed bored with and disdainful of Hemingway scholars for reasons I could understand.

For a time, I imagined writing books about under-appreciated American writers who seemed to have fallen off any listing of canonical contributors to modern literature, despite their accomplishments. As my first project, I assembled a collection of writings by and on the American writer Erskine Caldwell. His novels *Tobacco Road* (1932) and *God's Little Acre* (1933), both experimental in their way, had sold millions of copies (Jack Kirkland's 1933 stage adaptation of *Tobacco Road* is still the second-longest-running non-musical in Broadway history); *Trouble in July* (1940), like Faulkner's *Light in August* (1932) and *Intruder in the Dust* (1948), laid bare the Deep South's brutal racism; his short stories were remarkable for their terse power and stylistic inventiveness; and his collaborations with photographer Margaret Bourke-White—*You Have Seen Their Faces* (1937) and *North of the Danube* (1939)—remain landmark text-photo works. When Caldwell and Bourke-White married in 1939, they were both celebrities, popular and provocative in part because of their leftist politics and their questioning of American cultural norms (many Southerners were furious about Caldwell's depictions of the South). On June 22nd, 1941, the couple were in Russia when the Germans invaded; they were the first Americans to do radio reporting on the Russian front.

I had come to know Caldwell by the time my *Critical Essays on Erskine Caldwell* was published by G.K. Hall in 1981, but at that late date I couldn't imagine the book having any real impact on the general awareness of his career. Caldwell seemed appreciative, but my goal to have my work matter in some substantive way still seemed out of reach. However, since Caldwell's work, like Hemingway's, often focuses on dialogue as action, I continue to see Caldwell as a contributor to what soon became my commitment not just to interviewing, but to a conception of an interview with an accomplished filmmaker as a work of literature. And more generally, I can also see that researching, then getting to know an accomplished, widely recognized literary artist helped give me confidence to confront independent filmmakers with my questions.

Because Caldwell is far less known now than he was even in the 1980s, I've included my essay on the uses of repetition in his short stories in the hope that it may draw some attention back to a remarkable career.

* * *

James Dickey has said that Thomas Wolfe's work is "so rhetorical that it is almost a shameful act. But there should be such rhetorical writing, as the indication of a kind of limit."[1] The converse might be said about Erskine Caldwell's short fiction. In many of his stories Caldwell's style is so spare and so completely unadorned that the reader learns just how few of the traditional literary devices a writer can use and still create stories which are meaningful and effective. While the hallmark of Caldwell's prose style is simplicity, however, a careful investigation of the stories in such collections as *American Earth*, *We Are the Living*, *Kneel to the Rising Sun*, *Southways*, *Jackpot*, *The Complete Stories*, and *Georgia Boy* shows that Caldwell has worked successfully with a variety of technical devices. Particularly impressive is his extensive experimentation with repetition.[2]

With the exception of Gertrude Stein, there has probably never been a writer more fascinated with the possibilities of repetition than Erskine Caldwell. While the amount and the kind of repetition used in Caldwell's stories varies considerably, repetition itself is both the most obvious and the most important literary device in much of his best work. Some of the repetition in his stories is a reflection of the Steinesque idea that people continually repeat themselves in conversation, that, in fact, repetition is one of the most fundamental qualities of speech. Nearly every character in Caldwell's fiction habitually repeats seemingly offhand phrases and sentences which often serve as indices to aspects of the character's personality. Further, instead of purposely avoiding repetitive detail in descriptive passages, Caldwell normally presents the reader with a few well-chosen aspects of a scene and then repeats them whenever the setting needs comment. The result is simple but vivid description often made memorable by the degree to which the simplicity reflects the unsophisticated lives of the characters.

In much of Caldwell's short fiction repetition also functions in more complex and unusual ways. In many stories a limited number of repeated phrases and sentences are used to emphasize various types of structure. In "The Automobile That Wouldn't Run" and "Saturday Afternoon," for example, action begins at a certain place, moves to a second location, and then returns to the starting point. In both stories the style reflects this movement. Certain words and phrases are repeated during the first paragraphs of each story. When action moves away, these repetitions cease but are apparent again at the end of the story when the characters are back at the original place. By using repetition in this manner Caldwell gains two results. First, he brings the stories to a decisive conclusion, and second, he creates a strong final emphasis on the basic immovability of the central characters. In "A Swell-Looking Girl," a story in which Lem Johnson tries to prove to his country neighbors that his new wife wears fancy "little pink things" under her dress, a different kind of structure is emphasized by a fairly simple pattern of repetition on the part of Tom, the first-person narrator. As the events of "A Swell-Looking Girl" are presented, the phrase "a swell-looking girl" is repeated periodically, and with each repetition the phrase becomes more emphatic.[3] The regular recurrence of this line not only stresses the growing excitement of the narrator as he watches Lem raise his wife's skirt higher and higher, it also creates an overall pattern which adds coherence to the story.

While repetition is the most important stylistic device in the stories which have been discussed so far, the amount of repetition in these stories is not particularly heavy, at least not for Caldwell. In some of Caldwell's best stories repetitious style is used far more emphatically and results in three different general effects. First, in such stories as "The Medicine Man," "Where the Girls Were Different" and "August Afternoon," heavy repetition emphasizes erotic excitement. In other

The immense popularity of Caldwell's often ribald novels has tended to obscure both his skills and his fundamental seriousness as a prose artist.

Caldwell's short stories were, and are, less widely known than his novels, but his interest in prose experimentation is more obvious in the stories than in the novels.

stories a consistent barrage of repeated lines creates a feeling of almost insane frenzy. Finally, in some stories heavy repetition causes conversations to take on symbolic implications.

The most important aspect of the repetition in the humorously erotic story "The Medicine Man" is the fact that as Professor Eaton and Effie Henderson become increasingly involved in their mutual seduction, repeated words and phrases become more and more emphatic. As Effie takes her clothes off so that the Professor can make what he calls a thorough medical examination, Professor Eaton continually asks if "perhaps" Effie will remove her blouse, if "perhaps" she'd like to hear more about the miraculous powers of Indian Root Tonic, and, when she hesitates to take everything off, if "perhaps" he should go. To reassure Effie, the Professor explains again and again how important it is for her "to place yourself entirely in my hands," or a slight variation, and nine times in about three pages he assures her that everything will be "absolutely" all right. The Professor's repetitive cajolings and assurances are punctuated by Effie's continual questions: "Do you want me to take—"; "And this, too, Professor Eaton? This, too?"; "Professor Eaton, do you want me to take off all of this—like this?" The tension created in the story by the repetition builds until Effie exclaims, "You make me feel so funny, Professor Eaton. And are you sure—." The Professor assures her, "Absolutely, Absolutely," and urges her one last time to "place yourself completely in my hands" before her brother arrives with his town-marshal's pearl-handled revolver. The frustration of the Professor (and the reader) at the brother's arrival is reflected perfectly in the style for the repetition stops as completely as the sexual excitement does.[4]

Still heavier repetition creates the rising excitement in "Where the Girls Were Different," a humorous story about a young boy's adventures when he goes across the county to meet some girls who are supposedly "different" from the girls around home. The general concentration of repeated phrases which is evident all through the story is given direction by Caldwell's use of what might be called verbal counterpoint. The most frequently repeated phrase in the story is "were different," which in some form is used about sixteen times in the five pages of the narrative and creates one rhythmic pattern. A second pattern is developed as Fred drives to Rosemark and gets a date. Only one word is involved at first ("gee") but because it is an emphatic word, Fred's repetition of it is noticeable. "Gee" is used first when Fred explains that he hated to lie to his parents about where he was going, "but—gee—I had to go down to see those girls in Rosemark." As the story continues, and Fred's excitement grows, the author's use of the word becomes increasingly noticeable. Fred explains how the girl he asks for a date says "Sure" and he goes on to comment, "Gee, this was the way to see girls." Later, when Betty sits very close to Fred, he exclaims, "Gee, she was different!"

The rhythms created by the two patterns of repetition are made particularly emphatic by the fact that Caldwell uses the patterns in closer and closer proximity. This is clear, for instance, in the third repetition of "gee" mentioned above and it is clear in subsequent instances as well. After Fred has begun to gain confidence with Betty, for example, he decides to try and kiss her:

> Gee whiz! I reached down and kissed her and she wouldn't let me stop. The old car rocked from one side of the road to the other as dizzy as a bat. I couldn't see to steer it because Betty wouldn't let me stop kissing her, and I had to wait until we ran into a ditch almost before I knew which way to turn the wheel. Gee whiz! The girls in Rosemark were certainly different, all right [413].

Caldwell brings the two patterns together one final time when Betty asks Fred why he has stopped kissing her. When Fred kisses her again, she puts her arms around his neck and her legs across his lap, and Fred exclaims, "*Gee, whiz!* I didn't know girls did like that! Ben said the girls down in Rosemark were different, but I didn't expect anything like this to happen to me. Holy Cats!" It is just after this especially emphatic use of "gee" in connection with "were different" that Fred pulls into Betty's driveway and is rudely chased away by her father who has been following in the family car. As is true in "The Medicine Man," in "Where the Girls Were Different" the stylistic heartbeat created by the repetition ceases just when the erotic involvement does. The resulting frustration of the protagonist is thus reflected by a calmer style.

A final instance of Caldwell's use of heavy repetition to create erotic excitement occurs in "August Afternoon," a story in which Caldwell's ability to work effectively with different types of repetition is especially apparent. In "August Afternoon," Vic Glover's young attractive wife Willie is courted and won by a man with an eleven-inch hairy-handled knife, while Vic and Hubert, a black friend of Vic's, look on. Most of the types of repetition mentioned so far in this study are used in "August Afternoon." There is a generally heavy concentration of repeated descriptive detail and conversational statement, and a specific line is repeated throughout the story in the manner of "were different" in "Where the Girls Were Different": the five-fold repetition of Hubert's question, "We ain't aiming to have no trouble today, is we?" creates a rhythmic refrain which helps to organize the story. In addition to the previously discussed kinds of repetition, however, "August Afternoon" uses two which have not been mentioned. One involves the fact that as Caldwell's characters grow more tense, their manner of addressing each other changes. For example, when Hubert gets worried about the possibility of violence, he begins to address "Mr. Vic" in an unusually repetitive way:

> Mr. Vic, I'm trying to tell you about Miss Willie. Miss Willie's been sitting there on that high step showing her pretty and he's been looking at her a right long time, Mr. Vic. If you won't object to me saying so, Mr. Vic, I reckon I'd tell Miss Willie to go sit somewhere else, if I was you. Miss Willie ain't got much on today, Mr. Vic. Just only that skimpy outside dress, Mr. Vic. That's what I've been trying to tell you. I walked out there in the yard this while ago to see what he was looking at so much, and when I say Miss Willie ain't got much on today, I mean she's got on just only that skimpy outside dress, Mr. Vic. You can go look yourself and see if I'm lying to you, Mr. Vic [441].

The seven-fold repetition of "*Mr.* Vic" creates a pounding rhythm which is emphasized by the five-fold repetition of "Miss Willie" and by Hubert's frequent emphasis on how little Willie is wearing. Several times during "August Afternoon" the tension Hubert feels is revealed in similar passages.

A very different type of repetition is used in the two conversations Willie has with the stranger, one of which begins this way:

> "How old are you?" Floyd asked Willie.
> "Fifteen."
> Floyd jerked the knife out of the wood and thrust it deeper into the same place.
> "How old are you?" she asked him.
> "About twenty-seven."
> "Are you married?"
> "Not now," he said. "How long have you been?"
> "About three months," Willie said.
> "How do you like it?"
> "Pretty good so far."
> "How about another kiss?"
> "You just had one."
> "I'd like another one now."
> "I ought not to let you kiss me again."
> "Why not?"
> "Men don't like girls who kiss too much."
> "I'm not that kind."
> "What kind are you?"
> "I'd like to kiss you a lot" [443-44].

The erotic excitement this conversation creates during the story is emphasized by the repetitive format of the characters' brief questions and responses and by the combination of this rhythmically suggestive format with the characters' repetition of specific words. The two conversations between Willie and the stranger are particularly noticeable since the many exchanges between Vic and Hubert are composed of generally much longer statements. Both conversations occur at crucial moments in the story and raise the level of tension substantially. All in all, the various kinds of repetition work together in "August Afternoon" to intensify events and to create excitement. Little meaning in a philosophic sense is developed during the story, but for sheer joy in the possibilities of repetition, "August Afternoon" is a *tour de force*.

A second effect Caldwell develops by using heavy repetition is evident in "Country Full of Swedes," Caldwell's famous story about the arrival of a family of exuberant Swedes in a normally quiet valley in rural Maine. "Country Full of Swedes" uses repetition differently from previously discussed stories. No complete sentences or long phrases are repeated consistently throughout the story in the way "We ain't aiming to have no trouble today, is we" is repeated in "August Afternoon." In "Country Full of Swedes" Caldwell repeats single words and short phrases literally dozens of times to create an overwhelming feeling of frenzy.

The most frequently repeated word in "Country Full of Swedes" is "Swedes." Hardly a paragraph goes by without a character referring to the Swedes in one way or another. The intensity of this repetition varies somewhat but is probably heaviest when Stan takes his first careful look at the new arrivals:

> There were Swedes everywhere a man could see, and the ones that couldn't be seen could be heard yelling their heads off inside the yellow clapboarded house across the road. There wasn't any mistake about there being Swedes there, either; because I've never yet seen a man who mistakes a Swede or a Finn for an American. Once you see a Finn or a Swede you know, God-helping, that he is a Swede or a Finn, and not a Portuguese or an American.
>
> There was a Swede everywhere a man could look. Some of them were little Swedes, and women Swedes, to be sure; but little Swedes, in the end, and women Swedes too, near about, grow up as big as any of them. When you come right down to it, there's no sense in counting out the little Swedes and the women Swedes.
>
> Out in the road in front of their house were seven-eight autos and trucks loaded down with furniture and household goods. All around, everything was Swedes. The Swedes were yelling and shouting at one another, the little Swedes and the women Swedes just as loud as the big Swedes... [7].

The seventeen repetitions of "Swedes" in these few lines give the passage an especially frantic effect, an effect not only apropos for the frenzied action which is going on, but also quite expressive of the specific event involved at this point in the story—Jim's discovery of how many Swedes there are. The story is as full of "Swedes" as the country seems.

Other phrases are repeated over and over and give other sections of "Country Full of Swedes" an equally frenetic feeling. One of these phrases is "Good God"; others include the adjectival combination of "God" with other words, as in "God-awful," "God-helping," and "Goddamn." While these phrases are not repeated quite as often as "Swedes" is, they appear again and again, sometimes in combination with "Swedes." Early in the story, for example, Stan hears gunfire:

> "Who fired that God-awful shot, Jim?" I yelled at him, leaping down the stairs quicker than a man of my years ought to let himself do.
>
> "Good God!" Jim said, his voice hoarse, and falling all to pieces like a stump of punkwood. "The Swedes! The Swedes are shooting, Stan!"
>
> "What Swedes, Jim—those Swedes who own the farm and building across the road over there?" I said, trying to find the buttonholes in my shirt. "Have they come back here to live on that farm?"
>
> "Good God, yes!" he said, his voice croaking deep down in his throat, like he had swallowed too much water. "The Swedes are all over the place. They're everywhere you can see, there's that many of them."
>
> "What's their name, Jim?" I asked him. "You and Mrs. Frost never told me what their name is."

"Good God, I don't know. I never heard them called anything but Swedes, and that's what it is, I guess" [5].

The heavily repeated phrases mentioned so far, when combined with the less frequent, but still relatively heavy repetition of such phrases as "one-two," "of a forenoon," "yellow-headed," "yelling and shouting," and the repetition of longer phrases and sentences during specific paragraphs, make "Country Full of Swedes" a story of humorous but nerve-wracking frenzy.[5] The style of the story perfectly reflects the hysteria of the narrator, who is unable to understand or adjust to his exuberant new neighbors. The only comparable effect this critic is able to think of is created by the cinematic device called "pixilation," that method of shooting single frames of an activity and running them at normal speed so that characters seem to dance around on the screen like puppets.

In "We Are Looking at You, Agnes," heavy repetition is used to create a different kind of frenzy. Agnes, the protagonist and narrator of the story, is obsessed with the idea that she is being judged by her family for having become a prostitute. Her obsession is clearly reflected by the mad persistence of a series of paranoid thoughts which are presented and emphasized by the very heavy repetition of such lines as "don't sit there all day long and look at me like that without saying something about it" and "Ask me, Papa; I'll tell you the truth."

A final effect created by Caldwell's use of heavy repetition is apparent in "Daughter," a story in which the extreme intensity of repeated phrases and sentences results in the creation of symbolic narrative. "Daughter" is about Jim, a black man who has been jailed because he murdered his young daughter when he could no longer stand her being hungry. In presenting "Daughter," Caldwell uses repetition of several types. Certain statements by Jim and other characters are repeated consistently through much of the story. The most important of these repeated statements is Jim's, "Daughter's been hungry though—awful hungry," which with slight variations is repeated eight times. Often, the statement is followed by Jim's averring, "I just couldn't stand it no longer" or by a slight variation of this sentence. The sheriff also repeats himself fairly consistently throughout the story. Because he is afraid that Jim will get excited and dangerous, the sheriff says again and again, "Now, just take it easy, Jim boy" or "Now, don't you get careless, Jim boy," or a similar statement. Other phrases and sentences are repeated during specific sections of the story to emphasize certain points. Early in the story, as the townspeople try to determine exactly what happened, their question, "It must have been an accident, wasn't it, Jim?" is repeated three times in about a page. Later, when Jim indicates that he had no money to buy food, the townspeople say four times "it don't seem right" that Jim should have killed his child when he might have asked for food, and Jim defends himself by responding several times, "I made enough for all of us to eat," emphasizing the fact that he didn't want to ask for handouts since he had worked and made money he never received.

Finally, in addition to the many repetitions in conversation, Caldwell uses frequent repetition in his descriptions of events. The most important and most noticeable aspect of the repetition in "Daughter" is the fact that the repeated statements and descriptive details occur in a very limited space. The story is five pages long and most of the repetition occurs in the first three pages. As a result, there are passages during which nearly every line is a repeated line. In addition to creating tension, this extremely heavy repetition causes "Daughter" to seem at times less like a straight narrative than a kind of chant, something akin to the responsive reading during a church service or to the dialogue between character and chorus in some Greek tragedies. Through the process of repetition, lines like "Daughter was hungry" and "It don't seem right" take on symbolic power as capsulations of regional realities, and the almost ritualistic repetition of these statements by the crowd, the sheriff, and Jim causes their whole dialogue to have significance as a general statement about racial injustice and exploitation. All in all, the heavy repetition in "Daughter" helps to expand a single confrontation between a black man, a sheriff, and a group of townspeople into universal—or at least national—significance.[6]

Another general aspect of Caldwell's experimentation with repetition is his blending of repeated statements with colloquial diction, rhyme and rhythm to create stories which might be called prose folk ballads. The most successful of these stories are "Candy-Man Beechum" and "The Fly in the Coffin," both of which are attempts to portray aspects of black life in the South.

Caldwell uses colloquial diction in "Candy-Man Beechum" and "The Fly in the Coffin" in an unusual way. Most stories about blacks written by both whites and blacks are presented by narrators who use standard white American English. In "Candy-Man Beechum" and "The Fly in the Coffin," however, Caldwell uses third-person narrators who present events in a convincing rendition of black English. The opening paragraphs of the two stories illustrate Caldwell's method:

"Candy-Man Beechum":

It was ten miles out of the Ogeechee swamps, from the sawmill to the top of the ridge, but it was just one big step to Candy-Man. The way he stepped over those Middle Georgia gullies was a sight to see [23].

"The Fly in the Coffin":

There was poor old Dose Muffin, stretched out on the corn-crib floor, dead as a frostbitten watermelon vine in November, and a pesky housefly was walking all over his nose [576].

While the colloquial diction in these paragraphs is not obtrusive, the phrases "it was just one big step," "was a sight to see," "poor old," and the down-home simile, "dead as a frostbitten watermelon vine in November," create a feeling that the reader is not simply observing events involving black people but that he is listening to tales which are products of black folk culture.[7]

Caldwell uses repetition to develop a prose chorus in each story, and he carefully controls its appearance to emphasize aspects of the action. The chorus in "Candy-Man Beechum" is the periodic repetition of someone asking, "Where you goin', Candy-Man," "What's your big hurry, Candy-Man," or a variation of these sentences, and of Candy-Man's response: "Make way for these flappin feet, boys... Here I come!" or a variation. Each repetition of this chorus brings Candy-Man closer to town and to the danger his confidence obviously creates for him in a locale where, as one character puts it, "the white-folks is first-come." By the end of the third repetition of the chorus, the reader has become accustomed to the exuberant rhythm created by the repeated lines. The result is that when the fourth chorus begins with the white policeman's question "What's your hurry, Candy-Man?" and is not followed by Candy-Man's customary response, the stylistic rhythm is as abruptly interrupted as Candy-Man's journey is. For a moment the reader wonders if Candy-Man's confidence has been shaken, if the black man will give in and be taken to jail. But Candy-Man has the triumphant last word. When the policeman warns that if Candy-Man keeps arguing, he'll be forced to "hurry him on" to death, Candy-Man replies, "If that's the way it's to be, then make way for Candy-Man Beechum because here I come." The triumph of Candy-Man's refusal to compromise the vitality of his life is beautifully emphasized stylistically by the completion of the formerly interrupted chorus.

In "The Fly in the Coffin," a yarn in which a dead man interrupts the joyous celebration of his funeral to demand a fly-swatter so he can kill a fly which has gotten trapped in his coffin, the chorus is a three-statement conversation between Aunt Marty and Woodrow. Three times Aunt Marty says, "You, Woodrow, you! Go look in that corncrib and take a look if any old flies worrying Dose" or a slight variation; three times Woodrow hesitates to obey her; and three times Aunt Marty assures Woodrow that he must protect Dose from the flies. The repetition of this conversation creates an expectation in the reader which is frustrated during the last third of the story. After Aunt Marty gets a swatter and Dose lies back down in the coffin, the story ends with a series of rhythmic paragraphs but without a return to the chorus. Caldwell's decision to conclude the story in this manner is perfectly appropriate; the story trails off stylistically just as the party and the dancing continue on into the night.

The ballad-like feeling created in the two stories by Caldwell's combination of colloquial diction and repetition is enhanced by his unusual use of rhyme and rhythm in specific sentences. When Candy-Man is unjustly stopped by the "white-boss," for example, he says, "I never bothered white-folks, and they sure oughtn't bother me. But there ain't much use in living if that's the way it's going to be." The rhyme of "me" and "be" is made particularly emphatic by the rhythmic similarity of the two sentences. In some passages rhythm alone is used effectively. Near the middle of the story, for instance, the narrator explains "Eight miles to town, and two more to go, and he'd be rapping on that yellow gal's door." In "The Fly in the Coffin" Aunt Marty's explanations of why Woodrow must keep flies away from Dose are always rhythmic and in two instances they rhyme: "Dead or alive, Dose cares about flies" is one of these; "Dose sees flies, he dead or alive" is the other. Rhythm alone is used effectively in such sentences as "Poor old Dose, dead a day and a night, couldn't say a word," and "The jumper was dry, the coffin was thrown together, and the grave was six feet deep."

The development of the rhythmically musical folk ballad form for "Candy-Man Beechum" and "The Fly in the Coffin" is particularly apropos. Both stories not only portray aspects of black life in the South as black people might tell of them, but also dramatize positive responses of black people to their situation. "Candy-Man Beechum" portrays a man who heroically ignores social limitations and lives a life which, while tragically short, is vigorous and full of good humor. In "The Fly in the Coffin" even the reality of death fails to kill either the vitality of Dose, whose hatred of flies is so strong that it enables him to come back to life, or the energy of Dose's neighbors, who are able to wring joy out of tragedy and limited surroundings. The syncopated musical style of the two prose ballads emphasizes this theme of people rising above apparent limitations by reminding the reader of that tradition of the spiritual and jazz which itself represents the triumph of black vitality over societal oppression. The style of these two stories, in other words, is a reflection of the idea the stories present.[8]

While the fundamental quality of Caldwell's prose style is simplicity, a careful investigation of his short fiction shows that he has experimented with various kinds of simplicity. The most important stylistic experiments in the stories discussed, as well as in a substantial number which have not been mentioned, involve repetition.[9] Caldwell controls both the number of repeated words, phrases, and sentences and their distribution to create a wide range of effects, many of which are exciting and unusual. He also experiments with colloquial diction and with rhyme and rhythm and blends these aspects of style with repetition to create vibrantly musical folk ballads, prose pieces which may be unique in English. All in all, Caldwell's ability to work with the possibilities of style is noteworthy even in a period of American literature which includes such brilliant stylists as Gertrude Stein, Ernest Hemingway, and William Faulkner.

"Repetition as Technique in the Short Stories of Erskine Caldwell" was published in *Studies in American Fiction* 5, no. 2 (Autumn, 1977): 213-25.

---

1 James Dickey, *Sorties* (New York: Doubleday, 1971), 117.
2 Although most critics who mention Caldwell's short stories seem impressed with their quality, almost nothing has been written about them except for a few reviews and introductions. Even James Korges, who calls Caldwell "one of the American masters of the short story," spends only one paragraph on the short fiction in his pamphlet on Caldwell. See *Erskine Caldwell* (Minneapolis: University of Minnesota Press, 1969), 45-46. A few critics have mentioned aspects of Caldwell's style. Joseph Warren Beach describes what he calls the *"naive* style," and Henry Seidel Canby discusses Caldwell's use of understatement and the strong emotion it often disguises. See Beach, *American Fiction: 1920-1940* (New York: Macmillan, 1941), 247; and Canby, "Erskine Caldwell," an introduction to *A Day's Wooing and Other Stories* (New York: Grosset & Dunlap, 1944), vii-xiii. Randall Jarrell mentions Caldwell's heavy use of repetition, a quality which Kenneth Burke feels is Caldwell's greatest vice: "He seems as contented as a savage to say the same thing again and again," but Burke also suggests that repetition in Caldwell's prose "is so extreme as almost to perform the function of rhyme in verse." See Jarrell, "Ten Books," *Southern Review,* (1936), 404; and Burke, *The Philosophy of Literary Form* (Baton Rouge: Louisiana State University Press, 1941), 360. More recently, C. Hugh Holman has called Caldwell's style, "simple, direct, with underlying folk rhythms, resulting in part from repetition and in part from a folk vocabulary." See "The View from the Regency-Hyatt: Southern Social Issues and the Outer World," in George Core, *Southern Fiction Today: Renascence and Beyond* (Athens: University of Georgia Press, 1969), 29-30. Finally, in his interesting and painstaking review of French criticism on Caldwell, Stewart Benedict suggests that Caldwell's stylistic discipline is what makes him an important figure in the eyes of the French. See "Gallic Light on Erskine Caldwell," *SAQ*, 60 (1961), 390-97.
3 All quotations are from Erskine Caldwell, *The Complete Stories of Erskine Caldwell* (Boston: Little, Brown, 1953). Because of the brevity of most of Caldwell's stories and because of the

nature of much of the quotation in this essay, specific page references would often be distracting. As a result, only long quotations include page references. These are included in the text.

4   The ending of "The Medicine Man" involves a final punch line. Having agreed at gunpoint to marry Effie and having been made something of a fool in the process, the Professor is so much the optimistic salesman that when Effie exclaims, "Just to think that I'm going to marry a traveling herb doctor. Why! all the girls in town will be so envious of me they won't speak for a month!" he immediately returns to his former glory: "'Absolutely' Professor Eaton said, pulling tight the loosened knot in his tie and adjusting it in the opening of his celluloid collar. 'Absolutely. Indian Root Tonic has unlimited powers...'" The Professor's final repetition of "absolutely" is the funniest line in the story, and it is funny because it is a repeated line, and because it emphasizes the impossibility of interrupting for long the Professor's irrepressible blarney.

5   "One-two" is an adjectival combination expressing the idea "approximately one or two." Caldwell also uses "three-four," "four-five," etc. Such combinations were presumably common in rural Maine when Caldwell wrote "Country Full of Swedes."

6   "Masses of Men," a story which originally appeared with "Daughter" in *Kneel to the Rising Sun*, is similar to "Daughter" in the way it uses repetition. "Masses of Men" is not a totally satisfactory story, but it contains a brilliant, brutal scene in which a poverty-stricken mother sells her nine-year-old daughter as a prostitute to a man who pays her twenty-five cents. The scene uses the extremely heavy repetition of several lines in much the way "Daughter" does to build breath-taking tension and to elevate the sordid events into a kind of ritualized general statement about the dehumanizing effects of poverty, cold, and starvation. *God's Little Acre* also uses repetition in this manner in those chapters during which Will goes to the factory to "turn on the power." See *God's Little Acre* (New York: Viking, 1933), 227-54.

7   Similar use of colloquial diction can be found in such stories as "Big Buck" and "Nine Dollars' Worth of Mumble," though it is not used as consistently or as effectively as in "Candy-Man Beechum" and "The Fly in the Coffin."

8   Like "The Fly in the Coffin" and "Candy-Man Beechum," "The First Autumn" is made memorable in part by Caldwell's development of a chorus which helps to create a ballad-like feeling. The chorus is a series of three-fold repetitions: of "Woof! Woof! Woof!" when the children and father are playing bear; of "Neigh! Neigh! Neigh!" when they're playing horse; and of "Boo!...Boo!...Boo!" when the children and their mother sneak up on the father when they think he's asleep. The strange mood created by the chorus is enhanced by Caldwell's unusual juxtaposition of the third-person narrator's use of diction one normally expects of a child—the narrator, for example, refers to the father as "Daddy" and of the use by the children of diction which sounds very adult. Fittingly, the juxtaposition reflects the reversal of roles the story is involved with. The father dies while playing games with children who are playing at being adult, and the reader assumes that as a result of the father's death at a comparatively young age, the children will soon be forced in reality to become more adult.

9   Some stories which have not been mentioned in which repetition is an important device are "Blue Boy," "Dorothy," "An Evening in Nuevo Leon," "The Growing Season," "Horse Thief," "Indian Summer," "Kneel to the Rising Sun," "The Mating of Marjorie," "Mamma's Little Girl," "Meddlesome Jack," "Memorandum," "The Negro in the Well," "Over the Green Mountains," "Picking Cotton," "Slow Death," "Yellow Girl," and "A Woman in the House."

Young boys seen during the journey up through the layers of film emulsion in J. J. Murphy's *Print Generation* (1974). Murphy asked his film lab to make contact prints of contact prints of his one-minute 16mm diary, until the contact printings removed, layer by layer, virtually of all the emulsion. Then he organized fifty contact prints so that for the first half-film we "travel" from celluloid surface up through the layers of emulsion as they accumulate until the original print is seen; then he flipped the image to maintain composition, so that viewers "travel" back down to the celluloid. The sound is a tape recording of ocean waves that is retaped and retaped… then organized in reverse-order from the imagery.

1977

J. J. Murphy: In Progress

I met J. J. Murphy somewhere in the mid-1970s when he was teaching filmmaking and film history at Kirkland College (Kirkland became part of Hamilton College in 1978). At the time, I was teaching American literature and film appreciation at nearby Utica College. I believe the first Murphy film I saw, at a screening at Kirkland, was *Print Generation* (1974) and I was immediately fascinated. Murphy and I became friends and I was delighted to be able to explore his films. The films puzzled me—they seemed so different from conventional movies—and soon I was excited to try writing about them.

At some point I completed what I thought was a sensible interpretation of Murphy's films (maybe just of *Print Generation*) and sent the essay to him, thinking he'd be interested and grateful. When I phoned him some days later, assuming he would have read the piece, I asked him what he thought. He said, "I have a problem with it." I was taken aback, "What kind of problem?" "I have a problem with the approach." I felt disappointed and was dumbfounded about what he might have meant.

In time, I came to understand that Murphy, quite correctly, realized that I had written about *Print Generation* as if it were a literary work. As a result, I was blind to fundamental elements of the film and how Murphy himself understood his filmmaking. Any cineaste who would see *Print Generation* now would recognize that fundamentally Murphy was conducting an experiment to see what he could find out about how the emulsion on a 16mm filmstrip was constructed. Those of us who projected 16mm prints of films were continually aware of the fragility of the emulsion, since any scratch on the print was visible and the depth of scratches sometimes revealed the complexity of emulsion chemistry.

Of course, screenings of *Print Generation* are rarer now than they were when many of us were finding our way into the world of avant-garde filmmaking in the 1970s. Indeed, 16mm films have become difficult to show, not only because good, undamaged prints are rare, but also because so many 16mm projectors no longer work. During recent decades AV technicians at most colleges and universities have deep-sixed 16mm altogether, considering it no longer a viable projection technology.

Of course, a digital version of *Print Generation*, if there were one, would seem a betrayal of the original film. Whether 16mm projection can have a revival—comparable perhaps to the revival of vinyl recordings of music—remains to be seen. Pip Chodorov tells me that 16mm remains more fully viable in Europe than in the United States (email to the author, June 19, 2024).

What follows is one of my first film essays and, especially when I get to my interpretation of *Print Generation*, a clear demonstration of my tendency to approach cinema as a form of literature, rather than as its own artform. I'm not sure this is exactly the essay I sent to Murphy—but it might have been. Perhaps I published the piece, then showed it to Murphy, hoping for his approval—or perhaps I sent him a draft of the piece which was revised afterword.

Note: the two parenthetical comments in the version of the essay printed here were originally footnotes. A few spelling errors have been corrected, several commas have been added, and in a few instances capital letters have been replaced by non-caps.

* * *

One of the great joys of exploring contemporary film is that just when you think, well, now I've seen the best work of the most interesting filmmakers, you discover half a dozen new filmmakers and a dozen new films of interest and realize that these lead the way to dozens and dozens more. In the past week I've seen Nathaniel Dorsky's *Summerwind* and Peter Foldes' *Hunger*, and today I discovered *In Progress*, a film co-made by Ed Small and J. J. Murphy, a filmmaker whose work has interested me for some time. While this constant process of discovery is exciting for the viewer, however, it reflects a situation which must be frustrating for many filmmakers. *Summerwind* was finished twelve years ago; *In Progress* five years ago. I've been reading several periodicals which review experimental film, and I've looked through most books on the area, and until this week I'd never heard of Dorsky, and while I've known J. J. for a while, it is only because he has been teaching nearby at Kirkland College in Clinton, New York. Sometimes when a filmmaker's work is "discovered," it stays in that limited portion of the public eye which experimental film commands pretty consistently for a while. Too often, however, filmmakers who rank with the very best are noticed momentarily, only to find their work overlooked almost before the smell of new prints has disappeared. This has been the case with Murphy's work. There is no question of its significance, but while it is occasionally rented here and there (more on the West Coast than in the Northeast), and while Murphy himself makes appearances at colleges and museums (most recently at Swarthmore and Utica College), it is quite possible to be pretty well acquainted with experimental film without knowing his name or anything about his films.

If someone unacquainted with Murphy's films were looking through the Canyon Cinema catalogue, where the widest selection of his work is available, he or she would probably be most tempted to rent *Highway Landscape*, since it seems to be the most widely screened of Murphy's films and the one which has garnered the most awards. The catalogue listing, however, tends to create a false picture of the overall quality of Murphy's work. *Highway Landscape* is an impressive and meaningful meditation on the inevitability of death and natural process even in a fast-paced, highly technological society, but is far from the only significant film in the catalogue. The fact is that all five films listed are very interesting, and three of them—the three most recent—are magnificent (actually, *In Progress* was begun before any other film listed in the Canyon Cinema catalogue, but it was not finished until after *Highway Landscape* and *Ice*).

In Progress is in a genre with Larry Gottheim's *Barn Rushes*, *Doorway*, and *Fog Line* (the last two of which are much-too-infrequently screened): it balances an investigation of a specific Iowa landscape over a period of nearly a year with self-reflexive revelation of the fundamental components of the filmmaking process. With the exception of the first and last shots, the film is made up of approximately three-second images of a basically not-very-spectacular rural landscape taken from a stationary camera. A wide range of variables is developed. There are variables in the weather during individual seasons and of the seasons themselves and frequent variations in exactly what we see in the landscape in the way of people, cars and other objects. Other variables include the constant alterations in the amount, quality, and direction of light, the frequent alterations in the color of various parts of the imagery, the repeated changes in foreground-background relationships, and such directly reflexive aspects of the imagery as the film grain, which dances in various parts of the imagery in different shots, and the reflections of parts of the camera and room behind it in the window the camera is shooting through. All these aspects of the film's imagery combine to create a constantly fascinating and very moving meditation on the infinite visual possibilities which result from the combination of film and even a limited section of a single rural landscape. While the overall pace of *In Progress* is serene and the overall effect one of wonder, the changing of shots every three seconds creates a tension in the viewer, who frequently wants more time to examine what he's seeing. This tension, however, helps to emphasize a central theme of Murphy's work—the constancy and inevitability of change and the need for the artist to help us sensitize ourselves so that we can see the beauty of things as they flash by us, always too quickly for us to capture, but slowly enough for an alert sensibility to feel and enjoy them.

Sky Blue Water Light Sign is best seen in total innocence. My guess is that if one knows what he or she is looking at before seeing this little film, half of its excitement and a good deal of its meaning disappear. Seen in total innocence, though (and maybe I'm exaggerating the importance of this), *Sky Blue Water Light Sign* is a wonder. With Gottheim's *Blues* and Frampton's *Lemon*, it is one of the happiest, most uplifting short films I've ever seen. Also, it confirms the thematic direction taken in *In Progress*; all that we see during the brief film is constantly changing, disappearing as we see it. The implication is that the best the process of film can do is to help us see the changes more clearly.

Murphy's most accomplished film to date is the fifty-minute *Print Generation*: in it an exploration of the process of contact printing forms the basis for his most complex and insightful dramatization of the lovely evanescence of the good things in life. To make *Print Generation* Murphy produced a one-minute film of sixty one-second images, personal images photographed during the summer of 1973. He made a print of this film, then a print of the print, then a print of the print of the print, and so on. Since each generation of printing subtracted from the photographic quality of the imagery, it was inevitable that if he printed prints of prints long enough, the images would ultimately disappear. Having made fifty print generations, Murphy constructed the film so that we first see the one-minute collection of images in an extremely disintegrated state and then follow every second print generation until, halfway through the film, we see the images fully developed. During the second half of the film, we move through the other generations back to the point where we began.

(Sound adds an important dimension to *Print Generation*. Murphy tape-recorded ocean waves breaking, then recorded the recording, then recorded that recording, and so on. As the film begins, we hear the waves clearly; as the minutes pass, we hear the sound in more and more disintegrated form, until, halfway through the film, it reaches a point of maximum distortion. During the second half of the film, the process is reversed. Thematically, as we move to and from the opening visual images, we are reminded that all life, all generation, ultimately began in the sea.)

The imagery in *Print Generation* is constantly engaging. The slow changes the shots go through are not simply a means to the "finished" images. When I remember the film, I don't think of the finished images, but of specific images at various points of re- and decomposition. Further, Murphy creates a fascinating counterpoint of rhythms. The one-second pulse of the changing shots is one level; the various movements within each image are a second; and the eyes' creation of bridges between movements in one shot and to movements in the next is a third. Again, as is true in earlier films, in *Print Generation* the process of change itself is the interesting thing, not any specific result change brings about. All change can bring anyway, Murphy suggests, is more change of differing kinds.

All in all, the film's stately movement from faint dot patterns to completed images back to dot patterns forms a metaphor for cosmic changes of which we are a tiny part and certain crucial aspects of our personal experience of events. As the sixty images move, one each second, to and from more recognizable form, we are reminded that not only are all those people and objects that surround us changing as the seconds go by, but that everything from the beginning of time, when the first particles of matter cohered, has always been changing and will continue to change as long as it exists. For Murphy the fundamental fact of constant change is not at all depressing: it is simply a fascinating reality which, if approached with alert senses, thoughts, and feelings, can be productive of great gestures, perceptions, moments. And before we have a chance to grasp these lovely but fragile memories, we are moving back through decomposing print generations, finding it very hard to remember what we saw. The point is that to

J. J. Murphy and Scott MacDonald in the late 1970s.
Photo by Steve Liebman.

the extent we look ahead to what deceptively appears to be the culmination of changes we are undergoing, we merely realize too late that life has gone by, the "culminations" most quickly of all. However, if we can recognize that life *is* change and train our perceptions on the process of the change itself, we can more fully enjoy the riches available to our senses, thoughts, and feelings.

"J. J. Murphy: In Progress" was published in *Ideolects*, no. 5 (April/May/June 1977), 9-12. The issue was edited by Vincent Grenier and Bob Schneider; it included essays by Myron Adams, Jacqueline Austin, David Cohen, Coleen Fitzgibbon and Robin Winters, Grenier, Jim Hoberman, Taka Iimura, Helene Kaplan, Ann Knutson, David Tafler, Lynne Tillman, plus "Home Movie Comics" by Art Spiegelman.

Murphy's films are available, as 16mm prints, at Canyon Cinema. He no longer makes films. His *Rewriting Indie Cinema: Improvisation, Psychodrama, and the Screenplay* was published by Columbia University Press in 2019; his *The Florida Project*, in 2021 by the University of Texas Press as part of its 21st Century Film Essentials series. He founded and runs an art gallery in New York City (jjmurphygallery.com).

1983

Letters from Scott MacDonald to Marjorie Keller

In 1983, *Idiolects*, no. 13 ("letters") was published. It was conceived and edited by filmmakers Marjorie Keller and Mary Filippo. Keller's May 20, 1983 letter is the preface to the collection. She explains:

> Dear Readers,
> My idea for this issue of *Idiolects* was to try to collect many kinds of writing about film intended for an audience of one, written with the grace and urgency that letters often are. Mary [Filippo] and I partially succeeded. The letters dug out of people's files were chosen for their wit, intensity or historical interest. Some of the letters were written for this occasion and are included because the editors found the whole or parts of them to deal with a trend, a quirk, or an individual in an interesting (if sometimes neurotic) way. Many letters have been left out. Those that seemed fictional, blatantly journalistic or self-promotional, with little else to recommend them were excluded. A number of letters were written on the same subjects—the state of the art, specific films or filmmakers. I tried to choose one of them in order to keep the range of the magazine broad. And finally, many letters were left out simply because there was not space enough. Perhaps a second issue...

Seventy-six one-to-three-page letters from filmmakers, programmers and critics are included. Amos Vogel writes to Keller, "Who is this man Spielberg...and why is he making films?"; Hollis Frampton writes two letters to Annette Michelson (one on palindromes); Su Friedrich tells Leslie Thornton about really *seeing Gently Down the Stream* for the first time; Robert Breer writes to Sidney Peterson to applaud Peterson's book, *The Dark of the Screen*; David James writes to Paul Arthur and Paul Arthur writes to David James...

At the time, I was in the throes of my excitement at having found a field—independent cinema—that I'd come to feel I might be of service to, and I sent the editors the "letters" that follow (I no longer have any idea why I blacked out certain names or titles or even who or what they were).

* * *

Dear Margie,

I like writing letters, so I'm sending three.

I'm finding this a very confusing period. A lot seems to be happening, but I'm not at all clear where it's all going, or exactly where I think it should go. I am seeing a lot of films I want to come back to. The first ones that come to mind are Patricia Gruben's Sifted Evidence, ▮▮▮▮▮, Manuel De Landa's Harmful or Fatal if Swallowed and Robert Nelson's Thick Pucker (which are interestingly similar in the way that Hollis Frampton's Manual of Arms and Vivienne Dick's Guerillere Talks are similar), George Romero's Creepshow, Charles Barnett's Killer of Sheep, Jackie Raynal's New York Story, Bob Huot's Dr. Faustus' Foot Fetish, Diana Barrie's The Annunciation and Magic Explained, Werner Herzog's Every Man for Himself and God Against All (I finally got to see it), Timothy Asch's films about the Yanomamo (The Ax Fight, The Feast . . .), Ernest Schoedsack and Merian C. Cooper's Grass (an ethnographic film they made eight years before King Kong), Taka Iimura's Talking Picture (which I haven't actually seen—I read the script), Morgan Fisher's Screening Room (a 1970 film installation which I've read about.

I love discovering interesting new films, and new old films, but it also creates a certain frustration. I always feel drawn back to films I've been familiar with for some time, but I rarely find the time to really indulge my desire to explore them. Some of the films I'd most like to spend more time looking at/writing about are Peter Watkins' The War Game (which is much more subtle and complex than it's usually thought to be, particularly in its way of dealing with the effect of the mass media on major events), Morgan Fisher's Production Stills, Ernie Gehr's Morning, Jackie Raynal's Deux Fois, Babette Mangolte's What Maisie Knew, Robert Nelson's Blue Shut, Jonas Mekas's Diaries Notes & Sketches: Lost Lost Lost, Robert Huot's Super-8 Diary--1979, and the whole mini-genre of single-shot films: Andy Warhol's (I guess--I've never had the chance to see Warhol's films), Robert Nelson's The Awful Backlash, Morgan Fisher's Phi Phenomenon, Production Stills, ▇▇▇▇▇▇▇, The Wilkenson Household ▇▇▇▇▇▇▇ Fire Alarm, Larry Gottheim's Blues, Corn, Doorway, Harmonica, J. J. Murphy's Highway Landscape and Skyt Blue Water Light Sign, Robert Huot's Snow, Michael Snow and Joyce Wieland's Dripping Water and Snow's Breakfast, and a number of Barry Gerson's films; and, of course, the Lumière films and that long, apparently continuous 1906 trolley shot that Ernie Gehr used as the raw material for Eureka. I wonder if there are interesting single-shot films available from the Library of Congress. Also, I'd like to do more serious research and some writing about the horror film, about Keaton and the other silent comedians, etc. etc.

The other week
I tried "magic mushrooms"
(feels silly to type that) agai
n. (Somehow I was never in contact
with people who were exploring hallucin
ogens in the sixties, so this sort of thing
is pretty new for me.) Anyway, I was sitting
on our livingroom rug, looking at the space in f
ront of me and seeing   it glow and quive
r, and feeling as i   f something
was hovering just   behind
it, just around   the
edge. It wasn't
anything like t
he commercial m
ovie zoom-zap r
epresentation o
f "trips"; it w
as more lovely
and more serene
than I had expe
cted. I was li
stening to Terr
y Riley's In C
(a perfect choi
 ce, it turned o   ut).
  As I sat there e   nthral
  led, I remember   ed seeing
   the feeling I wa   s experiencin
    g in Tom Chomont'   s films: A Persia
     n Rug, Aria, Lifest   yle, Minor Revisions.
      .. Then, by coincidence, this past week I show
      ed his Ophelia and The Cat Lady on a program w
      ith Tod Browning's Freaks. The Cat Lady w
       as a knockout, and I realized that I'd
        not known how interesting it is be
         cause I'd only seen it on my
           tiny workroom screen a
                t home.

Hope all's well.

Scott MacDonald

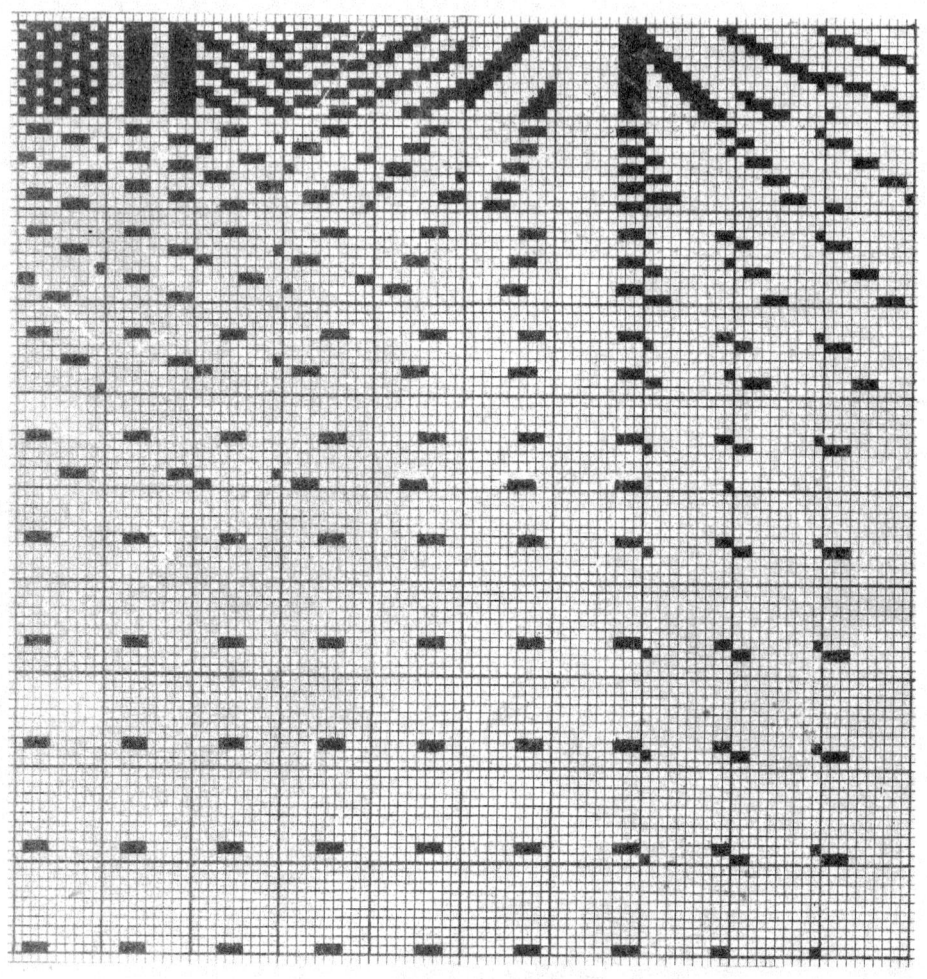

Map of THE VOY AGE

Back cover ("the Map") of
Emmett Williams' *THE VOY AGE* (1975).

1985

ALL HAN ZON DEK!: A Reading of
Emmett Williams' *THE VOY AGE*

I do not remember when I became interested in visual poetry (a.k.a. "concrete poetry"), though I'm sure that my interest must have been at least partly instigated by e. e. cummings who I was aware of as an undergraduate, originally because of the clever eroticism of his poem "she being Brand," and subsequently because of the verbal/visual play in other poems in *100 Selected Poems* (New York: Grove Press, 1959). I continued to come back to cummings for many years.

Even earlier, part of my pleasure in movies, from the late 1950s on, was the increasingly inventive use of visual text in opening credit sequences: *Psycho*, most obviously, and in other, earlier films by Hitchcock, as well as in the James Bond and Pink Panther series and later, particular films: *Easy Rider* comes to mind. And still earlier, as a child, I loved the roadside Burma-Shave signs, where one read a series of six signs placed at equal intervals along two-lane roads: "he tried/to cross/as fast train neared/death didn't draft him/he volunteered/Burma-Shave" "on curves ahead/remember sonny/ that rabbit's foot/didn't save/the bunny/Burma-Shave" "slow down, Pa/sakes alive!/ Ma missed signs/four/and five/Burma-shave" (see Frank Rowsome, Jr., *The Verse by the Side of the Road* [New York: Dutton, 1965] for the story of the Burma-Shave signs and the texts of all 600.)

During the 1960s and 1970s, visual language of new kinds was in the air, pretty much the same cultural air that was sustaining avant-garde filmmaking. Emmett Williams and Richard Kostelanetz published their own work and the work of other visual poets from many nations in extensive edited collections. And when George Maciunas instigated the Flux Film Anthology in 1960, he included Paul Sharits' *WordMovieFluxFilm* (Flux Film 28) along with many other films that were primarily or largely visual text (verbal or numerical), including Maciunas' own *End After 9* (Flux Film 3), *10 Feet* and *1000 frames* (Flux Films 7 and 8), James Riddle's *9 Minutes* (Flux Film 6), George Brecht's *Entrance to Exit* (Flux Film 10). There is also Sharits' unnumbered text: "pull down roll fold into pad wipe until clean drop into toilet flush away paper"! All these Flux Films are part of the collection "Flux Film Anthology, available on an Anthology Film Archives/Re-Voir DVD.

I tried my hand at writing visual poems, mostly for friends and colleagues—and even had a 2-page spread in Richard Kostelanetz's *A Critical (Ninth) Assembling* (New York: Precisely 6789, 1979), in which I pitched a number of independent films that made inventive use of visual text, then responded satirically to Kostelanetz's clever but annoyingly sexist visual poem, "Nymphomania." My survey essay "Text As Image (in some recent North American avant-garde films)" was published in *Afterimage* (Visual Studies Workshop) 13, no. 8 (March 1986): 9-20; and was followed, nine years later, by *Screen Writings: Scripts and Texts by Independent Filmmakers* (Berkeley: University of California Press, 1995). An interest in experimental text, particularly visually experimental text has stayed with me.

For the January 1985 issue of *Afterimage* I wrote a piece on Emmett Williams' book *THE VOY AGE*, published in 1975 in an edition of 1000. Williams was prolific as a publisher, writer, and performer, but for me, *THE VOY AGE* remains his most remarkable work—it brings the history of literature and the history of moving-image media together in an efficient, amusing, and imaginative way. That the book is not currently in distribution is for me an ongoing frustration, and including the Williams essay for this collection has felt Quixotic. Yet I long to share THE VOY AGE with students and hope to draw enough attention to Williams' wry epic—the sea voyage in this odyssey takes about fifteen minutes to read—to instigate its re-publication.

Note: the two footnotes that were part of the original publication of my essay have become parentheses for this publication.

* * *

I continually hear complaints about the paucity of interesting art making its way into the world. Yet I always feel completely besieged by work I want to see, or see more of. Year by year, the gap between my exposure to artwork and the opportunity to do at least a bit of writing about it grows larger. At the present rate, I won't get to respond to what's interested me most during the last couple of years—Marlene Gorris' *A Question of Silence*, for example; Diana Barrie's revisionist versions of Georges Méliès; Barbara Kruger's photographs; and Wayne Wang's *Chan Is Missing*—until the mid-1990s! The whole problem is exacerbated by the tendency—often the commitment—of many artists of the 1960s and 1970s to avoid traditional categories and the oversimplification these categories may help to foster. Whole areas—mini-traditions—have grown up *between* other, more traditional media, and individual artists have felt free to move continually from one set of intersections to another. With so much activity of so many kinds, interesting, even break-through achievements are always in danger of slipping through the cracks. One such work, which I have a special concern about, is Emmett Williams' visual-poetic epic, THE VOY AGE (printed in an edition of 1000 in Stuttgart by Hansjörg Mayer in 1975).

Williams has been a leading figure in the development of visual (or "concrete") poetry, that mini-tradition lying at the intersection of literature and graphic design, since the 1950s. His *Anthology of Concrete Poetry* (New York: Something Else, 1967) was a valuable early sampling of what had come to be a nearly worldwide phenomenon; his *Selected Shorter Poems 1950-1970* (New York: New Directions, 1975) is full of interesting work, as is *Schemes and Variations*, a book-length documentation of a show at the National Gallery of Berlin—where Williams lives (the catalogue was published by Hansjörg Mayer in 1981). Best of all, his book-length visual "epics"—*sweethearts* (Hansjörg Mayer, 1967, and New York: Something Else, 1968) and THE VOY AGE—are the two most accomplished longer visual poems I'm acquainted with. According to Williams' introduction, THE VOY AGE was written during the winter of 1975, in Halifax, Nova Scotia, while he was conducting a seminar at the Nova Scotia College of Art and Design: "I can remember sitting in my studio, following the slow progress of ships in the harbour, musing that a painter of seascapes could have used the studio to much greater advantage." The poem Williams had envisaged, a long poem about the adventures of "Two Buk Tim in Tim Buk Too" suddenly took a new direction. "Two Buk Tim fell overboard somewhere... He was replaced by an outspoken sea salt of a captain, and THE VOY AGE... metamorphosed into a trip through the inner space of a poem." In the traditional poetic epic, the formal dimensions of the poetic experience function to dramatize, clarify, and empower the narrative of the sea voyage.

```
  T E N   N Y E   A
T E   S E M   S I X
  F I E   F O E   F
U M   T W O   O N E
  A N D   O F F   W
E E   G O E   N O W
  Y O U   A N D   E
Y E   A W N   D I S
  F A N   T A S   T
I C   V O Y   A G E
```

```
    E Y E      G O T
    R H Y      T H M
    Y O U      G O T
    R H Y      T H M
    B U T      A W N
    D I S      V O Y
    A G E      A L L
    W E E      G E T
    I Z Z      L O G
    R H Y      T H M
```

```
              N O W
              W E E
              G E T
              O U R
              P O E
              E M M
              A L L
              I N N
              O N E
              R O W
```

Pages of *THE VOY AGE* (1975).

In *THE VOY AGE* the relationship is reversed: the "sea salt of a captain" who narrates the poem functions as a congenial guide through a wide range of formal devices.

The most fundamental formal device in *THE VOY AGE* is the rigorous grid structure Williams devised to contain the poem. It involves using words (real words or improvisations that suggest them) of only three letters each, set into a series of a hundred 100-space grids: "The only way to navigate was to break up language into 3-letter units. These triads move about in an invisible grid of one hundred squares via a mathematical progression. At the outset the triads are separated by single space; on page two, by two spaces; on page fifty, by fifty spaces—and on and on and on…" By "page" Williams means individual grid, the front side of each two-sided leaf of the volume—nothing is printed on the opposite side. The pages are not numbered in the text; Williams' numbering here refers only to the 100 grids. Particularly in the early pages, Williams' progression allows/forces the triads to create a series of overall designs, though after grid 12 or so, the number of triads is too small to maintain this design element. By the forty-ninth grid, the number of spaces between triads has grown too large to allow more than a single triad in the grid at a time, and by grid 100 no triads at all are left.

The length of *THE VOY AGE* is extended by one final formal device: each of the 100 grids is framed by a square outline that, along with the letters set within the grids, gets smaller each time the reader/viewer turns a page. When the number of spaces between the triads reaches 100, no letters remain in the grid, but *THE VOY AGE* continues until the "framing" square has become so small that one level smaller makes it disappear altogether. The book ends once we've seen the square at its smallest—as though it's become a period. The entire grid structure is presented as "Map of *THE VOY AGE*" on the back cover.

Even though Williams' elaborate grid structure allows him only 299 triads, he gets considerable mileage from the words he is able to make (the structure of *THE VOY AGE* results in six instances where fewer than three characters remain at the end of the final text line of the grid. GO fills the single two-character spot; punctuation marks are used in the remaining five). In fact, the challenge of seeing what could be done was central in Williams' conceptions of *THE VOY AGE*:

> Writing in three-letter units doesn't come naturally. of course. Neither does the sonnet form, or *Wuthering Heights*, or *Nu Descendant Un Escalier*. But this very restriction is part of what the poem is all about. I was startled by the range of possibilities such a tight form opened up. What a happy accident, or discovery, in a visual poem, that the pronoun *I* has to be written *eye* and that the seaway gives way to a *see way*.

Despite, and/or because of, his self-imposed limitations, Williams is able to develop not only a credible narrating character, but a range of witty, enjoyable word plays perfectly appropriate to what he calls his "pleasure cruise." In many instances, the word plays relate in obvious or subtle ways to the idea of a visual epic; in other instances, the poem seems to produce playful excesses, relevant—so far as I can see—only to Williams' interest in giving the reader/viewer an expanded visual

```
      D A
T      W
 S
F U N
  M O N
     A M I
        B U T
         I Z Z
            I T T
             A R T
```

```
  C A M
            E R A

  P O E
            T R Y

  A C T
            I O N
```

```
  A W N

        D I S

                V
O Y

    A G E
```

experience. The design of the title, as we see it on the cover and title page, can serve as an example. "THE VOY AGE" is organized into three vertically arranged triads. When read normally—left to right and down—we have the title. But the grid arrangement of the letters teases the eye into reading vertically and diagonally as well. This leads to the discovery of the vertical word EYE (and perhaps allows the reader's eye to construct phrases: THE EYE VOY AGE; THE EYE AGE) and several less relevant words: TVA (I suppose the idea of damming up rivers has at least a marginal connection to Williams' gridification of a sea voyage), TOE, HOG and VOY (Spanish for "I go"— a Spanish word makes particular sense for a voyage of discovery). The stencil-like typeface used for the title and throughout *THE VOY AGE* encourages the viewer's tendency to read Williams' pages as vertical/horizontal/diagonal graphic spaces as well as the more conventional literary way. Further, the "stenciled" typeface brings to mind the no-nonsense labeling characteristic of ocean-going shipping crates.

During approximately the first third of the poem, the reader/viewer is primarily involved in deciphering, responding to, and discovering the implications of the triads. Because of the limited options afforded by the 299 triads and the fact that many essential words (VOY AGE, for instance) require two or more triads, Williams makes use of slang (DIS for this, DAT for that), foreign words (MON AMI), an abbreviation (SOS) and a wide range of misspellings that communicate not only the word meant, but a feeling of dialect as well: AWN for on, and TAW KIN for talking, WAN TEW for want to, CUM for come, POE EMM for poem. The first-time reader must go through the enjoyable process of figuring out the individual words (I still have a tendency to say them aloud or mouth them) and how they fit together into sentences. The variety of designs engendered by Williams' grid, the free-form spelling, the fact that (especially well into the poem) individual sentences may require the reader to turn several pages, and the overall uniqueness of this entire project impede automatic comprehension.

As one discovers the specifics of the text, the nature of the voyage grows increasingly clear. The Captain is concerned to get the ship moving, but as he does, he confronts and comments on the strange poetic territory Williams' "map" has led him into. Grid one moves quickly and we seem to be underway: TEN NYE ATE SEM SIX FIE FOE FUM (a play on the giant's "fee fie fo fum") TWO ONE AND OFF WEE GOE NOW YOU AND EYE AWN DIS FAN TAS TIC VOY AGE. But immediately the Captain runs into trouble. Grids 2 and 3 tell us: EYE GOT RHY THM YOU GOT RHY THM BUT AWN DIS VOY AGE ALL WEE GET IZZ LOG RHY THM; AND MAN WEE GOT DAM LIT TLE LEE WAY AWN DIS WAN DER ING SEE WAY! The Captain's awareness of his difficult straits is continually punctuated by puns which relate to the experience of reading this visual poem: EYE GOT RHY THM is an allusion to the old Broadway tune, and it's perfectly relevant to the space/triad/space graphic rhythm in which the eye reads it. The use of BYE to spell by in grids 5 (YES LET TER BYE LET TER AND LET TER BYE LET TER) and 6 reflects the fact that, as the number of spaces between triads increases, each page will have fewer letters.

```
    OUR

              HEE


    ROW

                IZZ
```

```
         THE

                    P
    OE

              EMM
```

```
    SOS



              SOS
```

After a dozen or so grids, the Captain seems to betray frustration that as the voyage continues, the diminishing number of triads seems in danger of slowing it to a halt: ALL DIS SLO MOT ION & (grid 14) BRO KEN SYM BOL ISM (15) WHY NOT CUM OUT AND (16) SAY ITT ... (17). But actually, all this is in the way of helping the "crew" to fully understand the destination by empathizing with their possible concerns and difficulties. He soon explains: WEL ITS DIS WAY (18) ... AWN DIS VOY AGE (21) OUR HEE ROE ["row," also as in 10-row grid] IZZ THE POE EMM (23). In this poem, it's not the ocean's ebb and flow that decides the nature of the voyage; it's the EBB AND FLO (27) of . . . ERR (25) ANT SYN TAX (26), a syntax that does ebb and flow—graphically—in these grids. The Captain finds this situation both ROW MAN TIC (29) AND SEE MAN (30) TIC TOO! (31). From here on, each grid contains only two, then one word. As a result, we become more aware of the gradually decreasing size of the square margin line. As the Captain puts it: BUT ANY (36) VOY AGE (37) HAS ITS (38) LIM ITS (39).

It is both fitting and structurally ingenious that the first single-triad grid occurs just halfway through the poem, on the forty-ninth "page" and that the word WOE (implicitly both woe as in "woe is me" and *whoa*) is the only individual word repeated in two successive grids. From this point until the ninety-ninth grid, the nature of the reader's experience is fundamentally different, so different in fact that when the Captain nears the change, he warns the crew: SOS SOS (42) All HAN (43) ZON DEK (44) DEW YOU (45) SEE WUT (46) IZZ COM (47) ING ? (48). What is coming is the fact that, once the poem is down to one word per page, the action of holding the book with one hand (or laying it on a flat surface) and turning the pages one by one is so slow that it makes the sentences difficult to comprehend. Most readers I've observed (and I continue to use this method myself) reorient the book in their hand so that the book can be bent (to my knowledge, *THE VOY AGE*—unlike *sweethearts*—exists only in a paperback edition) and the pages released, one by one, but more quickly. I hold the back of the book with my left hand while my right hand holds the pages in much the same way I hold a DEK of cards when I shuffle. Just as the Captain warns, from here on we'll need both hands (AWL the HAN Z we have).

Once the reader/viewer has shifted the position of the book so as to get through the pages more quickly, the lone triad seems to move horizontally to the right, grid line after grid line, almost as if animated, as the GEO (51) MET (52) RIC (53) FOR (54) CES (55) GOB (56) BLE (57) UPP (58) OUR (59) POE (60) EMM (61) BIT (62) BYE (63) BIT (64) WEE [the words are very tiny by this time] (65) SEE (66) ITT (67) VAN (68) ISH (69).

When the poem is down to only three grid lines, the Captain and crew can see that, soon, they'll run out of words. YET (70) AWN (71) AND (72) AWN (73) WEE (74) TRA (75) VEL (76) DEE (77) PER (78) DEE (79) PER (80) TOO (81) FAR (82) OUT (83) FOR (84) RES (85) CUE (86). In fact, while the map on the back cover sees us through the 100 grids, we finally go beyond the terrain that's charted for us—BUT (87) POE (88) EMS (89) DEW (90) WUT (91) DEY (92) MUS (93) DEW (94). With a hardy NOW (95) OFF (96) WEE (97) GO (98) ! (99), the text ends [goes off the page].

```
                ALL
                              H
 A N
```

```
               ZON

 D E K
```

```


                          O F F
```

The text ends, but not *THE VOYAGE*. The book goes on for 26 more pages, as the margin line gradually disappears. The rigorousness, the density, and the subtlety of the voyage thus far makes these extra pages somewhat puzzling. Why did Williams decide to use that margin line if it was going to deviate so radically from the otherwise precise grid structure? The answer, I believe, is implied in the text and by the way in which the reader tends to experience the wordless pages. In the twelfth grid, the Captain calls CAM ERA POE TRY ACT ION. This reference to film becomes particularly suggestive when (and if) the reader notices that the last turning of the pages after grid 48 animates the remaining triads. Nearly every reader I've watched read *THE VOYAGE* deals with the final twenty-six pages the same way. Since the poem seems to have run out of words, there's no point in dealing with the pages one by one any longer: for first-time readers, the question is, are there words on those remaining pages? The quickest, most convenient way of finding out is to use the same way of holding the pages that was used in the middle part of *THE VOYAGE*, but to let them go more quickly—after all, one no longer needs to go slowly enough to read even one word per page. It may already be obvious, but when the reader accelerates the pace of the flipping, *THE VOYAGE* has entered into the realm of cinema. It becomes a flipbook, in which we watch a little square disappear—or, to put it in Hollywood terms, sail off into the horizon.

This final part of *THE VOYAGE* has a number of implications. For one thing, when we consider it with the rest of Williams' book, it dramatized an aspect of the overall process of reading—particularly reading long epic poems or novels—and perhaps of taking long trips as well. We begin slowly—or at least feel we're moving slowly; at first, we're conscious of just how much reading we'll need to do to finish the book. But the further we read, the more engrossed we become, until suddenly (WOE WOE) we realize that the world we've journeyed into is about to come to an end. But we're too far out to stop and too interested in learning the outcome, so we move quickly to the conclusion. The experience of *THE VOYAGE*, in other words, can be seen as recapitulating the structure of the reading experience. Moreover, since the experience of reading books is itself a recapitulation, a miniaturization of human experience in general (I mentioned travel but I could also have mentioned the process of the school year—the first three weeks of a semester always seem the longest—or the process of seeing a film), Williams has provided the traditional "eternal verite"—albeit a structural one—as the reward for the reader's involvement.

A second implication of the poem's overall structure involves the historical relationship of books and film. The shift from reading individual pages to flipping through a flipbook and animating characters parallels the nineteenth-to-twentieth century shift from writing to film as the primary source for the traditional narrative experience. In fact, if we want to push this idea a step further, we can see the process of deciphering the Captain's dialectic speech as suggesting the oral narrative period that produced the original poetic epics. Thus, our movement in *THE VOYAGE* from speech to writing to animation can be seen as a minimalist excursion through the history of some of the ways in which humans have experienced fictional voyages.

This idea may be confirmed by Williams' inclusion of an implicit perspectival device: once the text has disappeared, the margin line becomes a square that seems to move away from the reader, DEE PER DEE PER into the page. The shift from the flat graphic space of the early grids to the implicit perspectival space can be seen as a

WEE

GO

parallel to the shift from flatness to perspective during the Renaissance, which was part of the same cultural "voyage out" that included the development of printing and book techniques.

One final filmic dimension of *THE VOYAGE* needs to be mentioned. While Williams' visual epic poem refers in at least a general sense to the development of animation and, subsequently, film narrative out of the reading experience, the area of film with which it has most in common is not the commercial narrative history established by Georges Méliès, Edwin Porter, D. W. Griffith, and other early filmmakers. Williams' decision to establish a rigorous grid structure within which he can explore formal dimensions of the reading experience came during a period when any number of American filmmakers were using rigorous grid organizations for films that reveal and explore (often very playfully) formal dimensions of the film experience. Some examples are Hollis Frampton's *Zorns Lemma* (1970)—like *THE VOYAGE*, this is a largely textual work, partly about the process of coming to know something—Ernie Gehr's *Serene Velocity* (1970), Robert Huot's *Rolls: 1971* (1972), Taka Iimura's *Models* (1972), and J. J. Murphy's *Print Generation* (1974). Of course, there are precedents and parallels in other fields as well: Carl Andre in sculpture, Frank Stella in painting, Ray K. Metzker (and Eadweard Muybridge) in photography. Even Williams' own *sweethearts* is an important precedent, as are any number of his visual poems. But the fact that his mode of procedure has precedents does not diminish the achievement of *THE VOYAGE*, which manages to be sophisticated and easily accessible at the same time.

This essay was first published in *Afterimage* 12, no. 6 (January 1985), 4-6; then in Emmett Williams, *My Life in Flux and Vice Versa* (London: Thames and Hudson, 1992), 316-323.

"Apple Advancing *[var. Northern Spy]*," from *Sixteen Studies from VEGETABLE LOCOMOTION*, by Marion Faller and Hollis Frampton—their wry response to Eadweard Muybridge's Animal Locomotion photographs. Courtesy Marion Faller.

1986

Frames of Mind: Recent Filmmaking in Central New York

For at least two decades, my friend and longtime collaborator Patricia Zimmermann (1955-2023) and I toyed with the idea of producing a monograph focusing on the cinema and media history/geography of Central New York State. Patty had been surprised, when she was teaching in Singapore, that her students wondered what it was like to live where modern media had developed. After all, Eastman Kodak in Rochester had invented flexible-roll film; IBM had begun outside of Binghamton; T. W. Case, at the Case Research Lab near Auburn, was crucial in the development of sound film; and the Everson Museum in Syracuse may have been the first American museum to exhibit video art.

Also, by the 1970s, the New York State universities at Buffalo and Binghamton were bringing new kinds of filmmaking and film theory into prominence: Tony Conrad, Hollis Frampton, Paul Sharits, James Blue, and Woody and Steina Vasulka were teaching film and media studies in the department Gerald O'Grady had founded in Buffalo; and by 1970, Larry Gottheim had instigated a Cinema Department in Binghamton and he and his colleagues Ken Jacobs, Ernie Gehr, Nicholas Ray, and Ralph Hocking were producing graduates who soon were expanding media awareness nationwide, including Jim Hoberman, Alan Berliner, Steve Anker, Richard Herskowitz, Daniel Eisenberg, Bill T. Jones, Phil Solomon, and Mark McElhatten; Mark Graff, Ken Ross, and Phil Weisman would found the Collective for Living Cinema in New York City, and Ralph Hocking would found the Experimental Television Center.

By the mid-1980s, the annual Robert Flaherty Film Seminar, which had begun in Vermont, had found a home at Wells College in Aurora, New York, where it remained (with occasional visits to other sites) until 1998, when Vassar College became its regular home. In 2008 the seminar moved to Colgate University, where it remained through 2019.

I would begin to discover this history soon after I moved to Utica in 1971, and quickly learned that, even in the Utica-Rome area of the western Mohawk Valley, a good deal was going on. J. J. Murphy was teaching at Kirkland College; Patrick Clancy, at Colgate (Clancy moved to New Mexico in 1980); and in 1981, filmmaker/animator/graphic artist John Knecht joined Colgate's Art and Art History department and was instrumental in forming CNYPRG (the Central New York Programmers Group), which toured filmmakers through the region. Over in Syracuse, Owen Shapiro was making films, teaching film history, and hosting a film festival. Hollis Frampton was teaching in Buffalo but regularly commuting to Eaton, NY, where he lived with photographer Marion Faller; and Robert Huot, who was teaching at Hunter College in New York City, regularly commuted to his farm near New Berlin. Sculpture Space in Utica was bringing sculptors to Utica for residencies and hosting a range of cultural events. And the Munson-Williams-Proctor Art Institute (now "Munson") owned and exhibited the original version of the proto-cinematic series painting, Thomas Cole's *The Voyage of Life* (1839-40; a later version of the series hangs in the National Gallery of Art in Washington; see Paul D. Schweizer, *Thomas Cole's Voyage of Life* [Utica: MWPAI, 2014] for information).

From the mid-1970s on, I had been bringing filmmakers to Utica College to present their work (after 1981, also to Hamilton College) and I'd curated shows of painting, photography, and film by Hollis Frampton, Patrick Clancy, Robert Huot, Carol Kinne, and Marion Faller at Utica College. In 1986, I was asked by MWPAI to curate their annual Artists of Central New York show—we called the show "Frames of Mind: Recent Filmmaking in Central New York"—and to write an essay for the catalogue. The show combined a series of screenings in the Munson theater with a gallery show of other film-related work.

* * *

Over the past two decades, filmmakers working in Central New York have produced a body of work known around the world, wherever film is studied seriously. Ironically, however, this work has remained nearly invisible in the region where it was produced. The reasons why are not hard to discover. They have mostly to do with our conventional understanding of what movies are and how they function in contemporary society. When we hear the word "movies," most of us think of Hollywood and the systems of theaters housed in local shopping centers or the video outlets that have proliferated during the past few years. And even if we do think beyond Hollywood, it is usually to include the thriving film industries of Europe, Asia, Australia, and Latin America, and the types of films screened at college and museum film series like the series regularly sponsored by the Munson-Williams-Proctor Institute. Whether we are talking about American or foreign films, "the movies" means feature-length film stories spotlighting the skills of writers, directors, actors, cinematographers and editors.

We have every reason to be grateful for conventional movies. They have enriched our lives in many ways. They have regularly entertained us, and the best of them have challenged our intellects and our aesthetic and moral sensibilities. And yet, to enjoy and learn from conventional movies, and to want to see the American and foreign movie industries thrive, is not to say that these popular forms of film are the only ones we should experience. Since nearly the beginning of film history, there have been filmmakers working outside the commercial movie industry, attempting to offer alternatives to conventional films: to interest and enlighten audiences in new ways and to provide an ongoing critique of standard movie fare by exploring dimensions of human experience and of the film medium itself that commercial movies do not, or cannot, explore.

In the 1920s, the most notable alternative films were produced in Europe by visual artists—Hans Richter, Man Ray, Marcel Duchamp, Germaine Dulac, Fernand Léger, and Salvador Dalí and Luis Buñuel, among others—who have become known as the first film avant-garde. After World War II, North America became a leading producer of alternative forms of filmmaking; and New York (New York City and Upstate) became, and has remained, a perennial center for this activity. The alternative film history I am describing has produced such a wide range of films and types of film that there is no point in trying to detail all of them in this context. But we can begin to define the sorts of filmmaking that are the focus of the 48th Annual.

Most of the films, and the film-related photographs, Xerox prints, paintings, and other materials exhibited in this show, are instances of developments that began in the late 1960s, when a new generation of artists was turning its attention to film. Alternative film had already established itself in the American art world during the 1950s and 1960s and had produced hundreds of films and dozens of inventive filmmakers, many of whom had come to feel that conventional commercial movies underrated filmgoers' ability to perceive and understand visual imagery. These filmmakers of the 1950s and 1960s often produced films that barraged the eye and mind, on the assumption, I suppose, that even if viewers did not understand at first, their excitement with the films would draw them back for multiple viewings, in the way that poetry and other forms of "serious literature" often become ongoing explorations for readers.

Some members of the younger generation, however, were growing tired of visual assaults and were increasingly interested in producing films that would assist the filmmakers in reassessing their lives and in examining the film experience itself—films that would not overload the eye but would transform the screening space into a place for controlled investigation, for sustained thought, even for quiet meditation. One of the most productive concentrations of this younger generation of film artists is represented in this show. Some came to our region to live because they had found jobs at area colleges and universities: Larry Gottheim established the film department at SUNY Binghamton at the end of the 1960s, and he and Ken Jacobs have remained the nucleus of that department. Ernie Gehr was a visiting professor at SUNY Binghamton and Alan Berliner was a student from 1973 to 1977. Owen Shapiro has chaired the film studies department at Syracuse University for years. J. J. Murphy and Norman Bloom taught briefly at Hamilton/Kirkland College. Patrick Clancy, Marion Faller, and Susan Eder taught at Colgate University, where Lorna Lentini was a student; Carol Kinne and John Knecht teach there now.

Others bought property and homes here and commuted long distances to escape the urban settings where they worked. In 1970, Robert Huot began commuting regularly from New York City (where he still teaches in the art department at Hunter College) to his farm near New Berlin. In 1970, Hollis Frampton bought 30 acres of land near Eaton, and, beginning in 1974, regularly commuted from his job with the Center for Media Study at SUNY Buffalo to the home he shared with Marion Faller. Still others made films while visiting their colleagues or local art centers. During the 1970s, Phill Niblock was artist-in-residence at the Kirkland Art Center. He finished *Hundred Mile Radius* (the imagery was filmed within 100 miles of Clinton) in 1975. Bill Brand shot the footage used in *Chuck's Will's Widow* (1983) during a visit to the Adirondacks; Adam Mierzwa made *Suspended Animation* (1972) while living at Huot's farm; David Geary shot *Monkey Dream* (1977) at Sculpture Space during a visit to Utica. Working in communication and often in collaboration with each other, these artists produced a distinctive body of work which combines academic intellectual sophistication and a feel for Central New York—particularly for its lush, ever-changing landscape.

As these artists began to make films, they were determined to start from scratch in the hope that they could construct new kinds of film and photography and new kinds of viewing experiences. Not surprisingly, they found inspiration less in the contemporary commercial film they had grown up with than in some of the early experiments and discoveries that paved the way for film history. In the early 1890s, the Thomas Edison studio began making movies on the Edison Kinetograph (the first practical movie camera). The films were viewed on the Edison Kinetoscope, a peep-show box the viewer looked into.

On December 28, 1895, the Lumière Brothers presented the first public projection of motion pictures to an audience at the Grand Café in Paris (the Lumière Cinématographe was the first practical movie projector). Both the Edison and Lumière films used the most rudimentary film structure imaginable: each film was exactly one shot long. A subject was chosen and framed, the camera was turned on and off, and that was it. During the first public presentations in Paris, audiences would watch a series of such films. The technology of motion picture photography and projection was so new that these first filmgoers were thrilled to see the most everyday actions: a train arriving at a station, workers leaving a factory, parents feeding a baby, a stone wall being demolished. Conventional film history has usually seen the early one-shot films as "primitive," important only because they led quickly to more complex kinds of film storytelling.

For the new generation of alternative filmmakers, however, the directness and simplicity of the Lumière and Edison films were qualities to be emulated and explored. Larry Gottheim's first films—*Blues* (1970), *Fog Line* (1970), *Corn* (1970), *Doorway* (1971), and *Harmonica* (1971)—are all single-shot films. Though they are longer than the Lumière and Edison films, which lasted less than a minute, in some cases they seem even simpler than the earliest films: a bowl of blueberries is eaten; fog clears over a pasture; sweetcorn is husked and steamed. Even when Gottheim made his first multi-shot film—*Barn Rushes* (1971, 34 minutes)—he simply strung a series of eight continuous shots of an Upstate barn together. As simple as Gottheim's films seem, however, they are lovely to look at and dense with subtle suggestions about the film technology used in making them. Unlike the Lumière and Edison films, Gottheim's are meant to be food for thought and for meditation.

When Robert Huot moved upstate and began making "diary films," he too centered on the Lumière/Edison approach. His earliest diaries—*One Year (1970)* (1971), *Rolls: 1971* (1972), and *Third One-Year Movie—1972* (1973)—are full of continuous shots, a full roll of 16mm film long, many of which could stand alone as individual, minimal films. Hollis Frampton's *Zorns Lemma* (1970) concludes with three long, continuous shots edited together to form a single, unbroken continuity: we see Huot and a woman [Marcia Steinbrecher] walk across Huot's farm and into the woods; *Straits of Magellan: Drafts & Fragments* (1974) is made up of a series of continuous shots, including a reworking of the Lumières' *Demolition of a Wall* using an old silo instead of a wall; Murphy's *Movie Stills* (1977) presents 16 continuous roll-long shots of Polaroid photographs developing; Niblock's *Ten Hundred Inch Radii* (1972) presents long, gorgeous close-ups of Adirondack life; Shapiro's *Chameleon* (1978) begins with a 10-minute-plus shot of the female protagonist in her apartment; and Knecht's *Aspects of a Certain History* (1985) uses long takes and continuously looped shorter shots (which create much the same effect).

A second major inspiration for the films, photographs, paintings, and other works included in this show was the photography of Eadweard Muybridge, the photographer/scientist who discovered that he could analyze physical motion by using a series of still cameras. He invented the Zoopraxiscope (1880), a device that could resynthesize separate still images of phases of an action into the projected illusion of motion. The Zoopraxiscope showed a

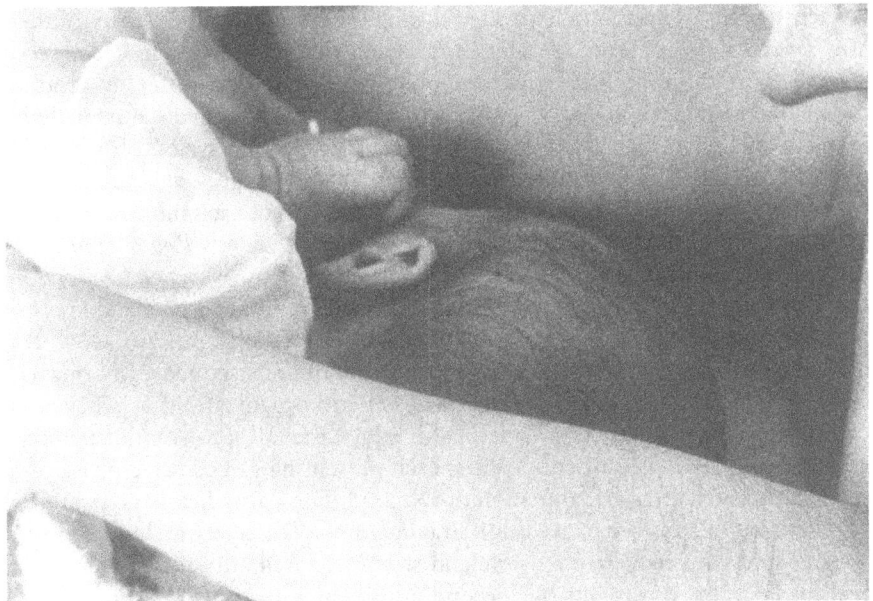

Twyla Tharp nursing Jesse Huot, in Robert Huot's film, *Rolls; 1971* (1972), shown during "Frames of Mind." Courtesy Robert Huot.

one-second-long "movie" over and over; it was an ancestor of the Lumière Cinématographe and the modern movie projector. Muybridge's excitement in being able to capture human and animal motion resulted in thousands of photographs, which were collected in 1887 in the eleven-volume *Animal Locomotion*. Throughout his photographic investigations, Muybridge used a consistent approach: he set up a grid of vertical and horizontal lines, in front of which animals and naked or nearly naked people would move—he wanted to photograph nude models so that their musculature could be studied against the backdrop of the linear coordinates. The animals and people would be photographed by a battery of cameras from several angles. The finished photographs of each particular subject were arranged in a grid so that the viewer could see all phases of the actions from all the viewing angles used, within a single frame. The fact that these experiments were a step more basic than the technological innovations of Edison and the Lumières, and the formal elegance of the motion photographs, made them doubly attractive for the artists in the 48th Annual. A consciousness of Muybridge—or the use of procedures reminiscent of him—is evident both in the films we are presenting and in most of the gallery work exhibited.

This influence is perhaps more obvious in the gallery work, much of which alludes to Muybridge's motion studies quite directly. The Marion Faller and Hollis Frampton series *Sixteen Studies from Vegetable Locomotion* (1975) is an elaborate, Central New York joke on Muybridge, in which the "movements" of various local fruits and vegetables are presented in Muybridgean photographic grids. Faller's *Local Conventions* series (1980) uses a grid organization to allow us to compare/contrast specific conventional ways in which Central New York residents outfit their homes and yards during the different seasons. Susan Eder uses several kinds of photographic grids. Each part of her *Crossed Sequences* series (1976-77) combines sequential photographs of two different actions. *Cloud Alphabet* (1978) presents photographs of clouds arranged sequentially in terms of the individual letters of the alphabet that particular cloud formations resemble, and the *Sky Calendar* series (1980) arranges imagery of clouds so that we can compare the look of the sky on sequential days of each month.

Related grid organizations are evident in Alan Berliner's *Photo-Film-Strip* (1976) and *Cine-Matrix* (1977); in Lorna Lentini's Xerox works, *Pea Conception* and *The View from 'Comealot'* (1980) as well as in *Frensch Window* and *Frensch Window* (Variation) (1980); and in Patrick Clancy's photoscrolls, where individual photographs are modules in long, continuous sequences of images, some of them 100 feet long. Filmmakers used grid organizations as a new and formally appropriate way of organizing film time; after all, a conventional movie is fundamentally a grid of still frames, each presenting a successive phase of a continuous movement for a fraction of a second. For *Zorns Lemma*, Frampton (whose essay "Eadweard Muybridge: Fragments of a Tesseract" includes seminal insights into the photographer's life and work)[1] devised an elaborate temporal grid made up of continuous one-second units. The long, central section of the film presents Frampton's immense collection of words filmed on New York City streets, arranged in alphabetic sets from A to Z: the viewer reads set after set of the words. Gradually, over a period of 47 minutes, the imagery in each letter's position is replaced by one-second images that show bits of progressive actions, but no words. The experience is fascinating and exhausting.

Grid structures are also used in Frampton's *Poetic Justice* (1972), where we read a series of 240 five-second shots of successive pages of a whacky screenplay; in *Less* (1973), where a one-second shot of a photograph is presented 20 times at equal intervals (in response to critic Jonas Mekas' statement that he wanted to see films 20 times before writing about them); and in *Straits of Magellan: Drafts & Fragments*, which presents a series of minute-long shots of domestic country life in Central New York.

Muybridgesque grids are also evident in Huot's *Turning Torso Drawdown* (1971) and *Rolls: 1971*. *Turning Torso Drawdown* is a filmic homage to Muybridge: we see shots of the torsos of nine naked people, arranged so that by the end of the film, each torso has been seen next to every other torso—seemingly for purposes of comparison/measurement *à la* Muybridge. *Rolls: 1971* uses a more complex grid: the film switches back and forth between 13 meditative roll-long shots of scenery and people, and highly edited passages of one-second sequential bits of imagery arranged so each kind of imagery is juxtaposed with all the other kinds. Elements of grid organization remain evident in Huot's *Third One-Year Movie—1972*, and in more recent diary films, including the five-projector, five-image *1983 Diary* (1984).

The eight successive equal-length shots of a barn in Gottheim's *Barn Rushes* form a simple grid, while the organization of *Horizons* (1973) forms a complex one. The four seasons are distinguished from each other not only by the seasonal differences in imagery but also by Gottheim's use of a different "rhyme scheme" for each season. Shots taken during the summer are arranged in pairs (each pair separated from the next by one second of green leader) which rhyme AA: that is, so that a visual element of the first shot is repeated in the second; the autumn shots are presented in groups of four (the rhyme: ABBA) separated by red leader; the winter shots in groups of four (rhyming ABAB) separated by blue leader; and the spring shots in triads separated by yellow leader (the triads rhyme BAB, CBC, DCD).

Still other grid-like organizations of film time are evident in Gehr's *Serene Velocity* (1970); in Murphy's *Movie Stills* (1977); in Mierzwa's *Suspended Animation*; in Norman Bloom's *Beaver Mountain Meditations* (1974), where Bloom "walks" through the woods to his home, covering an approximately equal portion of the walk each day for several months; in Carol Kinne's slide work *Bob's Elm* (1985), which presents a series of images of the same lovely elm for equal durations of time; as well as in other films included in the show.

A final important influence on the works in the 48th Annual is less specific than the Lumière/Edison and the Muybridge influences. It is the result of a general realization that in a certain very basic sense, movies are a modern form of the ancient scroll; movie projectors unroll imagery (and often text) from one reel onto a second. In fact, a most popular and little remembered forerunner of the modern film experience, the moving panorama shows of the nineteenth century, used canvas scrolls to present moving images to paying customers. Audiences would enter a room and sit in rows of seats facing a rectangular space at the front of the theater and would watch paintings hundreds of feet long move through the rectangular space (the paintings would unroll on one side of the screen and be rolled back up on the opposite side).[2] Like modern movies, these moving paintings were accompanied by music and sound effects and by modulations of projected light (the theater would darken for "storms" and "lightning" would flash). For a time, the moving panoramas were so popular that St. Louis became a mini-Hollywood where various studios battled to see which could produce the longest and best panorama. The most common topic of the panoramas was a voyage down a river. One show might "transport" the audience from St. Louis to New Orleans; the subsequent show would take the next audience back to St. Louis.

This popular form had an important impact on the fine arts, specifically on the Hudson River School of American landscape painting. Thomas Cole was apparently much taken with the panoramas, and their influence is evident in *The Voyage of Life* (Munson-Williams-Proctor Institute collection), where a panoramic trip down the river of life is "edited" into a four-image serial painting, in much the way that modern film editing is used to condense action.[3] *The Voyage of Life* creates meaning through its juxtaposition of "shots" of different stages of the protagonist's life. At the end of the nineteenth century, Lawrence W. Ladd ("the Utica artist"), and possibly others, painted smaller panoramas for Mohawk Valley audiences. One of these, according to one critic, was a "16mm version of the 'large' moving pictures" (it was 18 inches high and 200 feet long). The Utica panoramas were the subject of a recent show, "Panoramas for the People," organized for the Munson-Williams-Proctor Institute by Museum of Art Director Paul D. Schweizer.[4]

The scroll-like element of movies had a dramatic impact on several artists in the 48th Annual. Soon after Huot began making diary films, he began making "diary paintings." These would begin with a roll of canvas. Each day, Huot would roll out a successive section of canvas and paint it. Finished paintings would "unroll across floor, wall, space, and time," as Lucy Lippard put it.[5] Huot's unusual procedure and their resulting form allowed the diary paintings to make use of one of the central advantages of scrolls and movies. The image surfaces they provide are very large, but they can be rolled up for convenient transportation and storage. For Huot and for Clancy, whose 100-foot photoscrolls roll up and can be mailed in relatively small boxes, this convenience reflected a commitment to the idea that art should be able to function as part of practical, everyday life. Clancy's *Peliculas* (1979) is a different kind of scroll. It was made to be seen in two ways: as a normal, projected movie, and as a celluloid scroll that can literally be read, the way you will find it displayed in the gallery. A multicolored hand-written text begins by talking about itself, and then takes the reader on a strange trip to Mexico.

Alan Berliner's *Paper Film* (finished in 1976) also has obvious scroll-like qualities. Strips of calendar were rolled onto a reel—a joke on the way in which filmmaking and film viewing always involve a restructuring of time. For most of those film artists who came to this area to make new kinds of films and new kinds of film-related photography, the lush landscape and the challenge of the seasons became a source of sensual pleasure, a backdrop of self-examination and one of the subjects of perceptual/intellectual exploration. They brought to their work the respect for the land, which was a characteristic of the Hudson River School, but they found new ways of using twentieth-century technology to express this respect.

Even though much of the work reveals a spiritual dimension (their rigorous adherence to the temporal/spatial structures they set up has an ascetic quality), they were less involved with the idea that God had expressed Himself in the landscape than were their predecessors. Nevertheless, they were determined to preserve a deep reverence for the natural forces that sustained them, while maintaining a clear sense of the structure and implications of the photographic medium they had come to use.

I do not pretend that this discussion provides anything like an exhaustive survey of film activity in Central New York during the past 20 years. Most of

A strip of Patrick Clancy's *Peliculas* (1979, a film to be projected *and* read on a rewind). Courtesy Patrick Clancy.

the filmmakers mentioned have made many more films than there is opportunity to show. I would especially like to have included Gottheim's *Four Shadows* (1978), Huot's *Super-8 Diary—1979* (1980), other Frampton films, and Ernie Gehr's *Field*. No film by Ken Jacobs is included, though he has taught at SUNY Binghamton since the early 1970s and has a distinguished career as a filmmaker. I was unable to catch up with the one film Jacobs has made about Central New York in Central New York in time for the 48th Annual. Also, I have not seen much student work, though I know that students in the film departments at SUNY Binghamton and Syracuse University (and in other, smaller departments) have produced interesting films. Unnecessary to include, especially because of their wide dissemination over the years, are the commercial films, *The Sterile Cuckoo* (1969; directed by Alan J. Pakula), which was shot [on the Hamilton College campus] in and around Clinton, and *Slap Shot* (1978; directed by George Roy Hill), sequences of which were filmed in Utica.

A very different kind of film activity took place in the Mohawk Valley in the fall of 1984 when Peter Watkins shot several sequences for his new film, *The Journey* (known in this area as "The War Game 2"), an exploration of the thoughts and concerns of everyday people in eleven nations circling the earth, about the arms race and the many issues related to it. The Watkins film is in its final stages at the National Film Board of Canada.

This essay was published in *Frames of Mind: Recent Filmmaking in Central New York*, a catalogue published by the Munson-Williams-Proctor Institute (now Munson), on the occasion of their 48th Annual Exhibition, which ran from March 7-May 4, 1986.

---

1   "Eadweard Muybridge: Fragments of a Tesseract" originally appeared in *Artforum* (March 1973): 43-52. It was collected, along with other Frampton essays, in Hollis Frampton, *Circles of Confusion* (Rochester: Visual Studies Workshop, 1983).
2   To my knowledge, the two most useful sources of information about the moving panoramas are Richard D. Altick, *The Shows of London* (Cambridge: Harvard University Press, 1978), 198-210; and John Francis McDermott's *The Lost Panoramas of the Mississippi* (Chicago: University of Chicago Press, 1958).
3   See Elwood C. Parry III, "Thomas Cole's 'The Course of Empire': A Study in Serial Imagery," Ph.D. dissertation (Yale University, 1970), 7-8.
4   Paul D. Schweizer, *Panoramas for the People* (Utica: Munson-Williams-Proctor Institute, 1984), 13.
5   Lucy Lippard, "Full of It: Hasty but Fond Notes on Bob Huot's Diary Paintings," from a catalogue for an exhibition ("Robert Huot: Diary Paintings") held at the University Art Gallery, SUNY Albany, from January 19 through February 15, 1976.

1988

Avant-Garde Film: Cinema as Discourse

After a decade of exploring avant-garde filmmaking of the 1960s and 1970s and its antecedents, projecting the films in my classes, hosting visiting filmmakers, and writing about various films and filmmakers for journals that were receptive to this expanding body of filmmaking (most often, for *Afterimage*, but also for other journals: *Film Quarterly, Quarterly Review of Film Studies*), then finishing *A Critical Cinema: Interviews with Independent Filmmakers* (California, 1988), which would become a series, I had grown concerned that much of the academic world of cinema studies had become focused on applying new theoretical writing to the mainstream history of cinema. I felt that a pedagogical opportunity was slipping away and that I needed to redouble my efforts to promote the use of avant-garde films in film courses (whatever the topic). Avant-garde films tended to transform a classroom screening site into a more-fully-theoretical space.

The arrival of video cassettes, VHS and Betamax, was valuable in making a broader range of cinema available to a broader public, but I was soon concerned that this new way to access cinema might endanger the use of the theoretical films that had become so valuable for my teaching, many of which were predicated on what had been the academic dependence on 16mm (and 35mm and Super-8mm) projection.

Note: in the original publication, footnotes and works sited were listed separately. For convenience I have combined them here.

* * *

1

During the past couple of years, the talk in avant-garde film circles has centered on the question of whether the "movement" is dead. The two most prominent recent obituaries are Fred Camper's "The End of Avant-Garde Film" and Jim Hoberman's "Avant to Live: Fear and Trembling at the Whitney Biennial." Both authors begin their assessments in a similar and revealing way.

Camper:
> In 1963, when I was 15 years old and growing up in New York City, a friend of mine read a Jonas Mekas column praising a new "underground" film, went to see it, and was very impressed. He told me about it, and I went to the next screening of it with him. There was a certain adventure to all this for an adolescent: going to what seemed then like an out-of-the-way part of the city, sitting in an audience of older, somewhat strange-seeming people; seeing a film of a type I'd never even heard of before.
>
> But the real adventure began when the film was screened. I had never before imagined that the colors and shapes of the seen world, whose sensuality and texture had fascinated me since childhood, could be arranged into such a perfect expression. Every color, every object, every image seemed to gain energy from all that surrounded it. The time-crossing editing form was likewise unlike anything I had yet encountered. A whole new possibility for seeing and thinking, and most importantly

for understanding that seeing and thinking could be intimately related, interdependent acts, was opened. I came to see, feel, and understand my own capacities for eyesight, perception, thought, and imagination, far more deeply than I had before. My life was forever changed.[1]

Hoberman:
> The French call adolescence the age of filmgoing, and it may be that the movies you discover then set your taste forever. Certainly, my own life was altered in 1965, when I began frequenting a cruddy storefront on St. Marks Place and the even weirder basement of a midtown skyscraper. I knew movie-movies, but this was another world: oceanic superimpositions and crazy editing rhythms, films made from bits of newsreel and Top 40 songs, "plots" ranging from the creation of the universe to the sins of the fleshapoids, real people (often naked) cavorting in mock Arabian palaces and outer borough garbage dumps. Determined to learn more, I took out a subscription to *Film Culture*. That the first issue was half devoted to the grandiose schemes of a mad beatnik named Ron Rice only confirmed my sense that anything was possible.[2]

Part of me envies the experience shared by Camper and Hoberman (and presumably hundreds of others), and I can empathize with their disappointment that the cinematic adventures of their adolescence no longer seem possible.

There was a moment in the mid-1960s when some American urban centers—and, to a degree, people outside these centers—were discovering a range of non-conventional forms of cinema. Filmmakers who had been making films for a decade, and in some instances for two decades, were achieving recognition in areas of North American society that had previously not heard of them, and a host of new filmmakers were emerging. New York and San Francisco seemed the hubs of a cinematic movement in a manner analogous to the way Paris was the literary hub for experimental poets and fiction writers in the 1920s. And then in the early '70s, the excitement seemed to peter out. Jonas Mekas stopped writing his influential Movie Journal column in *The Village Voice*, and while experimental cinematic forms found some institutional homes, the social ferment which surrounded the celebrated screenings of the mid-to late-'60s evaporated.

If one defines the avant-garde movement as that special moment in the '60s when social excitement about alternative forms of cinema seemed greatest (especially in New York and San Francisco), then the movement is dead. But such a definition ignores a number of important realities. The most obvious, perhaps, is that that moment may not have been as special as it now seems to Camper and Hoberman.

Much of the history of earlier periods in the development of alternative cinema remains to be written, but we do know that a vital film avant-garde was underway in Europe by the mid-1920s and that, from the beginning, the influential London Film Society was offering its members opportunities to view avant-garde films in a context of other forms of cinema.[3] An American avant-garde movement was underway by the mid-1940s: Maya Deren and Alexander Hammid, the Whitney Brothers, Sidney Peterson, Kenneth Anger, James Broughton and others were making important films which were featured in the seminal Art in Cinema series held at the San Francisco Museum of Art, and subsequently, by Amos Vogel's Cinema 16, which presented film programs of remarkable diversity—programs which consistently included avant-garde films—to membership audiences in New York City.[4] At Cinema 16's height, audiences regularly filled a 1500-seat auditorium twice a night, as well as several commercial theaters, for monthly presentations. It is doubtful that at any other point during American film history—including the supposed heydays of the '60s—audiences of such size have ever been exposed to avant-garde work.[5] Large segments of the Cinema 16 membership may not have been enthusiastic about seeing early Anger, Peterson, Deren, and Brakhage, but they saw the films, and in contexts designed to keep them coming back. Like the London Film Society, Cinema 16 became a model for a nationwide network of film societies, many of which included avant-garde cinema in their programs.[6]

By the '60s, when Camper and Hoberman entered the scene, the exhibition climate already was changing. Along with new kinds of film came new approaches to exhibition, including the one-person show of films by the individual film artist—an approach promoted by the New American Cinema group.[7] The one-person show was useful in drawing attention to the achievement of many film artists, and yet, one could argue that the tendency of avant-garde screening rooms to adopt this exhibition model ultimately narrowed the public audience for alternative cinema. Thanks to federal and state subsidies during the '70s and '80s, some forms of avant-garde film have remained regularly available to paying public audiences in some cities and at some colleges and universities; yet, these screening rooms appeal to only a fraction of the audience which might have seen an avant-garde film at the London Film Society or at Cinema 16.[8]

It does seem clear that the mid-to-late '60s was one of the crucial periods for the production of alternative cinema; and it was an important period of discovery for many viewers. Nevertheless, the fact remains that for many of us who did not live in New York, San Francisco, and selected other urban centers, what seemed a movement to Camper and Hoberman was only one element in a changing film scene. My own first experiences with avant-garde cinema occurred during the same period as theirs, but that contemporaneity may be the only similarity. I did not experience my first avant-garde films as an adolescent (the films that had an impact on my adolescence were *A Summer Place*, *The World of Susie Wong*, and *Sundays and Cybele*!), but in my mid-twenties, when I saw a traveling program or two of "underground films" as a graduate student of American literature at the University of Florida, I was so entirely unimpressed with the films that I no longer recall an image or a title. I do remember being closed out of a screening of *Chelsea Girls*, only to hear later that I'd not missed much. For me the late '60s brought the discovery of European and Japanese film, and via Andrew Sarris' *The American Cinema*, of auteurs: Keaton, Lubitsch, Ford, et al.

My first important experiences with avant-garde film came later, at a weekend film symposium at SUNY Binghamton and a three-week seminar at Hampshire College in Massachusetts, sponsored by the University Film Study Center. In Binghamton I saw, on a single afternoon in the spring of 1972, in a program of "independent films," Ernie Gehr's *Serene Velocity*, Stan Brakhage's *The Act of Seeing With One's Own Eyes*, and Larry Gottheim's *Barn Rushes*. With the exception of

Barn Rushes, which seemed related to Monet, I understood nothing of what I saw, except that there was a good deal more to be understood about film than I had realized.

By the end of another year, I'd begun to use all three films in my courses, and by the time I arrived at Hampshire College in the summer of 1973, I was already enthusiastic about this "new" field. My excitement was fueled by Ed Emshwiller, at that time a good-will ambassador for avant-garde film, by filmmaker John Marshall (who began his seminar on ethnographic film with Peter Kubelka's *Arnulf Rainer*), by Sheldon Renan's fascination with Jordan Belson, and by seeing a sophisticated, "film-educated" audience walk out on the first three sections of Hollis Frampton's *Hapax Legomena*: *(nostalgia)*, *Poetic Justice*, and *Critical Mass*, films which simultaneously bored and annoyed me *and* put me in a state of thrilled receptivity which I can only call ecstatic. I was up half the night deliriously writing notes on the Frampton films.

My excitement with the avant-garde films I was seeing was largely a function of my teaching. As the field revealed its contours, each new curve of the terrain made possible new kinds of interaction with my students. Before I'd known about avant-garde film, I'd been in the position of delivering landmark commercial features and classic documentaries to classes and doing my best to enlighten students about the histories of these films and about their implications. Once I added avant-garde films to my courses, I found that my classroom became more fully a theoretical space, where all of us could directly confront the question of what a film *is* fundamentally and how popular cinema constructs us as viewers and as people. From the beginning, much of my admiration for avant-garde films was a function of what they were capable of revealing about conventional film experiences, by using strategies fundamentally different from the popular cinema. Or to put this another way, once I began to explore avant-garde film, the commercial cinema which had dominated my awareness became a set of cultural texts, and avant-garde film became an ongoing critique of those texts.

2

We can forget sometimes that film history is not simply a subject, or a series of cultural facts to be written about in essays and books. Film history is itself an ongoing discourse. The contribution of the long history of avant-garde cinema has been to increase the complexity and sophistication of this overall cinematic discourse. The North American avant-garde has produced its own pantheon—Brakhage, Conner, Snow, Gehr, Mekas, Rainer—and a variety of recognized genres: Dada and surreal film; abstract animation; the psychodrama and other forms of visionary cinema described by P. Adams Sitney; structural film; the diary film; the (usually sexually political) New Narrative—representing tendencies in which a cinematic discourse is developing, or in some cases has ceased to develop, at least for the moment.

Each of these avant-garde genres discursively interacts with other areas. For example, the New Narrative *à la* Rainer, Raynal, Mangolte, Mulvey/Wollen, Akerman, Potter, and Benning has developed partly in reaction to and through assimilation of the structural cinema of Snow, Gehr, and Frampton. And this complex avant-garde history has also interacted with popular cinema. By the late 1950s, George and Mike Kuchar had internalized Hollywood film of the '40s and '50s and were transforming what they had learned into tiny avant-garde trash epics which "commented on" the forms they had borrowed from and which influenced John Waters and a whole generation of "punk" filmmakers, whose design sense has had an impact on commercial cinema and television.[9]

Even if one were to agree that Camper's and Hoberman's experiences were the most dramatic way of discovering avant-garde cinema, there's no point in defining a cinematic movement according to the excitement viewers experienced during their earliest exposure to particular films. The question of the moment is whether the 1980s represent a diminishing of the power and complexity of the discourse of alternative cinema or a productive extension of what has gone before. From my very limited vantage point, I would argue that, regardless of one's sense of the state of alternative film exhibition, the production of avant-garde cinema has continued at a very high level. It may be true that the '80s have not produced a new pantheon, or a single filmmaker as remarkably inventive and prolific as Brakhage, but a number of the filmmakers who became well-known in the 1950s and '60s have continued to make interesting films (Brakhage is a good example), and impressive filmmakers and films continue to appear on the scene. An example, Su Friedrich: *Gently Down the Stream* (1981); *The Ties That Bind* (1980); and *Damned If You Don't* (1987).

In any case, there's no reason to assume that the achievements of the '80s are developing, or should develop, in the pattern that characterizes the innovative work of earlier decades. Up through the '60s, avant-garde cinema was pioneering work. For the most part, the individuals whose visions we so easily recognize now were moving into virgin territory. They had—or at least knew about—very few antecedents, and, since they rigorously avoided the approaches of the commercial cinema, it was almost inevitable that what they produced would be very different from any other films audiences would have had the opportunity to see. By the '70s the situation was changing.

Filmmakers interested in working outside the commercial mainstream entered a territory in which a good deal of filmic exploration had already occurred, and not surprisingly, their admiration of or frustration with the kinds of avant-garde cinema already available became a major factor in their development. As suggested earlier, a mixture of frustration with the limitations of structural film and excitement about the new rhetorical options offered by structural filmmakers is implicit in the feminist New Narrative. Other recent developments have grown from a recognition of the potential of other previously discovered forms. For example, Bruce Connor is usually credited with establishing "re-cycled cinema" (films edited from other films), a form which a number of recent filmmakers have explored with considerable ingenuity: for example, the Raffertys and Jayne Loader (*The Atomic Cafe*, 1982) Morgan Fisher (*Standard Gauge*, 1984), Alan Berliner (*City Edition*, 1980; *Myth in the Electric Age*, 1981; *Natural History*, 1983; *Everywhere at Once*, 1985; *The Family Album*, 1987); Yervant Gianikian and Angela Ricci Lucchi (*Karagoez-Catalogo 9.5*, 1981; *From the Pole to the Equator*, 1986); William Farley (*Tribute*, 1987).

In other instances, avant-garde filmmakers have extended the use of particular visual elements common in conventional and experimental cinema to such a degree that these elements become the foci of new forms. One of the most fully articulated of these forms is what might be called text-image cinema: films in which the act of reading printed or written texts is a (or the) central viewing experience. Early examples include Marcel Duchamp's *Anemic Cinema* (1926), Len Lye's *Musical Poster No. 1* (1939), and Carmen D'Avino's *The Big "O"* (c. 1953). Recent instances include Patrick Clancy's *Peliculas* (1979); Su Friedrich's *Gently Down the Stream* and *The Ties That Bind*; Michael Snow's *So Is This* (1982); David Goldberg and Michael Oblowitz's *The Is/Land* (1982); Rick Hancox's *Waterworx (A Clear Day and No Memories)* (1982); Leslie Thornton's *Oh China Oh* (1983); Peter Rose's *Secondary Currents* (1983) and *Spiritmatters* (1984); James Benning's *American Dreams* (1984); and Peter Watkins' *The Journey* (1987).[10]

There is no space here to provide a justification for the films, filmmakers, and tendencies I've mentioned, or for others that could be mentioned. But it does seem useful to say that since 1980 I've been unable to keep up with all the interesting avant-garde work I see, much less catch up on the past, much less explore the many films other critics I respect have found impressive. And there is also a sizable body of recent commercial and semi-commercial films with obvious historical and aesthetic ties to avant-garde cinema: for instance, Jim Jarmusch's *Stranger Than Paradise* (1984), Lizzie Borden's *Working Girls* (1986), Godfrey Reggio's *Koyaanisqatsi* (1983), and Ross McElwee's *Sherman's March* (1985). If the movement seems dead, I'd guess this is because the urban social surroundings for alternative cinema and the energy of traditional independent screening rooms seems to have diminished, not because of any paucity of interesting films.

3

I have always felt that the primary potential for alternative film rests with academe. One can attack the system of North American higher education in all manner of ways, but the fact remains that, despite the frequently conservative, potentially oppressive sources of capital that maintain our system of higher education, the academic environment remains one of the few substantial institutional frameworks within which serious discourse of any sort is at least intermittently encouraged. And it is the primary institutional home for the study of a number of subject areas roughly similar to avant-garde cinema. "Serious" poetry, short stories, novels, and plays have always had a rough time in the marketplace. Yet not only have these forms found a home in academe, they remain—for those people who study them—vital discourses. Film, especially "serious" alternative forms of film, should be functioning in a similar way. From my experience as a teacher, it seems clear that avant-garde cinema can be remarkably stimulating in the college classroom. But for the most part, so far as I can tell, the potential for a fully sophisticated film discourse, one that includes cinematic discourse on the cinema, has as yet not been realized in many colleges and universities.

Why hasn't it been realized? I have a number of suspicions. For one thing, the specialization of screening venues for the maturing North American avant-garde film was occurring simultaneously with the entry of serious film study into colleges and universities across the country. Since the increasing articulation of avant-garde film was less accessible—in both availability and comprehensibility—than the influx of foreign commercial cinema or the redefinition of Hollywood according to auteurism, the avant-garde tended to remain, for the most part, on the fringes of the burgeoning academic film establishment.[11]

The marginalization of even those areas of alternative cinema that "researched" crucial elements of the cinematic apparatus was confirmed during the '70s and early '80s by the incursion into academic institutions of new ways of reading mainstream cinema inspired by French theoreticians. Before cinema even had an opportunity to get its bearings in academe, to establish itself in a form analogous to other, roughly similar disciplines in the arts and humanities, film academics were besieged with a wealth of new, difficult theoretical texts whose potential for revealing interesting dimensions of popular cinema were considerable. Of course, there's no turning back the clock. And who would want to? Who hasn't profited from Barthes, from Foucault, from Mulvey's "Visual Pleasure and Narrative Cinema"? But while I have learned from some of those texts I've had an opportunity to read and understand, and while I often take pleasure in the brilliance of their insights, my pleasure is mitigated by a nagging feeling that to an extent what is happening, as these hundreds of primary and secondary writings absorb the attention and energy of academics, is that a new mode of literature is consuming cinema (or the limited time people have for experiencing cinema and thinking about it—that an essentially literary discourse is substituting itself for a cinematic one). Of course, I understand that people who write about film (or at least very few of them) want their writing to be a substitute for seeing film. Who could understand their writing then? And yet, there is a professional/economic/social value to writing and reading theory about film that does not seem to inhere in filmgoing or film exhibition.

Originally, I was drawn to film—and assume this is true for most people who come to care about cinema—because it provides an experience fundamentally different from reading literary texts. It was, and usually still is, a public experience during which a group of people enter a darkened room where their attention is focused on a specific set of visual/auditory stimuli. For me, this experiencing of film in the dark together is the issue. Since cinema takes place in time, we have become accustomed to the presence of narrative as a means for maintaining this experience of togetherness, but it is not for narrative alone that we pay our money. If it were, I'd argue that our dollars would be better spent on books: the great novels articulate narrative at a level considerably beyond film's current capabilities.

What we pay admission for, really, is to experience certain pleasures, shocks, and frustrations, and to be able to define the nature of our responses, immediately and directly, in relation to those of other people. And since film distorts whatever it presents in ways peculiar to its own apparatus, the imagery we watch inevitably confronts our sense of reality. Film provides a forum within which we must continually test our vision of things. It follows that if we only experience one kind of film, our testing of our sense of reality is very limited, but if we are present with audiences at a wide variety of types of cinema, the potential is there for the development of a much deeper sense not only of cinema, but of self, and of the communities in which we live.

Reading a written text which explicates or theorizes about a film or a set of films can be interesting and useful, even very exciting. But, no matter how ingenious the text, it cannot provide the same sort of direct revelation that occurs when an audience (student or otherwise), accustomed to a very limited cinematic discourse, is presented with a film which stands in an aggressively analytical or theoretical relationship to conventional cinema. Over the years I've screened a variety of films by Japanese avant-garde filmmaker Taka Iimura. It's a rare written text about film that can galvanize the level of energy produced by even a relatively brief Iimura film. Much of Iimura's work during the early '70s (he began as a surrealist filmmaker, and is working now primarily in video) dealt with the filmic experience of time. Generally, Iimura eliminated the usual sorts of film imagery, substituting various sign systems for measuring duration. The resulting films can function in a variety of ways: as meditative experiences (Iimura is much influenced by Zen) or as "durational sculptures" which shape time within the theater space. I've normally used them in my courses as cinematic "rulers" that measure out intervals of time in a regular, simple system.

Several years ago, as part of an Introduction to Film course at Hamilton College, I showed Iimura's + & – (1973), a 26-minute film (shorter Iimura films have the same effect) in which durations of darkness are added to one another: we'll see one bit of darkness, a + sign, then a second interval of darkness, then an = sign, and finally a duration of darkness equal to the first two. The equations proceed regularly, in a system which is quickly understood by the viewer. Once the 45 additions are accomplished, Iimura—with Zen irony—moves through a set of 45 equations during which durations of white leader are "subtracted" from durations of darkness.

Within five minutes of the beginning of + & –, Iimura's simple equations had catalyzed my students into a rage. People yelled, stood up, and stomped out of the room, slamming the door (this was a class that in all other circumstances was entirely quiet and orderly, maybe even a bit too elaborately respectful) and they continued to do battle with the film in their formal journals for weeks. Seeing + & – had demonstrated the size and something of the nature of the emotional stake these people had in the normal pleasure-giving functions of cinema, quickly and directly, from within the institution of cinema. The issues—cinematic and otherwise—raised by this experience haunted the classroom for the remainder of the semester, and allowed for a more alert perception of the more conventional films shown.

If the discourse of cinema—as distinguished from the literary discourse about cinema—is to remain vital, if it is to have ongoing productive impact, the theater must remain a dynamic space, if not in all sectors of the culture, at least in some. There's nothing very romantic about the recognition that the primary location where dynamic cinema programming remains possible is in academe. A vibrant "underground" in a mysterious corner of a great city is far more intriguing. But as with so many of our cultural traditions, the best present hope for much of alternative cinema remains the classroom. Of course, if we really want to maximize the potential of cinematic discourse, we will need to revise our priorities a bit.

I cannot claim to have traveled very widely in academic circles, but judging from the conferences I have attended and the colleges and universities I've taught at and visited, dynamic programming—for the public or in the classroom—remains far less common than one would wish. Even at film conferences, screenings often are viewed as a perfunctory fringe benefit, and sometimes are held in spaces totally unsuited for the presentation of important films. Further, it seems obvious that in the field of film teaching, a published article counts for substantially more than the experience of creative film exhibition. Academe remains the avant-garde's best hope, but at this point it is only a hope. For those of us convinced of the value and potential importance of the broadest articulation of cinema, the challenge is to demonstrate the excitement and value of using avant-garde films in a wide range of academic contexts, not simply on the fringes of academic film activity, but as one of its essential components. Hundreds of avant-garde films—old and brand new—are available, but unless we see a change in our priorities, much of this remarkable work may not be available to the next generation.

This essay was published in *Journal of Film and Video* 40, no. 2 (Spring 1988): 33-42.

---

1   Camper, in *Millennium Film Journal*: 16-18 (Fall/Winter 1986-87), 99.
2   Hoberman, in *The Village Voice*, June 23, 1987, 25.
3   In the Society's third program (December 1925), a silent comedy was shown with excerpts of a science film, with Robert Weine's *Raskolnikov*, and with *A quoi revent les jeunes films*. This last film is described in the program notes in a manner reminiscent of Camper's and Hoberman's descriptions of their first avant-garde screenings: the film apparently had "no plot, its interest centers in the shapes, value, rhythm and speed of the perspectives. All romance is banished, leaving place entirely to cinematography. By turns, arabesques and mirror reflections produce shapeless human forms, chaste as clouds, which emerge at last as faces of alloyed beauty, for which women well known for their charm and talents have consented to pose. One recognizes the Comtesse do Noailles, the celebrated French poet, the Princesse Bibesco, author of 'Seven Paradises' and 'The Green Parrot,' Mrs. Fellowes, Lady Abdy, etc. These faces fuse little by little into landscapes, crystal parks, frolicking lights in the night. Suddenly one bursts out of the dark to rush full speed round Paris, first by land and then on the water—vision becomes obscure—and finally the dream vanishes in a dazzling light." See *The Film Society Programs: 1925-1939* (New York: Arno, 1972), 11.
4   For more information about the Art in Cinema series, see Frank Stauffacher, ed., *Art in Cinema*, a booklet published by the San Francisco Museum of Art in 1947 which is included in Scott MacDonald, *Art in Cinema: Documents Toward a History of the Film Society* (Philadelphia: Temple University Press, 2006), a companion to MacDonald's *Cinema 16: Documents toward a History of the Film Society* (Temple, 2002)]. Censorship restrictions required that Cinema 16 be a membership society, but the only requirement for membership was buying a (reasonably priced) season pass.
5   One possible exception is mentioned in passing by Germain Clinton, in "The Canadian Federation of Film Societies," in Cecile Starr, ed., *The Film Society Primer* (Forest Hills, New York: American Federation of Film Societies, 1956), 71-2. In the 1930s, Vancouver boasted an immensely successful film society, which according to one report, showed "programs of great intrepidity."
6   According to George Amberg, in the introduction to *The Film Society Programmes*, the London Film Society "established the prototype for all subsequent cine clubs and societies that are now proliferating." For information about Cinema 16's influence on North American film societies, see The Film Society Primer, especially Armine T. Wilson, "Film Perspectives," Starr, ed., *The Film Society Primer*, 18-21. For more information on Cinema 16, see my "Amos Vogel and Cinema 16," *Wide Angle*, 9, no.3 (Fall, 1987), 38-51; and "Cinema 16: An Interview with Amos Vogel," *Film Quarterly*, 37, no. 3 (Spring 1984), 19-29.
7   In 1960 the New American Cinema Group (called together by Jonas Mekas and Lewis Allen) explored alternative types of distribution and exhibition for avant-garde and other non-mainstream forms of film—alternatives, specifically, to the procedures developed by Cinema 16. This

development was in some ways both understandable and healthy. Mekas and other members of the New American Cinema group (Brakhage in particular) had bridled at Vogel's insistence that avant-garde films be presented as part of what they called "potpourri programs" (see the "First Statement of the New American Cinema Group," *Film Culture*, 22-23 [Summer, 1961], 131-33) and at Vogel's assumption that he should continue to choose which of their films got distributed.

8   I remain deeply grateful to the little theaters which showed, and in some cases continue to show, avant-garde film, and to the dedicated enthusiasts who have kept them running (the combination of box office revenues and government grants rarely supply decent salaries for the administrators of avant-garde screening rooms). Without these theaters, the serious study of avant-garde film would be even more difficult than it is. Nevertheless, I would argue that this system has solidified the tendency since Cinema 16 to ghettoize avant-garde film. In some cases, the growing isolation of avant-garde film has produced a form of elitist pretension: only those films shown in avant-garde screening rooms are considered truly "serious," and those filmmakers (J. J. Murphy can serve as an example) who have moved toward narrative forms reminiscent of Hollywood are considered sell-outs by some, even when (as in the case of Murphy) their new work is in keeping with the filmmakers' basic commitment to the medium and is probably more financially and psychologically strenuous than their previous, "serious" filmmaking.

9   Of course, even the discourse of mainstream commercial film develops through an interaction between commercial films. For example, each new horror film we see either reconfirms or extends the experience and implications of previous horror films. *Nightmare on Elm Street* either does not frighten us, compared to previous frightening films, or it frightens us despite our previous horror training. Each new experience more completely articulates our sense of cinema horror. And each genre discourses with other genres: a horror film is a horror film precisely because it is not a musical, a comedy, a western, or a film noir—though inevitably some experimenters within the commercial industry will attempt to make the situation more complex by combining elements usually thought to be characteristic of separate genres.

10 For a more detailed discussion of text-image film, see my "Text As Image in Some Recent North American Avant-Garde Films," *Afterimage* (March 1986), 9-20 [This exploration would lead to my book: *Screen Writings: Scripts and Texts by Independent Filmmakers* (Berkeley: University of California Press, 1995)].

11 Obviously, there are exceptions. Avant-garde film has a distinguished place in some film departments at major universities (at NYU, for example). Nevertheless, I'd guess avant-garde cinema remains less familiar to film teachers across North America than any other major film tradition.

Title card of Luca Comerio's *From the Pole to the Equator* (1910) in Yervant Gianikian and Angela Ricci Lucchi's *From the Pole to the Equator* (1986).

Missionaries "civilizing" African children in *From the Pole to the Equator*. Courtesy Yervant Gianikian.

1989

Review of *From the Pole to the Equator* by Yervant Gianikian and Angela Ricci Lucchi

I'm often astonished by my own naivete. Perhaps this is just a result of my having been a literature student before becoming a film student. We continue to have easy access to many of the crucial writings of essayists, poets, and fiction writers of the past 2000-plus years, but often cannot manage access to recent accomplished works of cinema. Of course, our global literary access evolved over many centuries and I'm sure sci-fi aficionados can imagine a time when great works of cinema from many centuries will be easily accessible—in what forms, who knows?—to anyone with a desire to see them. Nevertheless, when I first saw Gianikian/Ricci Lucchi's *From the Pole to the Equator* at the 1986 Toronto Film Festival, I couldn't have imagined that a few decades later I'd not be able to show it to audiences.

As fully as we may feel culturally connected to Europe, I'm often surprised at how a good many American cineastes remain unaware of major European contributors to documentary and avant-garde (what I've recently tended to call "avant-doc") filmmaking. Even filmmakers with considerable filmographies—Nikolaus Geyrhalter, for example, and Sergei Loznitsa—don't always register, though it's not difficult to access their work online. In the case of the long-time filmmaking partners, Yervant Gianikian and Angela Ricci Lucchi (who died in 2018), even much of their best work feels generally out of reach.

There are DVDs of a number of major Gianikian/Ricci Lucchi films, including their World War I trilogy—*Prigionieri della Guerra/Prisoners of War* (1995), *Su Tutte le vetta è pace/On All Heights It's Peace* (1998), and *Oh! Uomo/Oh! Man* (2004)—though, so far as I'm aware, none of the DVDs or the film prints themselves are generally available. The war-trilogy DVDs were produced in 2004 by the Museo storico in Trento; MoMA's Circulating Film Collection once distributed prints of *From the Pole to the Equator*. But in general, there seems no current, practical way to access these films. One seven-minute short, *Diaro Africano/African Diary* (1994), is included in the 2021 compilation DVD, "Found Footage & Collage Films: selected works" produced by César Ustarroz of *Found Footage Magazine*.

Many of the most interesting Gianikian and Ricci Lucchi films, including their war trilogy and *From the Pole to the Equator*, allow us to see, and *see through*, films originally made in support of the Italian Fascist cause and more generally in support of colonialism and imperialism.

* * *

From the Pole to the Equator, the new film by Italians Yervant Gianikian and Angela Ricci Lucchi, generates a very complex viewing experience. Gianikian and Ricci Lucchi are collectors, of objects and memorabilia of various kinds, and most importantly for our purposes, of old footage.* For *From the Pole to the Equator*, they acquired the archives of Italian cinematographer Luca Comerio (1874-1940) who began recording exotic locations with Lumière cameras in the 1890s and continued to shoot (and collect) film through World War I. Gianikian and Ricci Lucchi reprinted selections from Comerio's 35mm films (they were still on nitrate stock),

---

* Some years ago, Gianikian and Ricci Lucchi toured the United States with films that catalogued items from their collections. As an accompaniment to their visuals, they burned scents from their collection of scents on Bunsen burners in the front of the theater.

frame by frame onto 16mm and added color to the imagery. The Comerio materials were then edited into an elaborate montage set to a score composed by Californians Keith Ullrich and Charles Anderson.

The audience of *From the Pole to the Equator* is able to retrieve some sense of how the original Comerio footage must have looked, and since Comerio was a skilled cinematographer with obvious artistic pretentions and achievements, this alone makes the film of considerable interest. We see well-made images of peoples, places, and experiences which were exotic enough when they were recorded for European audiences; with the passing of nearly a century, this footage has become as temporally remote from us as the locations it presents were geographically remote from audiences then—a fact regularly dramatized in the film by a variety of damages to the original 35mm materials carried over into the 16mm film.

The film divides into passages that are not explicitly distinguished in the visuals, though they are usually signaled by changes in the music (most of the sections are from 7 to 10 minutes long; the final section is around 15 minutes). Generally speaking, each passage is determined by a specific geographic locale. The opening section was filmed first from a train snaking through the Alps and subsequently from an Alpine tram car descending through the mountains into a village. The following section presents imagery Comerio filmed during an exploratory voyage to the South Pole. The focus is on the explorers observing and killing polar animals. The third section was shot at the frontier of the Russian and Persian Empires; in general, its focus is on a local army which is apparently working with the visiting Italians. The next section reveals Italian soldiers and church people working among African peoples: Africans dance for the Europeans, march in Europeanized outfits; a child is baptized, a group of African children follow a nun's orders in a school.

The film moves to India where we see street scenes, life along country roads, a woman dancing for the camera, a parade of European royalty and military, and the activities of Buddhist monks; then returns to African locations: first Tangiers, where we see street and harbor scenes, and later, after a series of portraits, to (again, I'm guessing) Eritrea, where local people seem to be performing a series of mock battles for the camera; and finally to Uganda, where Baron Franchetti—according to Gianikian and Ricci Lucchi, "the Italian version of T. E. Lawrence"—kills a variety of animals (generally we see Franchetti shooting and the animals in the throes of death) and moves his entourage from place to place with the help of dozens of Africans.

The final, somewhat longer section of the film presents footage from World War I: soldiers marching, riding horses and bicycles, and fighting in the field; in a number of instances, we see soldiers die. Just at the end of the section we see a panoramic view of the words "VIVA IL RE" (Long Live the King) spelled out by sheep herded together. The film ends with a shot of a nobleman holding a rabbit just out of the reach of two dogs, to his own amusement and that of several women.*

---

* While in general the imagery in any given passage is restricted to the particular location being explored, Gianikian and Ricci Lucchi do at times use shots from one location within a passage devoted to another. At the end of the polar expedition passage, for example, we see two shots which take place in a winterscape, but which, we realize later, are taken from the material on World War I. On first viewing these exceptions are no problem, but on subsequent viewings I've found them distracting—like a loose end.

The overall style of *From the Pole to the Equator*—both its editing style and its use of composition—developed in at least two stages. First, Gianikian and Ricci Lucchi worked with material included in Comerio's own finished films (the success of his fiction film *Rocambole* in 1908 enabled him to establish one of the most successful Italian production companies; his famous montage film, also entitled "From the Pole to the Equator," came later) and with materials Comerio had apparently planned to use in montage films that were not completed or have been lost. Though we cannot be sure of Comerio's editing style from what we see in the Gianikian/Ricci Lucchi film, it seems logical to assume that their montage film echoes his, at least in a general sense. On the other hand, we can sense the drama of Comerio's compositional style, which is evident through all the film's sections, from the dramatic pans over the Alpine landscape during the early train rides, to the careful framing of street scenes, to the frequently exquisite portrait filming, to the dramatic use of mattes in the hunting passages in Antarctica and in Uganda.

The second stage in the development of the style of the Gianikian/Ricci Lucchi *From the Pole to the Equator* involved their crucial decision to "analyze" the sequences they reprinted, a tactic which places *From the Pole to the Equator* within one of the central developments of recent avant-garde film. Traditionally, avant-garde film has functioned as more than an alternative to the conventional, commercial cinema; it has positioned itself in critical opposition to the dominant approaches and forms. While avant-garde filmmaking has continued to be economically marginal, it has used its marginality the way we use the margins of the pages of the books that are crucial in our lives—as free spaces within which we can develop a personally useful critique of the book's primary text.

For Gianikian/Ricci Lucchi, one element of this critical process has been to cinematically "rethink" areas of film history widely considered less than central. In recent years one of the most obvious of these areas has been what, not so long ago, was considered "primitive cinema": Edison, the Lumières, Méliès, Porter, Guy-Blaché, and other pioneers. From the late 1960s on, avant-garde filmmakers were seeing the pioneers' little films not merely as necessary simple first steps in the direction of sophisticated "important" (i.e., economically successful) cinema narratives, but as sources of inspiration and as works of complexity in their own right. In some instances, filmmakers made their respect for the early filmmakers explicit: Jonas Mekas dedicated *Walden* "to Lumière" and emulated what he saw as the personalness and directness of Lumière films; In *Tom, Tom, the Piper's Son*, Ken Jacobs used rephotography to explore an early narrative. In other instances, this respect was implicit in filmmakers' approaches: the Lumière and Edison equation of one shot = one film was emulated and extended by dozens of filmmakers (Robert Nelson, Larry Gottheim, Morgan Fisher, J. J. Murphy...) who developed single-shot cinema into a sophisticated and flexible form during the late 1960s and early 1970s.

Like so many American avant-garde filmmakers, Gianikian and Ricci Lucchi have been fascinated with early cinema for years. In the early 1980s they toured the United States with, among other films, *Karagoez-Catalogo 9.5* (1981), a two-part 16mm compilation film made up of excerpts taken from films once available in 9.5mm, an early European home-movie gauge with sprocket holes down the center of the film strip. As I remember (to my knowledge, the film is not available in the United States), *Karagoez* reprinted a variety of exotic imagery from commercial and other films.* In 1982, Gianikian and Ricci Lucchi completed *Das Lied von der Erde – Gustav Mahler*, again using Pathé Baby 9.5mm materials — in this instance, imagery recorded in various geographies, edited in an analogous relation to a reading of an essay on Mahler by Theodor Adorno. A version of the Mahler film was premiered at the 1982 Venice Festival, though it has not, to my knowledge, been screened in this country. The new film, *From the Pole to the Equator* (1986), is their most important work to date.

As suggested earlier, what makes *From the Pole to the Equator* remarkable is the subtle manner in which Gianikian and Ricci Lucchi analyze the Comerio footage in the process of presenting it. While we can see its visual beauty and power, we never see the Comerio imagery at a normal, "realistic" speed. Generally speaking, the finished film hovers on the line between stop-action and the illusion of motion; it is as though we are continually watching the images come alive, slow down, come alive — as if we are witnessing the events we see through a medium which is itself just coming to life.

More importantly, the particulars of Gianikian and Ricci Lucchi's precise control of motion continually foreground elements of the imagery which would probably not have been evident in the original material — or at least would not be evident had they presented Comerio's films the way the Lumière films are presented in the compilation reels made available by contemporary 16mm distributors servicing the academic market. When we watch the standard Lumière compilation reels, the individual films function simply as examples of a film history, a mode of film practice, now left behind: presentation of the films on contemporary equipment eliminates not only the dramatic effect of the fact of motion itself, which must have invigorated screenings in the 1890s, but any particular sense of the specificity of the experiences recorded. We tend to see (now) just a train — any train — arriving at a station, some workers leaving the Lumière factory, some children playing with boats in a Paris park.

In *From the Pole to the Equator* the slowed, irregular pace of the imagery highlights particular details of expression, gesture, and action, so that we seem to be making contact with people and events on a far more dramatic and revealing level than we usually experience when we see early films.** My guess is that in the Gianikian/Ricci Lucchi film we are making contact with people at a level Comerio would not only not have expected, but would not have wanted (according to Gianikian, Comerio hoped to become Mussolini's documentarian

---

* During that first American tour, Gianikian and Ricci Lucchi sometimes showed *Essence of Absynthe*, a short porn film from the period before 1910; as I remember, the film centered on two women and a man engaged in the standard for-the-camera blow job, but — touchingly, somehow — the three performers at times burst into laughter, seemingly at the absurdity of the process they're involved in.

** Much the same effect is achieved in much the same way in Ernie Gehr's remarkable *Eureka* (1979): Gehr reprinted what was originally a long single shot, filmed (for a Hale's Tours presentation) from the front of a trolley car traveling down Market Street in San Francisco to the end of the line, so that the details of the amazingly complex street are not merely entertaining (as they would have been for the Hale's Tours audience), but create a sense of Market Street as a microcosm of a nation in the process of cataclysmic technological and social change.

in the sense that Riefenstahl was later to become Hitler's).* *From the Pole to the Equator* re-presents Comerio's cinematography so that it comments on itself—on his original motivations for recording the imagery we see and on the moral and political implications of these motivations. It seems fair to assume that when Comerio originally recorded the imagery, his sense of the meaning of what he was doing was tied to notions of the "civilizing" impact of the European entry into African and Asian cultures and of the heroic nature of those explorers who lead expeditions to exotic places. The killing of animals in the polar and African sections was, no doubt, meant as a demonstration of the hunters' skill and prowess; and even the lovely portraits of exotic people seem part of a mindset bent on sophisticated domination in the interest of heroic, glorious colonialization.

Of course, even if we were to see his imagery unmediated by Gianikian and Ricci Lucchi, we would probably understand it differently than Comerio would, but their recycling dramatically extends the gap between Comerio's probable understanding of his images and ours. Their decisions about where to retard the imagery and which frames to highlight foreground the complexity of the exotic cultures and the humanity of the individuals who populate them. Comerio may have been fascinated with these people as representatives of a Difference to be overcome by the church and the military, but for contemporary viewers (at least for this viewer), this Difference is more to be admired than the power of those who would compromise it. In fact, because we see varied, complex cultures without the benefit (or detriment) of narration or any type of explanation—I assume the identities of some of these peoples would have been clearer to audiences at the original screenings, either because of informational intertitles or because at least some of the places and events would have been in the news—*From the Pole to the Equator* often reminds me of Trinh T. Minh-ha's *Naked Spaces: Living Is Round*.

Generally, the conquerors seem bored and boring, humorless and pretentious, almost oblivious to their surroundings. Near the end of the third section, we see a portrait of a young woman; then we see her doing a folk dance with a man before a crowd of people presumably native to the region. In the middle of the crowd sit two men: one is (I assume) some sort of elder representative of these people, the other is an Italian officer. As the dancers perform, Gianikian and Ricci Lucchi's reprinting of the shot emphasizes the dancers' gliding movements. Everyone in the shot seems to watch the dancers—except the Italian officer, who looks off-screen, seemingly unaware of the dance, daydreaming, one might infer, about future conquests or more "civilized" surroundings. In fact, while the individuals in the exotic cultures seem to enjoy what they do (the Indian dancer and musicians seem pleased to perform for the camera; the African men who assist the big game hunters seem proud of their part in events) and often seem happy to confront the camera's gaze, the Italians seem energized only by the pleasure of domination: we see them raise their guns to shoot, stand around rigidly in their military uniforms, ride in parades. They seem as unengaging as the bourgeois hunters in Peter Kubelka's *Our African Journey*, a film with which *From the Pole to the Equator* has much in common, at least thematically.

---

* Gianikian mentioned Comerio's interest in Italian fascism when he visited the Flaherty Film Seminar in the summer of 1987.

The subtle "analysis" provided by Gianikian and Ricci Lucchi's precise modulation of the speed with which we see the individual frames of Comerio's imagery (and by the more conventional gestures of their editing) is confirmed and extended by the soundtrack and by their use of color. The Anderson/Ullrich score is reminiscent of the serial music of Philip Glass, Terry Reilly, and Steve Reich, and its use in *From the Pole to the Equator* is reminiscent of the Glass soundtrack for *Koyaanisqatsi*, though the mood is darker. The Anderson/Ullrich music is eerie, haunting; it tends to emphasize the grimness of the events we are watching, even in instances where the imagery itself seems relatively neutral (The Anderson/Ullrich music is available on tape from Terry Cannon, at Little Sun, P.O. Box 1850, Monrovia, CA 91016.) The music helps to convey a sense of overwhelming sadness about the events Comerio documents, about what was lost through the colonialization and domination of people and animals.

The music also periodically dramatizes our historical complicity in the events; at times, the people we see seem to dance to the music we're hearing, particularly during the earlier passages filmed in Africa. These momentary synchronizations of image and sound reaffirm a fact which is implicit throughout: that we, sitting in a theater, fascinated with the people and events Comerio has captured, are the benefactors not only of his filmmaking, but of the processes of power and domination he documents for us. In fact, Comerio's footage dramatizes—as fully as any early footage I've seen—the degree to which the camera is one of the spearheads of empire. The Africans and Indians dance to the beat of our drum as fully as they danced for the conquerors, and in a historical sense we're probably no more prepossessing than the soldiers and church people whose commitment to colonialization many of us are likely to abhor.

The schizoid emotional quality of *From the Pole to the Equator* is emphasized by the obvious pains Gianikian and Ricci Lucchi took with color. In a general sense their color is reminiscent of that used in early film: monochrome tinting, and in a few instances, hand-coloring, frame by frame. But the way in which the color is articulated is different from the use of color in the few contemporary prints of early films I'm aware of. Most of *From the Pole to the Equator* is tinted, but while the color is monochromatic within any given frame, the color varies from moment to moment. A passage may be green, but the quality of green will continually change. More dramatic shifts in color separate sections of the film from each other: the move from the train section to the Antarctic section early in the film is signaled by a change from green-tinted imagery to cold blue-tinted imagery, which is made all the more dramatic by the fact that the train section has been exclusively greens and reds. However, dramatic shifts in color can occur anytime during a passage, and in some cases within a continuous shot. In other words, the use of tinting is not tied to the specifics of the content, as it is for example in the Killiam prints of Griffith's films.

The color in those infrequent passages when Gianikian and Ricci Lucchi forego tinting for multi-toned hand-coloring is realistic, but the fact of its being embedded in passages of tinted imagery renders it different in impact from a Méliès hand-colored film. The fact that the more painstaking use of multiple colors is confined to the section documenting India is probably no accident: the majority of multicolored moments seem to relate to the activities of Buddhist monks. It may be that Gianikian and Ricci Lucchi highlight the monks because, of all the Comerio imagery they reprinted, these images most nearly represent the philosophic opposite of the imperial quest so powerfully documented during the remainder of the film. Overall, the color in *From the Pole to the Equator* has a double impact which befits the film's complex mood: the color makes the film more sensuously beautiful, more watchable (certainly this is one of the most sensuously gorgeous films of recent years) so that we can more deeply experience the horror it captures and our complicity with it.

This essay was originally published in *Film Quarterly* 42, no. 3 (Spring 1989), 33-38.

1991

Process is Product, Product is Process: Peter Watkins' *The Journey*

From the 1970s on, I was an admirer of Peter Watkins' films. First, *The War Game* (1965), which I saw when I was a graduate student—driving home from the theater, thinking my car clock was off by an hour and gradually realizing that at 47 minutes, this film had had the impact of an epic-length feature. A decade later when, thanks to Joseph A. Gomez, author of *Peter Watkins* (Boston: Twayne, 1979), who brought the filmmaker to Utica, I saw other remarkable Watkins films—most memorably, *Punishment Park* (1971), *Edvard Munch* (1974), and *The Trap* (1975)—and was soon presenting these films, and hosting Watkins himself, at my Utica College film series.

In 1982-83, Watkins enlisted the assistance of those who'd hosted him at screenings to collaborate with him on what would become *The Journey*. Many of us who agreed to work with Watkins imagined that *The Journey* might have considerable impact—the kind of impact that *The War Game* might have had had it not been suppressed for twenty years by the BBC. Organizing and fundraising efforts took place during 1983, shooting during 1984. The editing was done at the National Film Board of Canada and the film premiered at festivals in 1987. That the final film was 14½-hours long (and slow moving for most viewers) made it controversial at festivals, though it garnered a good bit of attention, particularly in Berlin. The idea of a global film dealing with global issues was unusual and *The Journey* is full of memorable moments, though I believe Watkins' fundamental hope, a hope that had allowed him to devote himself for years to the project, was that he could successfully model a kind of global media attention and collaboration that might be more effective at informing global audiences and solving global problems than national commercial media corporations.

In August 1987, Watkins and several of those who had been involved with the production of *The Journey* were invited to the Robert Flaherty Film Seminar by Richard Herskowitz, that year's programmer. Herskowitz scheduled the entire film, some of it at normal Flaherty screening times, the rest during times usually used by seminarians for partying and leisure. There were grumblings throughout the days leading up to the Wednesday evening discussion with Watkins, and the discussion itself was brutal. Few of those present were willing to take the film or Watkins' hopes for the project seriously. For Watkins it was, I believe, a blow to his hope that *The Journey* might have the kinds of impact we had imagined. (An edited version of the Flaherty discussion is included in Zimmermann and MacDonald, *The Flaherty; Decades in the Cause of Independent Cinema* [Bloomington: Indiana University Press, 2017]: 177-83.)

What follows was written four years after the Flaherty debacle, at a time when I was still coming to terms with my personal disappointment at the film's reception, and beginning to recognize aspects of Watkins' conceptual design for *The Journey* that I'd not fully understood. Re-reading this particular essay is bittersweet for me. I'd worked with Herskowitz to bring *The Journey* to the Flaherty, never imagining what the response might be—this was my first Flaherty. The experience did damage to my relationship with Watkins that has never been fully repaired.

Note: In some cases, I've shortened paragraphs of the essay for easy reading and have made minor textual changes for clarity.

* * *

Peter Watkins has always been a director given to "excess." He has seen his job as testing limits, even the limits of those who complacently define themselves as open and experimental. In the late 1960s, when the BBC decided it wanted some of its young directors to deal with serious issues in new ways, Watkins responded with the devastating (and still powerful) *The War Game* (1965), which was refused the planned prime-time airing apparently because its attack on the 1960s arms build-up was so strong that some felt the 47-minute film could cause viewers to have the truly active response that was clearly Watkins' goal.[1] Nearly all the Watkins films that followed—*Privilege* (1967), *The Gladiators* (1969), *Punishment Park* (1971), *Edvard Munch* (1974), *The Seventies People* (1975), *The Trap* (1975), *Evening Land* (1977)—have been on the attack. None of these films, however, is as remarkable— and as monumentally "excessive"—as the recent, 14½-hour *The Journey* (shooting completed in 1986, premiered in 1987).

The Journey was/is a double-leveled assault on contemporary systems: on political/economic systems East and West, on the immense military systems that protect them, and on those communications systems theoretically charged with informing societies about contemporary realities: the mass media and organized education. At the first level of assault, the film's conception, practical execution, and completion are evidence that such a gigantic "process film" can be made. The second level involves the completed film, not simply as a discrete work, but in its implicit and explicit ongoing confrontation of contemporary systems of distribution and exhibition. On both levels, *The Journey* has precedents, and yet there is something quite distinctive about it.

The Journey developed out of the ashes of a project at one point called "The Nuclear War Film," an attempt to make an updated, contemporary version of *The War Game* in such a way that Watkins (rather than a production organization such as the BBC), would be able to control the resulting film's accessibility

Production stills by Sylvia de Swaan of Peter Watkins filming in the Mohawk Valley what became *The Journey* (1987).

to audiences. *The War Game* was produced on a limited budget, primarily with non-actor citizens of Kent, where filming took place. For "The Nuclear War Film" Watkins wanted to involve people throughout Great Britain, both in funding a much larger film and as non-actor citizens expressing their concerns through the making of the film. But as the potential costs of the project grew beyond Watkins' earliest plans, the original sponsors for the project (London's Central Television primary among them) pulled out, and the project collapsed—except for a crucial conceptual dimension which ultimately was the catalyst for *The Journey*.[2]

By 1983, Watkins' plan for setting up a grass-roots, activist system for the production of "The Nuclear War Film" had combined with a second concern he had long had about *The War Game*: though the Academy-Award-winning documentary was about the quintessential international problem, the action in the film takes place almost entirely within England (one brief sequence near the beginning of *The War Game* does supposedly take place in Germany, near the Berlin Wall, where tensions heat and boil over, resulting in the nuclear war that the film "documents").[3] Watkins began to organize all his resources for a film which would be truly international in as many ways as possible.

After *Privilege*, Watkins became an expatriate and didn't try to work in England again until "The Nuclear War Film." He moved from place to place making or trying to make films and, during periods when he was not involved in production, he toured Europe, North America, and Australia, presenting and discussing his films with audiences at colleges and universities and with community groups of various kinds and, in some cases, teaching formal courses in media and communications. Like other filmmakers who travel with their work, Watkins developed a network of friends and sponsors interested in and sympathetic to his films. For *The Journey* he decided to call upon this network, this time not simply as an alternative exhibition system but also as a loosely knit group of people capable of functioning in other ways, capable of participating in the production of a cinematic viewpoint as

well as of helping to sustain a system where some marginalized cinematic viewpoints could be seen and discussed.

Even at the early stages, *The Journey* project—Watkins called it "The Peace Film" at the beginning—sounded intriguing enough to attract a number of the people Watkins approached.[4] I was one of these people: the idea of working on a film (with a distinguished director whose films I had admired and taught) which would be shot in countries around the world and would deal with such issues as the arms race, hunger, racism, sexism, and the workings of the media and the educational system appealed to me immediately.[5] I agreed to help without fully understanding the conceptual implications of what was occurring.

From the vantage point of the completed film, it is clear that one of Watkins' primary themes is the issue of "objectivity" as it works itself out in much of professional life: that is, not simply as an adherence to the facts, but as a detachment from them. While it might seem the most obvious thing in the world to ask a person who teaches academic courses in literature and film to help make a film, Watkins' simple question as to whether I felt I could become involved in this project created a problem for me, and my guess is that one or another version of this problem confronted many of those who ultimately raised money for *The Journey* or appeared in it.

From my academic training, I had developed a commitment to a form of educated detachment which seemed to me essential for serious study and commentary. Though I had come to know some of the filmmakers whose films I wrote about—in the relatively small world of experimental/avant-garde cinema, some personal involvement is difficult to escape or resist—I had always avoided appearing in films by filmmakers I had a professional interest in and when this was unavoidable (when a filmmaker would be recording events I was part of for a diary film, for example), I consistently refused to write in any detail about the resulting film, on the assumption that my involvement, however unwitting, destroyed my objectivity, my detachment, and hence the credibility of anything I could write about that film.

As is obvious in the essay you are reading, *The Journey* plunged my earlier understanding of professionalism into crisis. I assume much the same was true for other local organizers, and I know it was true for many of the everyday people who appear in *The Journey*.[6] Watkins was particularly drawn to teachers at the elementary, high school and college level; his involving them in what they knew would be an openly political film was, I'm now convinced, a conscious part of his plan for the process film.

Each person approached for production assistance was asked to organize a fundraising group. Watkins made it clear from the beginning that if such a group were formed and if it raised any money at all, a portion of the film would be shot with those funds. The more money available, the more shooting would occur. It was also clear that groups in the more affluent countries (U.S.A., Sweden, Australia) would need to fund the

Poster designed by Robert Huot as fundraiser for the Mohawk Valley participation in *The Journey*.

shooting in countries where fundraising was not a practical or moral possibility. The optimum way of raising money, Watkins felt, was to host community events, some of which he hoped would relate to the issues the film would confront. Given the difficulty of raising money for a political film, it was obvious from the outset that, except for those technicians who would supply and run the film equipment, no one would be paid. Watkins also asked groups to organize crews for the shoot (hopefully with locals), to arrange for people he could consider interviewing on film, and—if it appeared a group would be able to raise sufficient funds for more than an extended interview—to assemble enough people to dramatize crowd scenes. In almost all instances I am aware of, all these jobs were carried out by people who had never done such work before. In other words, Watkins' process film created a "space" within which people could develop new skills and find the time for new kinds of personal action—all in the service of the film's international goals.

By the end of 1983, Watkins had been able to organize a grassroots, voluntary, international system committed to the production of a highly politicized film. Even at this early stage, the differences between *The Journey*'s procedures and the usual industry procedure were obvious. While there was no question that Watkins was in charge, the nature of his position as director was in most ways the opposite of the usual experience, in which an army of filmmakers arrives in a town and purchases the right to take over for a time, until it has achieved those ends necessary for its ultimate profit-making goals—an experience which often encapsulates the process of colonial exploitation.

Given the implicit challenge this project posed to traditional ways of doing things, those who agreed to work with Watkins did so on the assumption that the making of "The Peace Film" would be a means for activating some of their feelings and ideological stances and for communicating beyond their normal circle of acquaintances and institutional affiliations.

Watkins' process was, at the directorial level, analogous. Watkins has always maintained a rather schizoid stance toward his profession. On the one hand, he has consistently avoided fraternizing with other media makers in conventional professional settings such as professional conferences and high visibility festivals, on the grounds that his interest in making films has nothing to do with wanting to be part of a particular professional elite. Watkins has been so hostile toward many of those who are most secure in this professional world, in fact, that he has developed a rather widespread reputation for being "arrogant" and "difficult to work with." He has been more open to experimental/avant-garde filmmakers, and yet he makes little effort to know them or to keep up with their work, a tendency which I do feel has been somewhat counterproductive. On the other hand, when he discusses his films in public gatherings, Watkins is always careful to use "we," rather than "they," when referring to the professional media.

The procedure Watkins devised for himself as producer/director of *The Journey* reflects this rather schizoid attitude: although the procedure is highly experimental, it is clear in the finished film that Watkins feels his unusual procedure is a way of using media that "we" in the profession should learn from and elaborate on.

To be more specific, Watkins' procedure differed from conventional media procedures both in the amount and the kind of work he proved himself willing to undertake. In fact, the "performance" of getting the film made was easily as spectacular as anything in the completed film. During 1983 and 1984 Watkins functioned continually as an international person. He organized and filmed in three American locations (Portland, Oregon; Seattle, Washington; and Utica/Ilion, New York), in France, West Germany, and Norway, in the Soviet Union, in the Hebrides Islands and Glasgow, Scotland, in Mexico, on the Island of Tahiti (despite some French government resistance), in several Australian locations, in Mozambique, and in two Japanese locations.[7] He did not travel protected by an entourage; he moved from one nation to the next, from one language system to the next, alone, relying almost entirely on the good will of the people in the locales where he filmed.

Watkins was so committed to the diversity of cultural expression that he refused to simplify the international process even when it would have been easy to do so: for example, he asked the people on the Isle of Lewis to speak their native Gaelic during their community discussion, even though they could have spoken English. During the whirl of shooting in one location and the inevitable minor obstacles (in Utica the mayor refused police cordoning for neighborhood crowd scenes), Watkins was continually on the phone arranging for the next segment of the process.

When Watkins arrived at the National Film Board of Canada early in 1985 to edit the film, he had shot over 100 hours of material and, more important, he had demonstrated that an individual media professional could develop a film by moving through established boundaries—linguistic, political, cultural, and economic as well as national.[8] To put it another way, Watkins had enlarged the potential of the film director's (and/or producer's) job: he had shown that a filmmaker could interrogate contemporary systems not simply by accepting them and working within them, "doing what he/she could," but by moving across them, continually exceeding their limits, and finishing what some had assumed could not be done. His individual achievement in getting the film finished was a way of suggesting that all of us, whether we're involved in media or not, can and must do a good bit more than we tell ourselves we can do if we care about delivering a more humane, progressive world to our descendants.

At no point during the years when *The Journey* was being made and premiered was Watkins' "excessiveness" more obvious, at least to those of us who had collaborated on the film, than when we learned that the finished film was to be fourteen and a half hours long. I think it is fair to say that, despite the amount of shooting Watkins had done, none of us had ever considered that the film might be longer than a conventional feature or, at most, a conventional epic. For some of those who had collaborated with Watkins, this surprise turned to frustration, disappointment, and anger once they had seen the completed film.

My own experience reflected this pattern to a degree: I left the preview screening at the National Film Board feeling I had seen a very remarkable film, but I felt that it would have been an even "better" film had it been trimmed by a few hours. As the film made its way onto the festival circuit, the question of its excessive length was raised again and again. The fourteen and a half hours seemed a particular affront to viewers at festivals where film enthusiasts feel obliged to see as many films as possible in a very short time. The problem of the overall length was highlighted by the fact that *The Journey* moves very slowly; Watkins calculated later that the average length of a shot in *The Journey* is 45.9 seconds; and the film spends its extended time with people who would never be the focus of a commercial film or TV show or, for that matter, of an independent documentary: they're not experts and they're not bizarre in any way—except as cinematic personae.

As I have worked with *The Journey*, I have come to see that its "weaknesses"— its length and pace, in particular—are precisely its point. As a completed film, *The Journey* does have many strengths, the most obvious of which is its intricate, thoughtful structure. In general, *The Journey* is an immense filmic weave during which Watkins develops dozens of strands of discussion and information. Within any given passage we may see a portion of a discussion with one of the families; a rolling text presenting statistics suggesting the relation between world hunger and world arms expenditures; a reminiscence by a Hiroshima survivor; a bit of home-movie documentation of the White Train's delivery of nuclear warheads to the submarine base at Bangor, Washington; a portion of the Canadian group's coverage of the mass media coverage of the Reagan-Mulroney summit as interpreted by Watkins; a portion of a discussion with another family; and so on. As the film develops, each of these strands is elaborated, and resonates with other strands.

The Journey is divided into forty-five to fifty-minute "chapters" by question marks that appear on the screen. Overall, the film focuses on somewhat different aspects of issues during particular passages. For instance, during early "chapters," family discussions center on a set of large still photographs of the suffering and devastation at Hiroshima; during the final chapters, families see videos of the other families and discuss the general similarities in their responses to the same information. During any given viewing, one or another section of the film may seem strong or weak. In some cases, this has to do with decisions Watkins made as editor; in others, it's a function of the viewer's mood at the time.

Some sections seem consistently strong: for example, I am always moved by "Chapter 8," especially the conclusion, where a group of Norwegian children enact a frantic run to an air raid shelter. In any case, one need no more feel obliged to admire all of *The Journey* than one need admire all of Whitman's *Leaves of Grass* or Wordsworth's *Prelude*. My guess is that most viewers do admire sections of the film but find that the length (and pace) tend to cancel out their pleasure. But *The Journey*'s length and pace are not errors in aesthetic judgment; they have a significance that relates most crucially to Watkins' primary goals for the film.

As is obvious in *The Journey*, Watkins sees the world in an increasingly precarious state. The film's excessive length is not simply a way of saying that the problems it confronts are very important, requiring a symbolically greater length than films dealing with more trivial matters. And it is more than a way of including a wealth of information about the world arms race, world hunger, and related issues. Fundamentally, the length is a function of Watkins' commitment to those he interviewed and an attempt to suggest/demonstrate new ways of using media. In other words, the length is a function of the film-as-process rather than as perfect or imperfect product.

When Watkins was arranging and shooting the many interviews included in the film, he made it clear that he would treat what people said with respect. He then presented the interviewees with various kinds of photographic and statistical information and questioned them about their feelings and their own personal experiences. In his limited editing of the completed interviews, he demonstrated that he meant "respect" as more than metaphor: it was not a matter of choosing those portions of what people said that he found interesting or that he assumed viewers would find interesting, or that made the interviewees look good, or that he felt were correct. It was not simply a question of using people's statements to invigorate a predetermined cinematic or ideological structure. Rather, the structure was a means of giving people the opportunity to say what they felt they had to say at their own pace and as fully as possible without interruption (hence the extended length of individual shots) and, ultimately, for making the entirety of their comments available to the other interviewees and to those individuals around the world who would find their way to the film. *The Journey* is as long as it is, in other words, because of the primacy of Watkins' commitment to those he interviewed, and because of his assumption that we need to learn to listen to each other with a good deal more patience than we normally do.

Naturally, one might argue that while such ideas sound good, life does not give us time to listen to everyone: the mass media normally function as a means of intensifying and encapsulating human experience and dialogue so that we can know and understand more; only when we're informed can we take useful social/political action. For Watkins, however, conventional systems are bankrupt. The ever-presence of the media has not served to ameliorate the world's most serious problems; in recent years we've seen more images of starving people than ever before, and yet there are more and more starving people. Dozens of films have documented the spiraling arms race, and yet it continues to spiral. *The Journey* suggests that insofar as the mass media are concerned, the problem is with the system itself.

As is clear in the film's analysis of the Canadian media covering the "Shamrock Summit" between Reagan and Mulroney in 1984, current media structures don't really allow us to "study" world problems; we are left to hope those in power will see fit to protect us; for the media, the Summit was a spectacle (the majority of press time was spent on arrivals, ritual inspections, and on a gala entertainment); almost no time was spent on the issues of the summit—acid rain and greater Canadian involvement in American nuclear plans—and none at all on how individual citizens might work to effect the resolution of these issues.

For Watkins the crux of the problem—of all problems—is the necessity for individual action and the cooperation of individual citizens in accomplishing change. Just as his seemingly Herculean efforts in making the film are meant to be an example of what one committed media person can do by functioning as a citizen of the world, the efforts of the families and other groups recorded by the film to discuss the issues Watkins raises are presented primarily as role models for action, rather than as sources of entertainment or as interesting specimens for study.[9] With the exception of those individuals who recall their experiences during and after the bombings of Hiroshima and Hamburg and two young people from Algeria who discuss racism and sexism within French and Arab societies, most of those interviewed are visibly uncomfortable discussing issues.

It is clear that these families have rarely talked together at length about issues; often they cannot speak in an informed or coherent manner; they're not sure how to deal with the grisly photographs Watkins shows them in the presence of their young children. And yet, because of their commitment to the media process Watkins has enlisted their participation in, they try to talk together, to think about their potential part in the events they discuss, to inform their children about reality and to conceive of actions they could take as family groups in relation to these issues. These discussions are certainly not action in any conventional sense, and yet, since they could have a real impact on what these particular children and their parents do with their lives and on what they do together, the discussions reveal a potential for having a positive effect on specific circumstances. In the years since *The Journey* was shot, the William Hendricks family, focus of the Utica shooting, has opened their home at Thanksgiving to feed anyone who has no place to eat and gather with others.

For Watkins, the kinds of social change necessary for dealing with international mega-problems such as hunger and the arms race must occur as a wave of individuals helping their neighbors and joining with their neighbors to help *their* neighbors. Resources must be shared by individuals with other individuals until, person by person, family by family, neighborhood by neighborhood, region by region, a wave of human cooperation accomplishes a more humane future.

That everyday individuals can work through even the most frustrating international barriers is suggested by the developing friendship of the Smillies, a Scottish family, and the Kolosovs, a Soviet family. Watkins' process in making *The Journey* included videotaping messages from families to other families; by the end of the film Sam Smillie has flown to Leningrad to meet Alexander Kolosov, and the Soviet family looks forward to hosting the Scottish family during the "White Nights of Summer"; the excitement of both families at their accomplishment in getting to know each other is obvious.

Ultimately, I would guess, Watkins hoped that *The Journey* would function as a means for developing a new kind of media "network," a network of individual citizens from around the world using contemporary technology as a process of joining together for their mutual understanding and action. His hope, I'm sure, was that the process of getting to know people from other language systems, from other social systems, from economies more or less disadvantaged than one's own would, once it got going, replace the current rigid media superstructures which organize every second of the day according to a predigested one-way system.

The Journey's length is a way of suggesting that such a process should become a far larger part of our lives, that we need to change direction now in order to serve the future. And just as the film gave the interviewees practice in discussing serious issues with their families, it gives programmers/exhibitors practice in allocating time more flexibly for political films. Finally, it gives viewers practice in rearranging their time schedules to make room for progressive action: to see *The Journey* in a short time requires major rearrangements of the potential viewer's life for several days; to see it over a longer period requires an ongoing commitment.

To date, *The Journey* has not instigated any large social movement one can measure. It has changed the lives of some of those who collaborated on it; it has allowed for some interchange among people from diverse nations who would otherwise not have had an opportunity to communicate (a directory of those hundreds of people who took part in making the film is in the planning stages); it has been seen here and there at theaters, festivals, and on TV (Canyon Cinema distributes the film in 16mm and on video). Whether its direct impact will grow as years go by is impossible to say. Regardless of the size of the audience that ultimately sees it, however, I would guess that Watkins' efforts and achievements in functioning more fully as an international filmmaker will inspire others to attempt international projects and to break with the media systems and structures which have come to seem so normal. After all, *The Journey*'s excessiveness is a means of suggesting that the real spectacle is how, given the contemporary state of the world, we live our daily lives.

DVD copies of Watkins' work (French-only) are distributed by Doriane Films in Paris, France: www.capuseen.com. For other questions contact Watkins' sons, Patrick and Gerard Watkins, at peterwatkinsfilms@gmail.com. I have access to DVD copies of *The Journey* and some other Watkins films.

"Process is Product; Product is Process: Peter Watkins' *The Journey*" was published in a special issue of *Willamette Journal of the Liberal Arts*, Supplemental Series 5. The issue was edited by Ken Nolley, and includes Watkins' own "*The Journey*: A Voyage of Discovery" and essays by Nolley, Catherine Collins, Gregg B. Walker, James Welsh, and Mary Ann Youngren.

1 For more information about Watkins' early career, see Joseph A. Gomez, *Peter Watkins* (Boston: Twayne, 1979), chapters 1 and 2. James M. Welsh's *Peter Watkins: A Guide to References and Resources* (Boston: G. K. Hall, 1986) includes a biographical overview, a critical survey, a filmography, and a detailed, annotated listing of writings about and by Watkins.
2 For additional information see Welsh (1986), 21-22, and Nolley, "The Collapse of Watkins' Nuclear War Film," *Literature/Film Quarterly*, 11 (1983), 234-36.
3 The brief "German" sequence in *The War Game* and the implication that the Wall could be the catalyst for a nuclear war is still remembered in the German Democratic Republic, where officials refused to allow a mention of *The War Game* on TV during the 1987 documentary film festival in Leipzig, where *The Journey* was screened in toto, but at a site some distance away (a safe distance?) from the main festival.
4 The change from "The Nuclear War Film" to "The Peace Film" was a result of Watkins' growing conviction that, in the wake of *The Day After* (and other films and MTV videos which dramatized nuclear holocaust or nuclear explosions), further dramatizations of nuclear holocausts could only function to convince audiences of the inevitability of such events—and, thus, could only sap audiences' willingness to work actively for peace. From the beginning, *The Journey* was conceived as a film which would dramatize and catalyze peaceful alternatives.
5 My involvement with those portions of *The Journey* shot in upstate New York is discussed in "The Means Justify the Ends," *Afterimage* 14, no.9 (1987), 4-7.
6 Ken Nolley, who worked with the Portland, Oregon support group (and who participated in the Utica/Ilion, New York filming) had much the same experience as I did, as he explains in Nolley, "Making *The Journey* with Peter Watkins," *Cine/Action* (Spring 1988).
7 Watkins' idea of using the procedure of moving from one country to another as both a means of generating footage for a single film and as a structuring principle for a finished film has a good bit in common with the work of such experimental/avant-garde filmmakers as Warren Sonbert (*Divided Loyalties, Noblesse Oblige, A Woman's Touch, The Cup and the Lip*) and Johan Van Der Keuken (*The Way South*).
8 Once Watkins had arrived in Montreal to edit at the National Film Board of Canada, he worked with filmmaker Peter Wintonick and others in the Canadian support group to document the process of the commercial media "covering" the Shamrock Summit between Reagan and Mulroney.
9 Watkins' interest in interviewing nuclear families was questioned by the 1987 Robert Flaherty Film Seminar on the grounds that accepting the nuclear family as society's fundamental institution is not necessarily a progressive position. I assume Watkins would agree with this. *The Journey* is less a paean to the family than an implicit critique (one which is carefully respectful of the individuals he talks with) of its failure to function as a progressive force (educationally, politically) for its members.

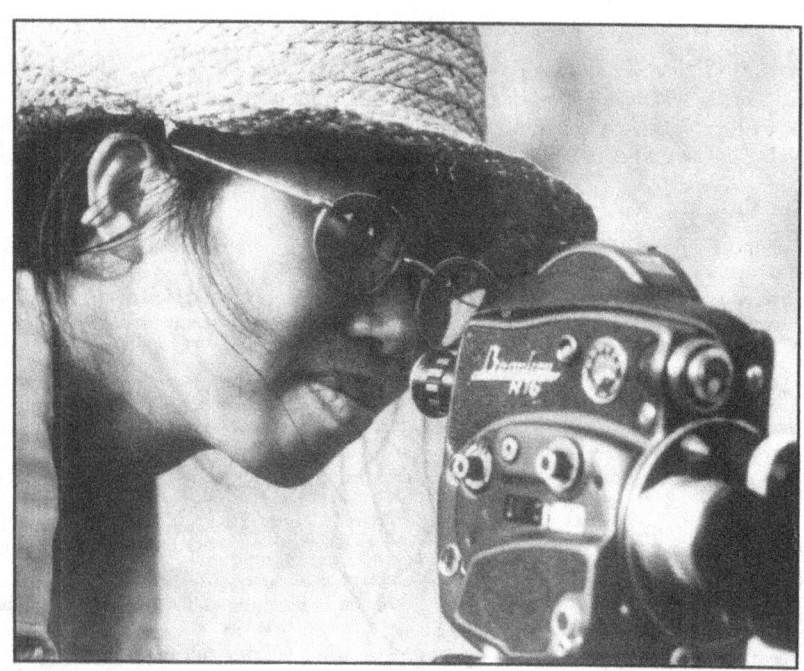

Cover of the catalogue produced in conjunction with
Trinh T. Minh-ha's residency, programmed by John Knecht,
at Colgate University in October 1994.

1994

Catalogue essay on Trinh T. Minh-ha, commissioned by Colgate University to accompany a film retrospective during an Artist-in-Residency, October 11-26, 1994

Looking back at the following essay after nearly 30 years, my defense of Trinh seems almost foolish; she has become, for most people interested in cinema history and media studies, a crucial figure. To recognize that her current status in the field was something of a work-in-progress, however, one need only read the post-screening discussion of her *Reassemblage* (1982) that took place at the Robert Flaherty Film Seminar in 1983, where a good many seminarians were sure she didn't know what she was doing [the discussion is available in Zimmermann and MacDonald, *The Flaherty: Decades in the Cause of Independent Cinema* (Bloomington: Indiana University Press, 2017, 167-71)]. By the time I was asked to contribute an essay to commemorate Trinh's visit to Colgate University, whatever early resistance she had encountered was disappearing. I was hardly the first film scholar to defend her; indeed, Patricia Zimmermann had come to Trinh's defense during the 1983 Flaherty discussion.

An irony here is that when Trinh returned for the 2017 Flaherty as a featured guest, some younger seminarians struggled with her work in ways familiar from the earlier seminar. Trinh: "Although there were, as always with my films, some among the viewers who were disturbed and eager to voice disapproval for anything they 'dislike' (and if you remember, these like-don't-like folks were mostly immature, unthinking newcomers—at least in 2017), there were also quite a number of experienced, accomplished filmmakers and film programmers there who respected the work…and gave strong, positively useful feedback. The surprise for me at the time came from a few film programmers who apologetically approached me at the end of the seminar to tell me they had learnt a lot and would seek out more of my work." (Email to the author, July 29, 2024.)

Note: I have shortened the paragraphs of the essay for ease of reading.

* * *

1

"I do not intend to speak about/Just speak nearby."[1]

From the standpoint of North American independent cinema, the 1980s and 1990s have been a paradoxical period, characterized, on one hand, by shrinking economic resources for production, exhibition, and distribution, and therefore by fewer opportunities for seeing films that provide in-theater critiques of commercial moviegoing; and on the other hand, by a surprising productivity on the part of the independent filmmakers themselves, and particularly on the part of filmmakers interested in rethinking not only the conventional, mass-market cinema and the audience it has created, but those traditions that have developed in large measure in reaction to commercial moviegoing: the traditions of documentary and avant-garde filmmaking.

For some, this re-thinking has led to a combining of elements from all three traditions—a way of suggesting both the limitations of these traditions and the fact that all the traditions have much to offer a filmmaker willing to separate the ideological and formal wheat from the chaff.[2] Trinh T. Minh-ha has pursued a related, but somewhat different course. She has tended to work between traditional categories, and particularly in the ideological and formal gaps between the histories of avant-garde and documentary film. Because of Trinh's success in revealing how large and humanly significant these gaps are, the result has been a remarkable and influential series of films that have frequently been the subjects of hot debate among filmmakers, film critics and scholars.

Reassemblage (1982), Trinh's first long film, and her first in 16mm (it had been preceded by three short Super-8mm films) was, and remains, a challenge to the histories of film in several ways. Most obviously—and this is true of all Trinh's films—*Reassemblage* defied the traditions of commercial moviemaking and conventional documentary by refusing to offer viewers either a simple, obvious focus of investigation or any form of resolution. Conventional mass market movies (and television shows), and traditional documentaries have at least one crucial characteristic in common: they are usually made to be understood completely, and in a single viewing, by a relatively broad audience. Commercial directors use composition and editing to be sure we always know exactly what we're supposed to be seeing and precisely what it means within the developing melodrama.

Documentarians may have less control over the development of their films than fiction filmmakers, who are free to create whatever they need to make their characterizations and plots at least momentarily believable, but traditionally documentarians have been able to count on spoken and written narration, generally by what has come to be called the "voice of god" (male) narrator, who directs our perceptions to what the filmmaker considers significant to the exploration of the history or issue being documented. In contrast, *Reassemblage* not only refuses to "get to the point," either in the narrative sense or the informational sense, Trinh's film is precisely about *not* getting to the point. *Reassemblage* is a dynamic meditation on various people and places Trinh observed during the time she lived in Senegal, but it comes to no specific conclusions about the complex world portrayed in the film. Indeed, she is quite open about this in the film: twice during her narration, she says, "A film about what? my friends ask. A film about Senegal; but what in Senegal?"

For Trinh, acceding to the tradition that filmmakers must answer all questions for their audiences, and that in documentary filmmaking in particular, the right to make a film is a function of the documentarian's expertise—defined as an ability to explain the subject of the film—is at best pretentious and at worst dangerous. When we "make sense" to each other about another, very different culture, whose sense do we make? The most Trinh pretends to do in *Reassemblage* is to be "looking through a circle [the circle of the camera lens] in a circle of looks": she looks at the Senegalese looking at her.

Of course, the paradox of *Reassemblage* is that while Trinh refuses to approach her subject using either the traditional melodramatic or informational approaches, and while she presents viewers with no particular conclusions, her stance outside the traditions of melodrama and documentary allows her to access, and to make accessible to us, a world conventionally marginalized by both traditions: the everyday world of women in general, and of African women in particular. During *Reassemblage* we see women hoeing, turning grain into food, taking care of children and of themselves, dancing, and interacting—living their lives. And as we observe them, we may remember that even the tradition of ethnographic documentary (of filmmaking in the service of serious anthropological research) has often been more intrigued by the adventures of men: their hunting, their battles with other men, their rituals, than with the experiences of women.

Indeed, my guess is that some of the original resistance to Trinh's African films—*Reassemblage* and *Naked Spaces—Living Is Round* (1985)—especially among male documentarians was a function of their embarrassed realization that so many of the most admired classic films about other cultures, from Robert Flaherty's *Nanook of the North* (1921) to John Marshall's *The Hunters* (1958) to Robert Gardner's *Dead Birds* (1963) to Timothy Asch and Napoleon Chagnon's *The Ax Fight* (1975) and *Magical Death* (1973) had been as male-centered as most Hollywood Westerns. By stepping outside both traditions, in her choices about what to film and in her decisions about how to organize her film for her viewers, Trinh was able to "reassemble" her North American viewers' (film) culture, through her commitment not to pretend to be able to shoot straight to the heart of other cultures.

2

> One sympathetic viewer at a festival told me that when she shared with others her admiration for the film, she was told that she should see *Reassemblage* first before offering any comment. *Reassemblage* had become a model!³

On one level, *Reassemblage* is deeply indebted to mainstream film history, especially the tradition of "montage" editing that was developed during the 1920s in post-revolutionary Russia by Lev Kuleshov, Sergei Eisenstein, Dziga Vertov and others, and subsequently exploited by filmmakers around the world. For Eisenstein in particular, the engagement of the viewer in films about progressive revolution was, at least in theory, a means of energizing filmgoers to leave the movie theater ready to sustain a progressive revolution or to create one. And this in-theater training was a function of montage editing: the more the viewer was faced with synthesizing the meaning of antithetical shots—that is, the more distinct from one another successive shots in a sequence were and the more shots per minute the viewer was forced to process—the more involved and sophisticated the viewer would become. Eisenstein's most famous "montage," the Odessa Steps sequence at the climax of *The Battleship Potemkin* (1925), became a model for filmmakers interested in making a moment in a film emotionally and politically overwhelming.

Unlike Eisenstein, Trinh did not embed a powerful montage within *Reassemblage*; rather, the entire film is a montage that confronts the viewer relentlessly with a wide variety of mundane and powerful images. For those committed to polemicizing about the marginalization of women, and particularly African women, the visual assault of Trinh's montage seemed perfectly appropriate, even exhilarating. *Reassemblage* was touted as a new feminist, ethnically alert landmark of political cinema, and at least some portion of Trinh's audience awaited the next, presumably even more powerful montage film that would further "reassemble" our thinking about issues of gender and ethnicity by applying the montage approach to other marginalized populations.

The most fundamental dialectic at work in Trinh's filmmaking career thus far, however, is her interest in following each film project with a very different project that can challenge viewers in new ways. When *Naked Spaces-Living Is Round* was finished, many of those who admired *Reassemblage* were disappointed: the new film didn't seem to pack the polemical wallop of *Reassemblage*. At the same time, other viewers, who had come to view montage-styled polemics with suspicion (the most pervasive use of the Eisenstein approach to editing, after all, is in television advertising and in the overall structuring of the American commercial television hour), found *Naked Spaces* even more interesting than *Reassemblage*, in large measure because Trinh's methods in the longer film (135 minutes) were quite the opposite of her approach in *Reassemblage*. *Naked Spaces* is as serene as *Reassemblage* is dynamic. Indeed, its meditative pace places it even further from conventional entertainment cinema—at least formally—than *Reassemblage*: it critiques not only the human gaps in traditional moviemaking (most obviously, the failure of Hollywood and of many conventional documentarians to focus on women), but on the experience of viewers themselves.

The meditative pace of *Naked Spaces* and its extended length (though only slightly longer than a conventional feature, the serene pace causes it to feel substantially longer) demands that we viewers confront our own impatience, our own frustration—the impact on us of the virtually inevitable, long-term training we have received from commercial film and television. For all its progressiveness, *Reassemblage* provides a variety of conventional pleasures in addition to its dynamic editing: most obviously, sensuous imagery of partially naked women's bodies. To enjoy *Naked Spaces*, we must leave even more of our expectations behind. Because of its viewer-confrontory approach, *Naked Spaces* caused considerable debate, among two different groups: documentarians, especially ethnographic documentarians, disapproved of the film not only because (like *Reassemblage*) it reveals Trinh's suspicion of the whole enterprise of anthropology, which Trinh seems to see as a function of the extension of empire, rather than as a corrective to it; but also because she disobeys the "rules" of ethnographic filmmaking: for example, in some instances, Trinh uses music from one African people as a soundtrack for visuals of a different people.

On the other hand, some avant-garde filmmakers and enthusiasts assumed that Trinh's use of a somewhat unstable, hand-held camera was a (failed) attempt to make a place for herself in the history of "personal," self-expressive avant-garde cinema—"failed" because Trinh was neither breaking new ground nor extending the personal in any significant way. The double-sided attack on *Naked Spaces* tended to assume that Trinh didn't know what she was doing. The irony, of course, is that the "failures" of *Naked Spaces* can just as easily be seen as dimensions of the film's cutting-edge critique of these two traditions of filmmaking that have often prided themselves on their sophistication as critiques of conventional mass-market industrial filmmaking.

Trinh's deviations from the "rules" of ethnographic filmmaking—especially her refusal to "explain" any particular dimension of the various West-African cultures she depicts, and her decision to structure her meditations on indigenous dwellings with a rather free-form poetic or musical organization instead of with the more traditional structure of an illustrated lecture—can be understood as a challenge to the assumption that traditional forms of cinematic investigation of non-industrialized cultures create "understanding" through the imposition of cinematic forms based on conventional Western logic. Indeed, Trinh's choice of a contrapuntal, musical structure for organizing image and sound seems more in tune with the sights and sounds of the diverse cultures she visits. Her "failed" attempt at "personal cinema," most evident in her use of a somewhat shaky hand-held camera, can be seen as a challenge to the personal tradition of avant-garde filmmaking—especially the claim by personal filmmakers that their films provide a challenge to Hollywood's hierarchical, collaborative production process. By using the hand-held procedure in an environment entirely foreign to the worlds generally depicted by either avant-garde or Hollywood filmmaking, Trinh demonstrated that both the mainstream and avant-garde traditions were equally parochial and (Western) culture-bound.

Naked Spaces is neither an ethnographic documentary nor a personal avant-garde film: it illuminates a space between these two traditions of critique and, at the same time, offers viewers a fascinating panorama of West African dwellings and life-styles (and, on the soundtrack, a variety of indigenous and non-indigenous ruminations on this kaleidoscope of cultures) that is not only a sensual pleasure, but an implicitly polemical demonstration that varieties of cultures in this sector of the world are at least as extensive and compelling as the varieties in any other geographic region, including those particular regions that have dominated the attention of Western filmmakers and moviegoers.

3

> When you walk from outside to the inside of most rural African houses, you come from a very bright sunlight to a very dark space where, for a moment you are totally blind. It takes some time to get adjusted to the darkness inside… To move inside oneself one has to be willing to go intermittently blind. Similarly, to move toward other people, one has to take a jump and move ahead blindly at certain moments of inquiry.[4]

With her third 16mm film, *Surname Viet Given Name Nam* (1989), Trinh appeared to return to her Vietnamese roots, but this movement into her personal ethnic heritage was simultaneously an expansion into the more diverse sense of contemporary geography and culture that she had developed through working and traveling in Europe, Africa, and North America. Indeed, *Surname Viet Given Name Nam* is a landmark contribution to two seemingly distinct but related tendencies that are, increasingly, the focus of serious discussion about world cinema: the developing fascination with new and historical contributions to film culture by ethnic communities marginalized by mainstream commercial moviemaking, and the increasing fascination with the "transnational," that is, with the crossing of ethnic, national, and linguistic boundaries as a fundamental structuring principle for motion pictures.

Trinh's awareness of the importance of her Vietnamese heritage is evident throughout her filmmaking, even in her African films. Her decision to narrate *Reassemblage* in her own Vietnamese-accented English, and to include herself as one of the three narrators in *Naked Spaces*, is evidence of this awareness and of her concern that we not forget that these depictions of African cultures are not presented from an exclusively Western—or African—point of view. At the same time, however, the fact that she speaks in a Vietnamese-accented English makes consistently clear that her sense of her own ethnicity is conditioned by her experiences as a transnational citizen of the world. In *Naked Spaces*, Trinh provides visual correlatives to this simultaneous sense of the ethnic and the transnational: those moments, for example, in rural Senegalese dwellings, seemingly quite far from urban centers where European and North American influences on indigenous African cultures are more obvious, when we see a blue plastic bucket or a yellow plastic tub. Indeed, these moments force us to consider that the ethnic purity that is often suggested by our concept of "indigenous" is as fully an illusion as Hollywood's assumption that certain forms of film entertainment are accessible to "everyone."

What we define as "indigenous" may be a complex interaction of particular, native cultural groups that, given our cultural and historical distance, we cannot perceive. And even if we were to imagine a cultural group that has had no contact whatsoever with any other cultural group throughout its entire history, this group could only be conceived in contradistinction to other, different cultural groups, and could only conceive itself by defining cultural distinctions within the group. In *Surname Viet*, the impossibility of the pure indigenous is less the issue, however, than the remarkable complexity of the transnational. Even Trinh's title suggests this complexity. Trinh's family (and family name) may be indigenous to the region of Southeast Asia we call Vietnam, but the French spelling of the "surname" Viet reminds us of the long-term French involvement in this part of the world and its inevitable effect on the Vietnamese sense of history and culture, an effect made even more complex and mysterious by the subsequent arrival of the American military who gave the region the nickname "Nam."

Of course, for Trinh the experience of her heritage is all the more complex because she left Vietnam, like so many other Vietnamese, and has been forced, and has forced herself, to be immersed in a wide variety of cultures, each of which has developed through its interactions with other cultures. It makes at least as much sense to define individuality as a function of the specific, myriad influences a particular person has experienced, as it does to try to account for an individual's distinctiveness as a function of her particular indigenous "roots." In a world where societies are increasingly made up of individuals defined more fully by their cultural "translations" from one region to another—either as a result of forced exile or freely chosen travel— it is crucial that we become attuned to the multiplicity of experience of any individual or cultural group. Filmmakers interested in using cinema to help us make contact with the real world can help us recognize the cultural simplicities trained into us by our conventional media experience.

Both *Surname Viet* and *Shoot for the Contents* (1991) provide this kind of cinematic retraining. The commercial film experience, and in large measure, the documentary experience as well, deals with cultural difference by romanticizing it, by allowing us to take various forms of sensual pleasure in the "exotic." In Trinh's two most recent films, moments that seem to fit these romantic preconceptions are developed only to be subsequently revealed as simplistic fabrications. In *Surname Viet*, our interest in the exotic romance of hearing women discuss the experience of living in postwar communist Vietnam allows us to believe what the film's various Vietnamese spokeswomen tell us. We may wonder that Trinh was able to return to Vietnam and get access to these women (several of whom offer telling critiques of life under communist rule), but their extremely accented English (so accented that Trinh superimposes textual translations of their comments over the imagery of the women speaking) tends to convince us of the reality of what we think we see. Since we virtually always understand everything everyone in a commercial film or television show says, we may assume that our difficulties in *Surname Viet* result from Trinh's inability to find women who speak better English, and that, therefore, we are seeing candidly filmed reality.

During the second half of the film, we discover that these spokeswomen are played by Vietnamese-American women (reading the reminiscences of other Vietnamese women, translated first into French, and later into English for use in this film), who themselves have been "translated" from Vietnam to the United States, and we have the opportunity to realize the superficiality of our original assumptions and the dangers of the pervasive media training that teaches us to expect easy translations of difficult cultural issues into simple resolutions. *Shoot for the Contents*, Trinh's most recent film, also focuses on translation, but in a different sense: not on translation from one language to another, or of people from one place to another, but rather on historical translation, from then to now—and what better geographic arena for such a topic than China?

Shoot for the Contents opens with an image that encapsulates the issues raised by the differences in the first and second parts of *Surname Viet Given Name Nam* and defines the focus of the new film. We see a man inside a rural dwelling singing a folk song. No sooner do we begin to see this moment from a position of romantic detachment, as a remnant of an irretrievable, exotic past, than an obviously artificial movie light illuminates the singer's face, revealing the artifice of the shot and the situation, which is then confirmed when he finishes a passage of the song, says "Second" to someone off-screen to our left, sings a second passage, with the help of a score that we can now see he is holding, and concludes with "O.K." What seems at first a "moment from the past" (we learn later he is singing an old folk song inside an ancient dwelling) is revealed to be very much a part of the present; and the illusion of the camera-as-invisible-window-on-the-world is shattered (just before the shot, during the title credit, we hear the sound of glass breaking and feet running) and transformed into the camera-as-instigator-of-a-modern-inter/intra-cultural-meeting-place.

Throughout *Shoot for the Contents*, China's complex history and the situation of this history within the political, social, and technological developments of the modern era intersect, as Trinh continues to explore the set of issues that inform *Reassemblage, Naked Spaces—Living Is Round*, and *Surname Viet Given Name Nam*, particularly the issues of gender, of cultural definition, and of the place of cinema in cultural studies. There is no telling where Trinh's filmmaking will take us next, but already she has taken us into a new genre of cinema that functions in the margins between the "accredited" melodramatic, documentary, and avant-garde film histories, to reveal that what may have once appeared to be a set of gaps between political, social, cultural, and technological "realities" are in fact a set of frontiers across which we watch each other and through which we can no longer help but try to find our way, at least if we mean to have an evolving sense of each other and of ourselves.

Trinh's films are available at Women Make Movies (wmm.com) and at Light Cone (lightcone.org). She has been widely published: *Woman, Native, Other* (Indiana University Press, 1989) and *When the Moon Waxes Red: Representation, Gender, and Cultural Politics* (New York: Routledge, 1991) were breakthroughs. I interviewed her for *A Critical Cinema 2* (University of California Press, 1992).

---

1 From *Reassemblage*. The scripts of Trinh's films up through *Surname Viet Given Name Nam* are available in her *Framer Framed* (New York and London: Routledge, 1992). The scripts of *Reassemblage* and *Naked Spaces—Living is Round* are also available in Scott MacDonald, *Screen Writings* (Berkeley: University of California Press, 1994).
2 Laura Mulvey and Peter Wollen (in their *Riddles of the Sphinx*, 1977) and Su Friedrich (in *The Ties That Bind*, 1984; *Damned If You Don't*, 1987; and *Sink or Swim*, 1990) exemplify this approach.
3 Trinh, in Scott MacDonald, *A Critical Cinema 2* (Berkeley: University of California Press, 1992), 375.
4 Trinh, in *A Critical Cinema 2*, 364.

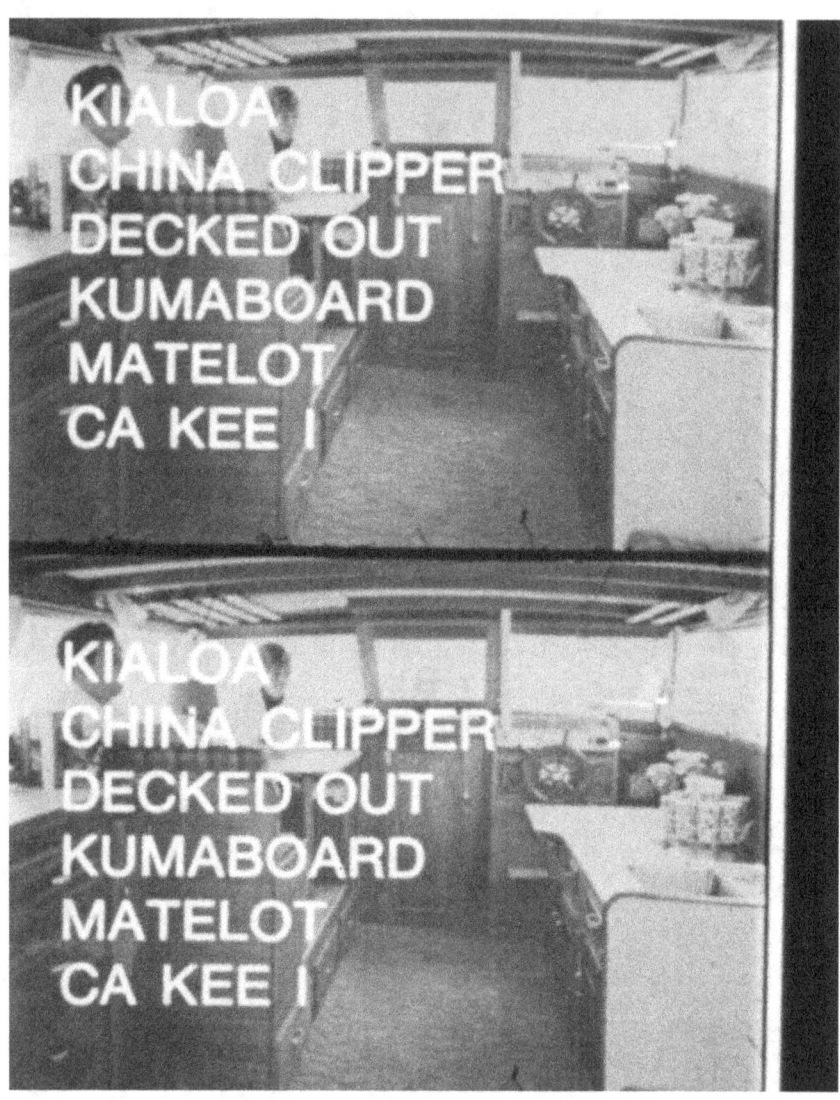
Boats and boat names from Robert Nelson's *Bleu Shut* (1970). Courtesy Robert Nelson.

2002

Fade In Fade Out: The Work of Filmmaker Robert Nelson

I recently checked to see if Canyon Cinema, which Robert Nelson had a hand in establishing, still distributes his films. It was a relief to see that they do—because there was a moment, not so long ago, when Nelson planned to destroy all his prints, thinking that when he died, what he had produced should die with him: "Carry it in, carry it out."

In August of 1981, I met Nelson as part of a weeks-long cross-country trip during which I showed single-shot films at Willie Varela's series at SWAMP (Southwest Arts Media Project) in El Paso, Texas, and at Terry Cannon's Pasadena Filmforum; and interviewed filmmakers: Morgan Fisher in Santa Monica; Bruce Conner, George Kuchar, and Robert Nelson in San Francisco. When I had written to Nelson to see if he'd be willing to do an interview, he wrote back, "J. J. [J. J. Murphy, who I'd interviewed in 1980] says you're a good guy. I trust J. J.—so let's do it." Nelson suggested we meet at the Cliff House, though I can't remember if we recorded the interview there.

Looking back, Nelson's choice of Cliff House—a historic building (over the years several buildings), perched above the cliffs just north of Ocean Beach in the Outer Richmond neighborhood of San Francisco—seems reflective of his Bay Area spirit, which was alive in his films. I had come to see Nelson (I doubt I'm alone) as the cine-spirit of the Bay area—in contradistinction to New York City's cine-spirit, which for me at that time was Hollis Frampton. Indeed, I came to see Nelson's *Bleu Shut* (1970) and the light-hearted game it creates for audiences as the inverse of, and geographic complement to, Hollis Frampton's *Zorns Lemma* (1970) and the more obviously intellectual game Frampton asks his audiences to play. I've often shown the two films together.

In 2002, Nelson wrote to say, "I won an award for being born in California and they want someone to write about me and my films. You were the one I thought of." The following essay is what I wrote.

* * *

> A good traveler leaves no tracks.
> Lao Tzu, *Tao Te Ching*

Not long ago, I received a letter from Robert Nelson, in response to my request to borrow prints of his *O Dem Watermelons* (1966) and *Bleu Shut* (1970) for a course I'm teaching at Bard College (Nelson withdrew his films from distributors some years ago). In the letter, Nelson explains,

> There is presently only one (1) print of *Watermelons*. It is A-wind struck from the original in about 1966. The color is perfect/pristine. The film has dozens of splices and is missing large chunks (about 15 feet from one section). All the other prints were B-wind (from internegs) that had become almost completely color*less*. I chopped them up and threw them away. That *one* print will not, cannot be loaned or rented or even shown. I'm saving it for a color referent and to have one print in case I ever become re-deranged and want to show something myself.

> *Bleu Shut* is almost the same story. I ground up several of the prints, almost all, and threw them in the garbage.

While the problem of film decay has been around as long as film itself, Nelson may be the first major figure in the history of modern American independent cinema whose work has entirely disappeared from public circulation. For those of us who know and love his work, this development is both sad and frustrating—*frustrating* because we now realize that our taking independent cinema for granted for so long is what has put us in this fix. Nelson himself is, as his letter suggests, ambivalent. His Taoist sensibility—he has been a serious student of Tao for years—seems to suggest to him that as *he* fades, what he's made might just as well fade with him.

Nelson's route to filmmaking was circuitous. He received a teaching degree from San Francisco State in 1954, taught high school students in San Francisco and in Europe for three years; then worked as a carpenter, all the while dabbling in painting and drawing. In 1956 he enrolled at what was then the California School of the Arts (it became the San Francisco Art Institute) and after two years transferred to Mills College where he earned an MFA in 1959. During the early 1960s he began making films, first with Gunvor Nelson, and beginning with *Plastic Haircut* (1963), on his own. During the next five years, working with shoestring budgets and high-spirited colleagues, Nelson made a series of films in and around San Francisco that implicitly challenged not only commercial cinema and television, but the somberness and pretension of much of the independent filmmaking of that era.

Nelson's first big success, and still his best-known film, was *O Dem Watermelons*, a collaboration with the San Francisco Mime Troupe. Ron Davis and Saul Landau asked Nelson to supply a short intermission piece for the Mime Troupe's new performance piece, *A Minstrel Show (Civil Rights from the Cracker Barrel)*, which used the minstrel show format to create a shocking confrontation of racist stereotypes. Choosing the watermelon as a symbol of American racism, Nelson and several members of the Mime Troupe generated a loose series of sketches in which they did everything imaginable to watermelons: melons were thrown off roofs, used erotically by a naked woman, crushed by construction machinery, disemboweled—all to the accompaniment of a soundtrack by Steve Reich that itself was a send-up of the often-racist nostalgia of Stephen Foster songs.

O Dem Watermelons was premiered as part of *A Minstrel Show*, but quickly became a nationwide underground hit, winning a prize at the Ann Arbor Film Festival, and laughter from audiences across the country. Nelson's tactic was not to "make some kind of diatribe on the subject of race," but to reduce the idea of racist stereotypes to absurdity, to make fun of the *stupidity* of racism.* *O Dem Watermelons* remains a rarity in American cultural history: a good-humored, thoroughly enjoyable film about our most serious and persistent social issue.

Making *O Dem Watermelons* confirmed an approach to filmmaking that would be typical of Nelson for much of the rest of his career. The *process* of filmmaking

---

* All Nelson quotations are from my interview with Nelson in *A Critical Cinema* (Berkeley: University of California Press, 1988).

has always been crucial for him: making a film requires that he can't know exactly what he's doing ("One of the things that has always been in my mind has been *not* making a film that expresses a meaning that I could already express, but instead to let the thing itself find out what it is") *and* that the experience of discovering the film "be alive in some way through all the processes." For Nelson the light-hearted, collaborative pleasure in *making* films has the best chance of creating films that are themselves light-hearted and pleasurable, regardless of the seriousness of the issues they deal with.

The success of O *Dem Watermelons* seems to have energized Nelson. During the two years following its release, he finished thirteen films (all Nelson's films have been made in 16mm), among them several that remain landmarks of independent cinema, including *The Awful Backlash* (1967) and *The Great Blondino* (1967). *The Awful Backlash* is a remarkable single-shot film. For fourteen minutes we watch, in close-up, as William Allan's hands untangle an impossibly tangled fishing reel. As the "backlash" in the fishing line is slowly removed, the untangled line is wound onto the reel. When the entire backlash is gone and the line wound on the reel, the film—our reel—ends. *The Awful Backlash* models a meditative sensibility; indeed, the camera is positioned so that our view is first-person, as if we are looking down at *our* hands untangling the line. Viewers can either be frustrated with Nelson's persistence in focusing on Allan's patience and dexterity, or we can relax and be grateful for this moment of cine-serenity, and consider the impact and effect of the films and non-film experiences we usually find ourselves entangled in.

The Great Blondino was the first, and the most elaborate, of several films Nelson co-made with the painter, William T. Wiley, and it remains a quintessential 1960s film. The central character (played by Chuck Wiley) moves through a colorful, surreal California cityscape, pushing a wheelbarrow. As "Blondino" (the name is a reference to Blondin, the famous nineteenth-century daredevil performer who crossed Niagara Falls on a tightrope) moves through the world, seemingly oblivious to the circumstances around him, Nelson and Wiley experiment with inventive and often amusing visual compositions and editing strategies: "we shot it in six or eight sessions. We'd work on weekends, though as usual, it wasn't really work. We had a good time. Lew Welch, Bill and Chuck Wiley, and I would go all over town. Off camera we were usually hysterical. It was wide open."

Those knowledgeable about the Bay Area film scene in the 1960s and '70s know that Nelson's interest in working with others went well beyond his filmmaking. He established and chaired the film department at the San Francisco Art Institute, and he taught filmmaking, first at the Art Institute from 1965 until 1969; then at the California Institute of the Arts (1971-73); and finally, as Professor of Film, at the University of Wisconsin-Milwaukee (from 1978-94). Filmmaker Peter Hutton, one of Nelson's students at the Art Institute remembers, "Bob was a great guy, an artist using film as a way of working with other artists; he made us feel comfortable, and his exuberance about filmmaking was inspiring—he was the perfect person to learn filmmaking with." Inside and outside the classroom, Nelson has always been a force for aesthetic freedom. When Anne Severson was first talking about "making a film about vaginas"—what became her ground-breaking feminist film, *Near the Big Chakra* (1972)—"men filmmaker friends listened to me with distaste. Bob Nelson was the first to support me. He became interested and, in a burst of enthusiasm, produced the title."*

Nelson was also deeply involved in the early evolution of Canyon Cinema, which began as a micro-cinema and developed into the San Francisco Cinematheque, one of the nation's leading exhibitors of alternative cinema, and into Canyon Cinema distribution, for decades the most dependable distributor of alternative cinema in the United States. Nelson was a founding member of the Canyon Cinema Corporation and served on the Board of Canyon for years. It was Nelson who steered Edith Kramer to Canyon (she had been a Nelson student at the Art Institute) where she became Canyon Cinema's director. Nelson was also a frequent contributor to Canyon's publication, *The Canyon Cinema News*, during the 1970s when it was one of the most influential film magazines in the country. Indeed, Nelson was more than a contributor; he was one of the primary spirits of the magazine.

After 1970 Nelson's output as filmmaker slowed, but he continued to make memorable movies—each of them quite different from the next: "As an independent filmmaker and artist, I *can* be very different. That's the freedom one has being outside of the commercial machinery. What I want is relative to the conditions I find myself in. I'm not interested in repeating myself." The most remarkable of Nelson's 1970s films are *Bleu Shut* and *Suite California, Stops and Passes* (Part I, 1976; Part II, 1977).

Bleu Shut is what P. Adams Sitney has called a "participatory film."** Basically, Nelson creates a game that most viewers cannot resist playing. Over the period of half an hour (a tiny clock in the image helps us keep track of the time), we see a series of pictures of yachts and, superimposed, five names. On the soundtrack Nelson and Wiley debate which of the five names is the correct one for each boat, and at the end of a minute a buzzer sounds and the "correct" boat name is revealed, after which the "contestants" discuss the outcome for a few moments; during the remainder of each second minute, we see bits of footage—some shot by Nelson, some recycled from other sources—until the next boat image and set of names appears.

"Bleu shut" is a variation on "bullshit," and so it is no surprise to learn that Nelson first invented a set of boat names; then recorded the conversations with Wiley, using random objects—ashtrays, glasses, whatever; *then* found magazine images of boats and matched them with the conversations. But even when we know the game is an illusion, the experience of *Bleu Shut* is entirely a pleasure: the "game" is fun; the Nelson/Wiley debates, infectiously funny; and Nelson's choice of imagery, other than the boats, quirky and amusing. It is easy to read *Bleu Shut* as a West Coast version of Hollis Frampton's *Zorns Lemma*, made the same year. Both films use visual/temporal grids to create films about epistemology, but while *Zorns Lemma* offers a traditional trajectory

---

* Anne Severson, in *A Critical Cinema 2* (University of California Press, 1992), 326.
** P. Adams Sitney discusses "participatory film" and Nelson's films in *Visionary Film* (New York: Oxford University Press, 1974), 354-60.

from darkness to enlightenment, *Bleu Shut* reveals, and allows us to enjoy, our gullibility within the pervasive absurdity of modern life.

While the structural grid of *Bleu Shut* is a kind of net in which a variety of images and sounds are snagged, the idea of California is the guiding principle for Nelson's longest film, the two-part *Suite California, Stops and Passes*. Informally organized, Nelson's homage to his native state provides a range of experiences. Part I focuses on Southern California; it includes a faux "foreign film," a Mexican border drama, in Spanish with English subtitles; a tour of Death Valley and other remote areas; a continuous take of a long line of Japanese tourists in front of the old Grauman's Chinese Restaurant; a visit to the Will Rogers Estate; the Edison Studio film, *Picking Oranges* (1898)... Part II focuses on Northern California and is the most autobiographical of Nelson's films. It includes home-movie footage of a Christmas pageant and Christmas Eve dinner; a portrait of Golden Gate Bridge (including Nelson's father talking about his role in building the bridge); imagery of Oona Nelson (daughter of Robert and Gunvor Nelson); and evocative home-movie footage of hunting excursions into the Sierra Nevada Mountains, made during various eras—all punctuated with bits of archival material (1903 imagery of Cliff House and Seal Rocks, and 1897 imagery of the Sutro Baths) and with panoramic views of the Bay Area.

Altogether, *Suite California* is a distinctive and memorable evocation of the Golden State—one of the most interesting evocations of place to come out of American independent film, and the most noteworthy depiction of California until James Benning's recent California Trilogy: *El Valley Centro* (1990), *Los* (2000), and *SOGOBI* (2001). Indeed, the two projects would work beautifully together as a diptych. *Suite California*, or at least my memories of it (I've not seen the film in years) has become increasingly poignant, now that there are no longer prints in circulation: like the California it records and evokes, the film is fading away, sadly, even from memory.

Nelson's most recent film, *Hauling Toto Big*, which won First Prize at the Ann Arbor Film Festival in 1998, is one of the strangest films I've seen in recent years. Many of the elements characteristic of Nelson's earlier films are evident—inventive use of visual text; a movement across diverse terrains (portions of the film were shot near Ithaca, New York, in Wisconsin, and in Southern California); surprising and sometimes amusing compositions; a diverse mixture of sources, including documentary footage of a man and a pet bull named Baloney and of men and women hawking a carnival girlie show, and a whacky enacted melodrama involving a character named Toto Big—but the mood is complex. Nelson's choice of black and white seems to locate the action in a different time, and yet there's an engaging immediacy to the film. Nominally the film is structured into four sections, each identified with a hexagram from the *I Ching* (Nelson has been exploring the *I Ching* for decades), during which we follow the story of Toto Big, but the nature of our experience is continually changing. *Hauling Toto Big* seems to have the logic of dreams; it creates something like an altered state. I'm still struggling with it, finding my way.

Several years ago, in response, I think, to one of my periodic requests to use a film no longer in distribution, Nelson sent me a print of *The Awful Backlash*, along with a note that the film had been revised. I strung it onto my 16mm projector and discovered that while William Allan's feat of untangling the fishing line was intact, the original soundtrack had been entirely reworked. The original track had been a man (presumably the man whose hands we see), talking quietly to himself, interrupted by periods of silence. As Nelson cut back and forth from silence to sound, the fabrication of the track was obvious—though unintended ("A lot of the elements in those early films are there because I didn't know any other way to do things"). The new track on the print Nelson had sent me was the noise created by Nelson's literally scratching out the original soundtrack—a premonition of what is in fact happening to Nelson's career.

The film experience is, by its very nature, evanescent; and it is powerful and poignant in some measure because this evanescence (of any particular film experience, of the film material) models the fragility of life itself. Whatever the confrontations and pleasures Nelson's films provided during the years when they were made, premiered, and widely circulated, Nelson's career has become a new kind of challenge. How can we honor *Nelson's* need to fade with dignity, even to be free of the work that has given us so much pleasure and awareness—a need that, after all, is merely a more mature version of the high-spirited unpretentiousness that made (*makes!*) his films so remarkable—while also honoring *our* need to keep these films and this remarkable career alive so that we, and those who follow us, can continue to enjoy, explore, and learn from them? One can only hope that honoring Nelson with the Phelan Award will contribute to a re-emergence of Nelson's films.

"Fade in Fade out" was published in *Release Print* (the magazine of the Film Arts Foundation) 25, no. 10 (November-December 2002), 30-32, as the issue's cover story.

Nelson's films are available as 16mm prints at Canyon Cinema. *The Off-Handed Jape* (1967) by Nelson and William T. Wiley is available on the "American Treasures IV: Avant-Garde Film, 1947-1986" DVD set.

The audience explores the 16mm projector beam during
Anthony McCall's *Line Describing a Cone* (1973).
Courtesy Anthony McCall.

2002

Professional Myopia: How Academe Is Failing Cinema

When I was informed, early in the fall of 2023, by Timothy Hicks, my (wonderful and always helpful) tech guy at Hamilton College, that after several failed attempts to get our last theatrical Eiki 16mm projector into working order (we'd already gone from a two-projector set-up to a one-projector set-up) that not one of the once-many classroom Eikis we had relied on for decades was working, I was shocked. I shouldn't have been, of course. And there was the further irony: those of us still showing 16mm in classes and at public events had been so worried about the safety of the prints we rented that we'd taken the 16mm hardware for granted. What good are good prints if you don't have the equipment to show them!

Anthony McCall's *Line Describing a Cone* (1973) has been a fixture in my film courses for decades. The crack-down on smoking inside college buildings chased my screenings of the film outdoors a decade or so ago, and I adjusted. But will my classes no longer have the experience of that film? And Peter Hutton's exquisite films—gone from my classes? And Benning's *13 Lakes* (2004)?

I'm working on it.

* * *

In the fall of 1982, I was invited to the Cinema Histories/Cinema Practices II Conference hosted by the University of Wisconsin-Milwaukee, one of a number of attempts in those years by the new generation of film studies scholars and teachers to come to grips with two remarkable cultural projects that had seemed to burst upon the American academic scene during the 1960s and 1970s: a considerable body of new, alternative film practice (with a variety of monikers: the New American Cinema, Visionary Film, Structural Film, Expanded Cinema, the New Talkies, Feminist Cinema) and a challenging set of theoretical approaches arriving from Europe with a range of cinematic applications.

My paper offered one simple argument: that by discovering and exploring so many new ways of *writing about* film, we might soon find ourselves in the same cul-de-sac as other, more traditional academic disciplines: there would be so much writing about cinema that scholars/teachers with normal academic responsibilities and personal lives would need to choose between keeping up with scholarly commentary about film and keeping up with film history itself. Or, to be more precise, we would need to choose between producing a literature of theoretical conjectures and theoretically informed analysis of films/Film, and using the screening space as a creative environment where various forms of film and film experience could critique and respond to commercial cinema and the audience it has produced and served—or to put it still another way, between scholarly writing and film activism.

Two decades later, I look back on my presentation with some embarrassment (it was more defiant than coherent), but I am surprised to realize that my concerns about what film scholarship might become were well founded, so well founded that with the turn of the new millennium we have arrived at a crossroads. If film studies continues on the path it has established during the past twenty years, we may soon see the disappearance of the very range of film practice that in 1982 seemed so exciting and invigorating to the film scholars who gathered in Milwaukee (invited guests included scholars/theorists *and* eight filmmakers: Diana Barrie, Manuel DeLanda, Joanna Kiernan, Robert Nelson, Yvonne Rainer, Jackie Raynal, Michael Snow, and Peter Wollen).

What I see as an increasingly troubling gap between film studies and film history is a function of the original challenge of finding a secure niche in academe for the serious study of cinema. In 1964, only six years before I would teach my first film course, I stood with a group of other undergraduate students and a professor at DePauw University, and laughed with the other students when the professor suggested that a college course in film might be interesting. Even at the end of the '60s, film study was a new idea for most American academics. With the nationwide demand during the early 1970s for film studies courses at the college level, colleges and universities were faced with the task of finding competent faculty who were expected to demonstrate their expertise in the ways faculty in other disciplines were required to demonstrate theirs; that is, by writing analyses of films and providing well-researched conjectures about film history and its place within modern culture. And with the help of the new theoretical paradigms arriving from Europe and elsewhere, those first generations of film academics were finding new, more sophisticated ways of talking and writing about film, and in some instances—in the deployment of Lacanian psychoanalysis by feminists, for example—were having insights about the relationships between cultural artifacts and human experience that were impacting older, more established disciplines.

Simultaneous with the flowering of more sophisticated writing about film in the 1980s and 1990s, however, was a decreased interest on the part of faculty in maintaining the regular public exhibition of a substantial spectrum of cinema in and around colleges and universities. I say "maintain" because for a period at the end of the 1960s and into the 1970s, nearly every urban area and most colleges and universities had regular access not only to Hollywood first-run releases, but to recent "foreign film," to revivals of classics from here and abroad, as well as some access to new forms of documentary and to a variety of forms of experimental and avant-garde work. Indeed, it became a prestige issue in some institutions to build theaters in which the very best screening conditions prevailed, and some filmmakers had the presumption not only to demand that their films be shown well, but to interrupt screenings when a projection problem was evident and demand that the problem be fixed before beginning the screening again. That is, for a time—at least in some of those academic environments where film was finding a place—film was taken seriously both as a series of "texts" worth writing about *and* as a set of in-theater experiences with the potential for perceptual/psychological/intellectual/spiritual engagement and transformation.

The past twenty years have seen a radical change in the commitment of academe, and film studies academics, toward exhibition. How *big* a change is suggested by two recent incidents:

—I am a visiting professor in a film department in a communications school at a major university, teaching a course on the depiction of American place in American cinema. When I am taken on my first tour of the facilities, I realize that there isn't a really good—even what I consider a passable—screening room for 16mm available at the school; most all screenings of film seem to be projected video and DVD in classroom environments. And further, no one seems embarrassed about this situation, or even to notice it.

One morning a few weeks later, I'm sitting in my office with a stack of 16mm film cans on my desk. A colleague pops her head in and, seeing the cans, exclaims excitedly, "Oh, you're actually showing *films*. Wow! Great!"

—I have just received word from a professor at a small college of the acceptance of my proposal to show a selection of independent films at the college in conjunction with a conference focusing on the Thoreauvian aspect of modern writing: my plan is to show films that use the screening room as a way of retraining perception and modeling a more thorough awareness of our environment. When I call the professor to ask about screening facilities, he thinks there might be a problem: he isn't sure if his campus has 16mm projection ("We do everything on video").

One day I get an e-mail with the good news that he and his audiovisual guy have found a projector, and that it works: "We weren't sure it would work, because Bill says it hasn't been used in ten years!"

I know these are conventional-enough stories, part of the now-considerable lore about the arrival of new video and digital technologies at the academic level. We've all watched new technologies arrive and revise our ways of doing things. Some last longer than others, but more and more we assume that, in a relatively short time, whatever technologies we use now will, in a few years, seem outdated, even embarrassing. On this level, the fact that 16mm may soon disappear is no more "tragic" than the replacement of any technology by another.

But the very obviousness of this ongoing technological evolution and its apparent inevitability hides another, troubling reality—one crucial for those of us who think of ourselves as film historians. For several generations 16mm production, distribution, and exhibition was the gauge of home-moviemaking and other more and less serious forms of amateur filmmaking; it was also the gauge used by educational institutions for the presentation of nearly all forms of nonfiction film, including political propaganda, medical films, cinema-verite documentary... And, most important for this discussion, it was the gauge of necessity/choice for "avant-garde" film artists who used it for a broad range of explorations of perception, psychology, intellect, and spirit. The avant-garde filmmakers in particular made/make films in 16mm, with first-rate, 16mm theatrical presentation specifically in mind.

(It is always a struggle to define "avant-garde" film, both because its history is so extensive and so various, and because the term "avant-garde" itself is so problematic: it *is* true that "avant-garde" cinema has, in many instances, provided a formal and ideological vanguard exploited later by commercial film and television, but avant-garde filmmakers have been at least equally likely to offer responses to new developments in popular entertainment. For purposes of this discussion, "avant-garde film" can be understood as that set of film practices produced by individuals or small groups working in forms other than the conventional narrative genres marketed by national film industries. While most avant-garde film has been produced in 16mm, there is also a substantial avant-garde history of 8mm and Super-8mm filmmaking, and notable 35mm productions as well.)

Were the arrival of the new moving-image technologies a guarantee that even the core film history produced in 16mm could and would be passed on to the next generation, we could celebrate each nuance of technological change. But in this case at least, the de facto decision of American academics to allow 16mm to be "replaced" by VHS/DVD is, in effect, the acceptance of a substantial narrowing of film history. When I'm told that a campus' 16mm projector has not been in operation for ten years, I know that the attention given to film in that institution does *not* include the remarkable history of avant-garde film, from its first flowering in Europe and America in the 1920s through the wildly productive half century that gave us Maya Deren, Sidney Peterson, Kenneth Anger, James Broughton, Stan Brakhage, Jordan Belson, the Whitney Brothers, Bruce Connor, Andy Warhol, Jonas Mekas, Jack Smith, Robert Breer, Ken Jacobs, George and Mike Kuchar, Peter Kubelka, Tony Conrad, Yoko Ono, Michael Snow, Joyce Wieland, Carolee Schneemann, Paul Sharits, Hollis Frampton, Larry Gottheim, Taka Iimura, Warren Sonbert, Yvonne Rainer, Laura Mulvey & Peter Wollen, Gunvor Nelson, Robert Nelson, Peter Hutton, Ernie Gehr, Gregory Markopoulos, Abigail Child, Robert Beavers, Trinh T. Minh-ha, Su Friedrich, Peggy Ahwesh, Martin Arnold, Phil Solomon, Leighton Pierce, and dozens of others.

Few who are even vaguely familiar with this world of cinema would be likely to argue that losing it would be a minor film-historical setback. Indeed, for teachers and scholars committed to this cinematic arena, the accomplishments of filmmakers working in the field, and the incomparable pedagogical value of the films they've produced, make avant-garde cinema one of the supreme achievements in all of film history. Its disappearance would be comparable to the loss of modern poetry from literary history, or fresco painting from art history. To ignore the current film-historical crisis on the assumption that the better 16mm films will be preserved by the newer technologies is naive, both about the financial resources available for such transfer and about the current academic commitment to this aspect of our cinematic heritage.

If, in fact, the abandonment of 16mm does result in the erasure of avant-garde cinema, or a considerable portion of it, from living film history, this would be the first major film-historical loss to occur since film studies became an academic discipline. Earlier losses of substantial dimensions of our cinematic heritage were caused by the instability of nitrate stock, by the refusal of many who had control of films to see that cinema might be more than a consumer good, by the devastations of war. But the abandonment of 16mm and the loss of the film experiences it makes possible would be a function of nothing more than, to be blunt, the laziness and irresponsibility of American academe, an unusual, but pervasive form of professional myopia that is the result of the widespread assumption that academic expertise is best demonstrated in scholarly publication.

It is one thing to regard writing about cinema as a crucial demonstration of intellectual expertise in the field of film studies; it is quite another to assume that writing is the *only* important such demonstration and that writers are responsible only to the written discourse of which they are a part (of course, even if writing *were* the only possible demonstration of scholarship and expertise, the loss of that film history available in 16mm would qualify the completeness and usefulness of this writing). Indeed, the myopic focus on written discourse ignores the double function of such writing and, by doing so, evades what seems to me a fundamental ethical issue. Scholarly writing about film *within academic discourse* should provide readers with a more thorough understanding of how cinema functions in the world. The function of scholarly writing *within the institution of academe*, however, is to serve as a way of measuring who receives tenure and promotion within particular colleges and universities and who earns mobility within the system of higher education. In the present context, scholarly writing has become largely a means of economic betterment and social climbing. Academics joke about how little financial remuneration scholarly activity brings, but in fact such labors do have economic value—indeed, written scholarship is *the* determiner of economic status within academe, at least for faculty.

I have no sweeping objection to this system: those who enrich our understanding of our chosen fields should be rewarded. My argument has more to do with the nature of film scholarship. As is true within any academic discourse about an art form, writers are, virtually by definition, dependent on those who produce the works written about. Without filmmakers, there are no film scholars. Further, since filmmaking has been one of the more expensive artistic endeavors, this intellectual dependency has also meant that the filmmakers make the risky financial investments that provide academic writers with the potential for economically improving *their* situations. Or, again to put it crudely, academic discourse exploits the labor and financial risk-taking of filmmakers, and at least in the United States, this exploitation is generally accomplished with no apparent sense of responsibility to filmmakers.

Of course, since a good many films exploited by written academic discourse are mainstream Hollywood productions, or the productions of major studios in other sectors of the world, the exploitation I'm describing is hardly a cause for concern among academics. In fact, many of us see ourselves engaged in forms of intellectual protection against the cultural power of the film industry. Any exploitation *we* do is minor, compared to the industrial exploitation of the mass audience and the toll on contemporary culture of its frequent sexism, racism, and classism. We feel free, even righteous, about exploiting in a small way the industrial exploiters of millions; we are Robin Hoods deconstructing the rich in the name of the masses. An often-ignored paradox here is that in order to protect modern culture *from* the industry, we focus our attention *on* the industry and support what we are determined to expose, both in the literal sense (colleges and universities rent feature films and buy videos or DVDs of major releases so they can be studied) and in the sense that ongoing academic attention in effect confirms the claim by the industry that it is the producer of virtually all films of any cultural import.

During the early years of film studies, this tendency to focus on mainstream cinema was, if not inevitable, at least understandable. There was an institutional and economic necessity to produce written discourse, and mainstream film was comparatively accessible: documentary, and especially amateur and avant-garde film, did not circulate through the culture—at least through academic culture—as consistently as popular mass-market cinema (of course, many of us did feel both a powerful psychic connection with the movies and a hunger to critique them for their obvious limitations). The problem is that once film studies had become established, this tendency to avoid less easily accessible forms of film had become habit. Some older scholars continue to pretend that avant-garde film is simply a lesser art, not truly worthy of sustained attention—at least compared to sophisticated feature narrative cinema. Many younger scholars are only marginally aware that there is a substantial history of avant-garde film. But nearly all scholars ignore alternative cinema, many of them, it would seem, in the hope, perhaps, that, in time, it will disappear, along with its challenges to mainstream movie history and academic film study.

In the other arts, the fact that accomplished work is obscure or difficult is usually seen as a challenge. In cinema studies, however, this has been true in only the most limited sense. The reasons are, no doubt, complex, but my suspicion is that it has to do with the tendency of much modern academe to ignore everything except intellectualization, the discourse of ideas. The arrival of video technology and DVD in academe confirmed an already obvious tendency to see films as "texts," of importance only insofar as they could be theorized and analyzed (and used as part of an effort to ascend the professional ladder). Increasingly, a commitment to alternative cinema by those few who do recognize its accomplishments and potential uses has meant a more direct engagement with films not simply as texts, but as physical objects that require more service than videotapes/DVDs. A 16mm print of a Brakhage film or a Snow film or a Friedrich film must be rented from a specialty distributor and must be shown on a clean 16mm projector that won't damage the print—that is, the film must be *cared for* and part of this care involves regular attention to the equipment necessary for its effective presentation. These forms of service to cinema are a form of unpaid, hands-on labor—a direct engagement with the machinery that produces cinematic experience.

Of course, it is precisely the carelessness of so much consumer culture that makes the achievements of avant-garde cinema so exciting, so worthy of our engagement. Here are hundreds of films that reveal a sense of the sacred within a medium addicted to the profane, that model healthy defiance in a world addicted to easy compromise, that provide illuminating interruptions in the smooth continuities and psychic repressions of industrial cinema, that foreground the perceptual and ideological limitations of conventional media experiences. Avant-garde film offers the best possibility of energizing the theater space, so that showing film and seeing it becomes a theoretical *experience*, revealing the conventional limits and unconventional possibilities of cinema. Here is the most underutilized major pedagogical resource available to film studies professionals, as well as to those in other disciplines—American Studies, for example, Environmental Studies, and Art History—who could and, I believe, would use these films if only their colleagues in film studies would take the time to show them what's available.

Surely it behooves educators to model an ethical relationship with the cinema we exploit for our pleasure, our enlightenment, and our economic mobility. There *is*, of course, an ethical dimension to scholarly writing that confronts socially irresponsible aspects of commercial culture. But we should also use the academic purchase we've written so hard for to demand academic respect and resources for those cinematic contributions that have little chance of surviving to the next generation without our intervention: that is, for the full range of cinema and film-cultural achievement *and* for those valiant, few distribution organizations—Canyon Cinema in San Francisco, the Canadian Film-makers' Distribution Centre in Toronto, the New York Film-Makers' Cooperative, the Museum of Modern Art Circulating Film Collection, and Women Make Movies in New York, Light Cone in Paris—that refuse to give up on avant-garde cinema.

Time may be running out for 16mm film and avant-garde history, but this writer continues to hope for a last-minute rescue that might take several particular forms. First, we must *not* abandon 16mm. While we can and should welcome new technologies that allow for more effective presentation and exploration of moving-image media, we need not, *must* not, allow an effective, proven technology, necessary for the correct presentation of a crucial dimension of alternative cinema, to disappear. Nearly all colleges and universities still have decent 16mm projectors, though in many cases audio-visual departments feel under pressure or exert pressure to switch campuses entirely to VHS/DVD, in order to avoid replacing older projectors and the costs of film rentals. We must exert a counter pressure in the name of maintaining the broadest and deepest representation of film-cultural history within academe.

Second, many larger universities have what at one time were rental collections of 16mm prints. Often these collections are now seen as white elephants, taking up space and resources, in a world gone over to video/DVD and the internet. And while it is true that many, even most of the films in these collections are outdated educational documentaries, the collections often contain prints of alternative films that (ironically *because* of the failure of Film Studies to commit to avant-garde cinema) are sometimes in better shape than current rental prints of these same films. Surely, there's a film studies professional in every major institution who could retrieve these valuable prints before these 16mm collections are destroyed and make them available to those distribution organizations that specialize in avant-garde film.

Of course, a true rescue of avant-garde cinema—and thus of cinema itself—also requires a new commitment to academic exhibition. Again, in large measure because professional advancement doesn't require it, often doesn't even recognize it, programming beyond the classroom has been left to students who—unknowingly following in the footsteps of film studies professionals!—focus, almost entirely, on recent commercial releases. Film studies professionals have the same obligation as professionals in other areas of the arts to provide opportunities for campus and local communities to access work generally outside their current awareness. Obviously, maintaining a serious exhibition schedule for a range of those forms of film generally unavailable (including 16mm and Super-8mm avant-garde film), along with video art and new digital experiments, requires not only research and creativity, but institutional resources, both money and time. Programmers need to be reasonably abreast of developments in media production; they need to create alliances across academic disciplines in order to develop audiences and financial resources for rentals and visiting artist fees; and they need to work with campus and local communications to alert the considerable potential public for alternative cinema. But surely, any serious program in Film Studies or Communications ought to have a first-rate exhibition component that delivers major new and revived film (and video and digital work, whatever) to the academic community and to the public, and, by doing so, models the activity of creative exhibition.

Obviously, such labors in support of the full spectrum of cinema history should be rewarded, not just financially, but in recognition that the field of film studies cannot simply restrict itself to written discourse that is confined, for reasons of convenience and self-aggrandizement, to the most easily accessible film history. We need to demonstrate to our students and colleagues that, while the popular cinema remains culturally influential and needs to be critiqued (and while it produces some remarkable films), an academically respectable, living film history must include the most inventive, accomplished work of all kinds. It is time for film studies scholars and teachers to make a new commitment to serving the field we represent, not only because an immense and crucial facet of film history is now in a most precarious position, but because this academically under-represented history is very much alive and continues to produce remarkable and remarkably useful work.

This essay was originally published in *Quarterly Review of Film Studies* 19, no. 3 (July-September 2002), 201-7.

The World Trade Center in 1979, originally filmed for John Knecht's *Continuing the Adventures of Adrian Block* (1980). In the wake of 9/11, the imagery became the focus of Knecht's *The Beacons of Aerolith* (2013). Courtesy of John Knecht.

2002

9/11, Critique, and Avant-Garde Film

I'm not sure how I feel about this essay, now, two decades later—it feels preachy in a way that makes me uncomfortable. But I don't want to suppress it since it does speak to the power of a particular moment and a particularly terrifying event, to reframe one's private thinking about, in this case, "independent filmmaking." The panel referenced in the following essay was part of a series of film/video events: screenings and a conference hosted by Queen's University in Kingston, Ontario, with panels and workshops that took place between October 9 and 25, 2001. The final panel of the conference was titled "Experimentation and Social Change"; presenters were Dorit Naaman (chair), Richard Fung, Lisa Steele, Judy Radul, and me.

* * *

As I sat at the panelists' table during the final session of the Tulips Conference, trying to listen to the panelist whose presentation immediately preceded mine, I was seized—again, as I had been all week—by misgivings about the relevance of the argument I was about to make, only a few weeks after the catastrophic attack on the World Trade Center and its world-shaking aftermath. Basically, my argument in "Professional Myopia: How Academe Is Failing Cinema" is that the widespread tendency throughout North American academe to give up on 16mm projection and switch to video and digital presentations of film is destructive of film history, since it endangers most forms of alternative cinema. Further, I believe that this de facto decision results from the laziness of academics whose definition of "professional" is the use of critical and theoretical writing, ostensibly in the name of cinema, as a means of accruing power and status within the academic social system. But on that October 21st my paper seemed so frivolous that I considered not giving it at all and opening a discussion of how avant-garde media could fit within what seemed a frightening new world.

Of course, even before the Tulips Conference, I had realized—though I was embarrassed to admit it, even to myself—that watching the Twin Towers collapse had changed my own thinking, even about the politics of alternative cinema. The attack had toppled two of what had seemed, for forty years, my most fundamental assumptions: that while I was no communist revolutionary, I was anti-capitalist; and that my job as a teacher and scholar was to critique the problematic dimensions of American military and economic power as this power was encoded within the commercial media. I realized that my thinking had already changed, just a few days after the attack, when I received an email sent by, perhaps originated by, a group of New York City artists. It said, "Islam is not the enemy/War is not the answer/Break the cycle/Pass it on."

Instead of speaking for me, as it might have before 9/11, the message annoyed me, and while I didn't have the words to respond at that point, by the time a friend sent me the same message a few weeks later, I was able to send a curt reply: "No, Islam is not the enemy, but certain forms of radical, fundamentalist Islam do seem to be; and at the moment, I have no faith that our peacefulness will do anything but invite further attacks." Much on my mind during those weeks was the image of the group of peaceful souls on the Odessa Steps in *Potemkin* whose appeal to the czar's soldiers is quickly met with further violence."

In the wake of the attack on the Trade Center, the thing that seemed most obvious to me was that the perpetrators, whoever exactly they were, had planned to kill as many people as possible. As the second tower collapsed, I had said to my partner, "There go twenty thousand people." It was Guernica on a massive scale. In the end, the number was, thankfully, nothing like twenty thousand, but the point had been made: those who had planned and carried out the attack were interested in mass destruction, and had they been able to kill a million people, or to level New York City altogether, they would certainly have done so.

As a result, during the following weeks I found myself frustrated at the nature of many of the responses of alternative media people to 9/11 and the subsequent war in Afghanistan. What condemnations of the Trade Center attack I did hear or read seemed, at best, pro forma—something said only to demonstrate the speakers' humanity, so that they could make the real point, which took a variety of forms. The crudest versions went something like this: "Those capitalist pigs [who worked in the Trade Center] finally got what they deserved: payback for all the shit they've been responsible for"; "The towers shouldn't have been built in the first place; they were just two giant capitalist phalluses." More common were statements that, while the terrorist attacks were horrific, we (capitalist Americans) certainly had it coming; an attack on America was long overdue. Indeed, we deserved to be attacked, and so much so that any military response from us was entirely unjustified—still further evidence of the belligerent capitalist imperialism that had just come home to roost.

I was surprised by my lack of patience with a set of attitudes that, for much of my life, had seemed my own. But the World Trade Center attack had demonstrated the obvious: that there are people in the world, other than Americans, other than capitalists, who are willing to effect horrific atrocities, including the unapologetic mass destruction of men, women, and children, seemingly without misgivings, in the name of God. When much of the artistic community rushed to blame the United States as at least the indirect cause of the attack, this community revealed its own fundamental attachment to a sterile nationalism, even a kind of negative imperialism: "No one else in the world is responsible for anything," this community seemed to say, "Only our nation can be responsible for a horror of this magnitude, and only the suffering we cause and our embarrassment and self-hatred are real."

In mid-October I went to New York to attend the New York Film Festival avant-garde programs organized by Mark McElhatten and Gavin Smith, and, like so many others, made a pilgrimage to Ground Zero. After circling the site of the attack, we walked to Wall Street to see the Stock Exchange with its giant flag—and I was amazed to hear myself think a silent prayer: "Don't let the nation collapse; hang in there." During the month between 9/11 and my visit, I had been haunted by two images of Lower Manhattan. One was that ubiquitous view from Brooklyn across the Brooklyn Bridge toward the financial district that for a generation or two had been the most iconic image of New York. The other was more "private," a view down East Broadway in Chinatown toward the Woolworth Building and the Trade Center, an image I had come to associate with a transformation in my life during my early thirties that had brought me storybook romantic love and a new professional passion: exploring and serving the wide world of avant-garde cinema.

Those two views had become my quintessential images of the city around which my life had always circled and in which, during the late 1970s, I was discovering a world of new possibilities. Or to put it in a truer, if more melodramatic way, 9/11 had revealed to me that I had—not exactly subconsciously, but not exactly consciously, either—come to see New York City as a "sacred space" and to feel that the city's energy and beauty, its ethnic and historical multiplicity, its artistic pre-eminence were encoded in those two images. By the time of my visit to Ground Zero, the connection of the attacks to a certain strain of fundamentalist Islam had come to seem quite clear, and I remember thinking that, whatever else one might say about the United States, we had not nuked Mecca and were not (I hoped, assumed) even considering such an action, despite the terrorist attack on my "Mecca" and its obvious implications. It had come to seem quite evident that the target of the attacks was the most visible symbol, not just of capitalism, but of modern life in an industrialized society and the many good things this life has made possible—including a living discourse of all kinds of cinema.

By the time I drove to Queen's University a week after my visit to New York and Ground Zero, I was increasingly troubled by the fact that, over a period of three decades, the primary justification for independent cinema had become its ongoing critique of American capitalism and bourgeois life. Of course, I had used this justification endlessly: my ongoing series of filmmaker interview books is called "A Critical Cinema." In avant-garde film, at least American avant-garde film, a critique of capitalism—as exemplified and propagandized by Hollywood filmmaking in particular—has been a badge of honor for decades. And in American academe much of what is considered sophisticated writing is implicitly, and sometimes explicitly, anti-capitalist and anti-American. It is true that in recent years I've been growing more conscious of the ironies of this situation, which seem particularly evident in academe, where new spins on Marxism, new forms of anti-Americanism and anti-Westernism, are of particular use in moving up the ladder of academic power and prestige.

Granted, I don't read as much academic writing as many of my colleagues, but I've never read an academic book or essay that, in its critique of capitalist patterns in commercial cinema and modern industrial society, also critiques what its own real purpose within a capitalist economy is. It may be argued that many of these essays and books are meant to be calls to action, but, in most instances, the action that seems most called for is a further immersion in the increasingly complex—and for most readers opaque—language of academic discourse.

In avant-garde filmmaking, the same paradox is evident, particularly in the most pervasive avant-garde approach of recent decades, "found-footage" or "recycled" cinema, where many filmmakers feel free, even obliged, to steal whatever imagery and sound they want from whomever they want (other than Disney!) as a means of mounting a critique of commercial media by turning its own absurdities and excesses against it. I have always been in sympathy with this Trojan-Horse strategy, but I am also aware that for many of these anti-capitalist warriors, "success" is measured, at least in part, by the acceptance of their work at festivals and in museums that are usually underwritten by (who else?) "The Enemy." And when it seemed that in *American Beauty* Sam Mendes had stolen the image of the plastic bag from avant-garde filmmaker Nathaniel Dorsky, few in the enraged avant-garde community seemed to see the irony of the situation. Dorsky later explained that he wasn't sure he should use the image since it was so common in poetry.

At some point during the Tulips Conference, in response (as I remember) to several pro-forma attacks on capitalism as *the* problem in world affairs, Peter Harcourt stood up and announced that he was not an anti-capitalist and that his hope was not for an end to capitalism, but for an "enlightened capitalism," a more humane and decent capitalism. It was precisely what I had been wanting to say, and Harcourt's statement brought to mind some lines from Emerson's "Self-Reliance":

> Great works of art have no more affecting lesson for us than this. They teach us to abide by our spontaneous impression with good-humored inflexibility than most when the whole cry of voices is on the other side. Else to-morrow a stranger will say with masterly good sense precisely what we have thought and felt all the time, and we shall be forced to take with shame our own opinion from another.

Continuing to argue for a global revolution—either in the name of communism or of fundamentalist Islam—seems to me as fully a form of political suicide as was the World Trade Center attack. As a result, I must, and do, hope for changes in the nature of capitalism, which I believe can be effected (and in some past instances have been affected) by creative human beings of courage and good will. I've come to believe that what I long understood as a progressive critique of capitalism, by media scholars and media makers, is often implicitly reactionary—and disingenuously reactionary at that. It assumes that the best that media scholars and makers can do is react to the status quo—model a hatred of capitalism and whatever it supports (except perhaps those systems that benefit makers and scholars).

As a result, activities that might develop or maintain spaces within capitalist societies for more progressive alternatives are increasingly ignored. It's simply easier—and often more profitable—to produce "radical" written critique of what one doesn't like than to create and support vital alternatives within capitalist economies. How else are we to account for the paradox of academe's production of a huge anti-capitalist (institutionally supported) literature critiquing mainstream film, and of fewer and fewer opportunities for students and the public at large to experience truly progressive moving-image media on a regular basis in a public forum?

I've become convinced that so long as film critique is grounded in a knee-jerk anti-capitalism, and in a hatred of the United States as the most visible representative of capitalism, it can never play a progressive role in an improvement of media or society. At most, it can lead only to endless complaint and self-righteous frustration—and to an expanding literature that may serve the careers of academics, but does not serve film history or expanded media awareness in any practical way.

On the other hand, if we could accept that alternative media could play a role in the development of a more humane form of capitalism, and, by doing so, help enable an ever-expanding world to deal with its many problems more effectively, we would have a less frustrating and more useful rationale for presenting a broader range of media art. We could express our revulsion with the more decadent tendencies of commercial cinema without damning commerce itself, which makes all media possible; and we could be clearer about how avant-garde film/video provides evocations of a more gentle, generous world, and more energetic in our efforts to be sure that these evocations reach those for whom they can be transformative.

What we need now is a new commitment to making what we consider the best and most progressive films/videos/digital works available and attractive to a growing audience, and a new generation of scholars who can see, tease out, and communicate the visions of progressive media makers so that a new generation of viewers can find their way into this work.

My deepest respect as a film historian and programmer has always gone to those films/videos that demonstrate most dramatically the quintessential lesson of avant-garde media: that magnificent works can be made from minimal financial resources. Indeed, many of what seem to me the most intelligent and memorable films and videos reveal the decadence of most Hollywood filmmaking, and so much of modern life, in both their production process and in the experiences they create for audiences.

Of course, avant-garde film- and video-makers have developed myriad ways of transcending limitation. If I am most deeply attracted to films/videos that model a retraining of perception (so that I can live more fully in the limited time I have, with the limited resources at my disposal), I remain in sympathy with all those makers who use the often limited resources available to them within capitalist economies to produce something substantial—and who, by implication, suggest we can do the same in our lives as teachers and as citizens.

There is, of course, a considerable history of organizational models for expanding academic and public awareness of alternative media, many of which were developed by individuals or small groups with very little to work with. The most obvious of these models are the major North American film societies of the 1940s and 50s—Cinema 16 in New York, Art in Cinema in San Francisco, and probably the Vancouver Film Society (I've not yet seen any detailed records of this venerable organization's work)—which created large and vital communities around the presentation of alternative media during an era as politically and economically conservative as our own.

These organizations didn't rely on government funding or even angel financing; they modeled community organization and action on the basis of a commitment to the use of media as a means of expanded awareness and more informed citizenship. The results of their efforts included new audiences for a wide range of cinema, a network of smaller film societies each of which developed its own audience, and the widespread distribution of forms of film that might never have been seen otherwise. That so much of this history has been ignored by so many in academe—even in an era when masters and doctoral theses about cultural history abound—is both typical and frustrating.

Ultimately, what a good many alternative films/videos demonstrate to those of us who find our way to them is that our quality of life—once our basic needs are met—is not a function of accumulation or extravagance, but of a deeper, more complex attention and awareness. This is, above all, the lesson that capitalism, in its more corrupt manifestations, doesn't want us to learn, and it is this lesson, above all others, that so many of us within modern industrialized societies have the opportunity to teach ourselves, our students, and our larger communities. Generations of inventive, courageous filmmakers have produced a body of work we have only begun to deploy in this quest. It remains for us to become a true avant-garde again, and show how cinema can model movement toward a world order that neither embarrasses nor frightens us.

But we can only do this if we're willing to move beyond the cul-de-sac of endless written critique of and complaint about what we don't respect, and serve the field of creative media by working to develop vigorous communities, inside and outside academe, around the informed, inventive, regular exhibition of what we do admire.

"9/11, Critique, and Avant-Garde Film" was published in a special issue of *Public*, 25 (2002), "Experimentalism," edited by Gary Kibbins and Susan Lord.

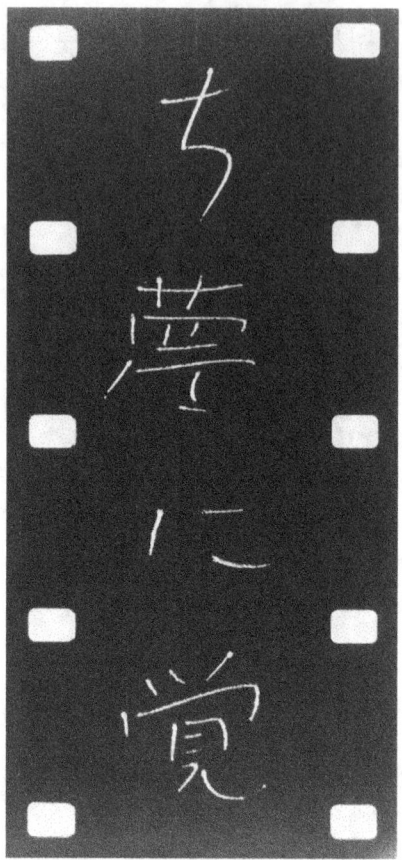

Filmstrip from Taka Iimura's *White Calligraphy* (1967).

Image from Iimura's *24 Frames Per Second* (1975-1978).
Courtesy Taka Iimura.

2003

Essay for Shiho Kano

My discussion of Kano's films was written for a screening of films by Sakumi Hagiwara and Kano at the Image Forum Cinematheque, Tokyo, Japan, in 2003. The discussion is preceded by some thoughts about Taka Iimura (1937-2022), in memoriam.

When Taka Iimura died at the end of July 2022, independent media lost one of its most distinctive figures. Beginning as a cine-surrealist and for a moment a cine-visual poet—*White Calligraphy* (1967), for example—Iimura was lured to New York City by the flowering of what P. Adams Sitney called "structural film": that body of work, produced mostly by American, Canadian, and British filmmakers, from the mid-to-late 1960s into the early 1970s, which focused on the apparatus of 16mm filmmaking. Salient instances include Tony Conrad's *The Flicker* (1965), Michael Snow's *Wavelength* (1967), Ernie Gehr's *Serene Velocity* (1970), Anthony McCall's *Line Describing a Cone* (1973), J. J. Murphy's *Print Generation* (1974), Morgan Fisher's *Projection Instructions* (1976), and the series of time-focused films produced by Iimura in the early 1970s, including *1 to 60 Seconds* (1973), *+ & –* (1973), and *24 Frames Per Second* (1975).

In 1980, the American Federation of Arts asked film scholar, Donald Richie, to create a film series focusing on the history of experimental film in Japan. Richie worked with Katsue Tomiyama, then director of Image Forum in Tokyo, to produce "Japanese Experimental Film 1960-1980," two programs of short films that toured the United States in the early 1980s. Program 2 included Iimura's *A Dance Party in the Kingdom of Lilliput* (1964). By the time the series toured, I had already interviewed Iimura about his turn to structural filmmaking and Richie's program note in the tour catalogue suggests that he too was aware of this later work, but perhaps resistant to celebrating it:

> This anarchistic, iconoclastic film contains echoes of dada and surrealism. Its incongruous images are set to the sound of the ubiquitous athletic instructor. Elaborate stairway sequence, lots of visual puns, nudity, charm, some criticism (if Lilliput perhaps means Japan). Even in this early work, the filmmaker's way of ordering film is already apparent.

I have two particularly fond memories of Iimura. I began interviewing independent filmmakers in 1976-77 and Iimura was one of the first five interviews I conducted (Hollis Frampton, Larry Gottheim, Robert Huot, Carolee Schneemann, and Iimura). Writing about and interviewing filmmakers was a challenge for me. I'd come out of a traditional academic graduate school system and was teaching in the English department at a small college, so exploring the strange new world of experimental filmmaking and speaking with accomplished artists about their work was still a challenge. Whatever else I had done and as passionate as I'd become about the films I was discovering, I was still a novice interviewer.

In those days, I used an old reel-to-reel tape recorder and in 1979 drove to New York City to speak with Iimura on two successive mornings. When back in my room after the first session, I checked to see how the recording sounded, only to discover that nothing was on the tape. I must have figured out what had gone wrong with the tape recorder, and decided that, during my second session with Iimura, I would bury camouflaged versions of my first-day's questions within the second day's questions, hoping he might repeat himself. Of course, Iimura cannot not have noticed that I was having us repeat much of what we had done the previous morning—but he never said a word about this and in no way revealed that he realized what must have happened. It was an act of remarkable kindness that I'm still grateful for.

The second memory is of a screening of *1 to 60 Seconds*—the final film shown at a well-attended, in-person Iimura presentation at Utica College. Several of Iimura's early surreal films had been shown and I had decided to run the minimalist *1 to 60 Seconds* as the last film before Iimura talked with the audience. The 30½ minutes of the film are measured out in a rigorous sequence. Iimura had scratched a series of numbers into single frames on the black-and-white filmstrip. As the film is projected, each of the numbers flashes on screen in the dark theater and its flash takes several seconds to fade from the viewer's retina. Also, a scratch on the soundtrack edge of the print creates a sonic blip each time the first number is seen.

The numbers are presented in pairs. The first number indicates the number of seconds of darkness that have just passed; the second, the total elapsed time to that point: that is, 1; 2, 00:3; 3, 00:6; 4, 00:10; 7, 00:17, up to 58, 59, 60. In other words, during the final minutes, the screen and room remain dark for fifty-eight, fifty-nine, and sixty seconds.

I had not shown the film publicly before and did not know what might happen. A few minutes into the film, audience members began to leave the theater. This continued, until by the 15-minute mark, the theater was empty. Neither Iimura nor I were exactly surprised; we knew showing the film might be seen by the audience as a not-so-amusing prank. Then, just as I was beginning to adjust to the now-empty theater and what had begun to seem a wholesale rejection of the show, I noticed that some members of the audience were returning. Others continued to come back into the theater. Indeed, at the end of *1 to 60 Seconds*, virtually everyone was back to see Iimura walk to the front to take questions. I remember being thrilled with the audience and fascinated with the entire experience.

It was clear that, as they watched the sequence of numbers, audience members had calculated approximately how long the film would be and implicitly understood that, so long as they remained aware of the time, they would still be part of the audience, even if they weren't in the theater. *1 to 60 Seconds* had generated an experience that provided an in-theater questioning of cinematic convention and a different kind of communal experience from what was common at more conventional screenings. Iimura had designed not only an unusual kind of intellectual/sensual cinematic activity, but a cine-conceptual time-sculpture.

Looking back, I see something of an irony in Richie's choice of an Iimura film that was resonant of the 1920s outrage created by Dada, when Iimura's later, more interesting and challenging films were available by the time the American Federation of Arts series was organized.

I lost touch with Iimura's work when he began exploring video's distinctiveness from film—like some other cineastes, I was a bit of a snob about early video. I regret this now. Iimura did continue to make films, in addition to working with video and video installation. His *MA: Space/Time in the Garden of Ryoan-Ji* is an engaging introduction to the tradition of classic Japanese gardens and the concept of "MA."

Note: Iimura's 16mm prints are available at Canyon Cinema (canyoncinema.com) and at New York Film-Makers' Cooperative (film-makerscoop.com), along with DVD collections of Iimura films and videos, published by Iimura himself: "On Duration in Film" includes *1 to 60 Seconds*.

* * *

My admiration for the films and videos of Kano has been conditioned by two experiences: one of them a film-historical experience; the other, my one visit to Japan. My memory of most of the films in the two programs that Richie made available has faded, but I do remember that the most pleasant surprise was *Kiri* (1971) by Hagiwara Sakumi, an eight-minute, single-shot film during which a misty landscape slowly clears, revealing a bit of a distant mountain. *Kiri* was a particular pleasure for me since I had recently begun to write about *Fog Line* (1970), by the American Larry Gottheim, an eleven-minute, single-shot film during which a foggy landscape begins to clear, revealing trees, bushes, and other details of a pasture. Certainly, there are differences between the two films—*Kiri* is black and white, *Fog Line*, in color. The landscape in *Fog Line* is more fully mediated by technology—and yet, I found it interesting, even poignant, that on opposite sides of the globe two filmmakers had had virtually the same idea at the same time and produced two lovely, serene films. I have long regretted that Hagiwara's films are not in distribution in the United States.

I experienced something of the same pleasure at the 2003 Images Festival in Toronto, when I saw three films by Kano—*Joukei* (1998), *Still* (1999), and *Rocking Chair* (2000)—in a program of Japanese experimental film curated by Chris Gehman. I was particularly taken with *Rocking Chair*, a thirteen-minute, color, sound film that reminded me of some of the then recent films and videos of Leighton Pierce, whose work I had been studying and writing about for some years. As was true of my experience with *Kiri* and *Fog Line*, I could see obvious differences between Pierce's work and *Rocking Chair*, but, once again, I was moved that these two artists, working on different continents, should be motivated to make beautiful work so obviously consonant in spirit and impact. Fortunately for Americans, Kano's work is finding its way into distribution here [*Rocking Chair* is available at Canyon Cinema].

Of course, the fact that Kano's work is being presented on a program with Hagiwara's and the fact that Hagiwara's work has been an important influence on Kano's makes this set of connections all the more interesting for me.

> Kano: "I doubt whether I really understood it at the time, but the power of Ito Takashi's *Spacy* [1981], the serenity of Hagiwara Sakumi's *Time* [1971], the stoic beauty of Matsumoto Toshio's *Shiki Soku Ze Kū* [1975]—all these diverse experiences deeply influenced and dazzled my high-school-student self. I had never seen films so free from convention."
>
> Interview with Kano, in MacDonald,
> *A Critical Cinema 5* (California 2006), 350.

The second experience that has provided a context for my interest in Kano's work has nothing to do with film; it occurred when I traveled to Japan in January 1997 to visit my son, Ian, who was teaching English in Okayama in Western Honshū. At the time of this trip, I was working on what was to become *The Garden in the Machine: A Field Guide to Independent Films about Place* (Berkeley: University of California Press, 2001), which focuses on an American tradition of independent filmmaking and videomaking dedicated to providing audiences with meditative and/or contemplative experiences that function as Edenic respites (as

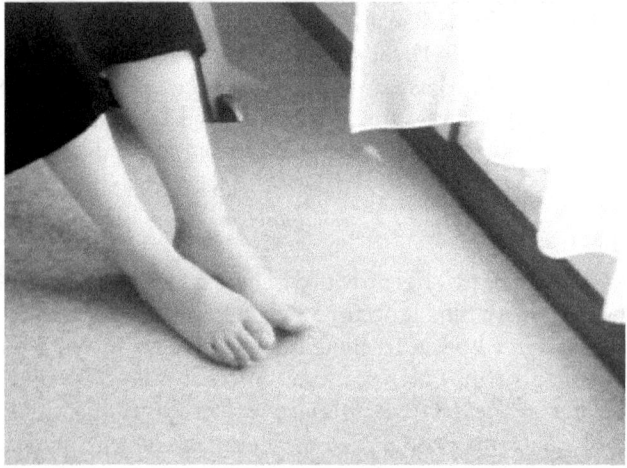

Images from Kano's *The Rocking Chair* (2000). Courtesy Kano Shiho.

"Gardens") within the pervasive hysteria of modern life ("The Machine"). As part of my research, I had been studying various traditions and accomplishments related to my theme, including the history of landscape architecture and particularly the work of Frederic Law Olmsted, the nineteenth-century landscape architect and designer who built New York's Central Park, Brooklyn's Prospect Park, the "Emerald Necklace" of parks in Boston, and so many of the major public parks across the United States.

During the weeks before my trip, I was excited to learn that Okayama was home to the Kōraku-en Garden, widely considered one of the most remarkable gardens in Japan, and I made plans to spend time there during my visit—as well as to visit gardens in Kyoto and elsewhere. When I rode Ian's bicycle through Okayama to the Kōraku-en Garden for the first time, I was surprised to discover that it was rather less extensive than I had imagined—though, of course, one of the accomplishments of the Kōraku-en Garden is the complexity of its beauty, its incorporation of a remarkably wide variety of environments and experiences within what might seem a limited space.

This first experience of the Kōraku-en Garden was confirmed a few days later when I journeyed with my son to Takahashi, a small town about fifty kilometers to the northwest of Okayama. While he spent the day teaching, I decided to visit the garden of the Raikyū-ji Temple, said to be the work of master garden designer, Enshū Kobori. For an hour I walked up and down the street where the garden was said to be located, unable to find it: no space seemed extensive enough for a garden that was considered a national treasure. Finally, I climbed an old stone staircase and discovered within the Raikyū-ji Temple the entrance to its exquisite garden, which, like so many Japanese gardens, is simultaneously enclosed within the energy of modern life—a main road, invisible to the eye, but continuously audible, passes by the rear end of the garden—*and* offers an opportunity for transcending the conventional demands of modern experience. The incorporation of Mount Atago, some kilometers away, into the design of the Raikyū-ji Garden embodies this idea, allowing the small garden to seem to extend as far as the eye can see.

These experiences are relevant to the work of Kano on several levels. Most obviously, her sensibility is related to the sensibility embodied in the history of Japanese gardens. She is interested in using the two media usually seen as the epitome of modern, urban, obsessively commercial life in order to transform limited expanses of space and limited durations of time into audio-visual experiences that offer lovely, sustained moments for cinematic meditation and contemplation. Further, compared with the American tradition of films that offer viewers "gardens" within the "machine" of modern life—I'm referring in particular to the films of Larry Gottheim, Peter Hutton, James Benning, Sharon Lockhart—Kano works not only within more rigid spatial limits, but without the idea of separating herself from modern urban/suburban experience.

Her best works—*Rocking Chair, White Tablecloth* (2000), *Incense* (2002), and *Rosecolored Flower* (2002)—do not involve literal escapes from conventional life; rather, Kano chooses sections of rooms within conventional urban living spaces, engulfed by the sounds of commercial life outside (automobile traffic, trains, and the like) and discovers/creates extended moments within which a particular quality of light, the subtle movement of a breeze, the wafting of a bit of smoke, a shade of rose reflected in a glass vase allow us to reconnect with the moment-to-moment incarnation of the world around us and to remember how much pleasure is available in even the smallest, least exciting moments and places.

Kano's films and videos (she is equally at home in both mediums) often suggest the origins of cinema—not surprisingly, since she has great admiration for cinema's pioneers:

> Personally, I think that all film stems from the primitive images that pioneers like Méliès and the Lumière Brothers left us. After film became somewhat established, avant-garde and experimental filmmakers self-consciously took on that same exploratory approach to film. Additionally, since we've come into contact with film, haven't we all experienced time and movement in a new way? What I am interested in is that most "primitive," basic quality that is a part of all film. I seek the same sort of experience and discovery in the present. I don't think that early film has become irrelevant and out of date; rather, I think we continually return there in order to come up with new discoveries.
>
> MacDonald interview, 354

The Lumière Brothers' matter-of-fact engagement with everyday life may seem particularly relevant to Kano's films and videos. But her work also suggests the trickfilms of Georges Méliès. Indeed, the moment we adjust to Kano's redirection of cinema away from plot, character, melodrama, montage, special effects—the usual components of commercial television and film experiences—and accept her meditative gaze, we are surprised by one or another form of subtle trickery that forces us to rethink what we're seeing and hearing and to recognize the artist's hand gently controlling our experience.

Near the end of *Rocking Chair*, for example, as we watch the hem of a white curtain moved by air currents in the room, we notice that for the first time we are seeing several layers of curtain, subtly superimposed—and these layers of curtain remind us that the visual-auditory experience of Kano's film, as direct and matter-of-fact as it may seem, has been constructed during several "layers" of time. A similar effect is created in *White Tablecloth*, as we discover that the water mark around the bottom of the cruet seems to ebb and flow, like a miniature tide: the cruet may have been filmed in continual, real time, but what we experience is carefully, almost invisibly edited so that the resulting video is simultaneously serene and mysterious, simple and surprising. In *Incense* the incense smoke wafts through the room and is lovely to look at, though as we enjoy this simple experience, we suddenly notice that the smoke is moving in reverse, that the incense stick is "un-burning," just in time to discover that the smoke is moving normally again.

There is also a musical, even theatrical dimension to Kano's work, especially in the way she choreographs her visuals and sounds. Doors open and close, allowing light into a portion of the space or removing some of the light; traffic sounds grow louder or soften; the light subtly modulates as a breeze moves through the space; Kano opens her aperture so fully that the image whites out, or she closes the aperture and the image fades to black; someone is seen, or heard, passing through the limited space revealed by the frame or somewhere close by. The resulting experiences are simultaneously open *and* in firm control, quiet *and* full of energy. They are reminiscent of various cultural traditions—the Japanese garden, the haiku, many North American avant-garde films (the slow zoom in *Rosecolored Flower* is evocative of Michael Snow's *Wavelength* [1967])—*and* aesthetically distinctive and particular to Kano's own place and moment.

See Shiho Kano's website (shihokano.info/en) for distribution information about her films, installations, and other work.

Cover of Amos Vogel's *Film as a Subversive Art* (1974).

2005

Forward to the 2005 Edition of Amos Vogel's *Film as a Subversive Art* (originally published by Random House in 1974)

A conversation with Amos Vogel about *Film as a Subversive Art*, recorded by phone on February 16, 2005; edited in 2024.

MacDonald: You know that Paul Cronin and I are trying to get *Film as a Subversive Art* back into print…
Vogel: I certainly do and it's wonderful! So what do you want to know?
MacDonald: What was the instigation for the book?
Vogel: Well, as you may know, Lord Weidenfeld is my cousin [George (Lord) Weidenfeld, 1919-2017, was a political journalist with the BBC and later established the publishing house Weidenfeld and Nicholson]. I had been thinking for quite some time about doing a book, but it never really crystallized. I mentioned this to him at some point, and he said, yes, it's a great idea; you should definitely do it. That gave me the final impetus to actually sit down and write the book. I must have been working on it in 1972-73, 1973 probably.

Just a second, Marcia wants to say something…
Marcia Vogel: You had the idea of writing a book sitting in you for years. Then you had a back problem and were stuck in bed for six weeks, and you did a lot of writing then.
Vogel: She's right, absolutely correct.
MacDonald: Formally, it's a very unusual book—really a text/image book, with three different levels of text. What do you remember about putting it together?
Vogel: To begin with, I felt I had a lot I wanted to say about many films. And I had a lot of files that I could consult; I'd begun filing information about films as soon as Cinema 16 got started. I also had, at that time at least, a very good memory.

I was not a stranger to writing. I had the notes I made when I first looked at each film and also what I wrote about that film for the program notes when it was shown at Cinema 16. The material was all at hand; it was simply a matter of going through sixteen years of Cinema 16 programs, picking out the films that I thought worthy of inclusion in a book. Then I added films I had come to understand and admire in the ten years after Cinema 16 ended in 1963, when I was co-directing (with Richard Roud) the New York Film Festival.
MacDonald: For a serious, theoretical film book in 1974, *Film as a Subversive Art* is unusually visual; it's full of images. Indeed, the images often take priority over the texts. I remember when I was first looking through it, I was often puzzled, even shocked by the images, and would access the texts looking for an explanation. Did you have a struggle with the publisher about the images?
Vogel: First, I absolutely never could have considered doing a book about this subject without copious illustrations. I'm a visual man. My obsession is film, the visual element in film. I'm not interested in a lot of heavy intellectual dialogue,

though I can take that, too—it can be very well done in film. But that's not the primary thing for me. What's primary is the liberty that film gives the artist to use visual materials. That's the exciting thing, the wonderful thing. So, I would never have agreed to publish a book without pictures.

Second, even a book with a few pictures here and there would not have appealed to me. I was given complete freedom to provide as many photographs as I wanted. Every image you see in the book was my decision.

Having said that, I also need to say something that may amuse you. In the original manuscript, there was one big still, spread across the top of two adjoining pages where I thought it would be best situated. It showed a naked man stretched out on his back, with an erect penis. This one still was vetoed by the publishers. And I was so eager to see the book published that I succumbed, I didn't want the book not published because of a single still. So in that one instance I was a coward.

MacDonald: Do you remember what film the image was from?

Vogel: I do not. When I think about this, it's very strange; I don't even know what happened to that still!

MacDonald: In 1974 It might have been from a porn film. Where else would you see an erect penis?

Vogel: I think you're probably right. I also think it's humorous that such a still would be the one image nixed by the publisher, since, without that organ and its ability to get stiff and erect, none of us would be here. To say that an erect penis cannot be shown is a violation of the most primary sort.

MacDonald: What's ironic to me about that image not being allowed is what *is* shown in the book. For example, there's candid imagery from the Otto Muehl's *Materialaktionsfilme*! And there are many penises in the book's imagery. Just not erect ones!

Vogel: There's nothing holier than the erect penis, right? That's the problem. Very dangerous. The censors are afraid of it.

MacDonald: In terms of sales, how did *Film as a Subversive Art* do?

Vogel: That's a difficult question for me to answer. I would say that in general it only did middling. I presented the idea of the book, then the finished book itself, to Weidenfeld, who owned the rights. He then contacted Random House and they published it. I had nothing to do with the arrangements with Random House.

Now, I'll say something that I'm not sure is wise of me to say—but then, I've never been known to be a wise man. My feeling has always been that Random House accepted the book, not because they really wanted it, but as a favor to Weidenfeld. Even though Random House was a first-class publisher, they didn't do a first-class job of getting the book into bookstores. I never said this, either to Random House or to Weidenfeld—but I don't give a damn anymore, so I'll say it to you. Random House took the book, but they did not *push* the book. I think they didn't want to push the book. I had difficulty finding it in bookstores.

And to this day, I don't understand why nobody reviewed the book. There was no review. I had difficulties wherever I went looking for the book in stores. In short, I think Random House was doing Weidenfeld a backhanded favor.

MacDonald: I certainly saw the book in bookstores, though I don't remember exactly where or when I bought my first copy—certainly during the early-to-mid 1970s.

Vogel: Maybe you have to take what I say with a grain of salt.

MacDonald: A specific question: right before the introduction, you have an "author's apologia." Three statements:

> This book is an approximation of a draft of a first edition; in short, a hint (to the wise).
>
> A still is not a film: it lacks the dimension of time and movement—indispensable components of film art—and represents only a small fraction of a single second of a given motion picture.
>
> Words are not the best way to deal with a visual medium.

Two of the statements I completely understand: a still is not a film, since it lacks the dimensions of time and movement; and words are not the best way to deal with a visual medium. But I'm not clear about the first statement.
Vogel: Well, I just think that a super writer would have written a better book. I did my best, but I was, in my opinion, just scratching the surface of a much bigger topic.
MacDonald: I see. Well, it's a hell of a book to be apologizing for! I found it fascinating, exciting, *freeing*.
Vogel: That's the sweetest thing you could have said to me.
MacDonald: Was it your decision to have the Makavejev image on the cover?
Vogel: Yes. It's a clear but complicated image—fantastic, surrealist, and serious all at the same time. It gave a good indication of what experimental films can be like. I remember looking at quite a few stills. But in the end, I had no doubt whatsoever about that being the cover image. It's hard to answer why; such choices involve the unconscious.

* * *

A generation ago, when I was a graduate student (during the 1960s), there seemed to be a reasonably clear distinction between a doctoral dissertation, the book-length study of a particular subject required of those who want to earn their Ph.D., and a book. The dissertation was where graduate students proved that they knew the field and were capable of conducting and reporting on research that would add to the general awareness of the chosen subject area. A scholarly *book*, which might be a revision of the dissertation, was where the young scholar eliminated those dimensions of the dissertation required to prove the author's intelligence and breadth of reading to specialists in the same field, and made contact with a larger public—a potential audience of intelligent individuals both inside and outside academe who were interested in the young scholar's topic.

During the past half-century, this distinction seems to have disappeared. In too many cases these days, doctoral dissertations on cinema, with seemingly only minor changes, find their way to bookstores, where unwary potential readers can hardly fail to be frustrated by the nature of the communication that occurs in so many of these tomes. All too often, they function like the gates in a gated community. Unless the reader has spent a good portion of a lifetime reading the same theoretical texts as the authors and developing the particular academic vocabularies the authors have become familiar with during several years of graduate work, these studies are sure to be confusing, sometimes even incomprehensible.

The result of our loss of the distinction between dissertation and book is that the world of serious scholarship and the world outside academe make a good bit less contact than they should. Academics often look with impotent puzzlement at a society seemingly addicted to the most absurd notions; and people outside academe see the work of scholars, at least in the humanities and the arts, as of no practical value or importance, and of no interest to anyone outside the inner circle of scholars and would-be scholars—a lose-lose situation for both academe and the public at large.

Most of my film education has come inside movie theaters and screening rooms, and from books that were written either before cinema became a full-fledged part of the academy or from a position outside the academy, books that function not simply to demonstrate the complexity of the research that went into them or the theoretical IQ of the author, but to introduce a broad range of readers to a more complete sense of film history and to instigate a deeper awareness of how cinema can function productively and progressively within society as a whole. Amos Vogel's *Film as a Subversive Art*, originally published by Weidenfeld and Nicholson in the United Kingdom and by Random House in the United States, in 1974, is among the most significant achievements of this more communicative, democratic form of film scholarship. After four decades, it remains as engaging as it ever was. Indeed, the passage of time may have made it a more valuable and important study than it was when it first appeared.

Film as a Subversive Art was part of a triumvirate of books published in the early 1970s that offered insight into the flood of cinema (film, video, multi-media) that had washed across modern society during the late 1960s and early 1970s. P. Adams Sitney's *Visionary Film* (New York: Oxford University Press, 1974) appeared the same year as Vogel's book; both followed Gene Youngblood's *Expanded Cinema* (New York: Dutton, 1970). Each of these breakthrough volumes was a detailed report on its author's exploration of a particular dimension of modern independent cinema; each was meant to instigate larger audiences for the remarkable accomplishments of media artists; and each grew out of a belief in the potential of modern media to provide society with enlightening, even transformative, experiences. Of the three books, *Film as a Subversive Art* remains the most accessible and, formally, the most remarkable—as well as the most revealing of the personal and professional history that produced it.

In a sense, Vogel's magnum opus was a final report on his efforts on behalf of independent cinema at Cinema 16, the film society he and his wife Marcia founded in 1947 (*Film as a Subversive Art* is dedicated "To Marcia, Steven, Loring [Vogel's two sons]—and Cinema 16"). Many of those who read the first edition of the book—I include myself—knew nothing of Cinema 16, but without that film society there could have been no book. Beginning in 1947, Vogel presented New York City film enthusiasts with regular programs of independent films, chosen and arranged dialectically so as to foreground the distinctiveness of the individual films *and* create a "meta-film" that would spark sustained thinking about cinema and its function in society.

Vogel's sense of what a film society might be owed something to his childhood in Vienna, where he was a member of a film society (until Hitler made it impossible for him to stay in Austria), and to his early contact with Frank Stauffacher, whose Art in Cinema film society began invigorating the Bay Area film scene in 1946. But from the beginning, Cinema 16 was infused with Vogel's commitment to a particularly wide range of independent cinema and his determination to find and screen what conventional film audiences would find challenging, a commitment that quickly required Cinema 16 to become a private membership organization so as to avoid the then stringent New York State censorship laws.

From 1947 until 1963, Vogel (with the assistance first of Marcia Vogel, and later, Jack Goelman) looked at thousands of films, searching for individual works that would productively subvert the film expectations of Cinema 16's growing membership. At its height Cinema 16 boasted five thousand members, including many of the cultural movers and shakers in New York City, and it became a major inspiration for what developed into a nationwide network of film societies that looked to Vogel's programming for ideas, and by the 1950s, depended on Cinema 16's distribution of otherwise unavailable films. Cinema 16 was a landmark moment in public film exhibition, open, like any public movie theater, to anyone who could afford the reasonable cost of a membership: $16 for 16 performances.

Vogel assumed that because the commercial cinema's mission is to make the maximum number of viewers happy and complacent, *his* mission was to attack complacency wherever he found it. The audiences that assembled for Cinema 16 programs represented a considerable range of politics and aesthetic preferences. While Vogel has always identified himself as a leftist and a modernist, he frequently programmed films that were sure to offend even those in tune with his political and/or aesthetic sensibilities: Cinema 16 was an equal opportunity offender. Nevertheless, those who were annoyed by the aesthetics of the new avant-garde films Vogel was showing, those who were bored with the social realist documentaries Cinema 16 presented, and those who were shocked by the sexuality of some films or by the political viewpoints of others continued to renew their memberships.

By 1963 the film exhibition landscape had changed and was continuing to change. Some of the kinds of films that, early on, had been audience lures at Cinema 16 were now increasingly available in public theaters, at screening venues that had developed to service aficionados of avant-garde filmmaking, and even on television. As these outlets opened up, Cinema 16 lost its ability to attract members at a price that could support the film society, until Vogel could see no way to continue. Cinema 16's final program was presented in May 1963. That same year, Vogel was asked to become co-director (along with Richard Roud) of the New York Film Festival at the then new Lincoln Center, a position he held until 1968. Vogel left Lincoln Center to become a faculty member in the Annenberg School of Communications at the University of Pennsylvania in

Philadelphia, where he taught film history and theory, and continued to present public programs at the Annenberg Cinematheque, which he established.

During the seventeen years when he ran Cinema 16, Vogel developed a habit of making notes on each film he saw and filing these notes so they could be accessed later on—a necessary procedure so that he could intelligently select the few dozen films there was time to present during a particular exhibition season. Vogel's dual habit of seeing many films and making careful notes on each of them continued even once Cinema 16 ceased operation. This habit would in time make *Film as a Subversive Art* possible. Of course, during the Cinema 16 years, Vogel had regularly written blurbs for the Cinema 16 brochures, program notes for individual presentations, and, from time to time, essays on film programming and on the social importance of independent cinema. And for some years, he had thought about using his experiences with independent film as the basis for a book. But it was not until he mentioned the idea to his cousin, Lord George Weidenfeld (of the British publishing house, Weidenfeld and Nicholson), and saw Weidenfeld's enthusiasm about the idea, that Vogel set to work on the project.

During the early 1970s, Vogel wrote *Film as a Subversive Art* using a general procedure reminiscent of his programming at Cinema 16. The book required him to select those films that seemed most significant as subversions of conventional expectation and then organize them into a coherent ongoing experience. Of course, while the book he envisioned could accommodate far more films than a year of Cinema 16 programming—in the end, several hundred—these had to be chosen from the thousands of films Vogel had seen and described in his notes.

Having labored over his selections, Vogel set about arranging his comments about cinema and about particular films into an overall presentation. Whereas most scholarly books adhere to a form that has become nearly as conventional as the various genres of commercial cinema, *Film as a Subversive Art* employs a highly unusual organization. Each chapter begins with a brief theoretical consideration of a particular dimension of film's capacity for subverting personal and societal complacency, and is followed by a series of brief comments on a set of films, chosen and arranged in more or less alphabetical order so as to reveal the considerable variety of ways in which a filmmaker can deal with this particular kind of cinematic subversion. Each chapter is profusely illustrated with imagery from the films, and each image includes a brief but informative and analytical caption.

On its dedication page, *Film as a Subversive Art* includes a brief "Author's Apologia" in which Vogel seems to ask forgiveness for whatever limitations the reader might find in his writing, and then makes several theoretical statements:

> A still is not a film. It lacks the dimensions of time and movement—indispensable components of film art—and represents only a small fraction of a single second of a given motion picture.
>
> Words are not the best way to deal with a visual medium.

That he apologizes for the limitations of stills, even before he indicates his reservations about the utility of words when it comes to the visual arts, reveals Vogel's fundamental commitment to the visual. This commitment is reflected in the experience that *Film as a Subversive Art* creates for readers, or really, readers/viewers. While there must be some who read the book from front to back, my guess is that most people approach *Film as a Subversive Art* in a manner unusual for a scholarly book. The imagery Vogel uses is generally so arresting—even at times, shocking—that readers are immediately confronted and engaged, *and then* find their way into Vogel's three-leveled verbal text as a way of coming to terms with what they've seen. Fortunately, Vogel's beautifully written essays, his perceptive discussions of individual films, and his useful captions do create a highly intelligent context.

Ultimately, the purpose of the unusual form of *Film as a Subversive Art* is not simply to dramatize Vogel's breath of experience or his intellectual sophistication, but rather to demonstrate how cinema, and especially cinema scholarship, should function in the world. Vogel's organization makes clear that the function of written film theory is to deliver the reader back to cinema, to the complexities of accomplished individual films, and to the social experience of filmgoing. Vogel is not primarily interested in compiling information about particular films or in assembling theoretical conjectures about cinema; he *is* interested in engaging readers/viewers so thoroughly that they will seek out, or even better, *will create*, opportunities for enjoying not just the movies that allow us to escape the pressures of our lives for a couple of hours on a weekend, but those moving-image experiences that can help us to live more completely, to know the world more thoroughly, and to function as more responsible citizens of humanity.

The decision of C.T. Editions to make *Film as a Subversive Art* easily available once again could not have come at a more appropriate moment. For one thing, while many of the films described and illustrated in *Film as a Subversive Art* are reasonably familiar, at least to aficionados of independent cinema, a good many others will be as new to contemporary filmgoers as they were to Cinema 16 audiences. And since new moving-image technologies have been making the older 16mm technology (the name, Cinema *16*, of course, was a reference to 16mm films) an increasingly endangered species, Vogel's descriptions and imagery may provide a valuable wake-up call for those determined to see that the most interesting 16mm independent films are available, in their original form, to future generations. It was Vogel's original mission to provide accomplished films with audiences and vice versa; my hope is that the re-publication of *Film as a Subversive Art* will help to revive this mission.

Equally important, the exhibition scene for independent film, especially for forms of cinema that subvert convention, has nearly disappeared. A few museums in major cities make a range of inventive programming available to an ill-informed public, and a network of "micro-cinemas" has evolved to provide opportunities for some independent filmmakers to tour with their work. But for the most part, there is little energy around alternative cinema; it is as if we are waiting for a new Vogel to appear on the scene and instigate a revival of serious moving-image spectatorship. There is no new Vogel as yet, but the reappearance of *Film as a Subversive Art* gives this eternal optimist hope that the original Vogel, as he is expressed in this remarkable book, may—once again—be able to instigate a new recognition of how entertaining and informative, and transformative, the public experience of the full range of cinema can be.

This forward was written for the 2005 paperback of *Film as a Subversive Art* published by C.T. Editions (London) and was included in several recent editions, including a Croatian language paperback edition, published by Mizantrop in Zagreb. A revised hardback edition was published by The Film Desk (New York) in 2021.

For more information on the film society movement and Cinema 16 in particular, see Scott MacDonald, *Cinema 16: Documents Toward a History of the Film Society* (Philadelphia: Temple University Press, 2002), which includes interviews with Amos Vogel, Marcia Vogel, and Jack Goelman, along with an extensive selection of documents from the Cinema 16 archives, plus a number of Vogel's other writings. For more information about Vogel, including many writings by Vogel, plus essays by Werner Herzog, Paul Cronin, Michael Omasta, Scott MacDonald, Tom Yoshikami, Michael Chaiken, and Bill Nichols, see Paul Cronin, ed., *Be Sand, Not Oil: The Life and Times of Amos Vogel* (Vienna: Österreichisches Filmmuseum/SYNEMA—Gesellschaft für Film und Medien, 2014).

Jackson Lake in Wyoming, the first lake seen in James Benning's *13 Lakes* (2004). Courtesy of James Benning.

2014

Nomination to the National Film Registry for James Benning's *13 Lakes* (2004)

I couldn't imagine not including something I'd written about James Benning in this collection—since I've written more and more frequently about Benning's work than about any other filmmaker, and have interviewed him for four different interview collections. I don't know whether the fact that we're close to the same age (both born in 1942) has anything to do with this; we've lived through exactly the same era. But it's been a pleasure to follow Benning's work for fifty years—though his move to digital has allowed him to be even more productive than he had been as a 16mm filmmaker, *so* productive that keeping up with his work is a challenge.

In 2014, I nominated Benning's *13 Lakes* (2004) to be part of the Library of Congress' National Film Registry. I worked at making the nomination as strategic as I could, and it apparently was successful—I do not know if others also nominated Benning that year.

* * *

Over the past half-century, Milwaukee native James Benning has become American cinema's preeminent landscape artist. Beginning in the 1970s with films like *11 x 14* (1975) and *One Way Boogie Woogie* (1976), Benning demonstrated a sensitivity to Midwestern landscape that evoked canonical American painters and photographers. In 1980 he moved to New York, then in 1987 to California to teach filmmaking and mathematics at California Institute of the Arts—and his range as a cine-explorer of American landscape and cityscape expanded with each move. While much of American commercial (and independent) media during the past several decades has been characterized by an increasing acceleration and density of action, along with a formal tendency toward image and sound overload, Benning's tendency has been to stretch his audiences' patience and offer them opportunities to refine their perceptual capacity.

Benning has always been committed to the long-duration shot. *One Way Boogie Woogie* is a 60-minute film composed of 60 one-minute shots; *11 x 14* includes three 10-minute shots; and each film in Benning's California Trilogy (*El Valley Centro*, 1999; *Los*, 2000; *SOGOBI*, 2001) is composed of thirty-five 2½ minute shots. Benning's interest in moving the audience toward patience and more careful attention reached a culmination in 2004 with the diptych *Ten Skies* and *13 Lakes*, which are composed, respectively, of ten and thirteen 10-minute shots. *13 Lakes* is the longest of Benning's celluloid films—after 2007, the move to digital video has allowed him to produce extended-duration images far beyond the capability of 16mm celluloid film: for example, the 2013 digital work, *BNSF* (the reference is to the Burlington Northern Santa Fe Railroad) is a three-hour-and-twenty-minute single shot! *13 Lakes*, however, remains Benning's most geographically expansive film and an epitome of his commitment to a meditative and ruminative cinema.

Each of the thirteen shots in *13 Lakes* is composed so that the surface of the lake bisects the film frame, and each image is separated from the one that follows by several seconds of darkness. In order, we see Jackson Lake, Wyoming;

Moosehead Lake, Maine; the Salton Sea in southern California; Lake Superior in northern Minnesota; Lake Winnebago in Wisconsin; Lake Okeechobee, Florida; Lower Red Lake, Minnesota; Lake Pontchartrain, Louisiana; the Great Salt Lake, Utah; Lake Iliamna in Alaska; Lake Powell, Arizona/Utah; Crater Lake, Oregon; and Oneida Lake, New York. The choice and order of this particular set of lakes has to do with the considerable differences between them. The move from Jackson Lake to Moosehead Lake to the Salton Sea at the beginning of the film, for example, jumps the viewer from one geographic region to another, from one kind of terrain to another, and from one kind of lake to another: Jackson Lake and Moosehead Lake were created by geological forces; the Salton Sea was man-made accidentally by a faulty irrigation system and subsequently by irrigation run-off from the Imperial Valley in Southern California.

Benning's choice of lakes also relates to his personal history. His Milwaukee origins are evident in the fact that three of the thirteen lakes are in the Upper Midwest; his choice of Oneida Lake in New York State has something to do with his frequent visits with close friends in the Central New York area; and for years he has been regularly drawn to both the Salton Sea and the Great Salt Lake. Indeed, the Great Salt Lake, especially Robert Smithson's *Spiral Jetty* (1970), is an important location in his *North on Evers* (1991) and *Deseret* (1995), as well as in *13 Lakes*; and *Spiral Jetty* is the subject of Benning's *Casting a Glance* (2007). But the most important principle at work in the choice and arrangement of the lakes is the creation of a complex and subtle variety in the kinds of perceptual experiences Benning can provide with these different locales.

This variety is evident in the sometimes obvious, sometimes very subtle visual experiences of the lakes. Benning likes to work at the very edges of perceptual awareness, and sometimes a visual development is so subtle that we wonder if we're really seeing it: the tiny lights of a moving car, far, far across the water in the Lake Winnebago shot, for instance. While other canonical filmmakers committed to representing American place—Peter Hutton and Nathaniel Dorsky are examples—have been devoted to the idea of cinema as a visual art, and therefore to silent cinema, Benning has always privileged sound. Each of the lakes in *13 Lakes* is different both in its visual characteristics and in the soundscape within which we observe it. Sometimes the sound is in the foreground of our attention, as it is in the shot of the Salton Sea, where two water scooters race, over and over, past the camera. In other instances, it is the subtle textures of sound that we come to notice.

Off-screen space is frequently as important in Benning's depiction of the thirteen lakes as the carefully composed imagery within his successive framings. The peaceful and gorgeous Lake Okeechobee shot is interrupted midway through by the sound of a train that we never see, which passes close enough to the lake to subtly affect the surface of the water—an allusion presumably to the train that passes by Walden Pond in Thoreau's *Walden* (a Benning favorite and subject of several Benning videos). In the Crater Lake shot, which serves as a visual climax to *13 Lakes*, off-screen gunshots cause the stunning image to have mysterious, potentially problematic implications.

The varied perceptual experiences in *13 Lakes* formally echo each other, while also revealing sometimes obvious and sometimes very subtle distinctions. During the opening moments of some shots, viewers may find themselves wondering how this shot is a useful addition to what has been experienced so far—only to realize, slowly but surely, that this new dynamic of image and sound adds considerably to what has gone before. As the depictions of the lakes accumulate, Benning develops a new form of cinematic suspense: as we grow more and more aware of the lake we're looking at and of the panoply of lakes we've already seen, we cannot not wonder how the next lake will differ from the one in front of us and what it will add to the ever-more-complex panorama provided by the film.

Ultimately, Benning's films are cine-therapy and a form of perceptual retraining for jaded modern cineastes. Watching *13 Lakes* in particular offers an opportunity for a kind of "cine-yoga," a stretching of our ability to see and hear with awareness and subtlety. For those who can meet Benning halfway, the experience can be exhilarating in its capacity to expand our awareness of motion picture imagery and sound—and of the beauty and perceptual and conceptual complexity of American Place.

Oneida Lake in New York State, the last lake seen in
Benning's *13 Lakes* (2004). Courtesy of James Benning.

This essay was published by, and is available at, the Library of Congress' National Film Registry site.

For rentals of Benning's 16mm films on digital files or any of the digital films, contact Benning at jbenning@calarts.edu. Benning's celluloid films, including *13 Lakes*, are available as 16mm prints from Canyon Cinema (canyoncinema.com). The Canadian Filmmakers Distribution Centre (cfmdc.org) has many of the films in 16mm, but not *13 Lakes*. Many of Benning's celluloid and digital films (again not *13 Lakes*) are available on DVD from the Austrian Film Museum (filmmuseum.at). Benning's work is also available through his European gallery, Neugerriemschneider, at Linienstraße 155, 10115 Berlin (mail@neugerriemschneider.com).

The cast of *My So-Called Life*.

2015

My So-Called Life—a cineaste's reading

This extended essay on *My So-Called Life* is the one text in this collection that was rejected by the publisher I had written it for—I'd hoped it would be a Wayne State University Press monograph. When I got word of the rejection, I figured that academic television studies had probably moved beyond the kind of writing I had done. I had other projects I wanted to do and a busy teaching life. Embarrassed by the rejection, I moved on.

As I was assembling writings for this new project, I decided to revisit the essay and to include it. *My So-Called Life* was aired thirty years ago and younger cineastes often seem unaware of the series. Watching *My So-Called Life* today reveals the many ways in which American television and American adolescence, along with the careers of Claire Danes, Jared Leto, and their colleagues, have transformed during recent decades—though the experience of the show itself still has its original power.

I can see how my decision to write about a television series for the first time was less a new writing adventure than a flashback to my years as a student and teacher of American literature and to the kinds of writing I did early in my career (indeed, my analysis of the dialogue in *My So-Called Life* evokes my discussion of Erskine Caldswell's dialogue in chapter 3 of this book). Re-reading the essay also reminded me of why, over the years, I've shifted my goal as a critic, from detailed analysis to inter- and meta-textual celebration and advocacy. Simply watching the 49-minute pilot, for example, probably reveals to any alert viewer the distinctive stylistic breakthroughs of *My So-Called Life* more efficiently than reading my analysis!

This long essay was an experiment for me, an attempt to see if I could find a way to write about a television series I admired (and still admire). It was not, I think, a totally successful experiment. Nevertheless, I hope my essay provides some valuable context; here and there, some useful insight—and that it attracts a few readers to a remarkable television series they may not be aware of.

* * *

I've been teaching film history at various colleges and universities since 1969, and it remains one of my greatest pleasures to be the person who introduces college students to *The Kid*, *M*, *Shadow of a Doubt*, *Blood of the Beasts*, *Window Water Baby Moving*, *Cabaret*, *The Flicker*, *Riddles of the Sphinx*... In my teaching I have generally made little reference to television, except as a way of demonstrating that the montage editing pioneered by Eisenstein in the 1920s has (ironically!) informed not only modern corporate advertising, but the shape of the American commercial television hour. Of course, like many of my colleagues I have enjoyed various television sitcoms and dramatic series over the years, but it was not until I planned my syllabus for Introduction to the History and Theory of Cinema in the fall of 2014 that I incorporated an episode from a television series into the course: the pilot for the series *My So-Called Life*.

Over the years, there have been very few television series that I've been drawn back to (I remember enjoying *The Honeymooners* some decades after loving it as a child in the 1950s), but for me *My So-Called Life* has become a special case. I did not see the series in its first run on ABC from August 1994 to January 1995; as I remember, I caught up with it when it was presented on MTV—and became a devotee. I videotaped many of the 19 episodes and returned to them again and again over the years, until the 2007 DVD release, which has allowed me to continue to re-experience the series. When I've discovered that younger friends and colleagues are not aware of *My So-Called Life*, I've regularly introduced them to it and, as is the case with the landmark films that amaze my students, this series seems to have considerable impact on first-time viewers.

Those familiar with *My So-Called Life* will be aware that the series can boast a number of "firsts." When it became clear that the show might be canceled because of low ratings (during its original airing on CBS, its competition was *Mad About You* and *Friends* on NBC, as well as *Martin* and *Living Single* on Fox)—there was also an issue with 15-year-old Claire Danes not wanting to continue with the show after the inaugural season. Fans organized a virtually unprecedented online campaign to save the series, and while the campaign failed, the impact of the original airing on those who saw the show and its re-emergence on MTV resulted in a considerable cult following (one listing has ranked it sixteenth among the 25 Top Cult Shows); and *My So-Called Life* continues to find its way onto listings of the best series, the top series canceled too soon, and so on.

Neither the failure of *My So-Called Life* to generate enough audience to instigate a second season, nor the post-cancellation accolades that the series continues to generate are of particular interest to me. Those of us who have studied and taught the history of literature and the history of cinema are aware that popularity or the lack of it cannot be counted on to reflect the accomplishment of a work. And by any conventional measure *My So-Called Life is* accomplished. The writing, much of it by series creator Winnie Holzman, is impressive, and was awarded an Emmy; and the acting (most obviously by Clare Danes, Jared Leto, Devon Gummersall, Devon Odessa, A. J. Langer, and Wilson Cruz) is more than impressive. And, given the recent sea change in American attitudes around gender and transgender, the character of Rickie Vasquez (Wilson Cruz) now seems remarkably prescient: Rickie may have been the first young, gay character featured on a continuing series.

Nevertheless, my decision to include the pilot episode as part of my course was neither the quality of the performances nor my interest in the characters. It was primarily a function of the pilot's unusual density and subtlety—typical of all the better episodes of *My So-Called Life*. What the pilot gets done in only 48 minutes remains astonishing to me. Obviously, any pilot is meant to provide a hook for potential viewers of episodes that will follow, but this pilot accomplishes both the standard range of functions—introducing a set of interesting characters, initiating potential plot lines, establishing a structure and style—*and* seems as complete a work of cinematic art as any series episode I can remember. Indeed, even canonical narrative films are rarely as efficient as this pilot. Of course, one of the ironies here is that the pilot (the only episode of *My So-Called Life* shot on 35mm) was not originally picked up by ABC—subsequent episodes did not go into production until a year and a half after the pilot was shot.

In any case, it is the stylistic particulars—the image and auditory subtleties—of *My So-Called Life* that I want to highlight. Because television is primarily a serial medium, our attention is usually focused on the ways in which the serial dimensions of a show play out over time, episode after episode, season after season—rather than on the distinctive elements of structure and style. Of course, as is true with any accomplished series, the successive episodes of *My So-Called Life* do offer an engaging trajectory, which will also be discussed. But within this trajectory the element that seems most unusual is the inclusion of distinct and distinctive moments of stylistic flourish, moments that are rather like lyric poems embedded within an ongoing prose narrative. One of these concludes the series pilot.

The Pilot

Written by Winnie Holzman and directed by Scott Winant, the pilot opens, implicitly in medias res, with a montage establishing the developing friendship between Angela Chase (Claire Danes) and Rayanne Graff (A. J. Langer), crucial to the change in Angela that is the impetus for the events that follow in this and subsequent episodes. Angela and Rayanne are goofing around on the street, pretending to be in trouble and panhandling from passersby. For the only time in the run of the series, these characters are addressing the camera and the viewers, as if we might be willing to respond to their requests. This opening portrait of the two girls helps to define the character of their relationship and the pleasure they take in each other's company. W. G. Snuffy Walden's score—a somewhat upbeat version of Carl Orff's *musica poetica*—confirms the rather romantic mood of the sequence.

As Angela and Rayanne run off down the street and into the narrative that follows, Angela explains her current mindset in a poetically timed narration that becomes a motif throughout *My So-Called Life* (I'm using ellipses to indicate Angela's dramatic pauses): "So I started hanging out with Rayanne Graff… just for fun… just 'cause it seemed if I didn't… I would *die* or something. Things were getting to me—just how people *are*, how they always expect you to be a certain way… even your best friend…" As Angela is saying "even your best friend," we are seeing her on the left side of a darkened frame into which walks Sharon Cherski (Devon Odessa), who fills the right side of the frame; the camera immediately pans left and a cut locates the two girls in their crowded high school hallway, where Angela and Sharon are walking to class.

As Sharon complains about a girl wanting to be "on yearbook" (that is, to be part of the group of students producing the Liberty High School yearbook) solely in order to be near a boy, Angela seems distracted. A slow-motion close-up on Angela surveying her surroundings is accompanied by a return to her narration: "Like with boys, how they have it so easy… how you have to pretend… you don't notice them… noticing you." A one-second subjective camera shot of Brian Krakow (Devon Gummersall) being bullied by some other boys, is followed by Angela's noticing several cheerleaders and commenting, as if to herself, "Like cheerleaders. Can't people just cheer on their own… like, to themselves?" Sharon continues her complaint to Angela, as Angela looks out a grated window and sees Rayanne and Rickie, in slightly fast motion, leaving school. When Sharon asks, "Who are you looking for?" Angela responds, "Nobody," but then completes the opening narration: "School is a battlefield… for your heart… so when Rayanne Graff told me my hair was holding me back, I had to listen… 'cause she wasn't just talking about my hair… she was talking about my life." The opening montage fades out.

Much gets done in this opening three-minute sequence. Most obviously, the movement from an older "best friend" and the more conventional "so-called" life Sharon (and, as will become clear, Brian) now represents for Angela to the new, more adventurous life represented by Rayanne and Rickie is established as the essential rite of passage of the series. And the sequence establishes the commitment of *My So-Called Life* to complex, layered stylistics, combining mobile camerawork and unusual transitions with poetically inflected narration and music. As the episode develops, other stylistic elements become clear.

After this first break, we see further evidence of the change in Angela. The second sequence begins with Angela (with the help of Rayanne and Rickie) dying her hair "crimson glow" red, and her mother Patty Chase (Bess Armstrong) arriving home to see this change and, awkwardly, meeting Angela's new friends. The dinner-table scene that follows that evening—Angela's father, Graham (Tom Irwin) and little sister Danielle (Lisa Wilhodt) are introduced—makes clear Angela's frustration and boredom with her home life and family ("I cannot bring myself to eat a well-balanced meal in front of my mother: it just means too much to her"; "My dad thinks every person in the world is having more fun than him, which could be true"). The introduction to Angela's home life concludes without Angela, as her parents discuss their concerns about her: for Patty, Angela is hard to look at now: "she looks like a stranger."

Snuffy Walden's music, which has been absent during the family scene—emphasizing Angela's boredom with her home life—begins a transition back into the now-more-romantic world of school and Angela looking off-screen (in a manner that subtly echoes her father's longing look at Patty at the end of the previous sequence), and in voice-over explaining, "I'm in love. His name is Jordan Catalano; he was left back... twice." As we see Jordan (Jared Leto) leaning against a wall, Angela notes, "He's always closing his eyes... like it *hurts* to look at things." After a moment when Sharon Cherski discovers that Angela, in cahoots with Rayanne, has changed her hair color, Angela joins Rayanne (and Rickie) in the girls' restroom, where she admits that Rayanne is right about her wanting to have sex with Jordan— "either sex or a conversation; ideally both."

A dissolve takes Angela to a meeting of the students working on the high school yearbook, trying to agree on this year's theme. The camera movement here, as in the earlier dinner-table sequence, is mobile—it circles close to Angela, emphasizing that we are seeing/hearing the events from her angle of view. When she sees Brian Krakow trying to photograph her—for a moment we see Angela from Brian's subjective view as he looks through the camera, trying to frame her—she hides within her sweater. That Angela is invisible to Jordan, but is Brian's focus, sets up a second, male-character dyad that will evolve during this and subsequent episodes. As Angela hides (with us) within her sweater, she is thinking to herself, "My parents keep asking how school was!" For Angela, school is like "a drive-by shooting: you don't care how it was; you're lucky to get out alive." When it's time to vote on the yearbook theme, Angela refuses, explaining that she doesn't want to be on yearbook. When the teacher (Nada Despotovich) asks why, Angela says, "I don't know why" and leaves the meeting—implicitly "getting out alive."

The episode fades in to the next morning as Sharon visits to retrieve her copy of *Anne Frank: The Diary of a Young Girl* before school and confronts Angela about quitting yearbook. At school, Angela is hanging with Rayanne and Rickie until the bell rings, then (sheepishly) leaves them to hurry to class—Angela is still torn between her good-girl life as a student and the adventure Rayanne and Rickie seem to represent. As she runs down the hall (in 1996 the natural, "unfeminine" nature of Angela's running seemed liberating), the camera tracks right to reveal a cheerleader crying—a metaphor for the emotional dangers of the phony security of conventional life represented by the annual yearbook and the regularity of the school routine.

An inventive sequence follows, efficiently providing additional information about Brian that balances the information we know about Jordan: jump cuts move us from a science class to a history class to a literature class, by means of Brian's always-raised hand. Each time a teacher calls on him to answer a question, his answer is a response to a question in the next class—it is clear that Brian is the most responsive, virtually the only responsive student, in some of his classes—and the opposite of the seemingly zoned-out Jordan.

In the literature class the topic is *Anne Frank* and even though Angela has told her father she is starting to like the diary, she, like most of the other students in English class, seems bored and distracted. As she stares up at a buzzing fluorescent light, the camera descends toward Angela and we see *Anne Frank* on her desk—the face of Anne looking off the book cover toward Angela as Angela looks up at the off-screen light. When the teacher (the same woman who was in charge of the yearbook meeting the previous day) asks, "So, how would you describe Anne Frank?" Angela says, to herself, but also out loud, "Lucky."

Angela's response surprises not only the teacher and the class, but the viewer—"lucky" seems not only defiant, but crude. When the teacher confronts Angela—"How could you make a statement like that?"—Angela self-consciously scans the stunned classroom (Brian and Sharon seem particularly taken aback), just as Jordan, apparently late for class, arrives. Seeing Jordan, the teacher rolls her eyes and continues, "Anne Frank died in a concentration camp; how could Anne Frank be 'lucky'?" Angela, implicitly defending Jordan and her feelings for him, responds, "I don't know—'cause she was trapped in an attic for three years with this guy she really liked?" Angela is saved by the bell ringing the end of class, and a dissolve takes us to an after-class meeting with the teacher, who is concerned that Angela is "getting off on the wrong foot." When the teacher asks about her decision to drop out of yearbook, Angela's response makes clear how deeply she has thought about the situation:

> It just seems like you agreed to have a certain personality or something. For no reason—just to make things easier for everyone. But when you think about it, I mean how do you know if it's even you?
>
> And I mean this whole thing with yearbook. It's like everybody's in this big hurry to make this book to supposedly remember what happened, but it's not even what really happened, it's just what everybody thinks was supposed to happen. Because if you made a book of what *really* happened, it'd be a really upsetting book.
>
> You know, in *my* humble opinion.

A fade-out is followed by a dissolve in which Angela's face is momentarily superimposed with the canonical cover photograph of Anne Frank, both girls looking off-image in a similar way.

While many viewers, especially older viewers, will react to the comparison of Angela's situation with Anne Frank's in much the same way as Angela's teacher does, the comparison also functions on a deeper level. For some years, one of my few reservations about *My So-Called Life* had to do with what seemed Angela's level of maturity and wisdom, particularly in her voice-over narrations. Could a 15-year-old girl really articulate her thoughts this way? However, *Anne Frank* demonstrates that, indeed, a young girl—Anne is a 13-year-old at the beginning of her diary—can think and articulate herself with considerable sophistication, and in particular about the trials and tribulations of being a teenager. Relatively little in Anne Frank's diary addresses the larger political situation that has entrapped her family: she is focused on her relationships with parents and especially later in the diary, with Peter—just as Angela is less concerned with what might seem larger societal and historical issues, than with the relationships within her immediate surround. At times, in fact, Anne's diary entries sound a good bit like Angela's voice-overs—for example, in her entry of Tuesday, March 28, 1944:

I'm in a very difficult position. Mummy is against me and I'm against her. Daddy closes his eyes and tries not to see the silent battle between us. Mummy is sad, because she does really love me, while I'm not in the least bit sad, because I don't think she understands. And Peter—I don't want to give Peter up, he's such a darling. I admire him so; it can grow into something beautiful between us; why do the 'old 'uns' have to poke their noses in all the time? Luckily, I'm quite used to hiding my feelings and I manage extremely well not to let them see how mad I am about him. Will he ever say anything? Will I ever feel his cheek against mine?

A transition to the evening after Angela meets with her teacher shows her reconnecting with her father—her mentioning to Graham that her school's version of "chili con carne" has no "carne" provides an opportunity for subtly critiquing the education offered by the school (there seems little "meat" in many of the classes we see) and for the father and daughter to share both affection and knowledge—presumably Angela's way of distracting herself from the embarrassment she has felt in class. Their subsequent conversation about Angela's tense relationship with her mother sets the stage for what will be the first of several lies that Angela uses during the pilot episode to free herself from her parents' control. She pretends that she's getting together with other students to do extra-credit school work, when in fact she is going to a party where she hopes to meet up with Rayanne and Jordan Catalano.

A quick transition reveals Angela arriving at the party, where she sees Rayanne at a distance, drinking and dancing, then gets knocked to the ground and into a puddle by an out-of-control boy who jumps off the stage of the performing rock band. Soaked and muddy, Angela goes inside, presumably to clean up, and finds herself in a room where Jordan is also escaping the party, watching a muted music video—the Divinyls' "I Touch Myself"—on television.[1] They have a minimal conversation—Jordan is unclear what day it is—after which he leaves the party with friends. A jump-cut returns us to Angela's parents who are arguing over Graham's refusal to be a disciplinarian with Angela, when Angela returns home. Angela's second lie assures them that nothing happened.

A fade-in on the following day to a cafeteria sequence, filmed, as Angela's voice-over suggests, like a scene from a prison film; once again, we see Brian Krakow, briefly, being bullied. Rayanne tells Angela about the club Let's Bolt, where she assures Angela that Jordan will be that night. In the evening, Patty attempts to interest the family in ice-skating and Angela explains that she plans to spend the night at Rayanne's house and Rickie's cousin will drive her there. Patty and Angela argue about Rayanne and Rickie, but within the confusion of the moment (it is clear that Patty is not sure Graham's claim that he is going out to see his brother is true, and Danielle is vying for attention) Angela convinces her parents that Rayanne's mother will be present and leaves for the evening.

The final climactic sequence begins with Angela hiding outside the Chase home, where she changes into a "tougher," more adult black dress—and waits to be picked up. Brian, who we now learn is Angela's neighbor, is riding around on a small bike; he sees what's happening and argues against her plans: "You're breaking like fourteen different laws!" When Brian tells her that her "adult" plans are "a stupid act," Angela responds, "Everybody's an act, including you"—as the car pulls up and Angela gets in. The juxtaposition of Brian on his bicycle and Angela getting into what looks like an old Cadillac confirms the transitional moment that Brian is resisting and Angela is embracing.

Outside Let's Bolt, Angela, Rayanne, and Rickie await Tino, who will, Rayanne claims, get them in. They are drinking, and to pass the time, Rickie asks the girls, "If you were about to do it, okay? What would you want the other person to say, like right before?" Rayanne: "This won't take long!" Rickie: "No, seriously!" Rayanne: "Don't I know you?" Rickie: "No, for real, like, like *romantic*." Angela, building on her observation about Jordan early in the episode, responds, "You're *so beautiful*, it hurts to look at you"; and Rickie, fully connecting with Angela for the first time, responds, "How'd you think of that? I really *like* that."

Rayanne, in reaction to this new connection and perhaps feeling awkward about not taking sex seriously, romantically, runs drunkenly into the parking lot, followed by the others, where she bumps into an older boy (Shane Powers), who offers to take the girls (and only the girls) for a ride. The older boy, seeing that Rayanne is interested and feeling his power, orders her to come over to him, which she does (all the while pretending she's not taking orders). The boy grabs Rayanne and, slamming her against the car, begins to molest her. Angela, momentarily stunned, says in voice-over: "Something was actually happening. But it was *too* actual"—and comes to Rayanne's rescue. Claiming that she can take care of herself, Rayanne throws her whiskey bottle at the boy, and when he moves to attack her, a cop (Cameron Arnett) arrives, sending the boy and his friend on their way; seeing the cop, Rickie tells Angela that Rayanne won't remember all this in the morning, and disappears. The cop escorts Rayanne and Angela into his police car—just as Jordan arrives at the club and, recognizing Angela, calls to her as the cop closes the car door. The cop drives Rayanne home, and, just before she gets out of the car, she tells Angela, "I'll always watch out for you; I'll always be there for you, so don't worry, okay? And you know, with your hair like that, it hurts to look at you."

Within the dialogue for the pilot, Winnie Holzman embeds what might be called "rhymes" that create a sense of conceptual continuity within the episode. One of the two most obvious is this play on the idea of things being painful to look at, which functions on several levels. At first, it refers only to how Jordan Catalano's somewhat wistful stance affects Angela's romantic sense of who he is; then, later, when Patty says it's "hard to look at" the stranger Angela is becoming, the idea represents the difficulty of facing changes in those we love. When Angela elaborates the phrase at Let's Bolt, it suggests both Angela's dream of romance with Jordan *and* the fact that, as becomes obvious just moments later, desire, particularly sexual desire, can "hurt" in very different ways: it can be the longing for romantic possibility, but also a source of danger, violence, pain, and oppression (Rickie leaves because he knows, apparently from experience, that cops can pose a danger to gay boys). And finally, Rayanne's repeating the phrase in relation to Angela's new hair color confirms that what has seemed Rayanne's toughness and nonchalant cynicism, especially about sex, hides a psyche that is fragile, unsure of the nature of its own sexuality, and lonely. Angela's voice-over indicates that no one was home at the elegant house where Rayanne and her mother live—no father has yet been mentioned.

As the cop and Angela arrive in her neighborhood, they are talking about *Anne Frank*. The cop hasn't read it, but here, Angela's excitement about the book is obvious, though it is clear that her excitement goes beyond what she had said, somewhat defiantly, in class. She explains, "See, the Nazis were going to kill her, so whatever she'd been like with her friends, or her teachers—well, that was just over. She was hiding, but in this other way, she *wasn't*; she'd like *stopped* hiding. She was free!" The cop drops Angela off near her home, where Brian (perhaps waiting for her return) is in a tree, reading. When the cop asks him, "Are you a friend of hers? Then act like it," Brian closes his book and drops down from the tree (his ivory tower) and faces the cop, who tells him, "Watch out for her"—echoing what Rayanne has said moments ago, though Rayanne's drunkenness makes her promise to "always watch out" for Angela at best ironic.

The cop drives off and Brian and Angela have a brief conversation that reflects their differences, but also the fact that both of them are dealing with painful transitions:

> Brian: Right, like you're not going to tell me what happened. Chase!
> Angela: These guys started hitting on us.
> Brian: What, like sexual harassment?
> Angela: Like guys.
> Brian: So they picked a theme. For yearbook.
> Angela: Who told you I liked Jordan Catalano?
> Brian: Nobody. So do you?

There's a pause as Angela has noticed something offscreen, then we (and Brian) see that Angela is looking at Graham and a young woman deep in serious conversation on the darkened street. At this moment, the R.E.M. song, "Everybody Hurts" begins to play—the song is simultaneously appropriate in complex ways and, in its interruption of the pilot's musical form (this is the first recycled musical bit, and it plays complete during the following sequence), it represents both a crucial interruption in the smooth continuity of Angela's previous life, as well as an even more personal climactic moment in Angela's now-growing recognition that looking at life's realities, especially those around passion and sex, can hurt.

The R.E.M. song also refers to Brian. In the brief conversation before Angela's new discovery, it is clear that he is taking the cop's request seriously: he can't watch out for Angela if he doesn't know what's going on, though when Angela tells him about the guys hitting on her and Rayanne, he sees it from within the intellectual concept of "sexual harassment"—something he has presumably heard about in school, without recognizing its living embodiment. Angela's response, "Like guys," suggests that she sees the danger of sexual harassment as far more ordinary than Brian does, and in his sudden self-consciousness (Brian would never sexually harass anyone—is he not a "guy"?), he returns to the moment before Angela began being pro-active about her freedom from convention: he tells her about the yearbook's banal theme. Yet Angela's question about who told Brian about her feelings for Jordan, and Brian's "Nobody!" confirms to us (and perhaps reveals to Angela) that Brian has an awareness about her that, at this point, only Rayanne shares.

As Angela and Brian walk a different route to the Chase home, Brian, to make conversation (perhaps to distract Angela from her thoughts about her father), says, "It's the year 2000—that's the theme, just what it'll be like." Realizing how trivial this is to bring up, he looks troubled, and apologetically says, "Angela..." (the first time he's not called her by the more formal "Chase"), and Angela responds, "I gotta go." The final shot of the sequence is a formally dramatic long shot of the misty, moonlit street with trees arcing overhead; Angela stands on the left, Brian on the right. Angela turns to say, "That's a pathetic theme," and Brian responds, "I know," and as Angela walks out of the frame, leaving Brian alone, a red stoplight (it could be the brake lights of a distant car) blinks on, just as a subtle dissolve places Brian more fully in the center of the shot, alone—as the R.E.M. song continues. The body of the pilot episode begins with Angela's introduction of Jordan, and it closes with Brian stopped at least for the moment from becoming emotionally closer to Angela—then with Angela's return home.

Angela quietly enters the house and climbs the stairs—without turning out the lights. Turning out the lights is a topic during an early scene, when Angela explains to Graham that Danielle is afraid of the dark and is the one who leaves the lights on. Has Angela's discovery of her father's involvement made her momentarily "afraid of the dark"? Is she leaving the lights on for Graham? Angela sneaks to her bedroom, removes her lipstick, and hides the sexy dress, then, after sitting alone with her thoughts, walks to her parents' bedroom. As "Everybody Hurts" dissolves to music more consistent with the rest of the pilot, we see Patty, who (like Brian) has presumably been waiting for Angela, and Graham.

Patty Chase has been the butt of Angela's frustration throughout the episode, but Angela's sudden doses of reality now allow her to empathize with what her mother would feel if she knew where her daughter has been and where husband actually is. When Patty asks how she got home, Angela tells her final lie, that Rayanne's mom brought her home, then in a return to voice-over, Angela thinks, "My mother's adopted. For a while she was looking for her real parents. I guess that's what everyone's looking for." The television is on, revealing a moment with George Bailey and his daughter in *It's a Wonderful Life*, implicitly a moment from the innocent past Angela is leaving behind, just as the erotic woman in the Divinyls music video Jordan is watching at the party suggests the new life Angela longs for. Angela's heartfelt apology for being rebellious and changing her appearance follows.

Patty, moved by Angela's sudden, surprising show of regret and affection, embraces her, and tells Angela that her hair will of course grow out, and that actually it "doesn't look all that bad—in my humble opinion." The repetition of "in my humble opinion" is powerful, not only because this scene is so well-acted, but because it makes clear both that Patty is resilient and honest with herself (as we viewers know, Angela looks fantastic in the new hair color!) and that Angela's rebelliousness toward her parents has incorporated both her father's frustrated longing for excitement *and* her mother's honesty and integrity. It is clear that both daughter and mother are poised in a transitional space: further changes seem to loom in both their lives. The care and subtlety evident in the use of "in my humble opinion" (the implicit assumption that we viewers will notice the repetition of the phrase and understand its various implications) is a powerful demonstration that *this* series will repay a kind of attention that viewers are rarely asked to give a dramatic television series, especially about young people.

In forty-eight minutes, the pilot episode has created a complex world, full of evolving relationships that form the context for Angela's move toward adulthood—a world that's presented with the care and subtlety we expect of serious literature and cinema. Angela is no longer hiding in a child's make-believe world. Ironically, the wild enthusiasm Rayanne reveals the next morning at school about the exciting "time" she, Angela, and Rickie had at Let's Bolt is her way of hiding the sad reality of her loneliness and what we suspect her emotionally empty sex life must be like. Of course, on one level Angela too is still hiding. Her lies to her parents hide the truth of what is going on in her life; but at the same time, her skill at learning to lie (each time we see Angela lie, she seems more comfortable with it, more *effective*) is, ironically, helping her move into a new, more adult, more authentic life.

Historical Contexts
For well over a century the United States has been fixated on adolescent life and transition. This fixation has been explored in literary works, in feature films, and, during recent decades, on television. Indeed, some of the most treasured artifacts of American culture focus on this particular period of transformation. Ernest Hemingway once famously claimed, "All modern American literature comes from one book by Mark Twain called *Huckleberry Finn*" (*Green Hills of Africa*, 1935). Presumably Hemingway meant that the American vernacular of Huck's narration was a crucial influence in the development of an *American* literature (as opposed to a literature in British English). He may also have meant that the essential subject of *Huckleberry Finn*—Huck's discovery of the pain and struggle underneath the conventional façade of the adult world (in this case, racism in particular)—is a, if not *the*, topic of much of modern American literature. Both meanings seem relevant to *My So-Called Life*: in the second paragraph of the Twain novel, Huck explains his current state of mind: "The Widow Douglas, she took me for her son, and allowed she would sivilize me; but it was rough living in the house all the time, considering how dismal regular and decent the widow was in all her ways; and so when I couldn't stand it no longer, I lit out. I got into my old rags, and my sugar-hogshead again, and was free and satisfied." Like Angela, Huck *bolts*.

Of course, when Hemingway canonized *Huckleberry Finn*, he was considering the American literature that had formed the context for his own development. His friendship with Gertrude Stein and his support of her fiction, particularly her *Three Lives* (1906) and *The Making of Americans* (1911), confirmed his commitment to the American vernacular; and his admiration for the early stories of Sherwood Anderson, and *Winesburg, Ohio* (1919) in particular, helped Hemingway understand that an adolescent boy's exploration of his small-town neighborhood's seemingly happy surroundings and his own secret desires could sustain serious literature. George Willard and the other adolescents in *Winesburg, Ohio*, struggle with many of the same issues as the young people in *My So-Called Life*, as does Nick Adams, the protagonist of the first five full-length stories in *In Our Time* (1925; the book intercuts between brief sketches and longer stories): "Indian Camp," "The Doctor and the Doctor's Wife," "The End of Something," "The Three-Day Blow," and "The Battler." The depiction of adolescents in *Winesburg, Ohio* is often poignant and romantic in much the way *My So-Called Life* is, whereas the Nick Adams adolescent saga is often shocking and generally stark.[2]

Salinger's *The Catcher in the Rye* seems more obviously, perhaps more consciously, in the background of *My So-Called Life*.[3] Holden Caufield's alienation from the privileged life that surrounds him is more relentless than Angela's, but when Angela meets with her English teacher after class during the brief moment the teacher has to eat her lunch, Angela, in voice-over, comments, "Seeing your teacher's actual lunch is like so depressing, not to mention her bra strap," it is hard not to hear an echo of Holden's visit (also in an early chapter of that narrative) to visit his teacher, "old Spencer": "He was reading the *Atlantic Monthly*, and there were pills and medicine all over the place, and everything smelled like Vicks Nose Drops. It was pretty depressing"; "old Spencer had on this very sad, ratty old bathrobe that he was probably born in or something." Of course, Holden is more acerbic than Angela and more deeply troubled, but there seems little question that the Salinger novel is in the background of *My So-Called Life*, as Nick Adams is in the background of Holden.

The theme of young adolescent girls finding their way into the underside of their comfortable worlds is also common in American feature films, from Nicholas Ray's *Rebel without a Cause* (1955—during episode 15 of *My So-Called Life*, Rayanne compares Rickie to Sal Mineo, who plays a comparable role in the Ray film), to Delmer Daves' *A Summer Place* (1959) and Elia Kazan's *Splendor in the Grass* (1961), to Terrence Malick's *Badlands* (1973) and *Days of Heaven* (1978), the John Hughes comedies with Molly Ringwald—*Sixteen Candles* (1984), *The Breakfast Club* (1985), and *Pretty in Pink* (1986)—and *Dirty Dancing* (directed by Emile Ardolino, 1987). Each of these films intersects in one way or another with *My So-Called Life*—*Rebel without a Cause* also focuses on a triad of teens rebelling against conformity, for example, and *Days of Heaven* uses an adolescent narrator who speaks in the American vernacular—though in each film the experience of adolescence is envisioned differently.

There is also Richard Linklater's widely admired *Dazed and Confused*, released in 1993, just as the writing and shooting of *My So-Called Life* was getting underway. The Linklater feature focuses more on boys than on girls, though it is like *My So-Called Life* in its creation of a group of students just entering high school whose lives are intersecting—and Jordan Catalano and his red car, might have driven right out of *Dazed and Confused*, though, ironically, Jordan seems more thoughtful and inward than any of the boys in the Linklater film. *Dazed and Confused* differs from *My So-Called Life* in that the events portrayed, though dramatized and filmed in 1993, supposedly take place on the last day of school in 1976. Linklater's nostalgic and comedic/mythic look at his high school years in Huntsville, Texas, foregrounds the drinking and pot smoking that were more commonplace, and somewhat more open among young people during that period. The raucousness of *Dazed and Confused* is closer to the family and high school scenes that open John Waters' *Female Trouble* (1974) than to *My So-Called Life*—indeed, the rebellious kids in *My So-Called Life* seem relatively conservative by comparison.

And of course, there is Amy Heckerling's remarkable feature, *Clueless* (1995), also completed during the same moment when *My So-Called Life* was being produced. In addition to the considerable insight into American adolescence that Heckerling and Winnie Holzman share, there is something in the spirit of the two projects that allows them to seem like complementary visions of American youth at a certain moment in history (to some extent, that spirit is a function of what seemed, at the time, an unusual range and use of music in a television series).[4]

There are obvious differences: like *Dazed and Confused*, *Clueless* is a comedy; *My So-Called Life*, a drama (though with frequent comedic moments); and the difference between Angela's middle-class family and Cher's wealthy widower-father is quite clear. Further, Cherilyn Horowitz, the protagonist of *Clueless*, is very different from Angela Chase—indeed, just the sort of girl Angela would not like. There are equally obvious similarities: for example, as in *My So-Called Life*, the adolescent protagonist in *Clueless* is both character and voice-over; and, more importantly, both Angela and Cher are, at base, deeply thoughtful girls, able to empathize and change—ultimately leaders within their own adolescent communities. In *Clueless* Cher is frequently satirized (she is often as "clueless" as anyone else in the film), but in some later episodes of the television series (episode 16, for example), Angela seems rather clueless herself.

The same historical moment that saw the release of *My So-Called Life* and *Clueless* also saw the completion of two independent films, both by women, that focus on the realities of adolescent life as experienced by female protagonists. Su Friedrich's *Hide and Seek* (1996) focuses on 12-year-old Lou, who is realizing that she is different from most of her friends and trying to make sense of what we can see is her incipient lesbianism. A bit younger than Angela, and without Angela's capacity for articulating her feelings, Lou struggles with her desire for her closest girlfriend who, to Lou's horror, is taking an interest in earrings and boys. In *Hide and Seek*, the several episodes from Lou's life are intercut with interviews with the memories of now-adult lesbians who, with considerable good humor, recall their own struggles in finding themselves during an era when being gay was considered unacceptable. Friedrich's *Sink or Swim* (1990), her formalist autobiographical film about her relationship with her father, also seems relevant here—and a premonition of Alison Bechdel's graphic novel and now Broadway play, *Fun Home* (2006).

In 1996 Jennifer Todd Reeves completed her short narrative, *Chronic*—like Friedrich's *Sink or Swim*, based on her own experiences as a young teen. Raped by several men at a college fraternity party, her protagonist Gretchen (played by Reeves herself) develops the habit of mutilating herself by cutting her skin with razor blades. In time Gretchen enters a mental hospital where she lives for two years, becoming part of a small community and achieving enough control over her obsessive behavior to leave the hospital. Soon after Gretchen learns that a close friend from the hospital has killed herself, we see her in a bathtub, possibly returning to self-mutilation or even committing suicide. However, while the ending of *Chronic* is at best ambiguous, Reeves' presentation of Gretchen's story, specifically the nature of her narrator, who speaks in the first person but is clearly neither family member nor friend, makes clear that, though Gretchen's experiences are not precisely Reeves', Gretchen is a *version* of Reeves at a certain moment in her adolescence (not only does Reeves play Gretchen in the film, but "Gretchen's" home movies and childhood photographs are Reeves' own)—and that Reeves herself has learned to redirect her personal demons into the production of the formally accomplished film we are watching.

Finally, more recently, there are photographer/filmmaker Sharon Lockhart's Pine Flat project, a collection of photographs and a feature film, *Pine Flat* (2006), focusing on adolescent boys and girls living in the Sierra Nevada mountains in California; and Richard Linklater's *Boyhood* (2015). *Pine Flat* is made up of twelve ten-minute-long shots, each focusing on an aspect of the lives of the boys and girls, seen within the landscape around them. More meditation than revelation, *Pine Flat* shares with *My So-Called Life* a feeling for the beauty of the moment before adulthood transforms American young people into citizens functioning within the general hysteria of modern life. *Boyhood* focuses on the evolution of a boy, Mason (Ellar Coltrane), over a period of twelve years (the film was shot from 2002 to 2013), but Mason's sister Samantha, played by Linklater's daughter Lorelei, is nearly as central to the film as her brother. I know of no film that captures the continuity of personality through the physical and psychic changes from childhood to adolescence, at least for boys, as skillfully as *Boyhood*.

American television has also been devoted to the onset of adolescence as a subject. In fact, shows focusing on young people are too many to name. Several series, however, seem particularly relevant to *My So-Called Life*. *Life Goes On*, for example, aired, also on ABC, from September 12, 1989 until May 23, 1993. Like the series it immediately predated, *Life Goes On* sometimes intercuts between the activities of a middle-class family and events in school, where a young adolescent girl, Becca (Kellie Martin) and her brother Corky (Chris Burke) deal with the usual school and social issues. Corky, who has Down Syndrome (and is played by an actor with Down Syndrome), is bullied at school and seems a premonition of Rickie in *My So-Called Life*; by his own account, Wilson Cruz's life, presumably like Burke's, was the basis for many of the events dramatized in the later series.

Whereas the relatively short life of *My So-Called Life* allowed the producers to keep the focus primarily on Angela Chase, during the 83 episodes of *Life Goes On* the general focus changed from Corky to Becca. *Life Goes On* is formally and stylistically typical of television series focusing on families during the 1970s and 80s, though it often dealt with significant issues. Corky's Down Syndrome made him a very unusual television protagonist, and in some episodes Corky was contextualized by other Down Syndrome characters/actors: the episode where

Corky meets Amanda (who he will later marry—she's played by Andrea Friedman) includes appearances by High Hopes, an accomplished Down Syndrome music group. During later seasons, episodes of the show focused on Becca's relationship with Jesse (Chad Lowe) who was HIV positive.

The producers, writers, and actors in *Life Goes On* deserve considerable credit for having the courage and tenacity to explore difficult topics—and indeed, the show's focus on Down Syndrome may have made a difference in the real lives of families. For all its accomplishments, however, *Life Goes On* lacks the subtlety and density, the formal inventiveness and psychological complexity of *My So-Called Life*—episodes often feel, to use the current vernacular, "cheesy": that is, both predictable and simplistic in their demand for maudlin emotional response. *Life Goes On* seems a later version of an earlier form of television melodrama that does, to its credit, tackle some unusually difficult topics. *My So-Called Life* seems a new kind of melodrama, a premonition of something innovative in television viewing. There is also the long-running, and to some extent contemporaneous *Beverly Hills 90210*. Created by Darren Star, Aaron Spelling, and E. Duke Vincent, *Beverly Hills 90210* premiered on Fox on October 4, 1990. From its opening moments, when Brandon and Brenda Walsh arrive for the first day of school at West Beverly Hills High School—their family has moved to Beverly Hills from Minneapolis—it is clear that *Beverly Hills 90210* is virtually the inverse of *My So-Called Life*: a slick, "glamorous," generally facile soap opera with little of the subtlety, poignancy or gravitas of the later series.

Of all the series devoted to youth, however, the one that seems most closely related to *My So-Called Life*, indeed in some ways an inspiration for it, is *The Wonder Years*, which ran on ABC for six seasons (115 episodes) from 1988 until 1993—concluding just before *My So-Called Life* went into production. Certainly there are significant differences between the two series. Most obviously, *The Wonder Years* is a half-hour sitcom, rather than an hour-long melodrama; and its protagonist is not a young girl growing up in the then present, but a young boy looking back twenty years on his years growing up during the late 1960s and early 70s: episodes during the first series begin with a montage of film images from that earlier time, in order to situate the viewer within the general social and political volatility of that earlier time period (the opening of episode 3 of *My So-Called Life* begins with shots of JFK's inauguration, being shown in class, in a way that recalls—perhaps consciously?—the *The Wonder Years* opening).

There are also significant similarities between the two series. In each, the central protagonist functions as both character within events and as a narrator who comments on various specifics and at times makes general philosophical observations. Claire Danes narrates Angela's comments, but since the events of *The Wonder Years* take place in retrospect, the voice of Kevin Arnold, looking back twenty years at his adolescence, is spoken not by Fred Savage who plays Kevin (at the time Savage's actual voice was still very much a young boy's), but by the adult Daniel Stern. The decision to have Claire Danes narrate *My So-Called Life* creates a level of intimacy, whereas the narration in *The Wonder Years* often creates an ironic detachment between then and now—an ongoing part of the series' wry humor. Nevertheless, the narrations do have a similar impact, both in the general sense that they represent an approach to storytelling on television that was, and remains, distinct, and because these narrations are often remarkably engaging and insightful. The implicit "narration" supplied by the use of music in both series is also similar, not just in the general sense that the music is used effectively, but because both films incorporate popular rock songs and musical interludes by W. G. Snuffy Walden, who won a BMI TV Music Award in 1988, 1989, and 1990 for *The Wonder Years*.

Despite the difference between the melodrama of *My So-Called Life* and the comedy of *The Wonder Years*, the two series have much in common. The poignancy of the best episodes of *My So-Called Life* is, if not comic, at least upbeat: the final minute of the pilot, where Angela reunites with Rayanne and Rickie after the near trauma of the night before, makes clear that, while the series will deal with serious issues, it will include both "tear" and "smile," as Chaplin put it in his famous introductory text to *The Kid* (1921). The general humor of the pilot of *The Wonder Years*—much of it supplied by the witty comments of the adult Kevin Arnold about his younger self—is made poignant by the sudden, surprising discovery near the end of the episode that Kevin's neighbor Brian, the older brother of his friend Winnie Cooper (Danica McKellar), has been killed in Vietnam: again, "smile" and "tear" (Brian's funeral opens the second episode). At times, because of their similar combination of humor and pathos, and the density of what they can accomplish in limited time, particular episodes of the two series have almost identical power: compare the *My So-Called Life* pilot with the density and power of the third episode of *The Wonder Years*, "My Father's Office."

I have not mentioned the Canadian series, *Degrassi High*, which was broadcast on CBC Television from November 1989 until January 1991. This series is especially interesting when compared/contrasted with *My So-Called Life*: it helps put the American series into a broader context, and is useful in defining its limitations and particular power. See the final section of this study.

Episodes 2 to 8
Once it seemed clear that *My So-Called Life* would be broadcast, the collaborators began fleshing out the implications of the characters introduced in the pilot, the storylines hinted at, and the elements of style and narrative structure that would come to characterize the series. The pilot develops several conflicts between characters that are picked up in subsequent episodes and are resolved—or if not resolved, transformed—by the conclusion of episode 8. The two most obvious conflicts, of course, are the gap between Angela and Sharon Cherski created by Angela's new friendship with Rayanne and Rickie; and the even more significant distance between Angela and her father, caused first by her development from child into adolescent and, more dramatically, by Angela's discovery of her father with a younger woman. At the conclusion of episode 2, "Dancing in the Dark," Angela comes downstairs and discovers her father, again in passionate and secret conversation, presumably with this woman. What Angela doesn't know is that there is a struggle going on between Graham and the woman; we know Graham has phoned the young woman to tell her he "can't do it"—that is, can't continue with this relationship. For us, Graham is, for the moment, in the clear; for Angela he has confirmed that he is untrustworthy and endangering their family.

The father-daughter conflict is not a factor in episode 3, which is focused more fully on Angela's school life, and on Rickie's struggles—though Angela's committing to her friendship with Rickie could be read as a substitute for her now problematic relationship with Graham, just as Graham's budding relationship with the young woman can be read as his attempt to replace the relationship with Angela that he feels he is losing. But the father-daughter relationship is central to episode 4, "Father Figures." In an attempt to confront Angela's coldness, Graham becomes friendly with Rayanne, sharing his love of cooking with her—and offering the girls two tickets to a Grateful Dead concert. Angela's decision to sell the tickets, at Jordan's suggestion, so that she can repay Jordan for her out-of-state driver's license (episode 2), is clearly a rejection of her father, though it also creates a rift between Angela and Rayanne. Ultimately, Angela tells Rayanne about her father's involvement with the young woman, to which Rayanne, whose father is long gone, responds: "my dad's had, like, eight different girlfriends since he left, so I'm used to it"—though we understand that her excitement to have gotten to know Graham and to have been given his ticket to the Dead is a function of her not being comfortable with her own situation and her envy of Angela's.

The conflict between Angela and Graham is finally resolved in episode 6, when Angela meets a teacher who, she tells her parents, is finally an adult she can look up to. Angela's admiration of Victor Racine is ultimately undercut by her discovery that he is on-the-run from his obligation to pay child support to the family he has abandoned. However, Racine's passionate teaching has inspired Angela to commit to an issue that goes beyond her personal problems with family and friends: she breaks Liberty High rules by publishing the *Liberty Lit*, the school's literary magazine, which has been censored by the principal. Just before Angela and her parents go into Mr. Foster's office to see what punishment Angela will receive, Graham assures Angela that there is absolutely no possibility that he will leave their family. Judging from subsequent episodes, Angela accepts what her father says (it is not clear whether she assumes her father is no longer involved with the young woman), since the rift between them that was created in the pilot is no longer in evidence.

The conflicts between Angela and Sharon, and between Sharon and Rayanne, take longer to resolve, though it is obvious, early on, that they will be resolved. It is evident, even in the pilot, that Angela and Sharon do still care deeply about each other, and during subsequent episodes—particularly in "The Substitute," Rayanne and Sharon bond over Sharon's sexy haiku, the cause of Mr. Foster's suppression of the *Liberty Lit* issue. Angela's friendship with Sharon is the topic of the culminating episode of the first wave of the series, episode 8, "Strangers in the House." The conflict between Angela and Sharon is brought to a head when Sharon's father has a heart attack and neither Sharon nor Angela can figure out how to deal with this situation or with each other. Once the danger is past, they come to terms with the fact that while they and their relationship are changing, they remain committed as friends. Throughout this episode Patty and Sharon's mother Camille (Mary Kay Place) are preparing to participate, as they have for years, in the mother-daughter fashion show—something Angela doesn't want to do. In the culminating sequence in this first wave of episodes, Angela, Rayanne and Rickie, and Graham, enjoy the fashion show, which includes Sharon and Camille, and Patty and Danielle. At this point, the narratives initiated by the pilot have all been, at least for the moment, resolved.

Episodes 2 to 8 also establish patterns of narrative structure and a range of stylistic motifs. Episode 2, "Dancing in the Dark" (like the pilot, written by Holzman and directed by Winant) develops the relatively conventional plot structure that is typical of the series: despite the inevitable conflicts between Angela and her friends and student colleagues and between the adolescents and the adults they come in contact with at home and at school, the episode is structured around parallel developments occurring, in this instance, within the lives of the kids and the adults. The title of the episode refers literally to the attempt by Patty and Graham to reinvigorate their marriage by taking up ballroom dancing, but also implies the "dance" between Angela and Jordan Catalano masterminded by Rayanne, who brings the two together, supposedly so that Jordan can supply Angela with an out-of-state driving license. It also suggests the "dance" between Angela, Rayanne, and Rickie (especially their contempt for schoolwork) and Angela's longtime neighbor, Brian, who is an obsessively good student.

The intercutting that structures the episode makes clear that while the adults and the adolescents are at different moments in their lives, these different moments are characterized by similar anxieties about romantic relationships. The two storylines do end somewhat differently—Patty and Graham ultimately overcome, at least for the moment, the anger and embarrassment they have felt when they discover that they cannot dance together, whereas Angela's first real contact with Jordan leads to Angela's anger, embarrassment and confusion, after Jordan, seeing Angela as just another typically too-talkative girl, presumptively kisses her in his car after giving her the fake ID (the episode opens with Angela's review of several previous kisses, all of which happened by mutual consent).

Early in the episode we see Angela and Brian working next to each other in biology class where the teacher is talking about the nature of experimentation. At the end of "Dancing in the Dark," the "experiments" in both plotlines conclude ironically. Back home, Angela overhears her father talking on the phone to the woman she has seen him with in the pilot; and Brian discovers that Angela has dropped her new ID outside his home and is the first to notice that the ID is useless since the dates on it indicate that Angela was "born yesterday"! The ballroom dancing and the ID, are or seem, at least for the moment, to have been failures—though here too there are ironies. Despite the embarrassments in dancing class, Graham seems to have committed to his marriage, even though his daughter presumes he is still involved with the younger woman; and Angela has in fact been alone with Jordan for the first time, the original goal of the request for the fake ID—though their rendezvous in Jordan's car has not worked out as she might have wished.

The heavy use of metaphor is one of several stylistic elements that become typical in the series, though this use of metaphor, as exemplified in "Dancing in the Dark" (or "dancing" in the "dark"), can sometimes seem so obvious as to be corny: the biology experiment the class is conducting involves *hearts, pig* hearts; Brian's extra-credit project involves a mouse and a *pressure* gauge (Brian's focus on Angela and Angela's on Jordan create emotional pressure); and Patty breaks her Cinderella statue, a treasure from childhood, as she is expresses her frustration with her current romantic life. Nevertheless, it seems foolish, even a form of looking a gift horse in the mouth, to complain about a 1990s television drama asking that viewers be alert to metaphor.

Other stylistic elements typical of *My So-Called Life* include the nature of adolescent conversation as depicted by the show, the way in which the characters dress, and a variety of particular visual and auditory motifs. One of the typical distinctions between generations is their speech mannerisms; indeed, adolescents tend to create idiomatic speech habits as a way of walling out the adult world. The adolescents in *My So-Called Life*—and here the series is similar to *Clueless*—have several speech tendencies, which may reflect American diction within the urban area of Pittsburgh, Pennsylvania, where the events supposedly take place, but certainly do become recognizable within the series where they often function as humor, sometimes as a kind of poetic rhythm, and sometimes both.[5] One of the most obvious of these tendencies is the use of "*What*!?" simultaneously as question and dramatic emphasis. When one of the characters senses that another is looking askance at her/him, "*What*!?" is the inevitable response—and while the young people of the series are particularly prone to his response, the adults sometimes use it as well, though in most cases the adult use of "*What*!?" is less emphatic and tends to suggest guilt, rather than an impatient, self-defensive response.

Other frequently used speech mannerisms include the interruptive use of "like," and the termination of sentences with "or something" and "or whatever."[6] In episode 4, "Father Figures," five different characters, all of them younger, use the interruptive "like" a total of ten times. Early on, as Rayanne, Angela, and Graham are cooking in the kitchen, Rayanne says, "I can't believe I am cooking something, like, not in a pouch," and a moment later, when talking about her mother's devotion to the Grateful Dead, "Before she had me, she lived in a bus for, like, months, with a girl named Pop Tart." The next day, when Rickie is talking about his meeting Graham the previous evening, he explains to Angela and Rayanne that "when I was leaving, he was there and I was, like, well, 'hi,' and he was, like, well, 'hi,' and I was, like, 'bye,' and he was, like, well…" before he is interrupted by Rayanne. That evening, Danielle, talking on the phone, tells a caller that "Mom's been on the phone, like, forever," and when Angela hides out in the Krakow family car, Brian asks her, "Are you, like, meeting someone in here?" The frequent use of "like" by adolescents is typical of the series and has subtly different emphases in different contexts. Still another vocal mannerism, consistent throughout the series, is the use of "Gotta go!" or "I've gotta go"—often used quite abruptly—when one character leaves another.

Often, the various vocal motifs are combined. In episode 8, for example, when Angela, to Brian's surprise, seems to be taking him seriously and giving him credit for being a friend to Sharon Cherski when she needed one, he responds, "What [here *not* emphasized], did you, like, give this thought, or something?" And the recognition of the vocal motifs on the part of characters evolves: the writers are alert to the way in which adults sometimes incorporate the new speech mannerisms of their children. By episode 14, "On the Wagon," when Rayanne asks Graham, "Do you actually, like, teach people how to cook?" Graham answers, "Yeah, I actually, like, do"—and both get the humor and implications of the interchange.

The ways in which the various characters refer to each other provides other motifs. "Tino" is an important friend, particularly for Rayanne and Jordan—but he is never seen during the nineteen episodes, though he is referred to frequently and often seems to have motivated important events. Jordan is usually "Jordan Catalano"—though Rayanne refers to him by his first name. Angela and Brian often refer to each other as "Chase" and "Krakow," and Sharon is frequently "Cherski." The principal is always "Foster." Only "Vic," the substitute teacher in episode 6, is referred to with affectionate informality.

The self-expression of the adolescents in *My So-Called Life* is evident not only in a range of speech mannerisms, but also in their body language and their dress. Perhaps the most evocative of the bodily gestures in the series is the tendency of characters who are moving away, often down the hallways of Liberty High, to turn and look back, seemingly at someone, but really at the memory of something that has just occurred, as if to assure themselves that what they saw or felt was in fact based in reality or to confirm that a change has indeed occurred. An example of this gesture is the final shot of episode 8, "Strangers in the House." After Angela and Sharon have regenerated their longtime friendship, though within a new and changed social world, they pass and acknowledge each other in a Liberty High hallway, and as the camera follows Angela, Rayanne, and Rickie continuing down the hall, Angela looks back, presumably at the receding Sharon, just as she and her new friends are turning a corner.

In terms of dress, Liberty High School is, for the most part, a grunge world: dress is informal and while particular individuals—especially those who are rebelling against convention, like Rayanne, Rickie, and Angela—dress in relatively distinctive ways, in general they share with their colleagues a love of plaid, presumably flannel shirts. It is also clear that the characters in the series have limited wardrobes, since we see individuals—Angela most obviously—wear some of the same outfits over and over, or at least the same clothing in varied combinations. Indeed, for aficionados of the series, the prevalence of plaid, like the frequency of "like" and "*What?!*" is simultaneously a way of embedding the characters in a particular historical moment *and* a source of humor—implicitly, perhaps, a way of subtly maintaining the fundamentally upbeat quality of the series.

The Substitute
Among the most memorable episodes of *My So-Called Life* is "The Substitute" (episode 6), the only episode of the series that focuses on the excitement of education itself. Most depictions of American teens in high school classrooms, including most such scenes in *My So-Called Life*, suggest that real education is virtually impossible in such a context. During early episodes, the fact that Brian Krakow is the only student who seems committed to his school work and the only one willing to participate in class (Sharon Cherski is the one other character who at least seems attentive) is a comic motif. In "The Substitute," however, Jason Katims and Ellen Pressman, who wrote and directed the episode, invert this motif. The arrival of Victor Racine (Roger Rees) in Angela's English class transforms the usual student routine of merely following directions and waiting for the bell to end class, into something more powerful and engaging—something worth paying attention to. In this episode, the comic implications of Brian's distinctiveness as a student are inverted: Brian is the only student who *cannot* engage the authentically personal, emotionally honest process of learning that "Vic" demands.

On his first day in class, Vic demonstrates his contempt for the students' lack of engagement with their own education, epitomized by the conventionality of the "creative writing" they've been doing in class and for the *Liberty Lit*, by throwing the writing assignments they've done for their previous English teacher—who, we may assume, quit teaching out of frustration—out the window. Vic's commitment as a teacher is particularly evident in his way of dealing with Jordan Catalano, who until this episode has typically been late for class or asleep in class. From the moment when Jordan stands up to leave, once Vic has said the students are in fact free to go, he senses Jordan's unconventional intelligence and willingness to act. Having dissuaded Jordan from leaving (by indicating that, once Jordan is gone, the class will talk about him), Vic goads Jordan into becoming responsive—and soon learns what apparently no other teacher has deduced: that Jordan cannot read.

The montage of classroom scenes that follows Vic's entry into the English class captures something of the pleasure of education and the excitement of learning that all of us who teach, whether at the high school or the college level, hope to inspire. Granted, this sequence is an exaggeration of the educational process—transformative learning rarely happens so quickly or so obviously. Nevertheless, the nature of Vic's personal engagement with the students, his way of inspiring the class to care about what they write and to enjoy the writing accomplishments of their colleagues rings fundamentally true—and creates in the audience for the series something of the excitement that the students and Racine feel.

When, after some time has passed, the now-engaged students are asked to read unsigned poems written by their colleagues, two particular poems are read in their entirety and function within the episode in what seems an unusual way, especially for a television series. The first of the poems is Angela's "A Fable":

> Once upon a time there lived a girl.
> She slept in a lovely little cottage made of gingerbread
>   and candy.
> She was always asleep.
> One morning she woke up, and the candy had mold
>   on it.
> Her father blew her a kiss, and the house fell down.
> She realized she was lost.
> She found herself walking down a crowded street,
>   but the people were made of paper, like paper
>   dolls.
> She blew everyone a kiss good-bye, and watched as
>   they blew away.

That this poem is a poetic transmutation of Angela's experience of learning that her father has a life apart from the family, a life that may be endangering the family, and that this knowledge has transformed her understanding of her own existence and of the "crowded street" of the school hallway, is obvious. But the assumption that viewers can be read a poem in the middle of a melodrama and be expected to understand its implications seems virtually unprecedented. Here is an unusual form of dramatic irony, at least for television: *we* understand this poem in a way that only Angela and Vic do—since the class doesn't know who wrote it and is unaware of the circumstances within which it was written.

The other poem, "Haiku for Him," is by Sharon Cherski:
He peels off my clothes,
    like a starving man would peel an orange.
His lips taste my juicy sweetness.
My legs tangle with his.
We become one being,
    a burning furnace,
        in the cold, cement basement of love.

When Brian refuses to read the entire poem, Vic finishes the reading and asks the class if the poem is actually a haiku. Rayanne immediately jumps in, recognizing that while it isn't formally a haiku, it is honestly expressive and should be included in the *Liberty Lit*. Vic agrees. Again, Katims and Pressman have assumed that viewers will be familiar enough with haiku poetry (later, in case some viewers are not, they have Vic explain to Jordan that in English a haiku is normally a fourteen-syllable poem) to see that Rayanne is aware of both the formal and the "moral" issues Sharon's poem raises.

The reading of "Haiku for Him" motivates the rest of the episode. It becomes an important element in the resolution of the conflict between Sharon and Rayanne (Sharon is terrified that everyone will find out that *she* wrote the poem; Rayanne wants everyone to think the poem is hers): the two girls conspire to maintain that the poem is Rayanne's. More importantly, it instigates a development in Angela that has considerable implications not just for this episode, but for *My So-Called Life* as a whole. The idea that the *Liberty Lit* might, and perhaps should, include a poem that celebrates the sexuality of a sophomore in high school, instigates a confrontation, first between Vic and Patty, whose shop is printing the *Lit*; then (after Vic has convinced her that "if these kids aren't afraid to put their hearts on the page, why should we be afraid of them?") and once the *Lit* is published, between Vic and principal Foster. At first it seems that Foster must have fired Vic — though, as Foster explains to Graham, Vic left, without being fired, once it was clear that Foster had learned of his taking an alias in an attempt to avoid paying child support.

Angela confronts Vic as he is packing to leave, learns that there are several truths (including that he abandoned his family), and that Vic believes she should get out of "that mind-control factory, that warehouse they store you in, because they don't know what else to do with you." Angela refuses the idea that leaving high school is sensible, but the next day, when the rest of the students are back in English class, now being taught by a more conventional teacher, Angela makes copies of the *Lit* and hands it out — causing Foster to call her in for discipline.

When Patty and Graham meet up with Angela to find out what Foster means to do (and Graham makes clear that he would never leave their family), Angela learns a lesson beyond the fact that speech isn't free for high school students. Foster, recognizing that to discipline Angela would be to reinforce her defiance, decides to offer no punishment at all. This appeases the parents, who have been ambivalent about Angela's decision to defy Foster's suppressing the *Lit*, despite their own political activity as young people in the 1960s. Angela's disappointment is obvious, and is reflected by her voice-over reading of much of her poem, now slightly changed, as her parents coddle her after the three leave the principal's office:

> Once upon a time there lived a girl.
> She slept in a lovely little cottage made of gingerbread
>   and candy.
> She was always asleep.
> One morning she woke up.
> She woke up.

That Foster is African American might suggest both his understanding of the value of social action and his realization, evident in episode 3, when he has a public relations problem because of the gun that has gone off in the school, that to exacerbate the situation might cause difficulties in the long run.

If we ask what Angela woke up to in this instance (originally it was clearly to the fragility of her middle-class family life), the new context suggests a new reading of the poem. Foster has said the episode is over, and, since Angela does not make copies of the *Lit* issue again, it is clear that, despite her disappointment at having the principal *not* punish her for doing the right thing despite her breaking the rules, her moment of defiance now seems over. And the visual of her parents coddling her demonstrates that her attempt to move beyond childhood, to *be* adult, has failed—at least for now. Here, what she has awakened to is less that her family life is fragile (that she lives in a gingerbread and candy home) than the fact that her middle-class status is dependent on her not making waves, that it is protected from doing the right thing both by her parents and by the school—essentially by the structure (Vic would call it "the factory") of American education. As the bell rings and Angela blends back into the crowded hallway, she is realizing that she has awakened, a second time, into a new, culture-wide, institutional "gingerbread cottage."

The fact that this is the only episode of *My So-Called Life* where political action is a topic allows Angela's advance and retreat to be read as a metaphor for the television series itself. For all its wonderful acting, engaging action, and formal subtleties, *My So-Called Life* is ultimately safe, in precisely the way that in the 1990s television generally remained. No matter how talented they reveal themselves to be in the nineteen episodes of the show, no matter how fully they have opened their hearts and drawn on their personal experiences in producing the show, the writers and directors of the series can only go so far, or will only allow themselves to go so far. They are compromised by the conventions of television and of American culture, in precisely the way Angela is coddled by her parents and Principal Foster. Angela's act of defiance is a beautiful moment, and *My So-Called Life* is beautiful in ways that no other television series in my memory has been. Nevertheless, like the committed substitute teacher Vic, the creators of "The Substitute" (and of *My So-Called Life* in general) can only provide a momentary escape from the romantic conventions of American television melodrama. *My So-Called Life* has implicitly dramatized its own limitations.

Lyric Television

The most distinctive element of *My So-Called Life*, especially during the first wave of episodes, is the use of lyric moments: visual/auditory flourishes that in one way or another encapsulate an unusual depth and complexity of emotion—the way the two poems in "The Substitute" encapsulate Angela's and Sharon's emotional states.

The first of these lyric flourishes concludes the pilot, following Angela's apology to her mother. Though her apology reflects her disappointment with her father's apparent relationship with the young woman and her new empathy for her mother (as well as the frightening events that happened earlier in the parking lot of Let's Bolt and the sobering discovery of Rayanne's lonely home), the focus of the pilot remains Angela's breakaway from convention, and the brief coda to the episode formally embodies the excitement of her transformation.

A jump cut from the scene in the bedroom (elided by Angela's narration) to the hallway of Liberty High School the next morning delivers the audience to a one-minute montage that not only confirms the "tear" and "smile" nature of the series but also functions as the After to the Before of the pilot's opening montage. We see how far Angela has come in her pursuit of adulthood in only a few days. That the montage begins with the sound of the school bell ringing a change of classes suggests both the wake-up call that the previous evening's events have been and the fact that Angela is now being schooled in ways that had been beyond her imagination.

To the accompaniment of W. G. Snuffy Walden's evocative upbeat score, Angela passes Jordan Catalano in the hallway. He says, "Hi" (for the first time acknowledging her at school) and jokingly asks if she's "out on bail?" Angela smiles and wonders how his weekend was, and Jordan avers that "it sucked." He leans against a locker for a moment, then says, "Gotta go," a final echo, this time of the final line of Angela's conversation with Brian the previous night—though with a different implication: Brian, who is fixated on Angela, is left alone, while Angela sees that Jordan is now including her within his life. Theirs is a minimal conversation, but one in which Jordan has revealed something of himself to Angela and to the audience: whatever we think of Jordan at this point, he can't be accused of pretending that he had a great time when he didn't—it is clear again, as it was at the party Thursday night, that, like Angela, Jordan is not satisfied to fit into the craziness around him; he too is searching for a more authentic experience.

Jordan's leaving is immediately followed by the reunion with Rayanne and Rickie, who are sharing their excitement about the experiences at Let's Bolt (or at least what Rayanne remembers of them), telling anyone who will listen what happened and that "We had a time!" Seeing Angela, Rayanne looks to her for confirmation. As the camera performs a dizzying tracking shot around the group, she asks Angela, "Didn't we have a time?" Smiling at the realization that whatever troubling events happened the previous evening and whatever awaits her in the coming months (and episodes), she is now part of an inner circle of interesting and sophisticated friends with whom she is beginning a more authentic and exciting life, Angela responds, "We did. We had a time." Like Anne Frank, Angela now knows she lives in a dangerous world, but she is making herself free to be with others who, like her, are no longer content to hide from the dangers. Ernest Holzman's camera tracks in for a now slow-motion close-up of Angela, who is glowing—and the episode fades to the credits.

It is a tradition within serial narrative of all kinds (one thinks of Dickens) that each chapter or episode ends with "hook" that is meant to ensure the reading or watching audience's return. What seems unusual about the hook at the end of the pilot of *My So-Called Life* is that it is not a hint of the next exciting events that will occur. Rather, it surprises us formally: the combination of music and complex camera movement (and the switch to slow-motion) is a demonstration that *this* series has a stylistic exuberance that we may want to continue to experience. And the opening of the episode 2 confirms this, with an even more inventive montage, one full of formal surprise.

The 3¼-minute sequence that opens "Dancing in the Dark" (it's the credit sequence for this episode, which was written by Holzman, directed by Winant, and shot, like all of the first eight episodes, by Ernest Holzman, Winnie Holzman's brother) begins in a classroom where a movie about the creation of the solar system is being shown, while Angela, in the rear of the class, is reminiscing about the three times she's been kissed. The sequence then intercuts between the events in the classroom and in the hallway presumably after this class and Angela's memories of the three events. Each transition within the sequence is subtle and imaginative.

The opening shot pans from the movie screen across the classroom, then tracks in on Angela whose mind is clearly elsewhere. A bit of light flickers on her face: at first, we assume it's a reflection from the movie screen, but as the camera moves closer, we see it is not the blue light of the screen, but yellow light, which a dissolve reveals is the campfire in her memory of the first kiss. A camp counselor leads a younger Angela away from the campfire into the dark, and when Angela takes a bite of the toasted marshmallow she is carrying, leaving a bit of the marshmallow on her lower lip, the boy tries to wipe it off with his thumb, then suddenly kisses her. As the kiss ends and the boy pulls away from Angela, a stunningly smooth transition, accomplished (without a visible edit) by a subtle change in lighting and the combined movement of the camera and Angela turning her head, returns Angela, and the viewer, to the classroom where Angela is embarrassed that what she's been thinking about might be visible to others.

The movie about the solar system has continued, and as the visual transition is occurring, we hear its narrator (his voice at first distant, then growing louder) describing how "under enormous pressure the inner core of the star now implodes, violently producing an explosion of unparalleled intensity." The words "unparalleled intensity" are accompanied by a visual of the star exploding, and a quick dissolve jump cuts Angela into the school hallway in front of a brightly lit window. That Angela's first kiss is compared with an explosion of "unparalleled intensity" is amusing, but suggests (as does her nervousness about someone realizing what she's been thinking about) the different "scale" of adolescent life—how a kiss can seem monumentally significant. And the transition itself is so surprising, so accomplished, as to be implicitly self-reflexive—a confirmation of the dexterity of the last tracking shot around Angela, Rayanne, and Rickie and the slow-motion close-up that concludes the pilot and another demonstration of the care and precision that the producers of *My So-Called Life* are bringing to this project.

Each of the three memories in the sequence is accompanied by Angela's voice-over thoughts about the circumstances of the particular kiss, and by a repetition of an extended phrase of Snuffy Walden's score, which (in an interview on the bonus disk of the DVD set) Walden describes as simultaneously helping to set a mood and to add a subtle velocity to what is being seen. Back in the hallway, Angela is still thinking about a second kiss, which occurred at a wedding in Milwaukee two years earlier. As she turns to walk into a classroom, the doorway brightens and she walks into the brightly lit remembered wedding, where we see Angela and a young adolescent boy walking through the wedding reception party into a corner where the boy quickly kisses her, then walks away: "Later, I found out he only kissed me because he had lost a bet." As we see Angela standing, alone, in the corner, framed by decorative flowers, a close-up of Angela's face, in the present, walks into the shot and the wedding scene disappears. Again, the transition is so unusual, so sudden and seamless, that its impact creates in the viewer something of the jolt that Angela's second waking out of her daydream of the past causes her—again, Angela looks around to see if the nature of her thinking has been evident to others.

Angela continues walking, then turns a corner, stops, leans against some lockers, and looking offscreen, remembers the third kiss, "the hardest to describe." In a brief succession of shots—the first, of the school hallway overlit by a distant window; the second, a continuation of the zoom into a close-up of Angela, still looking off-screen, followed by a fast dissolve into a combined image of the overlit hallway and an image from the past, where, in black-and-white silhouette, a lifeguard, presumably carrying Angela (here, no longer looking like a young girl), is walking toward her/us. Throughout this memory, "the most exciting" of the kisses, the imagery is mythic—something a bit outside of conventional time and space. In a medium shot, then an extreme close-up, we see the lifeguard kiss Angela (her voice-over explains, "Except it may not count as an actual kiss… since I was kind of unconscious"). Angela's auditory qualification occurs during still another remarkable transition. At the beginning of the extreme close-up, Angela is lying on the ground, the lifeguard's face coming into the frame from above to kiss her. Then subtly, there is a transition back into color as the lifeguard's face pulls away. The camera twists to the left, so that Angela-lying-on-the-ground becomes Angela-standing-by-the-locker, gradually becoming vertical, and moving back into normal life. In a verbal coda, she explains, "I've never had an actual boyfriend."

Like the sequence that concludes the pilot, the introduction to "Dancing in the Dark" has an impact very different from the preponderance of narrative action in the episode. Clearly the sequence cannot exist without its narrative context—it wouldn't make sense if we didn't already know who Angela is—but it stands out from the more usual articulation of the action, the way a poem's shape is distinct from a page of prose. It is not just an expression of a moment of remembering by Angela; it is memorable as a special cinematic moment for the viewer, a kind of lyric, poetic excursion/incursion within an ongoing story—and within the conventional storytelling that then characterized, and still characterizes, so much of American television.

A third lyric moment occurs two episodes later, at the conclusion of "The Zit." In this instance the sequence is a kind of climax to the action that has occurred during the episode, all of which is focused on individuals, primarily women, being dissatisfied with their physical appearance: Angela has a zit; Patty sees age lines around her eyes; Sharon is listed on the high school poll (put out secretly by some boys) as having the best "hooters," which causes her much embarrassment, and Rayanne is listed as having the most "slut potential" (her exuberance at being included in the poll hides embarrassment and insecurity). Two allusions create a more extensive context for this general theme: a civics class watches Malcolm X's speech, "Who Taught You to Hate Yourself?" and an English class reads Kafka's *The Metamorphosis*.

The climax of the show is the mother-daughter fashion show, a charity event for a local women's shelter. Throughout the episode Angela has resisted her mother's excitement about the event, feeling that the fashion show idea is corny but also revealing her insecurity about acting as if she thinks she is attractive enough for such an event. Of course, there is something a bit absurd about Angela (and Patty) being insecure about their looks, since both are obviously attractive. However, this absurdity works for the episode's premise: modern commercial culture does work relentlessly to make women and men feel insecure about their physical appearance, often creating insecurities about aspects of our physical make-up that are (or should be) virtually invisible to anyone else, and in any case are insignificant in any larger context. The somewhat crude title of the episode confirms this.

The lyrical moment that concludes "The Zit" is structured differently from the other lyrical moments I've described. It is introduced by an echo of the scene between Angela and Patty that concludes the body of the pilot. Angela comes into her parents' bedroom to apologize to Patty and suggests what the episode has made obvious all along: that Danielle, who wants to be thought of as a possible participant, should replace Angela at the fashion show. As Angela makes this suggestion to Patty, the pop song, "Return to Innocence" (released in 1993 by the German new-age group, Enigma) fades in and remains the accompaniment to the two-minute montage of the fashion show that follows.

The montage intercuts between various mother-daughter pairs (including Sharon and Camille Cherski and Patty and Danielle) walking the runway and the spectators (including Angela, Rayanne and Rickie, and Graham) enjoying the spectacle. The diversity of the pairs of models is considerable and the exuberance of the moment, combined with the music, celebrates the happiness of the mothers and daughters to be collaborating and their (at least momentary) acceptance of who they are. The climax of this climactic scene is Angela's poetic voice-over:

> Sometimes it seems like we're all living in some kind
>   of prison.
> And the crime is how much we hate ourselves.
> It's *good* to get really dressed up once in a while and
>   admit the truth:
>   that when you really look closely,
>   people are *so* strange and *so* complicated
>   that they're actually
>   beautiful.
> Possibly even me.

The episode includes a celebratory denouement after its lyric flourish: during the final credit sequence, Angela, Rayanne, and Rickie are seen in long-shot, fooling around in the room where Patty made the clothes for the fashion show.

One of the accomplishments of *My So-Called Life*, and particularly of the lyric moments I'm describing, is that they are emotionally moving without being saccharine. Television has not usually been friendly to what has been traditionally understood as the poetic. Indeed, the irony is that nearly all the moments on television that do feel poetic occur in advertisements (or in the standard opening title sequences that begin television series: the Stan Brakhage-esque montage, to the accompaniment of Alabama 3's "Woke Up This Morning" that begins episodes of *The Sopranos*, for example). However, while certain advertisements and title sequences can have powerful resonance, they differ from the lyric moments in *My So-Called Life* in that they are nearly always means to ends outside of the ideas they seem to express. The 2014 Apple iPad Air commercial, "What Will Your Verse Be?" is emotionally powerful—but ultimately a means to the end of purchasing an iPad (or to be more precise, to the end of celebrating the value of new technologies, as a way of creating more desire to buy an iPad). The title sequence for *The Sopranos* is simply an elegant form of framing for the narrative episode that will follow.

The lyric moments in *My So-Called Life* are powerful expressions of emotion and idea that have nothing in particular to do with commerce or with providing a recognizable frame for the following show (the individual episodes of *My So-Called Life* begin with such a montage, of images from the pilot). Rather, they are formal celebrations of transcendent concepts: the glory of youth, the excitement of transformation, the potential for overcoming self-loathing and loneliness, the pleasure of collaboration and community, the dignity of women—and the excitement of working on a television series with the freedom to experiment.

The haiku of lyric moments in *My So-Called Life* occurs about halfway through episode 7, "Why Jordan Can't Read." It's a 30-second moment that follows Angela's visit to see Jordan's band, Frozen Embryos, and Jordan's singing his song "Red," dedicated, we find out later, to his red car, but interpreted by Rayanne, Rickie, and Angela as dedicated to Angela and her red hair. Jordan drives Angela home and before Angela exits the car, they talk about Jordan's dyslexia and his fantasy of working at a ski resort—a rare moment of emotional intimacy and synchronicity. Jordan kisses Angela, then apologizes for interrupting her—making clear to Angela and the viewer that he has learned from his brusque treatment of her in episode 2. This realization is confirmed by the passage of Snuffy Walden's music that begins immediately after Angela says, "Thanks"—for the kiss and the apology, then, clearly in an ecstatic daze, exits the car. What happens next has not been predicted by anything in the first six episodes.

The orchestral articulation of the Walden score continues as Jordan drives away, then gradually builds. The camera remains in long shot as Angela turns toward the house. The music then implies an introduction, and Angela proceeds to performs a series of graceful dance moves in precise time to the music, as she negotiates the short walk up to the porch, reaches the door, and enters the house—the image and music fade out. Nothing in Angela's introspective demeanor to this point in *My So-Called Life* has suggested that she is capable of this short, but clearly accomplished dance routine (Clare Danes had studied dance for some years before being cast as Angela), and so the moment is a brief, very pleasurable surprise for the viewer— just as the kiss has been for Angela. This lovely interruption within the otherwise straightforward narrative of the episode beautifully expresses the way a moment of unexpected good fortune (in this case, what appears to be an expression of love) can transform us.

There is, of course, a particular poignancy in this lyric moment, since anyone who has already seen "Why Jordan Can't Read" will recognize that the red of Jordan's car, clearly highlighted for a moment as Jordan drives off, is a premonition of Angela's subsequent discovery that "Red," is, in fact, not about her. But this too is relevant to the brief scene: the lyric flourishes that distinguish *My So-Called Life* are only *moments*: they represent experiences that are memorable and powerful, often energizing and sometimes transformative, but almost always brief—and sure to be quickly tested by new realities and challenges.

One final lyric flourish concludes "Strangers in the House," the eighth episode (written by Jill Gordon and directed by Ron Lagomarsino). It has much in common with the fashion-show sequence from "The Zit." Angela and Sharon who have become strangers because of Angela's new loyalty to Rayanne and Rickie, are even further estranged when Andy Cherski, Sharon's father, is hospitalized by a heart attack—neither Angela nor Sharon knows how to respond, though the danger of Sharon's father dying brings the Cherskis and the Chases into continual contact. At the same time, a subtly growing tension between Patty and Graham is exacerbated by their needing to land an account for the printing business—an account that will mean Graham's expanded involvement with work he doesn't love to do. The combination of Andy Cherski's heart attack, Camille's explanation to Patty that while Andy does work hard, he *loves* his work (something clearly not true of Graham), and the increasing obviousness of Graham's feelings of claustrophobia cause Patty to revise her assumptions about their marriage.

Throughout the episode, petty jealousy has been a motivating factor: Patty is jealous of Graham's attention to Camille. Rayanne assumes that since Sharon is staying with the Chases, she and Angela are close again, and is jealous enough to do a good deed for Sharon, causing Angela to be jealous of Rayanne's ability to be pro-active about Sharon's situation. And when Sharon and Brian become close, Angela becomes jealous of their friendship. Once Andy Cherski is pronounced out of danger, these petty jealousies dissipate. Finally, Angela and Sharon have an authentic conversation about the pain and embarrassment they've been through and recommit to their friendship; and when Graham surprises Patty with the news that he has in fact landed the contract (but had resisted doing so because of what it would mean for him), Patty fires him from the printing business: he will have an opportunity to find work he can love.

The lyric moment begins just after Angela, now no longer jealous of Brian's short-lived friendship with Sharon, makes clear to Brian that she sees him as having been unusually mature about the situation—even though he feels embarrassed by Sharon's sudden abandonment of him and her return to her boyfriend Kyle, who, like Angela, has not been able to provide Sharon with the support she has needed during the crisis. As Angela walks away from Brian, who is fixing his bike, Snuffy Walden's music cues the transition into a final sequence, which is accompanied throughout by Angela's voice-over, and divided into three visual/auditory stanzas that are introduced by Angela's saying, "There are so many ways to be connected to people"—followed by a dissolve to a Liberty High School hallway and the first of the three stanzas:

There are the people you feel this unspoken
   connection to,
even though there's not a word for it.

This comment is accompanied by series of shot-countershot between Angela walking along the hallway with Rayanne and Rickie, and Jordan, leaning against a locker—making eye contact with Angela (Jordan's leaning is reminiscent of Angela's original description of Jordan in the pilot—but now, she literally has a new angle on him, is in touch with him).

The sequence in the hallway is followed by a direct cut to the doorway of the Chase home, where Graham is seeing Patty off to work: he opens the front door, kisses her, and hands her a brown-bag lunch—a scene reminiscent of the penultimate sequence in Mike Nichols' *Working Girl* (1988)—as we hear the second stanza:

There's the people you've known forever,
who know you in this way that other people can't.
Because they've seen you change.

A direct cut brings us back to Angela, walking along the Liberty High hallway, between Rayanne and Rickie, then to a shot of Sharon and new friends walking the same hallway: we see them in the same composition—that is, in both shots, the groups of friends are moving forward, toward the left of the screen, though in fact they are moving in opposite directions. Angela and Sharon smile at each other as they pass, and Angela's voice-over concludes:

They've *let* you change.

The sequence concludes with shot-countershot of Angela, smiling, walking; then of Sharon, smiling; back to Angela, then back to Sharon once more, who turns to walk with her friends—followed by a shot of Angela, Rayanne, and Rickie turning a corner, as Angela looks back. In this instance, the backward look (which earlier I described as a motif of expressive body language in the series) has particular resonance, because it is not only the conclusion of this episode, but of the various conflicts set up in the pilot. Important transitions in growing into a new, more satisfying life have occurred for both the adolescents and their parents—and the series has reached a kind of equilibrium: one could imagine *My So-Called Life* ending here.

I see the gesture of Angela's looking back at the conclusion of this lyric moment as evocative of "Sophistication," the final story in Sherwood Anderson's *Winesburg, Ohio*, where George Willard and his girlfriend Helen White are presented as moving into a new, more mature phase of life. Anderson explains, "There is a time in the life of every boy when he for the first time takes the backward view of life. Perhaps that is the moment when he crosses the line into manhood" (paragraph 4 of "Sophistication"). Angela is younger than George Willard, but her look back at Sharon, now moving away from her (but moving forward, just as she is) is also a look of sophistication: like George, Angela has learned something about friendship, and is now "looking back" from the perspective of a new, more adult moment of understanding, taking account of a phase of her life that has presumably concluded.

While there are exuberant moments during subsequent episodes of *My So-Called Life*, the conclusion of "Strangers in the House" is the last of what I've called the lyrical flourishes in the series. Whether this has something to do with Ernest Holzman's leaving the show (except for episode 10, "Other People's Mothers," Charles Lieberman was the cinematographer for the remaining episodes) or was a function of other circumstances is unclear. In any case, subsequent episodes would search, not very successfully, for other ways of creating emotional epiphanies.

Betrayals
Episode 17 of *My So-Called Life* is entitled "Betrayal"—referring to Rayanne's and Jordan's betrayal of their friendship with Angela in that episode. But the real betrayal in the series occurs much earlier, and, beginning with episode 9, "Halloween" (written by Jill Gordon and directed by Mark Piznarski), becomes something of an unfortunate motif during the final eleven episodes. The first eight episodes of *My So-Called Life* are distinctive in the way in which they take the complexities of middle-class American life, as experienced by parents and adolescents, seriously—without being pretentious, saccharine, or flip. This seriousness is evident in the writing, the direction, the acting, and in the formal design of the episodes (and is encapsulated within the lyric moments I've just described). "Halloween" participates in what has always seemed to me an unfortunate tendency in television series, motivated by a decision to exploit the fact that an episode will be seen on a day designated as special by the calendar.[7]

From its opening moments, "Halloween" redirects the narrative and stylistic devices that have come to characterize *My So-Called Life* away from the kinds of insight and pleasure the opening suite of episodes offers—into forms of fake suspense and embarrassingly lame humor that seem typical of the worst of commercial television and cinema. It is as if the producers of the series decided that, since no one would be watching anyway on this special day, they could goof around—the way the students in the classroom sequences in *My So-Called Life* goof around when no education is taking place. Or, if in fact these calendar-determined episodes *are* marketable, or are designed to attract new viewers to the series, I suppose the producers might have wanted to appeal to kinds of viewers who aren't interested in television shows that take themselves seriously: a larger audience might attract advertisers. Whatever the motivation, however, the Halloween episode feels aesthetically corrupt.

This corruption is evident in several particular ways, the most obvious of which is a fundamentally prurient attitude toward sex. Early in the episode, Brian Krakow is walking past the Girls Room and sees Rayanne, inside, shaving her legs. In this moment Rayanne is exposed physically in a manner unlike anything else to this point in *My So-Called Life*. While it is understood throughout the series that Rayanne is sexually promiscuous, she is never exhibited for the sexual titillation of other characters or the audience. Indeed, this is true for all the characters: even when in episode 5 Sharon Cherski's breasts are singled out by the boys' poll and attention is drawn to her as a result, the episode never uses this plot point as an excuse to expose Sharon. In the brief Girls Room moment, however, Brian and the viewer see Rayanne in what seems to me a manner exploitive of both character and actress. Much the same is true of the Sharon Cherski character in "Halloween," who like some other students and even some teachers has worn a Halloween costume to school to celebrate the day It is obvious that Sharon's attire was designed to exploit Devon Odessa's body—the "real" Sharon would never willingly exploit herself in this manner.

A similar reliance on sex as audience titillation, rather than as narrative issue, occurs in the sequences involving Patty and Graham Chase. Having forgotten (one of many inconceivable dimensions of the plot) to buy Halloween costumes to wear to Camille Cherski's Halloween party, they visit a store where they purchase a Rapunzel outfit for Patty and a pirate costume for Graham. While dressing for the party, Graham and Patty become sexually involved, only to have their attempts to have sex continually interrupted by trick-or-treaters knocking at their door. Ironically, these sex scenes are entirely non-erotic and it is merely the idea of sex that seems meant to be titillating: only actresses who play young adolescent characters (actresses, one suspects, who were considered to have more exploitable bodies) are exposed for our voyeuristic enjoyment in "Halloween."

Among the more annoying dimensions of the Halloween episode is the several attempts to connect the events with those that have occurred in the episodes immediately preceding episode 9. A brief conflict, never developed further than in this instance, between Patty and the young man she has hired to replace Graham at the printing business (she ultimately fires the young man, who never appears) builds on the final events of episode 8. In the opening school sequence, Angela is in English class where the new teacher wonders if anyone knows Jordan Catalano, who has apparently been skipping class, and Angela remembers that she has had seven conversations with him "and one really bad kiss, and one amazing one"—references to episodes 2 and 7. These connections serve only to embarrass the earlier episodes, especially since the producers of "Halloween" seem to be assuming that we don't already know these characters. When Angela tells the English teacher she "sort of" knows Jordan, it is as if episode 7 never happened and the connection between Jordan and Angela demonstrated at the end of episode 8 does not exist.

This mixture of connection and disconnection to the previous episodes is sloppy and confuses a narrative that has been carefully built through episode 8. And the various mini-narratives that seem meant to fulfill the requirement of a Halloween episode (Angela's involvement with the spirit of "Nicky Driscoll"; Brian and Rayanne being locked together inside Liberty High for the night—don't the doors open out?) seem altogether pointless and unrelated to anything else in the series. The booklet published with the DVD release of *My So-Called Life* describes this episode as "a surreal twist," but there is nothing surreal about the events, except in the least meaningful sense of "surreal." Surreal works are meant to surprise, even to shock conventional expectations; "Halloween" only shocks by reducing an unconventional series to a set of unbelievable and meaningless clichés.

Two other episodes embarrass the series. Episode 15, "So-Called Angels," was produced to be shown at Christmastime, and though it does attempt to deal with two serious issues, its Christmas context leads to some of the same problems that haunt "Halloween." Once again, the supernatural is invoked, here in the form of an angel who appears as a homeless girl—an attempt, it would seem, to evoke *It's a Wonderful Life*, which is seen on the Chase family television at one point. "So-Called Angels" opens with an unusually visceral shot of Rickie kneeling on the ground spitting blood and crying, apparently having just been beaten up. We learn that he has been kicked out of his house, though it is unclear whether Rickie has been beaten up at home or since he's been homeless. Wilson Cruz has said that enacting Rickie's situation was quite personal for him: on the commentary track, he explains to Winnie Holzman, "This had actually happened to me less than a year from when we actually shot this episode. So I had been kicked out of my house because I came out to my father the Christmas before this [that is, the Christmas before the episode was shot in October]..." Apparently, when the episode was aired, Cruz's father saw it and telephoned him after the episode, which is "the reason I have a relationship with my father."

The idea of Rickie getting beaten up is hardly new to the series—his fear of the police is evident in the pilot and the bullying he sometimes endures is central to episode 3, "Guns and Gossip." One might have imagined that the focus on Rickie, who spends time trying to find somewhere to stay on a cold winter night, might have sustained "So-Called Angels." However, in an apparent attempt to portray Rickie's homelessness as emblematic of a much larger, culture-wide issue, the homeless angel (played by singer-songwriter Juliana Hatfield) is introduced and, in effect, allows much of the episode to avoid both Rickie's situation and the issue of homelessness itself. One climactic moment occurs when Angela, who has seen the angel at school and in an abandoned warehouse where homeless kids hang out, wants to include the girl at Christmas dinner. When Patty resists, Angela angrily tells her mother, "*She* could be *me*!"—to which Patty, yells, "Oh, don't say that! She *couldn't* be you!" On the commentary track, Holzman and Cruz agree that this interchange is the heart of the episode—that is, that any of us, if we had a series of bad breaks, could end up homeless.

Of course, had "So-Called Angels" allowed the girl to be an actual homeless person and therefore a challenge to the Chase family's conventional Christmas, which the various characters might have dealt with in one way or another, the interchange between daughter and mother could have been meaningful. But since the girl is an *angel* and in fact needs no help—since, in other words, given the episode's own assumptions, she literally *can't* be Angela—this apparent attempt at empathy and engagement with the issue of homelessness rings hollow. In effect, the events involving the angel allow the producers to provide a spiritual *feeling*, but to escape responsibility to deal in a realistic fashion with the issue they have raised. When Patty and Graham overhear Angela telling Brian about the homeless kids at the abandoned warehouse, they contact the authorities, and when Angela returns, hoping to find the girl, all the kids are gone—no explanation is given as to what happened to them: their disappearance is simply a narrative convenience.

As is true in so many episodes of *My So-Called Life*, "So-Called Angels" develops a two-sided narrative: Rickie's homelessness, loneliness, and suffering is roughly parallel to Brian Krakow's situation: identified as Jewish for the only time in the series, Brian has been left alone at his own request by his parents—they're visiting his sister's family in Denver—and is feeling lonely and out of place, though he seems welcome enough in the Chase household. Hoping to talk with someone, he calls a helpline, where Sharon Cherski and Rayanne Graff are taking calls (Sharon has volunteered for this duty and has convinced Rayanne to join her). Rayanne answers the call, realizes it's Brian, who somehow never recognizes Rayanne's voice (the improbable coincidences in "So-Called Angels" are further evidence that the supposed seriousness of the episode is essentially pretense). In order to cheer Brian up, Rayanne jumps into a phone-sex routine, which apparently makes Brian feel better. That this scene comes immediately after the somber sequence where Angela returns to the now-empty warehouse and that it relies on the titillation of a fifteen-year-old girl doing sex-talk is further confirmation that, like "Halloween," "So-Called Angels" is not to be taken seriously. Ironically, while the story of Rickie's being beaten up serves to open the episode with visceral power, it is never actually dealt with—except in the sense that, at the conclusion of the episode, Rickie is accepted into the Chase family circle and into their home.

Ultimately, the betrayal of "So-Called Angels" is a function of the producers' attempt to stretch the series they have created into something beyond its emotional and moral capacities, solely, it would seem, so that *My So-Called Life* can conform, out of "respect" for conventional ideas of how Christmas should feel—ideas based, for the most part, on commercial pressures and on an overvaluing of supposed Christmas classics. The attempt by Chris Brooks to salvage the "Halloween" and "So-Called Angels" episodes by arguing that these episodes succeed "not because of their verisimilitude or proximity to real life, but because they *transcend* the mimesis for which the series is known" in order to touch "the supernatural or perhaps the magical"—that is, by demonstrating that they are instances of magical realism—seems a desperate attempt to justify the unjustifiable.[8] Brooks' assumption that the episodes provide *unconventional* viewing experiences that offer the "pleasure of seeing realism injected with just a bit of something else, something different, perhaps something magical" ignores the fact that the two episodes actually are not at all *different* in any meaningful sense from other commercial exploitations of the holidays. They are only different from the non-exploitive emotional realism that distinguishes most of *My So-Called Life*.[9]

Episode 18, "Weekend" (written by Adam Dooley and directed by Todd Holland), completes the triad of betrayals. Mercifully, there is no dependence on the supernatural here and no phony pretense that the series deals in a meaningful way with serious issues. Perhaps in a moment of relief to see that the shooting of *My So-Called Life* was finally coming to a conclusion, the producers decided to make a comedy. A double-level plot focusing on—what else?—sex is developed: Patty and Graham go away with Neil Chase and his new girlfriend to an inn for a fun weekend, leaving behind in the bedroom the handcuffs that Camille has loaned to Patty to rev up her sex life with Graham. Of course, Rayanne finds the cuffs, puts them on, and finds she is chained to the bed, requiring that all the other younger characters get involved. It is difficult to imagine a less amusing episode—or an episode in which capable actors do less impressive work. To discuss the episode further would be to give it more attention than it deserves.

Because television is a serial medium, and because in many instances, the men and women who write, produce, and direct individual episodes of a series change from episode to episode, certain kinds of consistency that we tend to expect from other narrative forms—especially from novels and feature films—can get lost. Indeed, a certain inconsistency seems virtually inevitable in any series. And if the poor quality of certain episodes can cause one to wonder if the more successful episodes are really as accomplished as they have seemed, perhaps one can also see these episodes as offering a contrast, a kind of lesson in what does and does not work—a lesson about the tenuousness and fragility of accomplishment. The fact that the spaces between what seem to me the failed episodes of the series grow shorter suggests that *My So-Called Life* was, in fact, gradually losing its aesthetic edge and emotional power. Fortunately, other than the three episodes I've discussed here, the overall quality of the series was generally maintained until the end—though with some noteworthy variations in approach.

The Second Wave
Episode 10, "Other People's Mothers" (written by Richard Kramer and directed by Claudia Weill) and Episode 11, "Life of Brian" (written by Jason Katims and directed by Todd Holland) mark a transitional moment in *My So-Called Life*. In these episodes, the expansion of the focus on characters other than Angela signals a loosening of the overall continuity of the series.[10] "Other People's Mothers" seems basically a development of issues explored early on in the series—the central focus is Rayanne's drinking—though Rayanne is more clearly the center of this episode than has been the case in earlier episodes, where Angela is the protagonist. Here, Rayanne's drinking (and perhaps by implication her cavalier openness about sex) is clearly depicted as a response to her father's disappearance from the family. With a small amount of money her father has sent to her mother, Rayanne hosts a party where she binges on alcohol and Ecstasy, leading to her hospitalization—and to a new respect on Angela's part for *her* mother, who saves the day. Subsequent writers and directors would continue to develop this expanded focus on Rayanne in episodes 14 and 17: "On the Wagon" and "Betrayal."

"Life of Brian," reveals even more significant changes in the series, though, of course, it also picks up on some of what viewers had already come to expect. For the first time since the arrival of Victor Racine, important new characters are introduced, and, unlike Vic, both will remain fixtures during subsequent episodes. Early in the episode, Sharon Cherski introduces Delia Fisher (Senta Moses), a student new to Liberty High, to Brian Krakow—Delia is clearly attracted to Brian and Brian's awkwardness cannot hide his pleasure in being, for once, an object of desire. In the next sequence, another new student, Corey Helfrick (Adam Blesk), wearing artistically painted shoes, enters a classroom where Angela, Rayanne, and Rickie are talking, and asks for information—Rickie is immediately attracted to Corey.

The most immediate surprise in "Life of Brian," however, is implicit in the episode title: for the first time in the series, someone other than Angela is the voice-over commentator. A long, slow pan and zoom reveals Brian at home, as his mother and father—a behavioral psychologist and a Freudian psychiatrist—

argue with each other as they speak to Brian from off-screen. Brian is behind his camera using a telephoto lens to look in on the more normal family situation of the Chases next door, as his voice-over describes his family and his interest in photography. Brian's voice-over punctuates "Life of Brian" in much the same way that Angela's does during earlier episodes, though unlike Angela, Brian doesn't offer serious philosophical insights. Brian is also a central focus in two of this episode's plotlines: his brief involvement with Delia which is short circuited by his deeper attraction to Angela, ultimately leaving him as lonely as ever; and his helping Graham wallpaper a room in the Chase home: as Graham considers what career he might like to commit to, Brian considers whether he should pursue Delia or Angela.

The expansion of focus in *My So-Called Life* can be related to two classic American literary works and to various attempts over the decades to assess the similarities and differences between novels and films, and in more recent years, between novels and television series. There is certainly historical justification for comparisons between the serial medium of television and the traditional novel. Early on, many novels were published serially—new episodes of a Dickens story would be marketed weekly or monthly, so that readers would engage an evolving narrative with numerous characters and varied plot complications over a substantial period of time—just as viewers of a television series do. Whereas feature films condense the experience even of long novels into a brief time spans (reading an epic novel can take many hours spread over weeks, an epic feature film lasts about three hours), serial television can maintain viewer attention on a regular basis for years: *Breaking Bad* lasted 62 hours, spread over a period of more than five years; and the British period drama, *Downton Abbey*, inspired by the great British novels of the Victorian era, included 43 episodes of various lengths that aired over four years.

Of course, there are also significant distinctions. The most obvious, perhaps, is that in most cases one assumes that the individual novelist understands from early on where his/her novel is going: that is, how the characters will evolve and how the various plotlines will converge to form a coherent conclusion. For the most part, television series begin and evolve without a clear sense of how many "chapters" will be possible and therefore, where the narrative will lead—since the duration of the series is dependent on its popularity and economic viability for advertisers. It is not unusual for an ongoing plotline to change direction on the basis of decisions determined by momentary marketing logistics. The original premise of *Breaking Bad* was that Walter White is dying from advanced, inoperable lung cancer. Had the show not been popular, Walter might have died at the end of the first series, but since *Breaking Bad* quickly attracted a considerable audience, White could find himself in remission—for as long as the show remained economically viable.

The nature of authorship is another difference between television series and both novels and feature films. Novels are written by a single person at that person's particular writing pace; and feature films are normally directed by a single director, who is in charge of dozens of collaborators organized within a hierarchical production team that is employed to work within in a more or less predictable span of time. However, even a television series that lasts only a single season, like *My So-Called Life*, can involve numerous producers, writers, directors, story editors, organized into constantly changing units; often particular sets of collaborators participate on only a small number of episodes. Winnie Holzman, the creator and lead writer of *My So-Called Life*, has a writing credit on only six of nineteen episodes: the pilot and episodes 2, 4, 12, 15 (a co-credit with Jason Katims), and 19. The largest number of writing credits for other writers is three (Jason Katims: 6, 11, 15; and Jill Gordon: 8, 9, 17). Mark Piznarski has directing credits on four episodes: 7, 9, 13, 17; Scott Winant, on three: the pilot, 2, and 15. The majority of *My So-Called Life* episodes were directed and written by individual men and women each of whom participated in the production of a single episode.

The only thing that the episodes of *My So-Called Life* share, in other words, is a consistent focus on the exploits of a particular set of characters usually involved in certain types of interaction that are presented with a relatively predictable tone and pace. It is as if the characters are musical instruments for which various composers create musical scores that various instrumentalists are hired for brief periods to perform. All in all, the loosening of the structure of *My So-Called Life*—evident in the tonality and focus of individual episodes after "Strangers in the House"—causes the series to seem less like a traditional novel (or a feature film) than like a collection of short stories—in particular, like those collections of short stories that are generally, but not entirely, organized around the evolution of a particular protagonist: Sherwood Anderson's *Winesburg, Ohio* and Hemingway's *In Our Time*, for example. Anderson's development of a fictional form in between a novel and a collection of disparate short stories seemed a breakthrough when *Winesburg, Ohio* was published in 1919—enough of a breakthrough that Hemingway, who was rethinking the style and structure of narrative fiction, could take it as a model in *In Our Time*.

Winesburg, Ohio takes place in a small Midwestern town, and focuses most consistently on George Willard, who is slightly older than Angela Chase and her friends, but is, as a senior in high school, struggling (as *his* friends are) with maturation.[11] More of the *Winesburg* stories involve George than any other character, just as the episodes of *My So-Called Life* involve Angela more consistently than any other character, but there are stories in *Winesburg* in which George is a minor, even a somewhat unattractive, character. "The Thinker," for example, focuses on Seth Richmond's conflict between his fascination with local girl Helen White and a desire to escape small town life. From the viewpoint of Seth (and within this story, from the reader's viewpoint as well), his friend George is rather shallow.[12]

The shifting focus of *My So-Called Life* during the second wave of episodes is quite similar in general structure, even in overall mood, to the canonical Anderson short story collection. In "Life of Brian" Angela is a secondary focus, the motivation of Brian's conflict between his enjoyment of Delia's attention and his attraction to Angela—or really, between his doing the right thing by Delia and doing what Angela wants in the hope that this will make him attractive to her. Seeing Angela's self-involved manipulations through Brian's eyes allows us to see her as less admirable than she has been during earlier episodes, and from the point of view of the series producers, perhaps, as no longer the moral center of the series—after episode 10 Rickie increasingly assumes this role.[13]

"Life of Brian" ends with a memorable climax—one of the most engaging and insightful moments in *My So-Called Life*. All of the characters in the episode gather in and around the Liberty High gym, where Sharon Cherski has organized a "World Happiness" dance—ironically, since all the characters we are acquainted with are struggling with various kinds of embarrassment, confusion, and loneliness. When Angela realizes that Brian is acting as if she is his date, and that he has probably embarrassed Delia in order to be with her, she calls him heartless and leaves to find Jordan. When Rickie realizes that Corey is waiting for Rayanne to arrive and that Rayanne has not told Corey she was not coming—in order to leave Rickie and Corey together—his fantasy of being with Corey evaporates, leaving him embarrassed and lonely. And when Angela finally meets up with Jordan, she is embarrassed when Jordan seems less interested in her than in his male friends. Even Sharon Cherski seems to have become bored with her boyfriend Kyle.

Then something magical happens: not a formal lyrical flourish as in early episodes, but a revealing and perceptive surprise, energized by the high-spirited Haddaway song, "What Is Love?" Delia and Rickie find themselves standing next to one another. Rickie asks Delia to dance and she accepts. They join the crowd on the dance floor where Rickie shows himself to be a confident and passionate dancer and Delia reveals that she is up to the challenge. As Brian looks on, realizing that Delia is more interesting than he had assumed, Rickie and Delia take over the dance floor—their disappointments and embarrassments now forgotten in the excitement of the dancing.

The triad of episodes that follow "Life of Brian" continue the expanding focus of the series. "Self-Esteem" (episode 12, written by Holzman and directed by Michael Engler) opens with a focus on Rickie and the introduction of another new character who will remain important in subsequent episodes: Mr. Katimsky (Jeff Perry) has been hired to teach English (and also apparently to take charge of the drama club). Rickie's immediate dislike of Katimsky reflects his instinctive awareness of a kindred spirit (Katimsky is gay). The episode focuses on issues of self-esteem, as experienced in a range of different ways. Katimsky immediately recognizes Rickie's dramatic personality and his low self-esteem; a female colleague flirts with Katimsky and is embarrassed when she's not taken seriously; Graham is annoyed that Patty seems surprised by his being asked to teach a cooking class, and Jordan's desire to make a secret of his make-out sessions with Angela in the school boiler room are recognized by Rayanne and Sharon as demeaning to her—and Angela is too embarrassed to admit the truth of their insight, until she is publicly embarrassed by Jordan's dismissal of her at a club where Buffalo Tom is performing.

The episode concludes with a double climax that begins immediately after Mr. Katimsky tells Rickie pointedly that "No one should... *hate* who they *are*." Buffalo Tom music cues an elaborate hallway sequence that begins with Rickie signing up for the drama club as *Enrique* Vasquez (signaling a new level of self-acceptance), then joining Rayanne and Angela. And Jordan, who has been moved by Katimsky's reading and discussion of Shakespeare's Sonnet 130, makes his relationship with Angela public: Jordan and Angela walk off holding hands, in slow motion, as Rayanne and Sharon, Jordan's friend Shane, and Brian look on. As is true of the climax of "Life of Brian," this ending is emotionally complex—

simultaneously happy for Angela, poignant for Rickie, Sharon, and Rayanne, and melancholy for Brian and perhaps for Shane.[14]

In "Pressure" (episode 13), Angela is, once again, the primary focus of an episode as she struggles with Jordan's pressuring her to have sex (the only other pressure in this episode develops when Hallie Lowenthal pushes Graham to agree to be the chef at a restaurant she hopes to bankroll). In her ways of avoiding a more serious sexual involvement with Jordan, Angela seems younger here than in any previous episode—in the final scene Angela is seen riding Brian's bicycle (in the final shot, beneath power lines); the bike has been a relatively consistent symbol of a resistance to the emotional demands of adult life throughout the series. Angela's reticence about sex may reflect the reticence of the series producers to commit to more adult territory: Angela remains a virgin. Holzman's writing is particularly skillful when Angela asks Sharon about her sexual experiences with Kyle, though the sequence where Jordan takes Angela to an abandoned house where other young people go to have sex seems silly. The idea that adolescents from the solid middle-class world where Angela lives wouldn't be able to find a private place to have sex seems a stretch. It does, however, confirm the tendency of the series to be rather cavalier in its depiction of place.

Nominally *My So-Called Life* takes place in Pittsburgh, and though reference is made to this supposed location from time to time (a character will be seen wearing a Pittsburgh Pirates jacket), these references seem perfunctory at best. During the decades before the Interstate Highway System was constructed, relatively few Americans had the opportunity to wander from one region to another, and filmmakers could create impossible landscapes that were accepted by audiences without question. In a number of John Ford films, for example, saguaro cacti are seen within the landscape of Monument Valley. For Ford the Monument Valley region of Arizona/Utah and the saguaro were convenient symbols of the West, and the fact that saguaros grow only in the Sonoran Desert region of Southern Arizona, hundreds of miles from the Colorado Plateau, didn't seem significant, since film audiences would be unlikely to recognize this strange elision. Of course, the physical location of the events of *My So-Called Life* doesn't really matter—young people struggle with the onset of maturity everywhere—and it may seem foolish to raise the issue in this context. Nevertheless, as early as the concluding moments of the series pilot, one can be distracted by the fact that the street Angela and Brian live on looks more like Pasadena than Pittsburgh.

Critical Mass
"On the Wagon" (episode 14, written by Elizabeth Gill and directed by Jeff Perry) is focused almost entirely on Rayanne, following up on episode 10 where she overdoses, an event referenced in episodes 11 and 12. Among the most interesting episodes of *My So-Called Life*, and certainly the most suspenseful, "On the Wagon" develops the one "bad guy" of the series: Rayanne's mother Amber Vallon, played effectively by Patti D'Arbanville-Quinn. Amber's irresponsibility about her daughter is, of course, already obvious in episode 10, particularly when she arrives in Rayanne's hospital room in hysterics. However, she's not hysterical when, in an early scene in "On the Wagon," she mixes daiquiris in front of Rayanne, whose struggle with addiction is obvious from the opening moments of

the episode. "On the Wagon" opens with her making light of her substance abuse counselor's comments about the possible dangers of her early success in avoiding alcohol. Amber, who is introduced in "Guns and Gossip" as a pro-active parent, is frustratingly self-involved in any pressure situation; she is one of few characters in *My So-Called Life* (other than several incompetent teachers at Liberty High) who are portrayed negatively.

For Angela, whose relationship with Jordan continues as a nonsexual friendship, Rayanne's new neediness is annoying—and the distance between the girls is exacerbated by Rayanne's wanting to replace Tino as the lead singer of Frozen Embryos. The boys in the band are so dysfunctional that while they accept Rayanne as lead singer for an upcoming audition, they never actually practice with her—and when they begin to perform (what else?) The Ramones' "I Wanna Be Sedated" at the Vertigo Coffeehouse, Rayanne freezes and runs off, leaving Jordan to take over. Throughout the episode the danger in Rayanne's more-than-usual frantic behavior and in her "jokes" about taking a drink is obvious. After we learn, during an uncomfortable confrontation between Patty Chase and Amber, that in fact Rayanne did not get drunk after freezing at the audition, as Rickie suspected she would, Patty drives her to school (as she leaves Patty's car, Rayanne thanks her for her life), where Rayanne is reunited with Rickie and Angela. The episode seems to be ending happily—before cutting to a final sequence that takes place at a movie theater waiting line. In high spirits, Rayanne sings a sultry version of the *Sesame Street* theme for appreciative bystanders, and as they applaud, she grabs a beer from a man standing in line and takes her first drink in over a month.

That the startling and powerful surprise that concludes "On the Wagon" immediately precedes "So-Called Angels," where Rayanne is a "comic" presence doing sex-talk on the help line, is evidence that even a remarkably sensitive series can reveal a sloppy narrative crassness on the part of its producers—and it is a premonition of the emotional fission that characterizes the final five episodes of *My So-Called Life*. The world of "So-Called Angels," suddenly inhabited by a supernatural entity, is fundamentally different from the world we see in nearly all other series episodes ("Halloween" being the one exception) though no one seems to notice: in "Resolutions" (episode 16) Rickie still has bruises from when he was assaulted in "So-Called Angels," but Angela seems to have no memory of the miraculous events of that episode—did she lose the flower the angel put into her notebook? Obviously we're supposed to understand that this is *television*—and that no one is supposed to take consistency too seriously. But what was and remains distinctive about *My So-Called Life* is precisely its refusal, particularly during early episodes, to be typical television.

More deeply frustrating is the mixture of moods in "Resolutions." Of course, a mixture of moods can be powerful, as Chaplin understood in *The Kid*. However, in "Resolutions," the attempts at humor often seem emotionally oblivious. The central focus of the episode remains Rickie's abandonment by his relatives who seem not only to have kicked him out of their home (just before the action of "So-Called Angels" begins) but then to have moved away without telling him, leaving him with no place to live. Writer Ellen Norman and director Patrick R. Norris are at pains to dramatize Rickie's frightening plight, and though Mr. Katimsky becomes involved in Rickie's situation (and with his own fear that if he and his partner take Rickie in, he may lose his job because of "what people could make of it"), his New Year's resolution to stop drinking coffee transforms him into an almost slapstick character. Here, humor doesn't provide a useful contrast to more dramatic action, it demonstrates that the producers are less serious about the dramatic action they've created than with being "entertaining" in the most superficial sense.

Similarly, the episode's admirable seriousness about the perils of being openly gay in an era when being gay could cause a competent and committed teacher to lose a job, seems cheapened by the focus on Sharon's discovery that she enjoys sex more, now that she's no longer in love with Kyle and their lovemaking is stimulated by Brad Pitt movies (*A River Runs Through It*, *Thelma & Louise*). This is less a reflection on an adolescent girl's life than the writers' unimaginative reliance on sexual titillation to provide generic, "entertaining" humor. Sharon's sexual revelations in "Resolutions" contradict the poignancy of her revelations about her sex life when she talks with Angela in "Self-Esteem."

That the wonderful "Betrayal" (episode 17), written by Jill Gordon and directed by Mark Piznarski, could be sandwiched between the pair of episodes that precede it and the nearly unwatchable "Weekend" attests to the sad fact that while it was still possible for the series collaborators to work in the mode of the early episodes, the motivation and commitment to do so had become intermittent at best. Complexity of emotion is the topic of "Betrayal." Angela tells herself that she is "over" Jordan Catalano, but when she learns that Rayanne and Jordan got drunk and had sex in Jordan's car (Brian, who is recording off-campus events for the yearbook, videotapes their tryst), she is devastated by their combined disloyalty—though it is also clear that both Jordan and Rayanne do what they do as a kind of revenge: Jordan, for Angela's refusal to have sex with him; Rayanne, for what she feels is Angela's abandonment of her.

The drama club's production of Thornton Wilder's *Our Town* forms the background of this episode: Rickie is already involved, as is Corey; and Rayanne auditions and is chosen to play Emily Webb—a character with a good deal in common with Angela. Meanwhile, angry at Jordan and Rayanne, and embarrassed about her own sexual innocence, Angela (in a hair-do with Rayanne-esque braids) arrives backstage during a rehearsal in order to help paint the set. Angela seems to be trying to channel Rayanne when she throws herself at Corey, who is embarrassed and rejects her.

In an inventive turn, the play's climactic speech—Emily's realization that "earth, you're too wonderful for anybody to realize you… Do any human beings ever realize life while they live it?" is also the climax of the episode. Rayanne says Emily's lines to Abyssinia who is playing the stage manager and to Angela who is standing in for the absent actor chosen to play Mrs. Gibbs. The role of Emily allows Rayanne a rare moment to function entirely without cynicism, and though Angela is clearly moved by the speech and by Rayanne's implicit apology, it is clear as soon as the reading is over that what might be forgiveness has been channeled back into anger, the way Rayanne's anger at her father's leaving the family has been channeled into empty sex, liquor, and cynicism.

Near the end of the final episode of *My So-Called Life*, "In Dreams Begin Responsibilities" (episode 19), written by Winnie Holzman and directed by Elodie

Keene, there is a remarkable (and amusing) moment. Patty Chase is awaiting a visit by her old boyfriend Tony—she has not seen him in decades but has recently dreamed about him. Suddenly there's a knock at the kitchen door. Patty readies herself, then opens the door—to find Jordan Catalano. Both are surprised (as are we), Patty not unpleasantly, since she has long wanted to meet Jordan, whom she has only heard about and seen from a distance. After a cutaway (to where Graham and Hallie are serving the meal they hope will convince potential investors to back the restaurant they want to start), we return to Patty, now getting off the phone with Tony, who has cancelled the visit.

In the following conversation it is evident that Jordan has told Patty about the letter that Brian wrote for him, that Patty understands that Jordan has never meant to hurt Angela, and that he now understands that his pose of being a loner has been a lie, a way of deluding himself that he is emotionally safe. When Jordan, noticing that Patty is unusually dressed up for an evening at home, suddenly asks if she always wears so much make-up, Patty explains that she was waiting for an old boyfriend, who has apparently taken an antihistamine and is afraid to drive (we assume this is just an excuse, that Tony is probably afraid to see Patty—perhaps protecting his own emotional safety): "This was a person who drove so recklessly when he was 17 that my parents wanted him dead." "Wow," says Jordan, "Ironic."

Earlier in this episode, Jordan has learned the meaning of "ironic" from Brian, in order to complete Mr. Katimsky's assignment to use several new words in sentences—and his deployment of this new word in such an appropriate way is a funny surprise that confirms what has been implicit throughout the series: that Jordan is more intelligent than his being "held-back, twice" might suggest, that he *can* learn, and that, in this instance, he is wise enough to see the humor in Patty's situation. "Ironic," which should have been the title of this episode, characterizes much of what occurs in it.

After two brief cutaways—one back to the restaurant where Graham and Hallie get good news from the potential investors; the other, to Angela being dropped off by Mr. Katimsky, having just learned from Rickie that Brian wrote "Jordan's" letter—a ringing phone takes us back to Jordan and Patty, as she gets a call from Graham with the good news. He wonders how the meeting with Tony went. Acting as if Tony did, in fact, come by, Patty tells Graham that it was like "old times," as she looks at Jordan, who wipes his mouth on his sleeve. It is clear that she sees that Jordan is Angela's "Tony" and the reincarnation of hers, and has realized that hers is probably no longer who she has imagined he might still be and might never have been. Patty is clearly moved by Graham's saying that he was a bit jealous to think she'd be seeing Tony.

The fact that we know that it was Hallie's suggestion to Graham that Patty might like it if he seemed jealous, that Patty *is* happy he is jealous, and that Graham is moved by *her* happiness is further irony, since in essence this is just a more adult version of what has happened with Jordan, Brian, and Angela. Hallie, who is clearly smitten with Graham, has helped Graham and Patty reconnect—though this, along with their success in impressing the would-be investors, has also brought Graham and Hallie more closely together, which is confirmed immediately after Graham's phoning Patty, when he and Hallie share a hug and nearly a kiss. Graham ends the awkward pause, saying "I gotta get home," and Hallie is left to deal with her emotions, just as Brian has had to deal with his as he has watched his input re-energize the relationship between Angela and Jordan. This pile-up of irony continues through the final scene.

After Katimsky drops her off, Angela questions Brian, who is riding his bike (again presumably waiting for Angela to return home). He avoids admitting that he wrote the letter until Angela begins to think he and Jordan were amusing themselves at her expense. Then he blurts out, "No, I meant every word. I mean the person who wrote it meant every word. Probably." Whether we interpret Brian's comment as an accidental slip or a subtle manipulation (earlier in the episode, he has been careful to let Rickie know that he's been helping Jordan woo Angela, knowing Rickie will probably tell her), the central irony in this sequence is that Angela is becoming more aware of Brian and more emotionally involved with him, just as Jordan, who earlier in the episode has tried to tell her he *didn't* write the letter, has demonstrated in his conversation with Patty that he is now capable of revealing his honest feelings for Angela. Jordan comes out of the house and joins Brian and Angela, and during the moments when Jordan opens the car door for Angela (a first) and they drive away, it is obvious that Angela is now no longer clear about whom she most cares for—as the scene, the episode, and *My So-Called Life* concludes.

Ironic
After alluding to a good many earlier moments of the series,[15] "In Dreams Begin Responsibilities" ends ambiguously, not only in terms of the relationships between Angela, Jordan, and Brian, and between Patty, Graham, and Hallie, but also because we must wonder what will happen now that Rickie lives with Mr. Katimsky and his boyfriend, as well as if and how the friendships between Angela, Sharon, and Rayanne will evolve. Of course, this is just the sort of ambiguity that seems meant to function as a final hook to catch the interest of viewers in the show's second season. That Winnie Holzman had begun to imagine what might happen seems clear. In the first paragraph of her introduction to the booklet produced for the 2007 DVD release of *My So-Called Life* Holzman explains that:

> I would have gotten somebody pregnant. Sharon's the obvious choice. I would have made Angela unable to resist turning to Brian Krakow for advice about her doomed relationship with Jordan Catalano, and I would have split Graham and Patty up, so Patty could fall into a deep depression—the kind where you can't get out of bed—so that Angela is forced to somehow run the household. I would have had Rickie move in with Mr. Katimsky… and when Mr. Katimsky is fired for the crime of giving a kid a place to live, I would have forced Patty out of her depression to defend him.

And yet there was no second season, and perhaps, ironically, there didn't need to be one. As Robert Lloyd has suggested:

Though the final episode...was written as though the series would return, there is an open-ended rightness to its abbreviation: What doesn't end, goes on. As in life, we're left in transit, in transition, with questions hanging. But we've been given enough: the world in 19 hours. As Angela says in the fan-canonized lines that cap the pilot episode, confirming Rayanne's description of their last night's adventure, "We had a time." Which is all anyone gets out of this so-called life...[16]

Lloyd's comments are confirmed by Holzman herself. In the DVD essay she concludes that it *isn't* a shame that the show was canceled: "It was perfect. It all worked out perfectly. We had a time, and I'm still having one."

The fact that "In Dreams Begin Responsibilities"—especially in its complex, layered ironies—is among the most successful episodes of *My So-Called Life* doesn't alter the fact that several of the final episodes are weak, and that, overall, the series might have been tending toward mediocrity. Of course, we'll never know. *My So-Called Life* is certainly not perfect, though I must admit that after twenty years of regularly watching the series, I find that the majority of the episodes continue to hold up, and that despite its few problematic episodes *My So-Called Life* is, as Ginia Bellavante has said, "more than a good TV show, it is a good TV show that attains the dimension and complexity of literature."[17] Perhaps, after all, the series is perfect enough.[18]

American commentators have generally focused on the seriousness and the comparative "reality" of *My So-Called Life* as something quite distinct from what had seemed typical of television shows dealing with adolescents. For example, when The N announced its decision to air *My So-Called Life* on the tenth anniversary of the show's original airing,[19] the official news release quoted a critical assessment of the show as "the only authentic portrait of a teenager a TV show has ever presented" and as having "a grasp of adolescence that's so real you can smell the Clearasil."[20] But *Degrassi High*, the series I mentioned earlier in this study as one of the predecessors of *My So-Called Life*, is at least as serious as the later series and in some ways more serious—at least if "serious" means dealing honestly with significant social and psychological issues.[21]

Issues that American network shows (even series not on the major networks) rarely confront are consistently invoked by *Degrassi High*. During its opening episodes, "A New Start, Part 1" and "A New Start, Part 2," Erica Farrell (Angela Deiseach) has an abortion at a clinic, despite the resistance of her twin sister and other classmates. This double episode candidly dramatizes a considerable range of attitudes toward the right to choose. The episodes that follow often reference Erica's abortion. In "Natural Attraction" (episode 11) Erica's sister Heather has nightmares that reflect her guilt that despite her moral reservations, she made it easier for Erica to have the abortion and Erica makes clear her lack of regret at having had the procedure. Far more consistently than *My So-Called Life*, *Degrassi High* recognizes that high school is a public space where deeply felt attitudes collide. *Degrassi High* did find its way onto American television, but when PBS aired the two parts of "A New Start," they had been re-edited so as not to show the abortion protesters that Erica must walk through to enter the clinic and so that no final decision as to getting an abortion was made. When The N broadcast the series, these episodes were eliminated completely.

Degrassi High presents a wider range of high school students than *My So-Called Life*, within well-written and capably acted half-hour episodes, and these high school students are as believable and have as much depth as Angela, Rayanne, Rickie, Brian and their colleagues and parents. If *My So-Called Life* seems more true-to-life than most other American television series about young people, within the context of *Degrassi High*, it seems remarkably romantic adult nostalgia for an imagined adolescence. And yet, for all this, *My So-Called Life* does seem closer to "the dimension and complexity of literature" than *Degrassi High*.

As I've suggested throughout this monograph, I've come to believe that the power of *My So-Called Life* over those of us who have become devotees is not primarily a function of its success in representing reality. In its best episodes, *My So-Called Life* is able to evoke something beyond the real struggles that adolescents (and parents dealing with adolescents) confront. *My So-Called Life* communicates the thrill of living itself, the exquisite pleasures (and terrors) of discovering and exploring our developing desires and needs. This thrill is communicated by the commitment to style that is evident throughout *My So-Called Life* and that is most obviously demonstrated in the lyric moments I described earlier. Perhaps it's because Holzman and her colleagues produced the series during a time when no one had agreed to air the show, when there were not as yet any clear deadlines. Perhaps this temporal limbo allowed them the luxury that serious novelists have, the time to struggle at moving beyond what will "do the job," what will be popular, what will attract sponsors—into something that might, from time to time, move us at the deepest level. But however we understand the formal decisions that give the series its special power, *My So-Called Life* radiates a stylistic glow that distinguishes it from nearly all other series (including *Degrassi High*), the way the "crimson glow" of Angela's hair distinguishes her from her colleagues.

The past two decades have seen a sea change in the quality of the serial dramas on American television, or at least in the narrative energy and visual/auditory style of shows like *The Sopranos*, *The Wire*, *Homeland*, *Breaking Bad*, *Masters of Sex*, and *True Detective*. Often it seems obvious that television, especially the long-form dramatic series, has become both more experimental and more accomplished than commercial cinema. Nevertheless, *My So-Called Life* continues to stand apart from even the most acclaimed recent series, as well as from most of commercial cinema, in the commitment of its formal density and subtlety not to excitement and shock, to various forms of physical and psychic brutality, but rather to a remarkable gentleness—to what Lincoln called "the better angels of our nature."

My So-Called Life is available on DVD.

1   Kelli Maloy, in her essay, "Their So-Called Scene: Uses of Popular Music in *My So-Called Life*," chapter 4 of *Dear Angela: Remembering My So-Called Life*, edited by Michel Byers and David Lavery (New York: Lexington Books, 2007 — the second book in the series Critical Studies in Television), explains that the music video Jordan is watching is the Divinyls' "I Touch Myself." In 1994 at least some viewers would have been familiar with this song (some might still remember it) and be able to recognize the relevance of the lyrics to both Angela's and Jordan's situations: "I don't want anybody else/And when I think about you/I touch myself"; "I close my eyes/And see you before me/Think I would die/If you were to ignore me." Maloy's essay is very useful in tracking the various recyclings of pop music in the series — though strangely, she doesn't discuss W. G. Snuffy Walden's score for the film.

2   Hemingway's "My Old Man," the penultimate story in *In Our Time*, is a more sophisticated version of the earlier Anderson story, "I Want to Know Why" (from Anderson's 1921 collection *The Triumph of the Egg*). Both stories focus on young adolescent boys discovering the corruption of the adult world around them.

3   In "Holden Caulfield in Doc Martens: *The Catcher in the Rye* and *My So-Called Life*," chapter 10 of *Dear Angela*, Barbara Bell explores the similarities, especially in the language used by Holden and by Angela and her friends, concluding that "in Angela Chase is much of Holden Caulfield reincarnated" (153).

4   For detailed discussions of the use of music (specifically, the recycling of popular music) in *My So-Called Life* and *Clueless* see "Their So-Called Scene: Uses of Popular Music" by Kelli Maloy, in *Dear Angela*; and "Clueless about Listening Formations?" by Ben Aslinger, in the *Clueless* dossier in *Cinema Journal*: 53, no. 3 (2014), 126-30.

5   In "'We've Got to Work on Your Accent and Vocabulary': Characterization through Verbal Style in *Clueless*." *Cinema Journal* 53: no. 3 (2014), Jennifer O'Meara explores the nuances of adolescent speech in *Clueless*. Though the films are more or less contemporaneous, the speech mannerisms emphasized are rather different. In both the TV series and the film, "like" is used as a kind of punctuation — but the more famous vocal particularities in *Clueless* — "As If!" for example, and the use of "way" instead of "very," "way harsh!" — are generally different. In a way this is surprising since both Holzman and Heckerling used visits to local LA schools as research for their dialogue. Melissa Lenos, editor of the "In Focus," section of *Cinema Journal* (53, no. 3), 123-51, describes a "Quote Along" with *Clueless* that she attended in Kansas City at an Alamo Drafthouse (123) — it would appear that the speech mannerisms in the film have caught on more fully than those in the television series.

6   In "Holden Caulfield in Doc Martens: *The Catcher in the Rye* and *My So-Called Life*," chapter 10 of *Dear Angela*, Barbara Bell explores the linguistic nuances of the adolescent speakers in the series, reminding us that Winnie Holzman "took a teaching position in a suburban Los Angeles high school so that she could 'research' the language and subject matter" of the series. See also Harry I. Waters' *Newsweek* review of the series (February 21, 1994).

7   In a review of the 2007 release of the DVD set, Robert Lloyd explains that "the series taps something deep and urgent and so brimming with feeling that when the action suddenly glides into a wider sort of reality — as in a Halloween episode, with ghosts, and a Christmas episode, with singer Julia Hatfield as a grunge angel — it never violates the show's fundamental honesty" ("The Gift of Growing Pains," *Los Angeles Times*, October 28, 2007). While I empathize with the urge to give *My So-Called Life* a pass on these two episodes, unfortunately they violate just what Lloyd claims they don't.

8   Chris Brooks, "My So-Called Magical Life: Magical Realism Joins the Chase(s)," chapter 9 of *Dear Angela*, 131. Brooks reviews some of the many negative reviews of "Halloween" and "So-Called Angels."

9   Ibid., 142

10 "Halloween" was the first episode in the series not shot by Ernest Holzman, who had been director of photography for the pilot and for episodes 2 through 8: he would DP one last time, for "Other People's Mothers," after which Charles Lieberman, who was DP for "Halloween" would be DP for episodes 11 through 19. This change resulted in a somewhat different look. Holzman's camerawork seems more free-form than Lieberman's, a bit more experimental: one remembers the tracking shot around Angela, Rayanne, and Rickie during the lyrical flourish that completes the pilot; and, earlier in that episode, the slow track into Angela's face, staring at a light bulb, then hiding inside her sweater.

11 Despite their difference in age, George Willard and his high school colleagues, who are seniors, and Angela Chase and her colleagues, who are just beginning high school, are dealing with similar issues — though with different emphases. The *Winesburg, Ohio* characters seem less sophisticated about and

less interested in issues of sex than the teens in *My So-Called Life*. Presumably this has more to do with changes in what has been acceptable to publish and broadcast in different eras of American history.

12 Hemingway's *In Our Time* begins with a series of stories that focus on Nick Adams, an adolescent boy dealing with unpleasant realities at home and early sexual adventures; then its focus expands, introducing other characters and situations, while periodically returning to Nick.

13 It cannot be an accident that the title of the episode is shared by the popular feature comedy, *Life of Brian* (1979; the full title is *Monty Python's Life of Brian*), directed by Terry Jones. Jones' comedy focuses on Brian Cohen (Graham Chapman), a young Jewish man who is born on the same day, and *next door to*, Jesus Christ. Might the title "Life of Brian" be a subtle way of confirming that, from Brian's point of view (in episode 15, Brian is identified as Jewish), Angela no longer seems a goddess and the potential savior for his loneliness?

14 Given earlier moments of interaction between Jordan and Shane, the juxtaposition of Shane and Rickie during this sequence may suggest that Shane may be gay as well—or at least, that his relationship with Jordan includes a repressed level of passion.

15 Many of these echoes of earlier episodes confirm the complex ironies of episode 19, which opens with Angela's description of a dream in which she tries to catch up to Jordan and speak with him, to no avail—she is invisible to Jordan just as she was when the pilot began.

Another instance: in the pilot Sharon is surprised and upset to see Angela with her new red hair, hanging out with Rayanne in the hallway as the school day opens; at the beginning of episode 19, Rayanne sees Angela with Sharon in the hallway as the school day begins and is surprised and embarrassed—though ironically the animosity between Sharon and Rayanne that is evident early on has mollified to the point that Sharon is now Rayanne's only friend. Early in the final episode Rayanne asks Rickie, "You think I'm unhappy?" Rickie responds, "In my humble opinion, yes." Rayanne tells him he's talking like Angela, but we know from the pilot what Rayanne doesn't: that both Angela and Rickie are talking like Patty.

In "Life of Brian" Brian devastates Delia by canceling their date, then awkwardly says, "Maybe we can go somewhere else sometime—I mean catch a movie, or whatever." Near the end of the concluding episode, Rickie tells Delia, "Maybe we should go somewhere sometime, you know like to a movie, or something." The two interactions are quite distinct, though ironically the words are nearly the same.

16 Robert Lloyd, "The Gift of Growing Pains," *Los Angeles Times*, October 28, 2007.

17 Ginia Bellafante, "A Teenager in Love (So-Called)," *New York Times*, October 28, 2007.

18 As the years have passed, it has also been a pleasure to see that Claire Danes' astonishing performance as Angela Chase was merely the first accomplishment in what has become a diverse and distinctive career; and that Jared Leto's taking the lead for Frozen Embryos in episode 14 was a premonition of his becoming lead vocalist for Thirty Seconds to Mars, the internationally successful alternative rock band he formed in 1998 (of course, Leto, like Danes, has also had a diverse and accomplished acting career).

19 The revival of *My So-Called Life* was to follow their Friday night airing of *Degrassi: The Next Generation*, then the most recent Degrassi series.

20 See "The N/Noggin (USA) Celebrates the 10th Anniversary of *My So-Called Life* as the Groundbreaking Teen Drama Joins the Network's Schedule Friday," April 2004.

21 *Degrassi High*, created by Linda Schuyler and Kit Hood, was the follow-up to *The Kids of Degrassi Street*, created by Linda Schuyler (its 26 episodes ran from September 12, 1979 until January 1986) and *Degrassi Junior High*, created, like *Degrassi High*, by Linda Schuyler and Kit Hood (its 42 episodes ran from January 1987 until March 1989)—a number of the actors in *Degrassi Junior High* continued into the subsequent series. Two further series followed *Degrassi High*: *Degrassi: The Next Generation* (renamed *Degrassi* after the tenth season; and *Degrassi: Next Class*, starting with the show's second incarnation) from October 2001 until August 2015.

Andy Warhol Superstar Ondine (standing far right) presents Warhol's dual-projection *Chelsea Girls* (1966) at The Funnel, 507 King St. E., Toronto, on February 16, 1980. Photograph by John Porter, included in *John Porter's CineScenes* (2016). Courtesy John Porter.

2015

Documenting Devotion:
A Brief History of North American CineScenes

My first explorations of independent cinema, beginning in the early 1970s, were pilgrimages, first to see films in Binghamton, New York; Amherst, Massachusetts; New York City, Buffalo—at special events and/or at theaters that focused on the cinema that commercial theaters did not. When I was offered the opportunity to contribute to what would become *John Porter's CineScenes: Documentary Portraits of Alternative Film Scenes, Toronto and Beyond: 1978-2015*, a photo-book, edited by Clint Enns (published by the8fest Small-Gauge Festival, Toronto, in 2016), celebrating Super-8mm filmmaker John Porter and his archive of photographs documenting alternative film exhibition sites in Canada, I was happy to contribute what I could. I decided to make an attempt at broadening the scope of the project by providing a skeletal history of alternative film exhibition in Canada and the United States, as I had come to understand it and, in many instances, had been able to experience it. I recognize that this history is partial, especially in its coverage of Canada, but I hope it's of some limited use.

I remain deeply grateful for the various institutions and private efforts that have allowed those of us interested in the full panoply of modern cinema accomplishment to experience the films we've felt we needed to experience, during times when there would have been no other way to access them.

* * *

All art-making, including all levels of the production of cinematic art, can be understood as a spiritual enterprise. Indeed, I would argue that the ongoing discourse of various forms and levels of film production that characterizes film history from its earliest moments represents, is in essence, a modern redirection of a deep human commitment to spirituality that in earlier centuries was primarily focused on religion. For those committed to the cinematic arts, one embodiment of spirit, at least until very recently, was the aesthetically/ politically committed inscription of light/Light on and through the ever-so-fragile strip of celluloid within the quiet, intimate darkness of the movie theater. Of course, over the decades the Hollywood film industry came to think of itself as the One True Church, and while few of the cathedrals of cinema built during the 1920s and 1930s remain, sizable multiplexes, now using digital projection, have become ubiquitous, and during the holidays (the holy days) they swarm with activity.

For many devotees of cinema, however, screenings of major industry releases at multiplexes have never been enough to adequately feed the spirit. As a result, during the century-plus since the emergence of the Cinématographe, various alternative forms of exhibition, dedicated to a wider sense of the history of cinema, have developed. They have provided "protestant" alternatives: opportunities for experiencing forms of cinema that explicitly and/or implicitly *protest* against industry dominance and its ways of representing the world.

In many instances, these alternatives have generated scenes devoted to progressive cinema, serving small, dedicated communities of cineastes.

Alternatives to the excesses and disappointments of industrial cinema have nearly always needed to find exhibition venues outside the network of commercial first-run theaters. During the 1920s, especially in Europe, many of those dedicated to cinematic resistance to industrial cinema and/or to a more inclusive form of cinephilia, found their way into the film society movement, which may have begun in France as a growing network of ciné-clubs dedicated to presenting films thought to be too aesthetically daring or politically dangerous for commercial theaters (Richard Abel's *French Cinema: The First Wave, 1915-1929* [Princeton: Princeton University Press, 1984] includes an excellent chapter on the development of the French ciné-club). The film society movement quickly spread across Europe, into the United Kingdom, and to a lesser extent, even into the United States and Canada. In 1929, Symon Gould's Film Guild in New York City was successful enough to open a theater designed by Friedrich Kiesler. This theater was part of the little theater movement of the 1920s, a small, loose network of theaters dedicated to the art of cinema (See Jan-Christopher Horak's "The First American Film Avant-Garde, 1919-1945," the introduction to *Lovers of Cinema* [Madison: University of Wisconsin Press, 1995], for more information).

By the 1930s, a Canadian film society movement had become a national phenomenon and in 1935 a meeting was held in Ottawa to establish a national film organization, which came to be known as the Canadian Federation of Film Societies (for more information, see the *Handbook for Canadian Film Societies*, published by the CFFS in 1959). Throughout North America, film societies made available—often to what would now be considered sizable audience—programs of short films not considered appropriate for commercial theaters and new and classic features that could not (or could no longer) get distribution. By 1937, the Vancouver Film Society, probably the largest in Canada, boasted 2,000 members. The film society movement in Canada, and the Vancouver Film Society in particular, seem fertile fields for research. While it is difficult to assess the nature of the scenes created by specific film societies, it is equally difficult to imagine that these alternative screenings did not create engaged communities of cine-aficionados.

The film society movement was slowed by the catastrophe of the Second World War, though ironically, the rise of Nazism and the aftermath of the war's devastation helped to instigate a substantial film society movement in the United States. After the war, Frank Stauffacher was stationed in Europe, where he was able to develop a sense of film history that reached beyond the mainstream commercial feature. When he returned to California, filmmaking had become a passion, and his hunger to find other filmmakers working outside the mainstream and to develop an audience for their films led to the establishment of the Art in Cinema film society at the San Francisco Museum of Art in 1946. Amos Vogel had been a member of a film society in his native Vienna, Austria, until 1938, when he fled the expanding Nazi influence, ultimately to end up in the United States, where he and Marcia Vogel founded Cinema 16 in 1947. By September 1947, Vogel and Stauffacher were in contact; they quickly became regular correspondents and collaborators and by the 1950s their leadership had resulted in a sizable network of film societies across the United States.

While Art in Cinema, Cinema 16, the Vancouver Film Society and other film societies across North America ministered to audiences far smaller than those that frequented commercial cinemas, almost from the beginning some of these organizations were able to attract what today would seem remarkably large audiences. Art in Cinema regularly drew five hundred members to the San Francisco Museum of Art and more than that to the University of California, once the Art in Cinema series expanded to a second venue in Berkeley in March 1947. Cinema 16 was even more successful, in part because early on, Vogel made Cinema 16 his livelihood and devoted all of his energies to it (Stauffacher worked as a commercial artist to support himself and his filmmaking; Art in Cinema was not a money-earning activity). At the height of its popularity and influence, Cinema 16 boasted 7,000 members who filled a 1,600-seat auditorium at the High School of the Fashion Industries in Manhattan's garment district for each of two shows once a month, plus two and sometimes three first-run theaters at various uptown Manhattan locations.

There were other alternative exhibition options between the 1920s and 1950s, including the network of cinema clubs that ministered to amateur filmmakers: men and women who often took their work quite seriously, but generally functioned outside both the commercial film world and the art world. By the late 1930s, the American Amateur Cinema League, founded in 1926, was ministering to thousands of non-professional filmmakers through amateur cinema clubs across the country (there were 250 clubs on its rolls by 1937), providing information, offering national awards, and also, as Patricia R. Zimmermann explains, sponsoring "screenings . . . by society people in their private homes" (Zimmermann, *Reel Families: A Social History of Amateur Film* [Bloomington: Indiana University Press, 1995], 72). During the Great Depression, Tom Brandon, founder of Garrison Films, which was dedicated to the exhibition of Russian communist films, established a circuit of screening venues across the American Midwest dedicated to laborers and farmers interested in unionizing. In 1934, Brandon reported on the way in which his network functioned: "The operator travels in an old Ford from town to town, but his 16-millimeter sound projector is new and does the job well. The farmers eat it up. They flock in from miles around, and see the pictures in barns, schools, town halls; once even in a big funeral parlor loaned by a friendly mortician" (quoted in William Alexander, *Film on the Left: American Documentary Film from 1931 to 1942* [Princeton: Princeton University Press, 1981], 37).

Of course, all these efforts to develop new possibilities for seeing a wider variety of films are a function of the fact that from the 1920s through the '50s, there were few places where Americans and Canadians could see anything but first- or second-run commercial features and shorts; and early on, television offered only the most limited kinds of programming. Film society members do seem to have been interested in what we would consider experimental or avant-garde forms of film, but only within wide-ranging programs that also presented, indeed highlighted, classic American shorts and features no longer in circulation, informational documentaries of various kinds, political films, and commercial features from abroad (often features that included more liberal attitudes about nudity and the depiction of sexuality)—that is, many of the forms of moving-image media that by the late 1960s and early '70s were becoming ubiquitous at film series at institutions of higher learning, and at museums across the country, even to a limited extent on television. As many of these kinds of film became more widely available, the nature of "alternative" screenings was continually redefined.

During the 1960s and '70s, a new kind of alternative screening venue developed that, for a time, seemed more stable than a film society: the new excitement about seeing *and making* forms of cinema that implicitly critiqued commercial moviemaking generated institutions, often supported by government arts funding, which provided both workshop opportunities and regular screenings. In New York City, there was the Millennium Film Workshop and The Collective for Living Cinema; in Toronto, there was Light Cone; in Minneapolis/St. Paul, Film in the Cities. These combined workshop/screening venues developed in many cities. The early film societies tended to be membership organizations—the only way to avoid the widespread censorship of film in those days. Generally, they seem to have been geared to audiences made up of art-interested, upper-middle-class adults (the membership of Cinema 16 was generated by an annual advertisement in *The New York Times*). These new organizations were geared to young people, and the (limited but crucial) governmental support they received allowed those who frequented the screenings or used the workshop facilities to do so at minimal cost. And just as important, they generated small communities dedicated to cinematic experiment—small but energetic scenes that enlivened the cultural landscape of their cities, and became, for those living further away, pilgrimage destinations where individuals living in more isolated circumstances could re-energize and feel part of a national-international network of like-minded cineastes.

While some of these experimental workshop/screening centers continue to exist (there is the Northwest Film Forum in Seattle, Washington; Squeaky Wheel in Buffalo, New York; and UnionDocs in Brooklyn, which specializes in experimental documentary), economic conditions during recent decades, as well as other developments, have redirected the interest in alternative forms of cinema and the desire for communities of cineastes dedicated to progressive media into new directions: most obviously, into the ever-proliferating world of film festivals and into what have come to be called "micro-cinemas."

The sheer number of film festivals has become remarkable, and of course, the best known of the festivals—Cannes, Toronto, Berlin, Telluride, Sundance, New York, Locarno—seem primarily geared to relatively affluent filmgoers. Less glitzy scenes have developed around smaller festivals, sometimes dedicated to particular forms of alternative cinema (the Chicago Underground Film Festival, for example; and the Camden International Film Festival in tiny Camden, Maine, which focuses on documentary; or the Images Festival in Toronto, which is dedicated to experimental film); as well as alongside major festivals (for some years "Views from the Avant-Garde" was a sidebar to the New York Film Festival—it is now called "Projections"—and "Wavelengths" is a sidebar to TIFF). These festivals provide crucial nodal points for cineastes who gather annually to share their excitement about the ongoing evolution of alternatives to mass-market cinema.

Judging from my limited experience with them, the recent micro-cinema movement is the embodiment of an attitude expressed by Tom Gunning in an influential article published in the Winter 1989-90 issue of *Motion Picture* ("Towards a Minor Cinema: Fonoroff, Herwitz, Ahwesh, Lapore, Klahr and Solomon"), where he argues that the younger filmmakers who most interest him forswear aspiration to mastery, fashioning from their marginality films that "assert no vision of conquest, make no claims to hegemony." While an earlier generation of filmmakers might have worked at breaking out of the avant-garde ghetto, these new filmmakers "proudly wear the badge of the ghetto." Contemporary micro-cinemas minister to audiences who accept and embrace their culturally "minor" status and that of the filmmakers they gather to see. Indeed, they attend micro-cinemas in part *because* of the intimacy of these micro-cinema scenes and because the films shown and the filmmakers who make them have chosen a more intimate way of functioning as film artists.

As "*micro*-cinema" suggests, this network of exhibition venues, now spread across North America, is made up of very small, intimate communities of women and men who gather to enjoy forms of cinema that have virtually no chance of being seen in first-run theaters, on television, or even within many educational institutions. YouTube and other online sites have made some work available, but, in general, at the cost of seeing the work as it was meant to be seen. During the past two decades, the micro-cinema movement has provided many audiences with momentary reprieves from a contemporary culture characterized by violence and hysterical consumption, and by doing so, have helped to maintain the vitality of the independent filmmaking movement that germinated during the 1920s and flowered during the second half of the twentieth century. That a number of micro-cinemas happen to be housed in now-defunct churches is a coincidence that supports my sense of the micro-cinema movement as a cine-spiritual development.

In the United States, one key pioneering project that was based on the valuing of intimacy (of the *micro*) as a component of filmgoing and that seems to have led the way toward the micro-cinema movement was Bruce Baillie's original Canyon Cinema. Baillie has described Canyon's beginnings:

> We started Canyon Cinema about 1960, in Canyon, California, over the hills from Oakland and Berkeley. Kikuko [Baillie's partner at the time] was paying the rent and giving me the chance to free up my time to make films. Immediately I realized that making films and showing films must go hand in hand, so I got a job at Safeway, took out a loan and bought a projector. We got an army surplus screen and hung it up real nice in the backyard of this house we were renting. Then we'd find whatever films we could, including our own little things that were in progress—"we," there wasn't really any we, just myself for a while—and show them.

So I made a *thing* of it. I had no occupation. I couldn't get a real job anywhere. So I thought, I'll invent my own occupation. I set up a little part of the house as an office. I had to call it something: I put up a little sign and it turned out to be "Canyon Cinema" with a light bulb next to it. Fairly soon, we had weekly showings. Kikuko made popcorn. The kids around the neighborhood gathered the community benches and chairs, and we'd sit under the trees in the summer with all the dogs and people and watch French or Canadian Embassy films and National Film Board of Canada stuff, along with our own. I let it be known immediately that I had a place to show films, if any filmmakers were coming through town. I let Jonas [Mekas] know right away.

> Baillie in MacDonald, *A Critical Cinema 2*
> (Berkeley: University of California Press, 1992), 113-14

The mood at Canyon Cinema seems to have been quite different from the scenes that developed around the 1940s and '50s film societies: Baillie was less involved in connecting filmgoers with High Culture than with invigorating local culture. By the mid-1960s, Baillie had been joined by Chick Strand, and Canyon had become a nomadic screening organization, presenting programs at various venues in the Bay Area, including Ernest Callenbach's backyard. Callenbach remembers:

We would set up Bruce's old projector and a screen of some kind on the other end of the yard, and invite all the neighbors—because the soundtracks were often pretty raucous. And people would come in. It was really a neat scene because Chicky Strand, who had, and probably still has, a real sense of drama, would wear a kind of witchy cloak and her long black hair down, and she would sit with a couple of candles in the garage that went through from the street to my backyard, and that was the "box office." She would collect the money and chat with people, and then they'd go on in, bringing sleeping bags and jugs of wine and so on. They'd sort of crash all over the deck and after a while we'd show the films to maybe thirty or forty people. Not immense, but enough—and they were pretty regular; they would come . . . maybe once a month. Some of them helped out with Canyon's operation in some way, but most people just showed up hoping to see something unusual.

> Unpublished interview with the author, 11/6/02

This seems the very spirit of the micro-cinema. Indeed, when Rebecca Barton and David Sherman established their breakthrough micro-cinema, "Total Mobile Home," in 1994—they hosted filmmakers and film screenings in their home in San Francisco, once a week from 1994 until 1997—they had Baillie's early Canyon Cinema in mind: during Total Mobile Home's first year Barton/Sherman organized a series of morning salons with Baillie where the connections between what they were doing and what Baillie had done were discussed.

One crucial distinction between the current network of micro-cinemas and the other American experiments in alternative exhibition that have been mentioned is a function of our film-historical moment. The film society movement in the United States was possible because of the advent of financially accessible 16mm prints and projectors (of course, Cinema *16*'s name is a sign of this). Once 16mm became more accessible in the years following World War II, it became the gauge of choice for avant-garde filmmakers and remained so for more than half a century. Indeed, it remains the gauge of choice for a good many filmmakers even now, despite the shrinking support system for 16mm production and exhibition. Micro-cinemas provide support for filmmakers still working and exhibiting in 16mm, and in smaller gauges as well. This is a particularly valuable service to the field, made all the more significant since American academe, which for so many years depended on 16mm exhibition, has for the most part allowed this tried-and-true exhibition technology to disappear from campuses—smaller film gauges were never embraced, at least in American academe. Given the fact that so much of alternative cinema history has been produced in 16mm (and 8mm and Super-8mm), specifically for exhibition in those gauges, this abrogation of responsibility on the part of so many academics has the potential to do long-term damage to our sense of film history. Fortunately, the current network of micro-cinemas, run and attended by true lovers of alternative media, is helping to keep the full range of film-historical achievement alive.

In general, individual micro-cinemas have limited financial resources; nevertheless, the ever-evolving micro-cinema network provides young (and not only young) filmmakers with a set of intimate screening spaces spread across North America where new forms of cinema and cinema-related activities find enthusiastic and appreciative audiences in tiny but vibrant cine-scenes. There are relatively high-profile micro-cinemas (some stretch the definition of "micro"): Light Industry in Brooklyn, New York, for example; but smaller venues have become ubiquitous. Some of them are well known: the Aurora Picture Show in Houston, Texas, for example; Craig Baldwin's Other Cinema in San Francisco; Toronto's CineCycle; Cinema Project in Portland, Oregon; and the mobile Balagan film series in the Boston area; others are in the process of building reputations: the Microscope Gallery in Brooklyn; Exploded View in Tucson, Arizona; Dominic Angerame's Art in Cinema in San Francisco…

Since micro-cinemas *are* micro, they tend to be under the radar for most conventional cineastes—and often the scenes they have created are ignored by glossy periodicals and major newspapers, even by periodicals devoted to cinema. Fortunately, there are those whose dedication to cinematic alternatives has expressed itself in attempts to create a broader consciousness of the remarkable work of the women and men who do the hard work of keeping the full range of cinema alive. Few in North America have been as dedicated in this regard as Toronto's John "Super-8" Porter, who has been not only a remarkably prolific filmmaker and a fervent supporter of alternative film venues in the Toronto area for decades, but a chronicler of the many cine-scenes he has been a part of and has visited over the years. The images in this collection capture the intimacy of alternative screening spaces and document the accomplished individual makers whose work continues to create unpretentiously vibrant cine-scenes across the continent. Porter's photographic tribute to alternative screening spaces and moments is a gift to all who love cinema—and a moving reminiscence of a life spent in spiritual devotion to what Stan Brakhage might call the Light of Cinema and the adventures of perception the wide world of cinema makes possible for us.

This essay was published in Clint Enns, ed., *John Porter's CineScenes: Documentary Portraits of Alternative Film Scenes, Toronto and Beyond, 1978-2015* (2016), in a first edition of 500, in conjunction with the8fest Small Gauge Film Festival, Toronto, Ontario, Canada.

Shirley (Stephanie Cumming) in Gustav Deutsch's *Shirley—Visions of Reality*, reading Emily Dickinson poems in a train car while waiting for the train to leave; with her journalist partner in a New York City apartment; and, having lost her partner, during the intermission of a film. The images are evocations of Edward Hopper paintings: "Chair Car," "Room in New York," and "Intermission." Thanks to Jerzy Palacz.

2015

Essay for DVD release of Gustav Deutsch's *Shirley—Visions of Reality* (2013)

Shirley—Visions of Reality (written, directed, and edited by Gustav Deutsch; key scenic artist, Hanna Schimek; cinematography by Jerzy Palacz) begins with a framing sequence, the first image of which slowly comes into focus: Shirley (Stephanie Cumming), the protagonist of the film, enters a train car, sits down and appears to be reading a collection of Emily Dickinson poems (a 1959 Edward Hopper painting, "Excursion into Philosophy" is the illustration on the cover). Each of the twelve sequences that follows the opening sequence, which is based on Hopper's "Chair Car" (1965; "Excursion into Philosophy," reappears as the ninth sequence) is a remarkably precise evocation of a specific Hopper painting. But while Hopper's individual paintings present a woman in relative isolation, without creating a narrative, *Shirley—Visons of Reality* dramatizes a somewhat surreal series of related moments in Shirley's life over a period of 32 years—surreal, because (like Orlando in Sally Potter's eponymous film) Shirley doesn't age, though her fashions change over the decades. In the end, *Shirley—Visons of Reality* returns us to the opening sequence and, as the train begins to move, we realize that the previous sequences have been flashbacks to events that have led up to Shirley's return to Paris (during "Hotel Room," the second sequence in the film, Shirley is making ready to return to New York after an apparently extended Parisian visit).

Each of the twelve central sequences is introduced by a fade-in from darkness, with visual texts indicating the date, year, time and place of the action, and a male voice-over that provides a gloss of three events that were news on the 28th of August in a series of years: 1931, 1932, 1939, 1940, 1942, 1952, 1956, 1957, 1959, 1961, 1963—a second 1963 sequence is dated the 29th of August. Visually each of the twelve five-to-eight-minute sequences is based on a Hopper painting painted the same year, and dramatizes an imagined extended moment in Shirley's life. In other words, the film embeds a skeletal narrative of Shirley's experiences both within a skeletal review of world events and cultural changes, and within a panorama of Hopper's paintings.

Watching *Shirley* in 2024, with an awareness of the history of the filmic "supercut" and especially Max Tohline's *A Supercut of Supercuts* (2024; see chapter 26), I see the film in a new way—as something like a feature-length (89 minutes) supercut. To make the film, Deutsch and Schimek explored Hopper's extensive *oeuvre* and selected, re-staged, and re-enacted a series of thirteen Edward Hopper paintings, each of which focuses on a young woman—in some paintings there are other characters, but it's quickly clear that in each instance "Shirley" is the visual focus (as well as a frequent narrator during the events portrayed). Deutsch's cinematic re-enactments of the paintings are organized in an obvious narrative sequence. But to the degree that one is familiar with Hopper's work and these particular paintings, it is obvious that at one specific moment during each shot, Deutsch is mimicking the composition of the original painting. That is, in addition to the narrative (syntagmatic) trajectory of Shirley's life, there are also paradigmatic dimensions to the film, including the choice of paintings (each focusing on a woman during a quiet, thoughtful moment) and our knowing, whether we can identify all of them or not, that within any sequence a particular moment will carefully echo the composition of the chosen painting.

In order, after "Chair Car," the Hopper paintings evoked are "Hotel Room," "Room in New York," "New York Movie," "Office at Night," Hotel Lobby," "Morning Sun," Sunlight on Brownstones," "Western Motel," "Excursion into Philosophy," "A Woman in the Sun," "Intermission," and "Sun in an Empty Room"—"Chair Car" closes the narrative.

Jerzy Palacz's cinematography was awarded the Austrian Camera Prize.

* * *

Cinema's engagement with painters and painting has a considerable history. There have been documentaries about painters at work (e.g., *Jackson Pollock 51* [1951], by Hans Namuth and Paul Falkenberg; Emile de Antonio's *Painters Painting: the New York Art Scene 1940-1970* [1972]; and Corinna Belz's *Gerhard Richter Painting* [2011]); and serious biopics (*Edvard Munch*, 1974) by Peter Watkins, for example—as well as a fascination with the private lives of painters, from Michelangelo (*The Agony and the Ecstasy*, 1965), Johannes Vermeer (*Girl with a Pearl Earring*, 2003) and Van Gogh (*Lust for Life*, 1956) to Frida Kahlo (*Frida*, 2002), Jackson Pollock (*Pollock*, 2000), and Jean-Michel Basquiat (*Basquiat*, 1996). And in 2011 Lech Majewski directed *The Mill and the Cross*, an exploration of the social context and ideological implications of Pieter Bruegel the Elder's 1564 painting *The Way to Calvary*, based on Michael Francis Gibson's book. But in the annals of films-about-painters/painting, so far as I know, there has never been a film like Gustav Deutsch's *Shirley—Visions of Reality* (2013). While earlier films have focused on artists-at-work and on painters as characters in melodrama, in *Shirley—Visions of Reality,* Deutsch uses carefully fabricated evocations of the paintings of Edward Hopper to rethink the work of the canonical American painter and create a new kind of film experience.

For those of us on the North American side of the Atlantic, *Shirley—Visions of Reality* seemed, at first look, unprecedented in Deutsch's work. We have known Deutsch as a cinematic "recycler," a film artist fascinated with the past history of film and interested in presenting elements of the global motion-picture archive within new cinematic forms—in such works as his *Film ist.*: parts 1-6 (1998); parts 7-12 (2002); and *a girl & a gun* (2009). As Tom Gunning has put it, in Deutsch's films images of the past "are refined and transmuted to yield a range of temporal experience, as a new present arises from fossilized films and the conjunctions of shots revitalize slumbering meanings" (See Gunning's "From Fossils of Time to a Cinematic Genesis," in *Gustav Deutsch*, edited by Wilbirg Brainin-Donnenberg and Michael Loebenstein [Vienna: Austrian Film Museum, 2009], 180).

But in fact, Deutsch has always been more than a master of recycled cinema. Trained in architecture, he has worked in a variety of installation modes, and in 2003 he collaborated with architect Franz Berzl to construct a camera obscura on the Greek island of Aegina. Deutsch's fascination with Edward Hopper has also taken "architectural" form: in 2008 he exhibited *Wednesday, 28 August 1957, 6 p.m., Pacific Palisades*, a full-scale installation based on Edward Hopper's *Western Motel* (1957) in the exhibition "Edward Hopper and Contemporary Art" at Kunsthalle Vienna; and in 2009, he exhibited *Thursday, August 28th, 1952, 6 a.m., New York*, based on Hopper's *Morning Sun* (1952), as part of a Hopper retrospective at the Palazzo Reale in Milan. By building the scenes depicted in *Western Motel* and *Morning Sun*, Deutsch revealed that the often-assumed realism of Hopper's painting in fact requires surreal distortions of physical reality.

Deutsch's ongoing considerations of Hopper's painting culminated in "Shirley—Visions of Reality," a major installation show, realized together with his collaborator and partner Hanna Schimek at Künstlerhaus, Vienna, as well as Deutsch's first feature-length narrative film. As different as *Shirley— Visions of Reality* can seem from Deutsch's recycled cinema work, it relies on an organization employed in many parts of *Film ist.*: the visual catalogue. Deutsch often arranges excerpts from early films so that a particular detail—one that might not otherwise be noticeable—becomes the focal point. For example, in the final piece of the second series of *Film ist.* (sequence 12.5) the focus is dogs that spontaneously make themselves part of imagery recorded in a very wide range of places and for a wide range of purposes. Something amusing about the nature of canines and their obliviousness to the purpose of filmmaking comes through this delightful sequence. Essentially, *Shirley—Visions of Reality* is a catalogue of cinematic recreations of thirteen Edward Hopper paintings, with which Deutsch creates a magical panorama of Hopper's work and a skeletal narrative that offers implicit commentary on the painter's life and the American history he was part of.

Cinema's "magical" ability to engage us in the lives of characters has long been a popular topic, but in *Shirley* the narrative, while engaging, is subsumed within a form of magic closer to that in Roméo Bossetti's *The Automatic Moving Company* (1912), where what is most obvious to a modern audience is the considerable labor involved in constructing the time-lapse illusion of furniture moving itself into an apartment without human assistance. The precision of Deutsch's evocations of Hopper paintings in *Shirley—Visions of Reality* cannot fail to astonish. Clearly, these cinematic recreations were a labor of love for Deutsch and Schimek—and on first viewing their courage and the research and labor involved in doing what they've done tend to be the emotional foreground of the experience.

I suppose it would be possible to enjoy *Shirley* even if one had no awareness of Hopper's paintings: the film would then be a formalized, visually arresting, temporal picaresque focusing on moments in a woman's maturation, from her visiting Paris in 1931 as a youth, to dealing with the aftereffects of the Great Depression, with her involvement in the Group Theatre and later on with the Living Theater, with her long relationship with photo-journalist Stephen, and at the end with her loss of Stephen and her preparations to start a new life in Europe where she hopes to rejoin the Living Theater. For anyone who does know Edward Hopper's work, however, Deutsch's implicit homage sends us back to the original paintings, in order to ruminate on crucial differences within the apparent similarities between painterly and cinematic imaging, and to see how the filmmaker has positioned the painter's compositions within a narrative framework.

While Hopper's paintings nearly always provide a vision of a single moment in time, often a moment of stasis when a character or characters seem to be coming to grips with some concern or a strong emotion, Deutsch's cinematic transformations of these paintings are presented in five-to-eight-minute sequences during which at some point the graphic organization of the original painting is, for a brief moment, quite precisely mimicked. Deutsch uses zooms-in and zooms-out and short panning shots to create a mini-narrative around the moment frozen in the Hopper painting, and through the use of sound (voice-overs by "Shirley," radio broadcasts, environmental noises, and minimalist music composed by Christian Fennesz) offers an imagining of the psychic context within which the frozen moment in the Hopper painting might have occurred. Purists might argue that it is precisely their ambiguity that gives Hopper's paintings their resonance, but Deutsch's contextualizing leaves much to the imagination—and of course we understand that his is just one possible reading of the context that might have surrounded the moments Hopper painted.

Once we begin to examine *Shirley* in detail, and move beyond our astonishment at the precision of Deutsch's versions of the Hopper paintings, we notice the inevitable differences between painting and cinema that, despite his efforts, Deutsch could not have overcome, even had he wanted to. Most obvious perhaps is the standard aspect ratio of modern cinema, which is substantially wider than the shape of Hopper's paintings. There is also the distinction between Hopper's painterly color, illuminated by reflected environmental light, and the cinematic color created by a combination of translucence and reflection: *Shirley* does evoke Hopper's distinctive sense of color and chiaroscuro, but Schimek reworked Hopper's color for the film by using only monochromatic colors, which gives the film versions of the paintings more of a Pop Art look. And most obviously, perhaps, by having the characters move around in the space delineated by the frame, Deutsch transforms the tendency toward flatness in Hopper's paintings into the illusion of three dimensions. Ultimately, Deutsch's re-creations are entirely distinctive within the history of cinema: if the similarities between the Hopper paintings and Deutsch's imagings of them are what first strikes us, the difference between the look of *Shirley* and the look of virtually all other films is impossible to miss.

As is true in many of the particular pieces in *Film ist.*, Deutsch is playful within the rigorous formal organization of the film, which is emphasized by his introducing each of the episodes with a textual indication of the date, time of day, and location; and a male voice-over providing brief excerpts of the news of August 28th in the years of Shirley's life (also, the years when the various paintings were completed). These regular bits of news are reminiscent of the "newsreel" sections of John Dos Passos' *U.S.A.* trilogy (1930, 1932, 1936), which Deutsch considered an influence on the film. From time to time, Deutsch surprises the expectations his organization has created: for example, in his re-creation of Hopper's *Hotel Lobby* (1943), Deutsch begins by treating the lobby (where an elderly couple on the left awaits a taxi to take them to the Schubert Theater in New Haven while, on the right, Shirley reads *The Skin of Our Teeth* by Thornton Wilder) like the other locations in the film: that is, as part of a straightforward narrative. Then, once the elderly couple has left, Deutsch transforms the space into a stage set with a spotlight on Shirley, who is rehearsing her role as Sabina in the Wilder play, which premiered in the autumn of 1943 at the Shubert Theater under the direction of Elia Kazan. The lifting of the columns in the lobby is a reference to *The Skin of Our Teeth*, during which parts of the sets disappear. Shirley then addresses the film audience with the same words that Sabina uses to address the audience of the play. For those familiar with Hopper's love of the theater, this sequence suggests the influence of stage sets on various Hopper paintings.

Deutsch's designation of his central character as "Shirley" may be a reference to Jo Hopper (Josephine Nivison Hopper, Hopper's wife) who called the woman in Hopper's *Office at Night* (1940) by that name—see Gail Levin's *Edward Hopper: An Intimate Biography* (New York: Rizzoli, 2007), 325—though Deutsch's Shirley is far more her own woman than Jo Hopper seems to have been. Indeed, Shirley can be read as Deutsch's subtle feminist response to the oft-troubled relationship between Edward and his painter wife in an era when gender assumptions seem to have constricted their ability to cooperate and collaborate in a manner satisfactory to both of them. Deutsch and Schimek worked together for nearly 30 years [Deutsch died in 2019] and they developed methods of working comfortably both separately and together. *Shirley—Visions of Reality* is their most impressive collaboration—and a thoroughly remarkable contribution to modern cinema.

This essay was originally published in the booklet that accompanies the 2015 DVD release of *Shirley: Visions of Reality*. Deutsch's films are available from SIXPACKFILM in Vienna, Austria. I interviewed Deutsch about his work, including *Shirley: Visions of Reality*, for *The Sublimity of Document* (New York: Oxford University Press, 2019), 51-72.

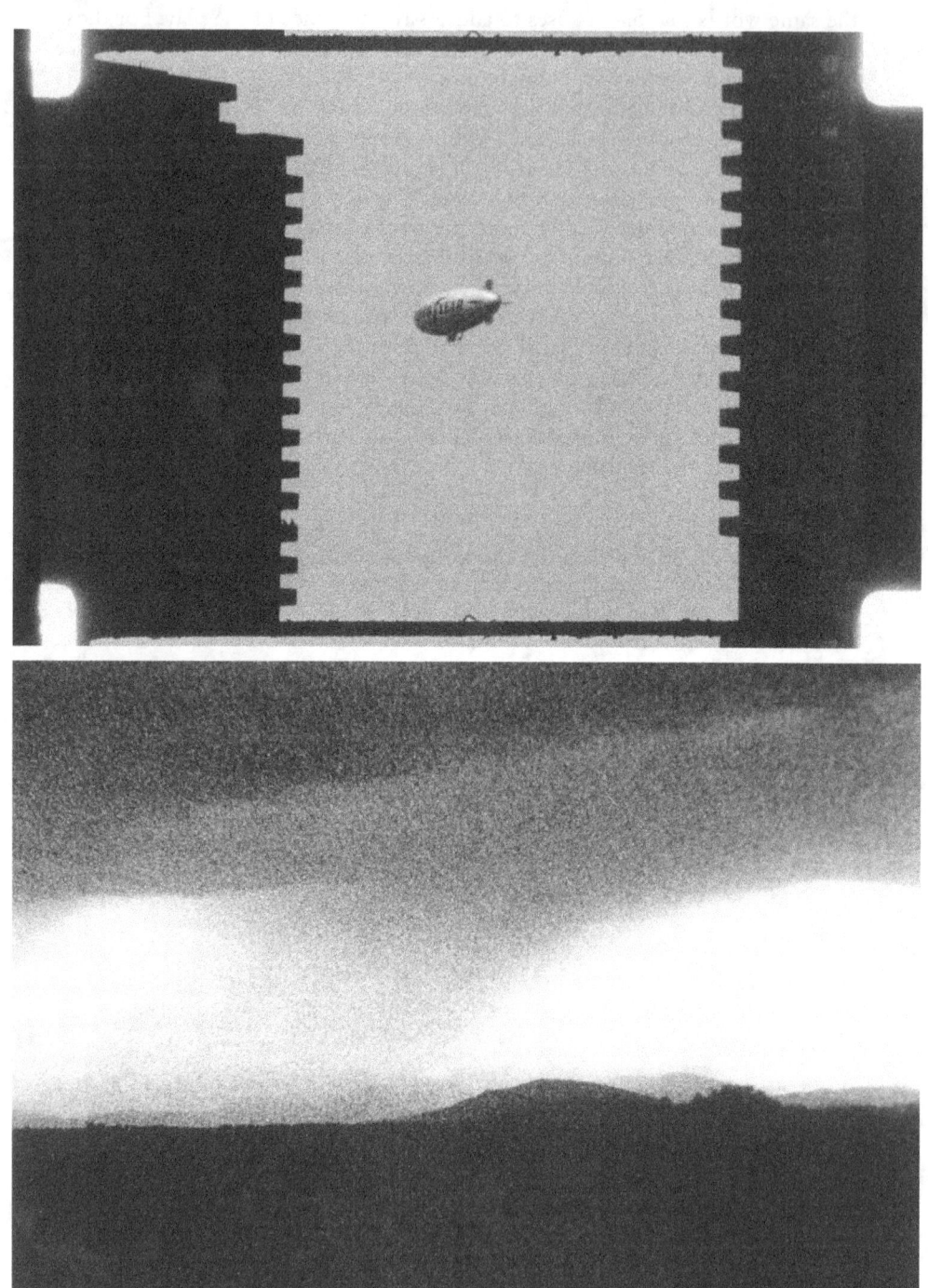

Stills from Peter Hutton's *New York Portrait, Part II* (1980) and *Landscape (for Manon)* (1987). All stills courtesy of Peter Hutton.

2016

Peter Hutton: Hudson River Filmmaker

When Peter Hutton died in 2016, we lost one of the preeminent American independent filmmakers and, with James Benning, the preeminent landscape filmmaker of our era. Further, since Hutton had worked almost exclusively in 16mm, and since good 16mm projection has become, at least in the United States, available only in well-equipped archives, our access to Hutton's films is, for the moment, in limbo.

Hutton's commitment to black and white, 16mm shooting, despite the availability of digital, had to do with the palette and texture of 16mm as well as the 16mm aspect ratio, and since Hutton's films are resolutely silent, the limitations of 16mm sound were not an issue for him. Hutton is not the only filmmaker who devoted himself to 16mm. Betsy Bromberg has continued to work in 16mm and my guess is that Hutton would agree with her reasoning, circa 2012, when I interviewed her about *Voluptuous Sleep* (2011):

> My filmmaking certainly reflects the fact that I'm working in a medium that's almost at its end. This inevitability has given me license to make the most of the medium, to saturate the film with as much light and color and sensuality as possible. The films I'm making now could not be made in any other medium, which is why I'm shooting them on film, while I still can.

Bromberg followed *Voluptuous Sleep* with *Glide of Transparency* (2017), another 16mm feature, this one a stunning color panorama of tiny vistas shot in the small gardens around her home in Tajunga, California; and in June of 2024, when I asked if she still felt as she did in 2012 about 16mm, she said:

> YES! I'm still hoping to finish the new one on film, but I'll have to see if it's viable when the time comes. But I can't imagine shooting at the front end on anything but film as long as it's available and I can afford it. For me, celluloid is both more intimate and more mysterious. And more fun! I've been sketching out my edit on digital before I move to cutting the workprint, but I find I need to periodically project the workprint to remember how the images really look.

Hutton did return to color shooting—his earliest film, *In Marin County* (1970) was in color—for *Time and Tide* (2000), *Skagafjördur* (2004), and *At Sea* (2007). His last film, *Three Landscapes* (2013), shot in 16mm and in color, is available only for digital presentation.

This essay was written for a catalogue produced in conjunction with a lecture and screening event on October 9, 2016, hosted by the Thomas Cole National Historic Site in Catskill, New York, commemorating Hutton's films as a modern contribution to the history of Hudson River landscape painting. The catalogue was made possible by the support of friends and long-time admirers of Hutton's work, including James Benning, Erin Espelie, David Gatten, Alfred Guzzetti, Tom Gunning, John Knecht, Sharon Lockhart, Robb Moss, Patricia O'Connor, Adele Pressman, David Rodowick, and Patricia Zimmermann.

The beautifully illustrated catalogue is available for sale at the Thomas Cole site.

* * *

Barbara Novak's famous distinction between two approaches to American landscape in nineteenth-century painting—"grand opera" and "the still small voice"—remains useful for twentieth-century cinema, and not merely as a theoretical construct that assists in distinguishing different kinds of work developing from different aesthetic sensibilities.[1] The two areas of contemporary cinema that conform to Novak's categories are responses to some of the same historical developments that produced the paintings in her *Nature and Culture* surveys; and their positions vis-à-vis contemporary culture are analogous to the positions occupied by the "grand operatic" painters and the "Luminists" (and a bit later, the "Tonalists") with regard to mid-nineteenth-century commercial development.

To a significant degree, the grand landscape epitomized by Frederic Edwin Church and the Rocky Mountain School (Albert Bierstadt, Thomas Moran, Thomas Hill) became, and has remained, the literal, as well as one of the historical backgrounds of commercial films, from the earliest attempts to interest filmgoers in natural scenes, to John Ford's depiction of Monument Valley in such films as *Stagecoach* (1939), *Fort Apache* (1948), and *The Searchers* (1956), and to more recent popular films such as *Dances with Wolves* (1990), *The Last of the Mohicans* (1992), *What Dreams May Come* (1998), and *Into the Wild* (2007); and it has played a major role in the history of independent feature filmmaking, from Robert Flaherty's *Nanook of the North* (1921) to Babette Mangolte's *The Sky on Location* (1983), Godfrey Reggio's *Koyaanisqatsi* (1984) and Robert Fricke's *Baraka* (1993) and *Samsara* (2011).

But the "still small voices" of Luminism and Tonalism are also alive, not as a major influence on commercial cinema but as sensibilities of considerable use in coming to terms with a number of accomplished American independent filmmakers of recent decades, including Larry Gottheim, James Benning, Sharon Lockhart, Nathaniel Dorsky, Leighton Pierce, and perhaps most obviously, Peter Hutton.

Art historians have defined "Luminism" in a variety of ways since John Baur coined the term in the 1940s, to refer to the work of John Frederick Kensett, Sanford Gifford, Martin Johnson Heade, and Fitz Henry Lane, and to selected paintings by Thomas Cole and Frederic Church.[2] Generally, Novak and others have described the Luminists as offering a more meditative route to the spiritual than that provided by the awe-inspiring paintings of Church, Bierstadt, and Moran: "In contrast to the operatic landscape, Luminism is classic rather than baroque, contained rather than expansive, aristocratic rather than democratic, private not public, introverted not gregarious, exploring a state of being rather than becoming."[3] Stylistically, Luminism is identified with a particular rendering of atmospheric effects—specifically, as Angela Miller puts it, a "[r]esonant, light-suffused atmosphere [that] melded topographic divisions into a visually seamless whole,"[4] often presented in comparatively small compositions extended along the horizontal. Generally, the paintings betray little or no evidence of the artists' "labor trail" so obvious in contemporaneous, European impressionist painting and in modernist work in general.

There seems little point in exploring the origins of cinema for a single progenitor of the Luminist sensibility evident in more recent independent films. Film scholars are in the process of reconstructing early American film history, and while landscape has, so far, played a relatively small role in this process, it is clear that even during the dawn of cinema history the depiction of landscape, or at least "landscape," was considered significant. While landscape is not a central issue in the widely known actualities and proto-narratives produced by the Edison Studio and the Lumière Brothers in the 1890s, the "landscape film" was an early genre of American filmmaking. The Library of Congress lists dozens of titles that claim as their central focus not only American landscapes, but also, in a good many instances, precisely those landscapes made popular by the Hudson River and Rocky Mountain painters of the nineteenth century: the Catskill Mountains and Kaaterskill Falls in particular, Niagara Falls, Yosemite Valley, Yellowstone.[5] However, while the titles of many of the early films identify landscape as their subject, it must be said that most of them are really about railroad travel *through* landscapes and are more fully focused on the railroad tracks than on the landscapes themselves.

Faced with the challenge of turning the new medium of cinema into a popular, economically successful enterprise, early filmmakers did the obvious: they attempted to impress viewers; and the last thing they could be expected to do is produce films that appealed to a meditative sensibility. By the late 1920s, however, as filmmakers began to reflect on cinema's high-speed commercial development and on modern development in general, premonitions of a more meditative sensibility are evident in Ralph Steiner's *H20* (1929) and in Henwar Rodakiewicz's *Portrait of a Young Man* (1931). In these two films, and particularly in *Portrait*, a sensibility close to what would later inform Peter Hutton's work is already in evidence.

During his nearly half-century as an independent filmmaker, Hutton made a meditative gaze, especially a gaze on qualities of light and atmosphere, his fundamental rhetorical gesture, and in many instances he, quite consciously, provided viewers with film experiences that stand in relation to popular movie-going and to the dynamics of most independent cinema, precisely as "the still small voice" of Luminist painting stands in relation to the more aggressive dynamics of the more widely popular "operatic" school of nineteenth-century landscape painting. Hutton says:

> Most people go to films to get some kind of hit, some kind of overwhelming experience, whether it's like an amusement park ride or an ideological, informational hit that gives you a critical insight into an issue or an idea. But for those few people who feel they need a reprieve occasionally, who want to cleanse the palate a bit, whether for spiritual or physiological reasons, these films seem to be somewhat effective.
>
> I've never felt that my films are very important in terms of the History of Cinema. They offer a little detour from such grand concepts. They appeal primarily to people who enjoy looking at nature, or who enjoy having a moment to study something that's not fraught with information. The experience of my films is a little like daydreaming. It's about taking the time to just sit down and look at things, which I don't think is a very Western preoccupation. A lot of influences on me when I was younger were more Eastern. They suggested a contemplative way of looking— whether at painting, sculpture, architecture, or just a landscape—where the more time you spend actually looking at things, the more they reveal themselves in ways that you don't expect.

For the most part, people don't allow themselves the time or the circumstances to get into a relationship with the world that provides freedom to actually look at things. There's always an overriding design or mission behind their negotiation with life. I think when you have the occasion to step away from agendas, whether it's through circumstance or out of some kind of emotional necessity—then you're often struck by the incredible epiphanies of nature. These are often very subtle things, right at the edge of most people's sensibilities. My films try to record and to offer some of these experiences.[6]

Each of Hutton's mature films offers an extended meditative experience made up of a series of individual meditations. *Landscape (for Manon)* (1987) and *New York Portrait, Part I* (1976) can serve as representative instances. *Landscape (for Manon)* is not literally "extended"—it is only eighteen minutes long; *New York Portrait, Part I*, sixteen minutes—but for most viewers the experiences Hutton provides in these films *feel* extended, as a result of his timing and the unusual serenity of his images and especially their remarkable silence. Earl A. Powell has discussed the "contemplative sublime" of Fitz Henry Lane and Martin Johnson Heade as characterized by the "stillness and serenity of frozen time" and, in the case of Lane's 1864 paintings of Brace's Rock, by "the extreme sublime of silence."[7] Hutton's films create an analogous silence, and just as the "silence" of the Brace's Rock paintings seems especially powerful because of the historical context of the Civil War, the literal silence of Hutton's films is particularly dramatic because of the nature of our era and the increasingly "noisy" way in which film generally functions in our lives.[8] For a contemporary audience weaned and socialized by television and the internet, Hutton's combination of a meditative gaze on serene, black-and-white imagery presented in total silence can be almost shocking.

Over the decades, Hutton shot films in a wide variety of locations: New York City, Boston and San Francisco; Poland, Thailand, China, Iceland, Ethiopia—and in New York's Hudson Valley, sometimes in conscious homage to nineteenth-century painting. Indeed, he understood that he was hired to teach at Bard College in some measure because Bard, located in Annandale-on-Hudson, has often marketed its Hudson Valley locale. After moving to Bard, Hutton completed a series of films conceived as tributes to Hudson River painting. Much of the imagery in *Landscape (for Manon)* is suggestive of Cole's Catskill paintings—some of Hutton's imagery was made in and around Kaaterskill Clove—and the title of a second film, *In Titan's Goblet* (1991), refers to Cole's 1833 painting, *The Titan's Goblet*.[9] The third and fourth of Hutton's Hudson Valley films, *Study of a River* (1996) and *Time and Tide* (2000), explore the Hudson River itself, often from positions *on* the river. Before Hutton moved to San Francisco to study sculpture, then filmmaking at the San Francisco Art Institute, he spent some years as a merchant seaman—and his experiences on ocean-going freighters ("Being on the ship forced me to slow down, and allowed me to take time to look") often carried over into his experiences traveling and filming from barges and other watercraft on the Hudson.[10]

Landscape (for Manon) is made up of twenty-two shots. The first and last shots frame the film as a tribute to Hutton's then young daughter, Manon Hutton-De Wys: in the film's delicate and arresting final shot, we see her face in close-up, double exposed with mottled light (the inscription "for Manon" concludes the film). The film's opening image of a toy train moving along the top of a single railroad track seen from above (that it *is* a toy train is not clear until late in the twenty-five-second shot) not only confirms that the film is a tribute to Manon, it also suggests that Hutton saw himself rendered a "visual child" by his move to the Hudson Valley—though, of course, the specific reference to the train is a reminder that his cinematic exploration follows a long tradition of industrial exploration and development in this particular region.

I do not know whether Hutton's decision to begin his first Hudson Valley landscape film with the image of a tiny train is specifically a nod to the train in Thomas Cole's *River in the Catskills* (1843) or just a fascinating coincidence, but either way, the two trains have a related function. In his study *River in the Catskills*, Alan Wallach has suggested that, "[p]ainted in the early days of steam traction, this scene along the short-lived Canajoharie and Catskill Railroad is probably the first serious oil painting in the history of art to incorporate an image of a train…"[11] For Wallach the inclusion of this train was not Cole's way of normalizing industrial development in the Hudson Valley, but an attempt at an "anti-pastoral": a break from the previous pastoral landscape tradition that expressed Cole's frustration with unrestrained industrialization. Hutton's image actually includes two references to trains: the tiny toy train is moving along a real train track (presumably a rail of the Amtrak line that follows the eastern bank of the Hudson). If, as Wallach suggests, Cole's train evokes an early moment in the industrialization of the Hudson Valley and provides an implicit warning, Hutton's double-train image suggests the longing of a postlapsarian artist for a return to a prelapsarian world—or at least for a recognition that cinema is not only a child of the industrial revolution, but that modern cinema can be redirected toward a retrieval of the purity of vision that Cole was afraid was being lost, for the benefit of a new generation.

The organization of the other twenty shots of *Landscape (for Manon)* is distinctive and memorable. With two exceptions, each individual shot is separated from the next by two to five seconds of darkness. The variation in the lengths of these moments of darkness seems a function of intuitive timing that has to do with allowing the viewer to "digest" one image and prepare for the next. The timing of the particular images is quite sedate, and indeed seems calculated to confront the tendencies of commercial film editing: in general, the more "exciting" a commercial film becomes, the more heavily edited the film is. In fact, the best-known contribution of the Soviet montage school of editing was the "montage" itself, a device for intensifying the density of editing in climactic sequences, so as to thoroughly engage viewers in their secondhand participation in the action depicted and force them to feel its symbolic import. The average length of a shot in a contemporary commercial film is under ten seconds, and, of course, in advertisements and in music videos, individual shots are often shorter. In contrast, the lengths of the twenty-two shots in *Landscape (for Manon)*, in seconds, are 25, 27, 11/27, 18, 27, 27, 15, 21, 38, 49, 49, 53, 45, 39/34, 26, 28, 15, 25, 19 and 31 (the slashes indicate two instances when one shot is followed, without a pause, by another). The particular length of any one shot is a function of the subtle events revealed in the shots, but even a cursory look at Hutton's overall timing reveals that *Landscape* opens at a serene pace and then dramatically *slows down*; the moments where the editing is least frequent occur almost at the center of the film.

The development of the overall timing of *Landscape (for Manon)* is confirmed by the specifics of the imagery. After the toy train shot and a remarkable shot in which a bare tree seems to develop a glow, shots 3 through 8 depict trees blowing in the breeze or, sometimes, a wind, in early autumn. These relatively active images lead to a series of much quieter images of landscape, most of which include views of the Catskills. Further, Hutton's landscape images generally develop in a manner that creates an unusual perceptual process. Some images can seem, at first, like still photographs (this is particularly the case once the film's first eight images, as slow-paced as they are, have provided immediately apparent motion). It is only if and when one accepts this apparent stillness that a subtler form of motion begins to tease the eye and mind, and we realize that what seemed to be still is actually a part of a much larger order of motion: the cloud masses are gradually, relentlessly shifting through the space defined by the frame; the subtleties of chiaroscuro and composition are continually evolving; and what originally appeared (at least to a commercial filmgoing sensibility) to be "dead" is, in fact, not only very much alive, but part of an order of motion that dwarfs the rectangular world delimited by the camera.

What the Luminists accomplished by making their presence as working artists invisible—except in the general sense that it is the implicit dexterity of their "frozen" views that allows particular spaces to speak directly to the spectator's senses, mind, and spirit—Hutton accomplishes by making his presence as filmmaker invisible: except for the play of the toy train image, the double exposure at the film's conclusion, and an inconspicuous moment of zooming at the beginning of shot 20, Hutton's only filmic "device" is spatial and temporal composition. Hutton allows a revelation of the motion of the world to speak directly to the viewer. Indeed, this perceptual subtlety and implicitly spiritual connection is Hutton's gift to the sleeping child in the film's closing shot, and to the filmgoer-as-sleeping-child. We are often more oblivious than children to the visual subtleties of the world.

While *Landscape (for Manon)* and *In Titan's Goblet* are Hutton's most obvious tributes to nineteenth-century painting, Hutton's Luminist sensibility is not confined to his landscape work in the Hudson Valley: *Skagafjördur* (2004), shot in the Skagafjördur region of Iceland, is among his most remarkable Luminist works. Further, Hutton's portraits of cities—*New York, Near Sleep, for Saskia* (1972); *New York Portrait, Parts I* and *II* (1980); *New York Portrait, Part III* (1990); *Budapest Portrait* (1986); *Lodz Symphony* (1993); and his depiction of his native Detroit in *Three Landscapes* (2013)—resonate with the same meditative approach evident in the landscape films. In several instances, in fact, his New York City images provide obvious parallels to the Luminists, especially to Heade and Lane.[12]

That a cityscape of Manhattan can remind us of a Fitz Henry Lane harbor is less surprising if we remember that what may seem a quiet location to early-twenty-first-century eyes—a harbor with sailing ships—was, a century ago, a dynamic industrial arena. Of course, Lane's handling of a harbor had the impact of freezing this activity into a proto-surreal frozen moment—an effect very similar to what Hutton achieves by choosing quiet moments in a metropolis and cinematically meditating on them in extended shots. In *New York Portrait, Part I*, this meditative sensibility is confirmed not only by Hutton's tendency to divide individual shots (or in a few cases, pairs or triads of shots) from one another by moments of darkness, as he does in *Landscape (for Manon)*, but also by his frequent use of fades in and out to introduce and conclude particular shots.

Several particular shots of *New York Portrait, Part I* deserve comment. In shot 6, for example, we observe a downtown Manhattan skyline in silhouette, stretching across the bottom of the image; above the buildings is a sky full of clouds. As happens so often in *Landscape (for Manon)*, the image is so still that, at first, we are not sure it isn't a still photograph. But the length of the shot allows us to adjust and realize that the clouds are gradually shifting through the space of the frame: instead of taking the conventional route of locating a moment of "action" within the "world" of the frame, Hutton implicitly locates the space delimited by his frame within the shifting forces of the larger world that surrounds his filmmaking—a strategy that evokes Thomas Cole's *View of Boston* (1837-39), in which the painter embeds the distant city within the rural landscape that surrounds Boston and within the cloudscape visible above the scene.

By far the longest shot in *New York Portrait, Part I* (2 minutes, 18 seconds) confirms the implications of shot 6. The image is a "skyscape": all we see are sky and clouds—and at first one, then several distant flocks of pigeons looping through the sky, moving in and out of the framed space and, within the framed space, in and out of the light so that at one moment the birds seem white, the next moment black. One minute into the shot, an even more distant airplane enters the frame and for a full minute is seen moving further and further away, from the upper left toward the lower center of the image. At some point during this accidental choreography ("accidental" because Hutton obviously couldn't control the particular motions of birds and plane; "choreography" because he chose the space knowing birds and plane would move through it), we become aware of a third "layer" of motion—visible in the distance beyond the birds and plane but implicitly conditioning every motion they make. Gradually shifting clouds are altering the look of the frame and breathing new graphic life into the space even as we focus on the activities in the comparative foreground. The shot is an emblem of Hutton's commitment to an intensification of our sense of the particular as a means of putting us in touch with the general, of helping us to see what is within our world as a means of providing us with a more complete, and deeper, awareness of the world he and we are within.

My arguing for an analogy between Luminist painting and Hutton's filmmaking has so far sidestepped an important dimension of Hutton's work, a dimension evident in many of Hutton's films, and especially *In Titan's Goblet*— a dimension of Hutton's imagery that, at least on one level, conflicts with what I have been calling his Luminist sensibility. While it is true that Hutton, as film artist, "gets out of the way" of the scenes he depicts, as fully as Lane, Heade, and Kensett efface themselves from the scenes they depict, Hutton is trapped, in a way the painters were not, by the limitations of the mechanical-chemical technology he uses. Hutton's attraction to low-light outdoor conditions sometimes causes his imagery to be somewhat grainy. This graininess is the mechanical-chemical version of the particulars of moment-to-moment perception that fascinated Monet, Seurat, and other Impressionists and produced paintings of rural and urban scenes that critics have seen as fundamentally different from Luminist work: paintings that reveal the fundamental transience of perception and experience, rather than—as in Luminist work—the fundamental, divine harmony and solidity behind, or within, momentary appearance.

The most useful art-historical analogy to this dimension of Hutton's work is not Luminism, but the somewhat later evolution of American Tonalism. David A. Cleveland has explained:

> In the four decades from 1880 to 1920 the Tonalist movement of intimate landscape painting flourished in America. Soulful, deeply expressive landscapes by artists such as George Inness, Alexander Wyant, J. Francis Murphy, Dwight Tryon, and Charles Warren Eaton—with Whistler's low-toned decorative Nocturnes an ever-tantalizing presence—limn the nostalgic uncertainties of fin-de-siècle America… The moody, often melancholy evocations summoned by Tonalist landscapes, in which autumnal, sunset, and nocturnal themes predominate, followed from the horrors of the Civil War, while the failures of Reconstruction, the anxieties of a boom-and-bust economy, and Darwinian doubts only added to the undertone of vague displacement that haunts these precincts of embodied memory.[13]

There is a Tonalist element to many of Hutton's films, and in some instances it reflects Hutton's concern about broader political issues (especially environmentally political issues). A smoky landscape midway through *In Titan's Goblet* may at first seem to be a lovely natural phenomenon, but in fact this was the smoke from a runaway fire in a rubber tire graveyard—not an environmental catastrophe but for Hutton an implicit recognition that landscape art sometime glosses over elements that endanger the beauty of the scenes depicted. The considerable graininess of the imagery in *In Titan's Goblet* is, of course, a function of Hutton's shooting in low-light conditions—but it also references the fundamental elements of emulsion-based photography in a manner that evokes the highly textural quality of the brushwork in Ralph Albert Blakelock's Tonalist "Moonlights."

Because Hutton, child of the twentieth century that he was, chose to be a *film* artist, he could not help but confront the implications of this choice, even when he was using his mechanical-chemical apparatus to achieve a meditative sensibility. Just as his meditative gaze makes no fundamental distinction between rural and urban locales—both are places in which people live, and both are in a continual process of transformation by societal and natural forces—Hutton makes no fundamental distinction between material realities outside and inside the camera. The function of filmmaking, for Hutton, is to use the camera as a means of creating moments that reveal both outer and inner realities, the material and the spiritual, as the fundamental unity that in fact they are.

Statue of Liberty through rainy window,
from Hutton's *Time and Tide* (2000).

Hutton's most elaborate Hudson Valley film, *Time and Tide* (2000), was his second film to document the river itself—*Study of a River*, finished in 1996, is a stunning evocation of the Hudson in winter (there is also Hutton's rarely seen 2002 comparative study of the Hudson and China's Yangtse River: *Two Rivers*).[14] *Time and Tide* was also, at 35 minutes, Hutton's longest film in twenty-five years, approximately the same length as two early films: *July '71 in San Francisco, Living at Beach Street, Working at Canyon Cinema, Swimming in the Valley of the Moon* (1971) and *Images of Asian Music (A Diary from Life 1973-74)* (1974). And it includes the first color imagery Hutton had used in his own work since *In Marin County* (1970).

Time and Tide is Hutton's first film to include "recycled" imagery ("recycled cinema," the making of films out of previous films, is a pervasive tendency in recent filmmaking). In this instance, what is recycled is a complete film from the early twentieth century: *Down the River*, produced by the American Mutoscope and Biograph Company in 1903. *Down the River* is actually what we would call a trip *up* the Hudson, from Haverstraw to Newburgh, in mostly pixilated imagery that emphasizes the river's commercial importance: boats zip around the river and trains along it, at impossible speeds, which nevertheless express turn-of-the-century excitement with modernity's exploitation of this natural resource.

Time and Tide was also Hutton's most candid confrontation of the ways in which filmmaking itself was a part of modern industrial society. After the presentation of *Down the River*, *Time and Tide* slows down to the meditative pace typical of Hutton, and moves us first down the Hudson and into various sectors of New York Harbor, then back up the Hudson all the way to a General Electric factory (identified by a large light-sign),[15] and finally back down to the Hudson Highlands area (south of Poughkeepsie and north of Haverstraw). As this description may suggest, *Time and Tide* includes imagery of the river and its natural surroundings *and* imagery of New York City, as well as industrial sites up and down the river.

There is no seasonal consistency in the imagery in *Time and Tide*: we see the Hudson in all seasons and weathers. In *Time and Tide* any change from one shot to the next may move us from black and white to color or vice versa, and from one season to another. The variability of the imagery in *Time and Tide* reveals Hutton's recognition that, year after year, year in and year out, the Hudson provided him with a continually evolving panorama that could never be taken for granted, either cinematically or environmentally.

As Hutton understood, his films, and emulsion-based photography and filmmaking in general, involve not only a chemical process, but a particularly dirty one. Early in *Time and Tide* a tanker passes Hutton's camera, from left to right, revealing its name in reverse, one word at a time: first, "Pioneer," then "Chemical Pioneer." This name encapsulates a crucial dimension of *Time and Tide*: Hutton's awareness not only of the historical complicity of cinematic beauty and environmental damage, but his recognition of his own position within this history. As a filmmaker, Hutton was, at least until his switch to digital in *Three Landscapes*, inevitably a *chemical* film pioneer. Though he used cinema to move us away from unmitigated "progress" (defined as an ever-accelerating consumption of goods, and of film imagery) and toward forms of contemplation typical of nineteenth-century landscape painting, his methods were made possible by the world's most famous photochemical company, Kodak. More fully and more obviously than any of Hutton's earlier films, *Time and Tide* reflects its maker's recognition that his travels on the river have brought him near to the heart of (environmental) darkness, represented by the elegant and playful GE sign, and that he, like all of us, would need to face the implications of this history. Hutton: "I purposely put an image of the General Electric logo in the middle of the film, just to say, 'There are other issues inherent in this very beautiful bucolic landscape; there is something underneath this surface that's not so beautiful.' GE polluted the Hudson River with PCBs for many years, within legal limits, of course, but with terrible consequences."[16]

Collage of images from *Time and Tide*, by Peter Hutton (2000?). Exactly when Hutton made this collage is unclear to me.

During the final years before his death in June of 2016, Hutton was expanding his work in several directions. Both *At Sea* (2009) and *Three Landscapes* are panoramic works that include three disparate locations and visual explorations. *At Sea* depicts the life of seagoing vessels: part 1 was shot in a shipbuilding facility in Okpo, Korea; part 2, on a container ship sailing from Montreal, Canada to Hamburg, Germany; and part 3 at a shipbreaking facility in Chittagong, Bangladesh. *Three Landscapes* includes a depiction of post-industrial Detroit, activities at the Afar Depression in Ethiopia (the lowest point in Africa), and autumn in the pastoral Hudson Valley. Each of these panoramic triads suggests a global awareness, but is also a rumination on the life cycle and on personal history.

At sixty minutes, *At Sea* is Hutton's epic. It powerfully reconfirmed for those who had followed his career Hutton's stature as a visual artist.[17] *At Sea* is unusual within Hutton's work since the three sections, though disparate in geography (and in formal ways as well), document a single meta-process: the birth, life, and death of ocean-going freighters and container ships. The ships within each section of the film are, of course, different ships—but all ships are at one or another point in this process. As in Cole's *The Voyage of Life* (1839-49), the distinct ages of commercial sailing vessels in *At Sea* are represented both by literal content and by the use of chiaroscuro and color: the shipbuilding sequence is in bright, almost childlike colors, and the ships under construction look almost like toys; the containers on the ship making the voyage from Montreal to Hamburg are colorful, though the seriousness of the voyage itself is obvious; and our view—Hutton films from behind the window of the bridge—is sometimes obscured by weather conditions. The shipbreaking sequence is filmed in black and white and focuses as fully on laborers doing demanding work as on the ships under deconstruction. That *At Sea* was made as Hutton neared conventional retirement age (he was 62 when the film was finished) may suggest a more personal reading of the film's three sections. Was Hutton feeling a bit "at sea" as he looked forward to the coming years?

The three sections of *Three Landscapes*, the final film completed during Hutton's lifetime, suggest, in somewhat different ways, an ongoing rumination on aging. The opening section is a meditation on the city of Detroit in decay—and since Hutton was born in Detroit and grew up there before the city's economic downturn, his depiction of Detroit reads as a visual dirge to the passing of time as it has affected both his hometown and himself. The second section, filmed during Hutton's pilgrimage to the Afar Depression—the site of an unfinished film by his longtime friend, filmmaker Robert Gardner—was Hutton's way of honoring their long friendship by completing a project Gardner had begun. The third "landscape," the last Hutton would complete, returns him to the Hudson Valley at harvesttime.

Hutton used the two panoramic films to move more fully into the gallery world. In 2015, Ed Halter curated an installation show, "Nature is a Discipline," at the Miguel Abreu Gallery in New York City; the show included installation versions of *At Sea* and *Three Landscapes*, as well as *Tulare Road* (2015), an installation by James Benning—though Benning and Hutton had been close friends and cine-philosophical colleagues for decades, this was the first time they had worked together in this way. And in February 2016, the Shoshana Wayne Gallery in Santa Monica opened a show, "Peter Hutton/Film Stills": Hutton's inventive photographic enlargements of frames from his films.

When Peter Hutton died (like Cole, too soon—and much too quickly) in June of 2016, he left behind a particularly distinguished contribution to modern cinema and to the long history of landscape depiction—and now to the evolving history of the Thomas Cole National Historic Site and to the record of Cole's accomplishments and influence on other artists. Of course, Thomas Cole was more than an accomplished artist. On a hilltop directly across the Hudson from the Thomas Cole Site is the Olana State Historic Site, the home and grounds designed by Cole's remarkable student, Frederic Edwin Church. The formative teacher-student relationship of Cole and Church is documented in *Master, Mentor, Master: Thomas Cole & Frederic Church*, a monograph produced by the Cole Historic Site in 2014, and explored in John Wilmerding's catalogue essay.

Like Cole, Hutton was a teacher. He worked with filmmaking students at various institutions: California Institute of the Arts, Hampshire College, Harvard University, SUNY Purchase, and from 1985 on, at Bard College in Annandale-on-Hudson—just across the river and a few miles down Route 9G from the Cole Site and Olana. As a teacher, Hutton was gifted and charismatic (and the chair of Bard's Film and Electronic Arts Department for many years). Throughout his teaching career, he was important to many young filmmakers, most famously, perhaps, documentary filmmaker Ken Burns, who studied with Hutton at Hampshire College and has called him "a powerful influence on me and dozens of others" and "a national treasure."[18] Indeed, the stately pacing of Burns' best work seems to reflect the persistent serenity of Hutton's films.

Because Hutton was committed to the textures and tonalities of celluloid cinema and resisted a move to digital filming until very recently, we are left with a collection of 16mm prints of Hutton's films (in most cases the negatives are, I believe, intact), most of which remain in good shape. Since options for showing 16mm films have diminished considerably in recent years, Hutton's films will, at least for a time, be less available to cineastes and art lovers than they should be—at least as they were meant to be seen (some of the Hutton films are available, in low-resolution versions, on YouTube). Surely the major film archives will continue to make Hutton's work available, and one can hope that before long, first-rate digital versions of the films will become feasible and allow the audience for this master of landscape and cityscape to grow—just as the audience for the Cole paintings that were so important to Hutton continues to expand.

Hutton's films are available at Canyon Cinema (canyoncinema.com). The catalogue for the Peter Hutton show is available at the Thomas Cole National Historic Site, 218 Spring Street, Catskill, NY 12414.

---

1   See Barbara Novak, *Nature and Culture: American Landscape Painting, 1825-1875* (New York: Oxford University Press, 1984), chapters 2 and 3.
2   Baur apparently coined "Luminism" in "American Luminism, a Neglected Aspect of the Realist Movement in Nineteenth-Century American Painting," *Perspective USA*, no. 9 (Autumn 1954), 90-98. Ila Weiss reviews discussion of the topic in chapter 1 of *Poetic Landscape: The Art and Experience of Sanford R. Gifford* (Newmark: University of Delaware Press/Associated University Presses, 1987); and the term is debated throughout *American Light: The Luminist*

Movement, 1850-1875, a collection of overviews edited by John Wilmerding and published in 1980 by the National Gallery of Art in Washington, D.C., on the occasion of a major exhibition.
3   Novak, *Nature and Culture*, 32.
4   Angela Miller, *The Empire of the Eye* (Ithaca: Cornell University Press, 1993), 243.
5   For a listing of these films, see Iris Cahn, "The Changing Landscape of Modernity: Early Film and America's 'Great Picture' Tradition," *Wide Angle* 18, no. 3 (July 1996), 85-100.
6   Hutton, in Scott MacDonald, *A Critical Cinema 3: Interviews with Independent Filmmakers* (Berkeley: University of California Press, 1998), 243-44.
7   See Powell's overview of Luminism, "Luminism and the American Sublime," in Wilmerding, *American Light*, 80, 81. See note 3.
8   Of course, commercial cinema was never truly silent: audiences have always made themselves heard, and musical accompaniment was a nearly automatic dimension of the film experience until sound-on-film made sound inevitable in commercial cinema. Even those silent films produced by American independent filmmakers of the 1960s—Stan Brakhage is the most prominent example—for whom sound seemed an expensive, and, for a visual artist, aesthetically unnecessary extra, were generally characterized by heavy editing (and sometimes shocking imagery), causing the films to seem visually "noisy," even without soundtracks.
9   The relationships between Hutton's film and Cole's bizarre painting are implicit. Much of Hutton's *In Titan's Goblet* focuses on a rubber tire fire that men on bulldozers are attempting to extinguish. The bulldozers are filmed from a considerable distance and the result is that they look like toys. This distortion in size echoes the even more obvious distortion of scale evident in *The Titan's Goblet*.
10 Hutton interview in *A Critical Cinema 3*, 252
11 Alan Wallach, "Thomas Cole's 'River in the Catskills' as Antipastoral," *Art Bulletin* 84, no. 2 (June 2002), 335. Wallach explains (in his note 4) that others have argued that J. M. W. Turner's *Rain, Steam and Speed* (1844) deserves this title.
12 Also, the fact that Hutton's urban images are frequently reminiscent of the Luminists doesn't mean that the Luminists were a conscious reference. In fact, the particular images in the *New York Portrait* films suggest not just painting, but nineteenth-century photography. Shot 7 in *New York Portrait, Part II*, seems an obvious homage to Charles Sheeler, whose painting and photography Hutton admired, and who—in collaboration with Paul Strand—made the breakthrough city portrait, *Manhatta* (1921), which intercuts between poetic texts and imagery of Lower Manhattan—a forerunner to Hutton's depictions of New York. And several images in *New York Portrait, Part I*, are reminiscent of Alfred Stieglitz. Indeed, the history of photography clearly plays an important role in Hutton's thinking: It's a relationship that could sustain a considerable discussion.
13 David A. Cleveland, *A History of American Tonalism: 1880-1920* (Manchester, VT/New York: Hudson Hills Press, 2010), xiii.
14 Hutton: *Two Rivers* "was the most ambitious thing I'd done… The *Two Rivers* project came out of my interest in the Hudson River and in Hudson himself and the various recollections of his journeys to the New World… When I wrote the proposal for Diane Shamash ["who ran Minetta Brook until she died"; she was "a fairy godmother to me and to a lot of other artists"], I commented on the environmentalist issues facing both rivers: the Hudson was very much in the news because of General Electric and the PCB controversy; at the time, I thought the dredging of the Hudson would be part of the film… There was also environmentalist resistance in China to the damming of the Yangtze and the resulting damage to the Three Gorges…

    I also thought this was a very interesting idea because my imagery of each river was preceded by a great painterly tradition: I thought it would be interesting to think about how these specific landscapes influenced particular aspects of Chinese and American painting." Interview with Peter Hutton, in Scott MacDonald, *Adventures of Perception: Cinema as Exploration* (Berkeley: University of California Press, 2009), 226-227.
15 Actually, the General Electric sign was not on the Hudson River, but on the Mohawk River in Schenectady—this break in the geographic continuity of *Time and Tide* (it would be visible to few outside New York State) confirms Hutton's commitment to a polemical use of the image.
16 Interview with Hutton in *Adventures of Perception*, 222.
17 In 2010 *Film Comment* published the results of a poll of aficionados of independent cinema, and *At Sea* was voted the best avant-garde film of the decade.
18 Ken Burns, letter to *The Independent* 20, no.2 (March 1997), 7.

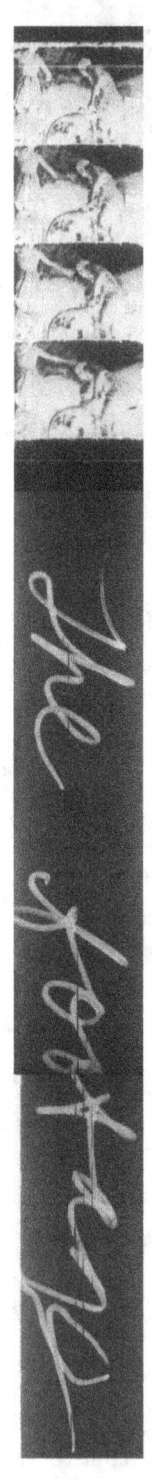

Filmstrip from Patrick Clancy's *Peliculas* (1979). Courtesy Patrick Clancy.

2019

Patrick Clancy's Early Photoscrolls— and (some of) what came later

This essay was written for a proposed edited collection of essays about Patrick Clancy that is now moving towards publication. When such a book does appear, it will have been long overdue.

I met Clancy sometime during the 1970s, when he was teaching at Colgate University and collaborating on various projects with his then neighbor, Hollis Frampton. My earliest memory of a Clancy artwork was an installation at the Picker Gallery at Colgate, where one looked out a window of the gallery at a section of the campus. Next to the tape-framed space on the window was a list indicating what (and who) one would be likely to see at certain moments during the day/week; Clancy had studied the space over time and had come to know what went on there. This seemed to me an inventive instance of conceptual art (how fully it "worked" I don't know—I couldn't stay in the gallery long enough to find out!). But it was also my first recognition that Clancy's interest was not in making art objects that could be sold or collected. He was interested in making art as an extension of thought, of curiosity—in this instance, of the then current (and still current) societal concerns about the issues of surveillance and privacy.

Clancy himself has no memory of the piece I remember so well.

Note: I have eliminated a paragraph on Emmett Williams' *THE VOY AGE* from the original essay; it appeared just after my discussion of Robert Huot's diary paintings and before the discussion of Clancy's *Peliculas*, as a work related to other works that straddle the gap between cinema and other modes of communication and expression. Chapter 6 discusses *THE VOY AGE* in detail.

* * *

The post-industrial cultural environment of signs, cities, and electronic media has replaced nature as the dominant paradigm of "reality."

Our experiences of this new "reality" are often discontinuous and at the same time repetitive. This is a change from the continuous spatial model of "reality" in which a causal, evolutionary cycle of primarily natural events was passed down from generation to generation. The experience of 30-second television commercials and driving along the highways of American culture with their neon signs, billboards, and urban architecture has shortened our attention span. It has accustomed us to the instantaneous reading of rapidly intercut information lacking a cohesive, overall context other than that of commercial manipulation.

Patrick Clancy, from catalogue essay for "Video As Attitude"[1]

Patrick Clancy has never been able to bring himself to take enough time away from thinking about and making art to effectively market what he's done. Of course, he's not alone in this—but he's a prime instance. As a result, he has produced a good deal of interesting work without receiving broad recognition. Clancy is no specialist (except at thinking about art and its relationship to the world). He studied painting at Yale, and for 5½ years (November 1966 to April 1972) was a member of PULSA (Yale Research Associates in the Arts): seven artists who collaborated on what Clancy has described as "large-scale environmental art, wave energies, video installations, and human interaction with machine intelligence."[2] In the late 1970s and early '80s, he worked in a form of sequential imagery that lies somewhere between still photography and motion pictures; he named the resulting works "photoscrolls." In February and March 1980, Clancy exhibited his early photoscrolls in a two-part show called "Marginal Works," at the Picker Gallery, Colgate University, in Hamilton, New York (February 8-March 2, 1980), and at the Barrett Gallery, Utica College of Syracuse University, Utica, New York (March 23-April 11, 1980).

It may seem strange, after all this time and given the many, varied kinds of work Clancy has done, to focus on one particular set of works made during a relatively brief moment within a half-century of art-making. But since most of these "marginal works" remain marginal in terms of our access to them, both physically and in memory, I've assumed that, at the very least, these works and the experiences they created/create need to be written into the record. Though my focus here is the photoscrolls included in the double show at the Picker and Barrett Galleries, other works were part of that show: at the Picker, *Seven Walls for Dziga Vertov*, a sequence of rubbings; the film *Peliculas* (see below); a large multi-person rubbing; some color-Xerox work, and a double "Lecture" performance by Clancy and Hollis Frampton; and at the Barrett Gallery, a multi-person performance and, subsequently, "evidence" from that performance.

Though the photoscrolls in the two Central New York galleries were installed in a variety of ways and have somewhat different functions, they were made in essentially the same manner. Rolls of 35mm film were shot and developed and printed *as strips*, so that what would normally have been cut into individual 3½ x 5-inch photographs became meta-photographs, 3½ inches wide but as much as a hundred feet long. Producing a photoscroll involved a rethinking of the process of making photographs. Having decided in advance that he would neither reduce the scrolls to separate, individual images, nor edit the scrolls, Clancy was forced to do a considerable amount of preparation before shooting. Generally, this involved a two-part process: first, thinking about the scrolls on a conceptual level, then setting up an experience or a performance out of which the scrolls would evolve. Since the scrolls were usually made outdoors, over periods of hours and sometimes days, human and natural events sometimes added unpredictable events and fortuitous discoveries, which Clancy could then incorporate into the thinking that determined the remaining images.

A viewer's experience of the scrolls tends to take place on a variety of levels. At the Picker Gallery show I was first aware of the scrolls' simple but grand minimal shapes and their rhythmic, serial division into five-inch units.[3] Since it is obvious, even from a distance, that the scrolls contain specific photographic information, spectators tend to be drawn into a double process of moving closer to the individual images, then horizontally along the strips, as the complex conceptual dimensions of the scrolls declare themselves. Generally, one conceptual dimension of each photoscroll involves the viewer's gradual recognition of the implicit performance involved in Clancy's recording the imagery.

Sandia Parallax (1979), for example, is made up of 21 images of different New Mexico residences, and behind them, what appears to be exactly the same profile of the Sandia mountain range to the east of Albuquerque.[4] The fact that the foreground constantly changes while the background remains the same implies Clancy's own movement in recording the images, the movement which our experience of moving along the scroll recreates at a further remove.[5] The overexposed sprocketholes visible within the first four frames at the left end of the scroll and the rhythmic overexposure in several frames at the right end of the scroll reference the scroll's nature as artifact. Implicitly, the sprocket holes are a microcosmic version of the regularity of the 21 images that make up the scroll, as well as of the regularities in the architecture of homes and streets in the neighborhood of Albuquerque Clancy moved through.[6]

From our perspective half a century later, we can understand the photoscrolls—simultaneously still photographs and a sequence of images arranged along a celluloid strip—as an instance of the ongoing evolution of thinking across the artworld, beginning in the 1960s and continuing into the 1980s, about the fundamentals of traditional modes of art-making, the distinctions between them, and the way one traditional art form can transition into or be imbricated with another. Two particular artists working in the years immediately preceding Clancy's turn to the photoscroll can provide some context.

During the 1960s, Robert Huot, Clancy's soon-to-become neighbor and friend in Central New York State, was one of a number of artists who were examining the fundamental nature of painting and its distinction from sculpture. How much paint is necessary for a work to be designated a painting? Can unpainted canvas stretched over a rectangular frame and hung in a gallery be understood as a conceptual "painting"—or is that a sculpture? Huot was soon considering conceptual relationships between painting and cinema. First, he used the celluloid filmstrip as a base for doing various kinds of work related to painting and printmaking: for *Scratch* (1967) he etched into the emulsion on a filmstrip; for *Spray* (1967), he spray-painted clear celluloid leader to create a film that, when projected, is an animated "painting." Growing fascinated with the fact that the traditional celluloid filmstrip was made up of a series of images arranged in a grid, Huot began to create paintings that are modularized strips (examples include *Untitled*, *Ins+Outs*, and *Scott's Scribble*, from 1967). By the early 1970s, once he had moved to Central New York State, Huot was making both film diaries—feature-length compilations of quotidian sights and activities (often with an inventive sense of chiaroscuro and visual design) and "diary paintings," for which he made painting and sculptural "entries" onto long strips of canvas over periods of weeks and months. For each entry, Huot would unroll a segment of the canvas and paint/collage within that segment, then, once the paint had dried, roll that segment up and move to the subsequent segment. The resulting diary paintings are essentially scrolls that can be rolled up for storage and unscrolled for exhibition.

Of course, there is also Clancy's own *Peliculas* (1979), a film/scroll/text/installation that combines two kinds of imagery recorded on a 16mm filmstrip: image clusters recycled from a short film his narrating character claims to have bought in a small store in a Central American town, and a multicolored text, written in cursive on the filmstrip. A complete experience of *Peliculas* involves seeing it as a projected film (shown at "silent speed": 16 or 18 frames per second) *and*, using rewinds, reading the filmstrip as a cine-scroll. If the projection comes first, one sees frame clusters of imagery apparently recorded on Latin American streets, but also that a text is recorded on the filmstrip continuously throughout the film. One can only wonder what the writing says, though in instances where Clancy repeats individual letters a frame at a time, we can understand bits of what is written.[7] If the viewer/reader first accesses the film as a scroll, the presence of the frame clusters makes clear that a projection will also be necessary if we are to understand what exactly is to be seen in the frames, though the found-footage frames are, as Clancy has said, "pretty subliminal" even at silent speed.[8] When we do access the full written text, we discover an amalgam of memory and narrative fiction, of cine-self-reflexivity and magical realism. Like Huot's diary paintings and films, and Williams' *THE VOY AGE*, *Peliculas* functions in between our normal categories, as a synergy of various media forms that are the ancestors of these works. As Clancy explained:

> Whenever *Peliculas* is looked at on rewinds it is a scroll. When viewed as a projection it is a film. When *Peliculas* is presented simultaneously on rewinds and projected, it is an installation. Although the projection can take much less time than the reading on rewinds, during the installation version people move back and forth between the two modes… *Peliculas* exists in the gap between, as well as the gaps within, both experiences.[9]

State Borders, "Pyr-A-Mid," Fringe of Consciousness—and Camera Obscura (1979)

Among the most engaging photoscrolls in the "Marginal Works" show was/is the 36-frame *State Borders, "Pyr-A-Mid," Fringe of Consciousness—and Camera Obscura* (the title echoes the scroll's organization and complexity). Like Huot's diary paintings and *Peliculas*, *State Borders* explores the "border" between different media. Perhaps the most sensible way to approach this photoscroll's considerable suggestiveness is to use the several elements of the title as clues to the various clusters of ideas signaled by the successive images.

The most elementary and obvious connotation of "state borders" is evident in the highway signs that appear in several frames. If one begins with the image furthest to the left and reads to the right (even if one approaches the scroll at a middle point, a left to right development quickly becomes evident), the road signs reveal that Patrick, Flora, and Raphael Clancy traveled westward, from Indiana (frame 1) to Illinois (2) to Missouri (3) to Kansas (12) to Oklahoma (17) to Texas (20) and finally, into New Mexico (23). Once it is clear that *State Borders* records moments during a specific journey, the photoscroll can be seen, at least on one level, as an ongoing diary. The viewer moves along the strip through picture after picture, just as the Clancys travel West along the highway through state after state, camping along the road, stopping at roadside stands, looking at the scenery—typical family activities on an automobile trip.[10] As is usually the case in what were, in 1980, more traditional forms of travel diary (snapshot albums, slide shows…), we are able to discover both the specifics of the trip and something of the personalities of the people involved. That there are no images of New York State or Ohio, suggests that the idea for *State Borders* may have occurred to Clancy once the trip was underway, instigated, at least in part, by the process of travel itself.

The opening frame of the photoscroll is a close-up of the Indiana State seal, subtitled "THE INTELLIGENT USE OF LEISURE TIME," which can be read as Clancy's wry comment on the project he has decided to pursue, what would become this photoscroll.[11] In general, the state boundaries recorded in the images don't identify any visible physical distinctions in the landscape itself; they are signals of invisible divisions between states of legal existence, which, in turn, effect physical reminders of these legal divisions: the signs, somewhat distinct in mood, that indicate the borders of the different states. Of course, since making the photoscroll was obviously a factor in determining the shape of the trip and since what was discovered along the way modified whatever expectations Clancy might originally have had, the relationship between the scroll and the trip is complex. We can "read" not just the literal journey of the family, but the conceptual journey of the imagemaker as he moved quickly from border crossing to border crossing at the beginning into a more complex awareness of his environment and its perceptual/conceptual potential.

Other implications of "state borders" involve reading "state" in a more general sense—as a state of being rather than a geographic entity. Much of Clancy's work reveals a consciousness of an idea Roland Barthes expresses in *The Pleasure of the Text*: "what pleasure wants is the site of a loss, the seam, the cut, the deflation, the *dissolve* which seizes the subject in the midst of bliss. Culture thus recurs as an edge: in no matter what form."[12] Each frame in *State Borders* is an index of the state of things at a specific moment, and the imagery within the individual frames tends to encode certain general themes that relate to various "states" and the "borders" between them. For example, Clancy explores the seam between the extensions of human technology—the road, the automobile, and the subculture the road makes way for (including Clancy's camera)—and the natural landscape (or the more-natural landscape) bisected by the road. For Clancy the shoulders of the highway are a fruitful source of information about the human content of the many landscapes we see, made apparent in the road signs and other human installations along the "margins" of the road: from the road signs, we learn where we are in human terms (within what humanly defined area we are, how far we need to go before we reach the next large group of humans); in the roadside stores, we find the products humans have made in, and of, the particular landscapes the Clancys drive through.

The "borders" between individual frames of the photoscroll are often conceptually dense. The "distance" between frames 1 and 2, for example, is several hundred miles and hours of driving and seems to reflect the fact that, early in this cross-country drive, the world the Clancys were passing through didn't yet seem worthy of particular attention: the terrain is familiar and they're concerned with getting the long drive underway. The seam between frames 7 and 8 is particularly subtle and rewarding; it builds on the series of images that lead up to it. Frame 4 is presumably a shot of the spot where the Clancys have decided to pitch their tent on the first night of their trip west; we see the tent in frame 5. That Clancy framed this image so that the tent seems to stand atop a print of the classic photograph of workers posing during the ceremony commemorating Leland Stanford's driving in the golden spike to mark the completion of the transcontinental railroad, represents both the temporal distance between the events of May 10, 1869, and the current moment in the Clancys' journey a century later, as well as the conceptual and historical relationship of the two projects. Clearly, Clancy sees his family's journey, and his own project of making this photoscroll, as an echo of that earlier project and ultimately a result of what it symbolized and made possible.

That Clancy brought this photograph with him on this trip or bought it during the trip makes clear that he was thinking about the history encoded in the photograph and his and his family's relationship to it. The transcontinental railroad opened the way not only for the easy movement west that the Clancys are taking advantage of, but also for the ongoing reshaping of what Europeans and their American descendants originally considered a wilderness, the transformation of natural life and process into products useful to the human cultures moving west from Europe. This relationship of present and past is confirmed by frames 6 and 7. In frame 6 we see the "golden spike" image, now in close-up, mounted on a board; and in the following image Flora and Raphael Clancy re-enact the physical positions of two of the figures in the photograph: Flora, a man in the background, standing at the front of the train on the left, reaching out with his arm (with a bottle of wine?) toward a man, on the right, also reaching out (with a glass for the wine?); Raphael, the man holding his lapels at the front right of the crowd.

This suite of images reaches a conceptual culmination in the seam between frames 7 and 8. While frame 7 is a long shot and frame 8, a close-up, the two images were (or are, even if Clancy didn't intend this effect—though I must assume he did) framed so that a tree branch in frame 7 seems to become the rope attached to a yellow tent peg in frame 8, evoking the transformation of plant life into the rope that is being used with a modern "golden spike," the plastic tent peg, itself a product of crude oil produced by the gradual transformation of plant life over millions of years, and accessed after centuries of scientific and technological development.

The triangularity of both the Clancys' tent and the arrangement of the crowd in the golden spike photograph is confirmed in frame 9, an image of David Macaulay's drawing, "Locating the Vanishing Point" (1978)—an amusing, surreal riff on the idea of vanishing point perspective.[13] Frame 10 returns us to the tent, now in morning light (as opposed to the evening light of frame 7), as Raphael, in the background, seems to be helping to pack up the car on the right. The "Boar Power" sales center sign in frame 11, with its extra-long arrow on the "O," confirms the hypermasculinity of the "golden spike" celebration. As far as I can see, the crowd in the photograph is all men, and there is also the phallic penetration into space by the railroad in the Macaulay drawing and by the shot of the highway that follows frame 11, where the Clancys cross a bridge into Kansas, presumably well into their second day of the drive.

"*Pyr-A-Mid,*" in the photoscroll title has, like "*State Borders,*" multileveled significance, and builds on the triangularity of the earlier suite of images. For one thing, the proximity of the close-ups of the three family members (frames 13, 16 and 19), with, superimposed, the syllables "PYR" "—A—" "MID," allows us to see how much the boy resembles his parents. Image 16 is framed so that Raphael is juxtaposed with a meteor, displayed presumably in a roadside stand of some kind, and a sign reading "1000 LB. SPACE WANDERER" (16), evoking the father's empathy with and lighthearted affection for his son, whose partially successful attempts to stay occupied during the trip are evident later in a pair of frames (28, 29), where Raphael—again, at least imaginatively, a "space wanderer"—is making paper airplanes. Though the Clancys' trip west has a definite destination, the images in this section of the photoscroll indicate that they have, from time to time, wandered into spaces along the margins of the road west.

Pyr-A-Mid" also confirms and expands the implication of the triangular shape of many of the earlier images. The triangular plastic container of the indoor beehive seen in close-up in frame 15 is framed so that two other triangular spaces are created by the edges of the plastic covers and the side and top frame lines. This motif of triangular/pyramidal shapes continues throughout the photoscroll; it is evident in the aforementioned paper airplane Raphael Clancy is making in frames 28 and 29 and in the triangular shape on the wall of the "Pyramid" porno shop (frame 27). But perhaps the most fundamental and significant "pyramidal" shape in the photoscroll is that made by the receding highway in Frames 2, 3, 12, 17, 20 and 22. The Interstate Highway System, begun during the Eisenhower administration, was a construction project comparable to the Egyptian or Mayan pyramids, a man-made wonder that in fact transformed the United States and remains among our most remarkable national accomplishments.

The suite of images from 13 to 19 also evokes a range of human methods for enclosing and/or controlling substances and processes found in nature, for both practical use and material gain. Frame 14 is dense with such imagery: to the right of the image two hams wrapped in cloth are displayed on the wall, above what appear to be jars of jelly and bottles of cooking oil. On the far right, below the hams, a Native American, "wrapped" in "American" clothing, gazes at the indoor beehive, framed at the center of the image and flanked by two display cases of honey. Of course, the Native American man reminds us that the American conquest of "the wilderness" involved the near destruction of a complex group of human cultures, and specific evidence of one of these cultures is evident in frame 13, where Flora Clancy holds an Osage orange, a fruit developed by the Osage tribe—we can tell it's an Osage orange by its mottled green skin.

The implicit enunciation of "pyramid" by the three family members is Clancy's reference to French inventor George Demeneÿ, who was a collaborator with Étienne-Jules Marey at the dawn of motion pictures. When Hector Marichelle, professor and director of the National Deaf-Mute Institute in France, asked Marey to make a close-up of filmed speech, hoping to teach deaf students to speak by means of lip reading, Marey gave the job to Demeneÿ, who produced an early cinematic instance of a medium close-up of himself, saying "Je vous aime." The implicit sequence of the three Clancys, each separated from the next by two images, can be conceptually animated into their enunciation of "pyramid." Of course, Marey (and Muybridge, at the instigation of Leland Stanford) would, in time, move from recording phases of motion in still images to reanimating still images into motion pictures.

The phrase "fringe of consciousness" evokes some of the same implications as "state borders"—a fringe being an edge or border—and it signals other ideas as well. Most obviously, there is the literal fringe in frame 31, photographed off a television screen (the TV's raster lines add a fringe-like texture) in the Desert Sands Motel, where the Clancys stayed when they first arrived in Albuquerque. There is no telling what the TV image means within its original context. A woman is looking up, apparently shocked by something we cannot see (she covers her mouth with her hand). Nor do we know what this fringe is a fringe of. The woman's shock does follow a triad of images: first, the image of the Pyramid pornography shop, then the two images of young, innocent Raphael making a paper airplane. Perhaps Clancy's use of the image of the woman's shock can be read as a wry, early-porn-era joke.

"Fringes," in one sense or another, are a motif throughout *State Borders*. There is the fringe of grass along the bottom of frame 8; the fringe of leaves around the "Boar Power" sign in frame 11; the "fringe" of ceramic cacti created by frames 25 and 26; the "fringe" of telephone poles and wires along the roads, and most obviously, the way the highways in the highway shots are sometimes fringed with grass. And of course, in a general sense, we can think of the strip of images on the wall as a fringe of photographic images, and of the considerable range of ideas these images give rise to as a conceptual fringe.

The literal fringe at the top of the TV shot can also be seen as an introduction to the triad of images that follow, during which Clancy is recorded, doing a rubbing of an outdoor wall of the motel. In the first frame of the rubbing triad, the rubbing paper has been carefully affixed to the rough contours of the wall and Clancy is working with the green chalk seen in close-up in frame 33. Of course, this rubbing is recording the rough edges, the "fringes," between the bricks of the wall. At the time, Clancy had become interested in the age-old tradition of making rubbings: in China, for making copies of Confucian texts; and in nineteenth-century United States, for memorializing the reliefs on gravestones. During the months before the trip from Central New York to northern New Mexico, Clancy had begun work on the piece called *Seven Walls for Dziga Vertov*:

> I was thinking about Vertov's work in the early 1920s with the Agitprop trains. The trains had poems by Mayakovsky and paintings by Malevich on the outside, and inside there were movie cameras and film processing equipment. Some works were more cultural; others, more propagandistic. Vertov's group included his brother, Michael Kaufman, and they would shoot film in a village and process it on the train; then, put up a sheet or some kind of wall and project the film in the next town, and repeat this for the duration of the trip. My journey and *State Borders* felt something like that.[14]

Clancy's interest in working on the *Seven Walls* project during the trip, as part of the trip, is confirmed by both Raphael Clancy's "working" on paper airplanes (the boy seems quite intense) and, perhaps, earlier on, by Flora Clancy's holding up the Osage orange: taking notice of Native-American artifacts was part of her research.

A further implicit reference in the double portrait of Raphael Clancy in frames 28, 29, and in the images of the Desert Sands Motel wall and rubbing (frames 32-34) is Béla Julesz's explorations of "cyclopean perception," discussed in his book, *Foundations of Cyclopean Perception* (University of Chicago Press, 1971), which Clancy was familiar with at the time. Julesz distinguishes between what we understand as normal visual perception, where our retinas can make sense of stimulation directly: that is, where binocular vision provides information directly to the brain; and "cyclopean perception," where normal visual stimulation cannot see the full perceptual reality of visual experiences. In his book, Julesz uses random-dot stereograms to demonstrate how particular perceptual realities can only be seen by the eye working with something beyond retinal imprinting. The double image of Raphael, where there is a tendency for the viewer to try to see a difference between the paired images, may be a wry reference to Julesz's work (Julesz pairs apparently identical random-dot stereograms throughout his book), while the red/green image of the rubbing in frame 32 evokes the red-green 3D-imaging that is illustrated throughout *Foundations of Cyclopean Perception*.

For Clancy, the art of rubbing, which is usually considered an early form of printmaking, also seemed related to what was then the new technology of color Xerox. The Xerox company in Rochester, New York, was offering artists opportunities to explore the creative possibilities of color Xerox, and Clancy visited there.[15] In fact, the announcements for the Colgate University and Utica College Marginal Works show used a color-Xerox image of Clancy's *American mystery: an image of revolution in the hemispheres* (1979—implicitly referencing the "hemispheres" of both the globe and the brain), from Clancy's "The Mummy's Virus" series. *American mystery* is, Clancy explains, a composite of multiple scans:

> an image of the Virgin of Guadalupe and a naked woman performing the "ward off" tai chi pose, are combined and below them is an image of a cow skull. It's a feminist work that celebrates the Virgin of Guadalupe—perhaps the first "miracle" that occurred in the Americas (the Catholic Church needed one)—and the woman warrior-athlete. In the original image of the Virgin, she is posed over the crescent moon, which in my image represents the horns of the cow: I was very interested in the Minoan paintings of the bare-breasted women vaulting over the minotaur's horns. I combined the two images into a single image of women's power, skill, and beauty—braiding the images together in a matrilineal past that had been overtaken by a socio/religious cultural hegemony.
>
> At the time, I had been traveling in Mexico and Central America and was very interested in the Euro-Spanish/Indian-Mayan "Idols Behind Altars," and continued to be. On other travels to Mexico I took a lot of these cards with me and left small stacks of them in historic churches in villages and cities.[16]

State Borders, "Pyr-A-Mid," Fringe of Consciousness—and Camera Obscura concludes with a photograph (frame 35) of a camera obscura image projected on the interior wall of the Desert Sands Motel by an opening in the window curtain, followed by a photograph (frame 36) of the section of the motel made visible by the pinhole image (now seen right side up). The history of the camera obscura relates to many of the images and ideas discussed here. Early in the seventeenth century Kepler used a camera obscura—in the form of a pyramidal tent!—as a movable solar observatory; and for the next two centuries artists used various camera obscura devices as an aid in making perspectival drawings (this relates to frame 9, a visual joke based on the tradition of Renaissance perspective, itself a crucial determinant in the grinding of camera lenses to create exactly the sort of deep-focus, vanishing-point perspective imagery so typical of the road images in Clancy's photoscroll). Of course, the camera obscura is a predecessor of both still and movie cameras; in fact, eighteenth- and nineteenth-century tourists frequently used a camera obscura to document their travels, in much the way Clancy used his camera to document his journey west.

That twenty-seven years after the Clancys stayed there, the Desert Sands Motel on Central Avenue in Albuquerque would become the site of crucial sequences in the Coen Brothers' *No Country for Old Men* (2007) now adds a strange and amusing "implication" to *State Borders, "Pyr-A-Mid," Fringe of Consciousness—and Camera Obscura*. The motel was demolished in 2017.

Atopia: No Man's Land (1980)

Installation of Clancy photoscroll at Utica College of Syracuse University (now Utica University) in 1980.

During the second half of the "Marginal Works" show, Clancy developed new and longer photoscrolls, all integral parts of what he considered a much larger work. Whereas *State Borders* is a physically minimal work that creates a conceptually "epic" experience, *Atopia: No Man's Land* involved not only an entire building, but the "margins" beyond the building, and a range of experiences. In particular, Clancy brought his conceptual resources to bear on what was then an unusual gallery space at Utica College of Syracuse University. Most of the time (when art shows were not ongoing) the space functioned as a pair of hallways between the administration building (DePerno Hall) and Gannett Library—at the college, this space was often described as a "square donut." To the north and south, there were solid cement-block outer walls, substantially longer than the east and west outer walls. On the eastern wall there were floor-to-ceiling windows at each end, next to each of two doors to DePerno Hall, divided by an expanse of solid wall between the doors; on the west end of the space, a double door in the center of the wall opened to the basement of the library. All four inner walls were glass; they enclosed an atrium, visible from inside the square donut and also from the outdoor plaza above the gallery. On the plaza level, the atrium opening was surrounded by a black metal fence and a concrete bench, and at the ends of the plaza there were doors to the second floors of the library and DePerno Hall. As he became acquainted with this unusual space, Clancy allowed his concept for a show to expand into it.

In recent years, I've been interested in Carl Akeley and the emergence of the diorama of animal life, ultimately climaxing in the white-tailed deer dioramas Akeley created for the Field Museum in Chicago and in Akeley's design for what became the Akeley Hall of African Mammals at the American Museum of Natural History in New York.[17] When one recognizes the amount of labor that went into these dioramas, both the painstaking collection and replication of the animals and plants that one sees within each diorama, and the relation of the individual dioramas to one another within the museum display, it is easy to see the diorama of animal life as a genre of the visual arts. Of course, it has become traditional to understand art museums and natural history museums as distinct kinds of exhibition sites, but in recent years a number of artists, most obviously, Damien Hirst, have designed and seen to the building of installations for art museums that are evocative of dioramic exhibitions in natural history museums—in a sense muddying the traditional distinction between the two kinds of exhibition and the two kinds of institution.

Clancy was already considering the conceptual liminal zone between these two ideas of exhibition by the time he designed *Atopia: No Man's Land*. He remembers sleeping for a night in the empty gallery, as he was beginning to conceptualize *Atopia: No Man's Land* and waking early in the morning when the gallery spaces were still dark, but the atrium brightly lit by the sunrise: he quickly conceived of the atrium as simultaneously a vitrine and an "event space" around which the gallery installations could evolve.[18]

For *Atopia: No Man's Land*, Clancy devised a skeletal plot involving guerillas capturing and indoctrinating hostages who eventually attack and capture their captors. Having gathered a cast of willing students (costumed according to his instructions), he shot a series of ten rolls of film as the students enacted the performance. In addition to recording elements of the performance, he included imagery from the surroundings and from a short photoscroll made in advance of the performance. Clues relating to the performance—a ladder, a black flag, a rifle, a pile of seeds through which one of the guerillas had been dragged—were left in the atrium.[19] The ten rolls were printed into a single, continuous, unedited 100-foot photoscroll, which was mounted on the southern wall of the gallery space.

When read from left to right, this first long scroll, like *State Borders*, can be seen as a narrative, of both the enacted plot *and* the process of executing and recording the performance: bystanders, for example, can frequently be seen in the background. Far from detracting from the "reality" of the photoscroll, however, this double-edged record reveals a series of conceptually provocative relationships. Clearly, playing a role in a drama is a different order of experience from actually being a guerilla; yet in both instances, people remove themselves from the normal circumstances of their lives, don costumes/uniforms, and carry out a series of preplanned activities intended to have a powerful effect on the community within which the activities occur. If one thinks of guerrilla activity as a means of subverting established institutions, the performance Clancy initiated not only symbolized subversive activity, but enacted a limited form of subversion by disregarding the "rules" established by Utica College: the "guerillas" climbed in and out of the atrium on ladders without (so far as I remember) getting permission from the College, something students and faculty were not allowed to do—stimulating some serious thought and discussion.

Atopia: No Man's Land was an ongoing process: each week revealed new facets of the work. During the week following the performance, Clancy developed the first long scroll and mounted it in the gallery, then made a second 100-foot scroll using the first scroll, this time by working "vertically," rather than on the "horizontal" narrative level. He used the new scroll to explore ideas which had been generated by the performance and by the first scroll. One of the more obvious areas Clancy explored involved the "institutionally established" 3.5 x 5 inch size of the standard photographic print. For the second scroll, which, when finished, was displayed on the north wall, he devised a variety of tactics for confounding the viewer's ability to distinguish individual frames: in some instances, we see what appear to be continuous spaces several frames long; in others, pictures include vertical lines which confuse the eye and make the real divisions between frames difficult to identify or superimposed images within the camera to create multileveled spaces.

By composing images and sequences of images so as to defy Kodak's single frame structure, Clancy engaged viewers in some of the same issues raised by the earlier narrative scroll, but on a more basic level. Isn't the process of culturally ordering activity on the basis of particular definitions and categories (and by means of the institutions and technologies generated by these definitions and categories) a "natural" process for humans—comparable to the patterns evolved by other species for dealing with the ever-changing continuum of nature? But if so, doesn't this "natural" process—by definition—posit the equally "natural" process of evading or invading any given cultural order? The ordering of human activity may be "natural," but so is any human activity that is not ordered according to established forms.

Relating this to photography, one might say that in making the scrolls Clancy accepted a highly ordered and ordering technology, but was driven to defy the order at every stage. By choosing to photograph a limited number of distinct images out of the potentially infinite images available in and around the specific performance space he chose, and by arranging them in a particular way, Clancy was able to generate conceptual experiences that in effect opened up the institutionalized space to amounts and kinds of thinking which would not have occurred otherwise. To put it another way, by *limiting* a given experience with this camera, Clancy was able to open the activities he photographed (both the enacted experience and the real educational context in which it took place) to almost *unlimited* speculation.

While the two 100-foot scrolls were the most arresting elements of *Atopia: No Man's Land*, other parts of the show helped to expand the implications of the scrolls themselves. These included a cordoned-off classroom installation, with chairs placed close together, facing a portable blackboard and a projection screen. During the performance the "classroom" was used by guerrillas in their indoctrination of the hostages; afterwards, the "classroom" was used for a continuous slide show, projecting images from the Stanford Prison Experiment, conducted by Philip G. Zimbardo, in which the students who were supposedly acting the roles of prisoners and guards crossed over an invisible "border" and became, at least symbolically, "real" guards and prisoners.

Sound was added to *Atopia: No Man's Land* during the final week. Clancy used two sources, located so that as people walked from one section of the gallery to another, they moved from one kind of sound experience to another. One was the narration that accompanies the Stanford experiment slides; the other was a tape of Clancy's performance, including his directions to the actors. Miraculously, Clancy's tape recorder accidentally picked up a Paul Harvey radio show, during which Harvey tells the well-known story of how, in the heat of the Mexican Revolution in 1914, Mutual Films sent film crews to record authentic battle footage and paid Pancho Villa $25,000 to guarantee that the fighting would occur in enough light for the cameras; ironically, when the producers saw the footage, they rejected it because it didn't look real enough![20]

Following the performance, Clancy mounted printed labels on the glass between the gallery and the central atrium, as if the atrium space were a diorama of the site of the guerilla attack. The atrium and the guerilla action for which it had been the location thus became the "text" and the scrolls mounted on the gallery walls became a complex series of notations about the "text," "written" within the "margins" of the atrium.

During the *Atopia: No Man's Land* show, the entire gallery space became, as the title of the show implies, a "no man's land," an energized, continually developing intellectual site located between the conventional "educational" processes housed in the surrounding host institution (processes that are a function of the contemporary cultural order) and the activities of guerillas, political or art-political, interested in confronting this cultural order. The pleasure of being involved in the Clancy show was that described in Barthes' *The Pleasure of the Text*. Ideological systems, according to Barthes, are "fictions," supported by "social jargons"—languages, ruled by the ruthless *topic* of fighting for hegemony: "The text itself is atopic, if not in its consumption at least in its production... There can be tranquil moments in the war of languages, and these moments are texts... Between two onslaughts of words, between too imposing systematic presences, the pleasure of the text is always possible, not as a respite, but as the incongruous—disassociated—passage from another language, like the exercise of a different physiology."[21]

Nouvelles Impressions D'Albuquerque (Open System) Cans > Canyons / INCONCLUSIONS FOR PATRICK CLANCY (1979-80)

A third part of the Marginal Works show was produced in lieu of a catalogue. Of course, the function of a catalogue is to introduce an exhibition by providing background on the artist and a general sense of the nature and history of the works included and how they fit within the traditions of art-making. For Clancy, however, a show of his work is merely a moment in an ongoing process, not something completed and in need of conventional forms of documentation. Each conceptual/material exploration generates the next foray into unknown territory. As Clancy writes at the conclusion of *Peliculas*, when his protagonist is considering walking to a cave that is 2000 feet above a lake in the mountains, at night, in order to attend a ritual, "the darkness is frightening—unknown but also mysterious and vital." There is no conclusion, only the next journey and the next conceptual immersion.

At first the Marginal Works show may have seemed (at least it seemed this way to me) a presentation of discrete photographic works (and works related to photography), but by the conclusion of *Atopia: No Man's Land*, it was clear that the photoscrolls were conceptual instigations, forays or riffs that assisted Clancy in thinking about the traditional concepts of nature and culture, educational institutions and creativity, what is "Art" and what is not. *Nouvelles Impressions D'Albuquerque (Open System) Cans > Canyons* already existed as a photoscroll, one of those exhibited at the Picker Gallery. It functioned as a kind of autobiographical follow-up to *State Borders*, where, having arrived in New Mexico after their cross-country drive, Patrick, Flora, and Raphael Clancy begin their lives in Albuquerque.

For his Marginal Works finale, Clancy teamed up with Hollis Frampton to produce a different kind of scroll. A black-and-white reproduction of the first twenty-eight images in *Nouvelles Impressions D'Albuquerque (Open System) Cans > Canyons* was combined with two texts: a rumination by Clancy on the imagery in *Nouvelles Impressions* and related texts/issues and an essay by Frampton, "Inconclusions for Patrick Clancy." The result, *Nouvelles Impressions D'Albuquerque (Open System) Cans > Canyons / INCONCLUSIONS FOR PATRICK CLANCY*, was produced as a double-sided paper scroll 5 ¾ x 37 inches, with the shortened *Nouvelles Impressions* scroll above the two texts; it is available (for $10) from Printed Matter in New York City (https://www.printedmatter.org/).

The two texts are organized into short columns, each corresponding to one of the twenty-eight images in the scroll. During the length of the scroll, Clancy intercuts between columns of his own text and Frampton's, producing a three-way juxtaposition of the scroll's elements: Clancy's comments refer to various elements in (or not in!) the photographs; Frampton's comments refer to Clancy's work in general and its position within intellectual history, specifically with regard to the history of artistic Modernism. Within their texts, Clancy and Frampton engage in something like a conversation with each other.

In "Inconclusions for Patrick Clancy," Frampton works to understand Clancy not as another photographic modernist, but rather as an instance of what was coming to be called "postmodernism":

> At a time when the received visual arts of painting and sculpture are supine, the energies invested in them at ebb tide, that compound practice within the arts that identifies itself to our attention by its piercing concern for the integrity of all intellectual discourse (together with the perilous random seas that surround it) gathers itself around a constellation of proscribed activities: photography, film, video; unallied performance; something called "writing," cursive and vernacular; something else called "sound," which comes from the unidentified muse of psychoacoustics.[22]

Frampton has long been considered a premiere theoretician of cinema and photography and among the most challenging writers to come out of the American avant-garde, so it is amusing and revealing to discover that for Frampton, *Clancy's* work is a challenge: "The pleasures of Clancy's work are the pleasures of the mind, given that the mind finds its greatest pleasures when confronted by problems quite beyond its powers, whose solutions are instantaneously paramount to its survival." That Frampton titled his piece "*In*conclusions for Patrick Clancy" confirms a sense that Clancy's use of photography (and color Xerox, and rubbings...) is not about producing finished works or a conclusive body of work, but is his way of documenting, or at least leaving evidence of, an ongoing consideration of how art-making relates to his personal experiences and the material/intellectual/historical/scientific world the artist travels through.

Nouvelles Impressions/INCONCLUSIONS begins (the scroll's design and the positioning of the title of the Frampton essay make clear on which side the scroll "begins") with successive images of what appears to be a small garden near an adobe wall on which, judging from the accompanying Clancy text, water from a sprinkler has made what looks like a wave, visible in each of the two images (in my quoting the texts in *Nouvelles Impressions/Inconclusions*, I have tried to imitate the graphic design of the quotes on the photoscroll—they're not exactly poetry, even concrete poetry, but not exactly conventional prose either):

> Two arcs of water cascade against the dry Adobe surface, which soaks in the damned Colorado River like the red desert sandstone where two waves hesitate — their momentum delayed due to some mutual attraction or arrangement between structure and process. (1)

camera, (2) waves, (3) desert plant, (4) recently planted saplings, (5) mulch. Which way do the sprinklers turn? I photographed the recently planted saplings outside the new addition to the city zoo. I didn't photograph the sign saying "zoo artist".

This opening functions as a kind of preface for the scroll, which itself is made up of two image/text "waves"—one on each side. The first two images on side one locate the scroll in the New Mexican desert where a traditional building material, adobe, meets a modern technology for providing water to desert plants and modern plantings. Frampton's "Inconclusions" begins beneath the second image of the garden, with his first comments on how the tradition of "esthetic modernism," the wave of artistic production that evolved out of late romanticism, "always encapsulated (and often managed to contain) latent contradictions…" As Frampton will suggest later in his essay, the "wave" of modernism has now instigated an increasingly less latent contradiction, the new "wave" of postmodernism, exemplified by Clancy and, in particular by *Nouvelles Impressions/INCONCLUSIONS*.

As is indicated in the title, *Nouvelles Impressions/INCONCLUSIONS* is an "*(open system)*"—meaning that Clancy has not predetermined how viewers/readers will access the work or how those of us who do access it will come to understand it. Each juxtaposition of image and image, of text and text, and of image and text can open various avenues for conjecture (the texts can sometimes feel like captions for the images and/or like the identificatory texts that accompany diorama exhibits in natural history museums). Indeed, the density of Clancy's thinking is such that to fully explore all the implications within his web of image and text is beyond the capacity of this discussion, though a few thoughts that relate to the scroll's overall structure may be useful.

Each of the two sides of the piece concludes with what is, at least in part, a narrative moment that demonstrates ideas that were of interest to Clancy. In the final images of side one—images 11, 12, 13 and 14—Flora Clancy performs a symbolic ritual. In image 11, she is seen in medium shot, standing in a grocery store aisle, holding a can of Joan of Arc Early Peas in front of a typical display of canned vegetables (each brand and type of vegetable having its own space on the shelves), acknowledging Patrick's camera. In shot 12, we see her—still acknowledging the camera—reaching with her left hand to take a can of Food Club Green Beans off the shelf, and shot 13 is a close-up of the empty space on the shelf that results. In shot 14, we see that Flora has placed the can of Joan of Arc Early Peas in the "wrong" place, with the green beans—an amusing rebellious gesture toward the overwhelming conformity of contemporary commercial life and a metaphor within *Nouvelles Impressions/INCONCLUSIONS* of the scroll's relationship to artworld categories and assumptions.

In the Clancy text underneath image 11, a further explanation, and a reference, is provided:

> Frame displacement (montage) for Hollis — Joan d'Arc Early Peas, August / 1979/ Albuquerque. All the cans in the store are perfectly aligned on the shelves. Peripheral flicker as you walk down the aisles. Cognitive patterns determine codes. A language of frames.

This textual gesture "for Hollis" relates to the passages of "Inconclusions" that sandwich Clancy's caption for the mini-performance, where Frampton writes about how modernist works of art distinguish themselves from the world that is *not* art by clear boundaries, and how his interest in Clancy's work involves Clancy's rebellion against this characteristic of modernism. For example, would another consumer, or an employee of the grocery store, see the Joan of Arc Early Peas can, embedded within the Food Club Green Beans display, as the result of a conceptual performance—that is, as a work of art—or as its opposite: random evidence of a lazy consumer? Patrick and Flora's mini-performance is also a reference to Frampton's own *By Any Other Name* series (late 1970s/ early 1980s), one aspect of which involved making color Xeroxes of the labels of grocery-store food cans (Blue Boy Chili Beans, for example, and Pine Cone Peeled Tomatoes) and repositioning these images into an art context (in homage perhaps to both Duchamp and Warhol).[23]

The four-frame performance is immediately "followed" by frame 15, on the opposite side of the scroll: an image of a bush, which, so far as I can see, has nothing to do with the grocery-store moment, except as an obvious disjunction from it. The image is accompanied by a Clancy text that includes its own radical disjunction:

> Intense heat of the desert sun separates interior from exterior. I take off my pants. The sun is hot, the canteen cold. I remember a time in winter when my hands were cold. I put them under hot water and still they were cold. While watching the Iranian turn the spitted lamb, I noticed that he was carefully positioning an umbrella between the lamb and the sun, even though it was being roasted over the fire.

How can we understand this bush in relation to the images that precede it and those that follow—two images of Clancy's pants and canteen?[24] Is the image of the bush like the Iranian's umbrella, "protecting" one reality (roasted lamb/shots 16-19) from another (sun/canned-peas-and-beans performance)? Within the open system of the scroll, the answer is, of course, up to us.

The eight-image sequence that concludes side two of the scroll and *Nouvelles Impressions/INCONCLUSIONS* is useful in evoking the scope of Clancy's thinking. After shot 20, where we see a wooden Indian chained against the space between two arched entries into a building, we begin to see images of Chaco Canyon. Originally designated Chaco Canyon National Monument in 1909 by the Theodore Roosevelt administration in order to preserve some of the most extensive pre-Columbian ruins in North America, it is now the Chaco Culture National Historical Park, which houses the remnants of an Anasazi culture, perhaps destroyed or relocated as a result of a prolonged drought in the twelfth century.[25]

Images 21 to 28 are organized so as to create a panoramic sense of the canyon landscape, where relatively flat land abuts increasingly formidable cliffs that in images 24 and 25 exceed the top of the image frame, then, in images 26 and 27, descend back, past ruins of kivas, to the flat land at the bottom of the canyon. The Clancy text that accompanies the image of ascension and descension created by these successive images first concludes an encyclopedic listing, beginning below image 19, of the principal lakes of the world as of 1979, listed in order of their size by name, location, area in square miles, length in miles, and depth in feet, beginning with the Caspian Sea and ending below image 23, with Europe's Onega Lake. A break in the text then introduces the story of an Anasazi shaman who, one day, slowly climbs to the top of a mountain, arriving at the end of the day, when he performs a strange ritual involving a pipe, a gourd, some "piki bread," a long golden wire, and a piece of flint; then, the next morning climbs back down the mountain. The Frampton text that accompanies this sequence focuses on Clancy's being a representative of a new tradition and on the challenge, for Frampton, of Clancy's thinking (quoted earlier).

The positioning of the Chaco sequence at the end of *Nouvelles Impressions/ INCONCLUSIONS* functions in various ways. Certainly, it suggests that visiting and learning about the Anasazi ruins was a highlight of the Clancys' arrival in New Mexico (the original *Nouvelles Impressions D'Albuquerque (Open System) Cans > Canyons* ends with 14 images of Chaco Canyon). Further, the sequence implicitly references the reason for the family's relocation to New Mexico from Central New York, instigated in part by Flora Clancy's research into pre-Columbian civilizations in the American Southwest and in Mexico and Central America, which led to her being offered the job at University of New Mexico. In 1980, during a Dumbarton Oaks symposium entitled "Interdisciplinary Approaches to the Study of Mesoamerican Highland-Lowland Interaction," she presented "A Comparison of Highland Zapotec and Lowland Maya Graphic Styles." I assume Patrick's sequence of low-to-high-to-low landscape images implicitly references Flora's essay.

Clancy rejoined Raphael and Flora in the fall of 1980 and began teaching at University of New Mexico. In the years that followed, he would continue to expand on the photoscroll, both on the size and complexity of individual photoscrolls and on his attempts to use the form within broader cultural contexts. In 1983 he finished *Hawaii nei: (Fish Out of Water)*, a 24-image/text piece, organized in a manner rather like *Nouvelles Impressions/ INCONCLUSIONS*.

Hawaii nei provides a conceptual excursion into a photograph from an advertisement in a travel brochure. The photograph depicts the arrival of a luxury cruise ship with a middle-aged couple in the foreground being greeted by a young Hawaiian woman in native dress. Clancy's camera frames various details of the advertisement, which are arranged as a series of disjunctive images, each accompanied by a text, presented directly below it, which in one way or another contextualizes that detail. At the bottom of each image/text unit, a city is named (Acapulco, Buenos Aires, Beirut, Peking, Buffalo...), followed by time of day, temperature, and an indication of the current weather, apparently in that city. Clancy creates a complex interplay between the fantasies of advertisement and the history of early European explorers who visited the Hawaiian islands, including Captain Cook, who named them the "Sandwich Islands"—a deed that "showed some foresight, but in an unintended and yet apparently fateful direction. Soon after the discovery he would die, in 1779, at the hands of 'cannibals'" (from Clancy text underneath frame 7).

In 1985, working with Gwen Widmer, Clancy finished a version of *365/360 (The Plowed Field)*, an epic photoscroll comprised of six horizontal strips of imagery and text.[26] Below each strip of sixty-one images is a double layer of often disjunctive text, printed in boustrophedon form so that the upper layer is read in normal right-to-left alignment; the lower, in italicized mirror writing.[27] At the end of the fourth strip of images, one image space is left blank: there are 365 photographs altogether, marking a calendar year; the "360" refers to the meta-panoramic shape of the work. As Clancy's colleague Ed Bryant was to say, "It takes considerably more than a cursory look to gain access to the contexts of this thematic material":

> The title *365/360* might give a clue, for it refers to those boundaries used by our self-centered culture to fix time, space and viewpoint. Denying any such closed concepts, Clancy has used the interweavings and cross-cuttings within this extensive visual amalgamate—of fact and fiction, of staged event and documented incident, of actor and poseur, of appropriated authentic evidence and sly deceit, of analogue and antipode—to spatialize time and push it inward as a direct experience of the content of our consciousness. The trip structured by the sequencing of these 365 stills is not rationally measurable, for its psychological time and space are created through our own experiential associations, emotional speculations, and cognitive dissonances.[28]

Presented as a wall installation, 5 x 35½ feet, *365/360* evokes, as its subtitle suggests, a series of furrows, where conceptual "seeds" have been planted and will grow with the viewer's engagement.[29]

A poignant instance of Clancy's attempt (again, in collaboration with Gwen Widmer) to work creatively within the commercial world with techniques developed in the photoscrolls involved a different kind of "seeding" of text and image for the January 1986 issue of *Albuquerque Living*. In a two-page spread, called "Front Pages" (actually pages 8 and 9 of the magazine) and subtitled "FRONTIER LIVING: Disappearing Space (Even in the West)," images and texts, similar in overall organization to the structuring of *365/360*, function to create a conceptual interruption within *Albuquerque Living*.[30] Readers who paid attention to "Front Pages" would have been led to re-see the magazine's cover image and the many advertisements within the issue that are reconfigured on "Front Pages" by Clancy/Widmer, in a manner that implicitly critiqued what was presumably understood as "normal" by readers of the magazine, raising the kinds of issues that these generic, locally-focused magazines routinely suppress. Clancy's contribution to a 1988 issue of *Cinematograph*, edited by Christine Tamblyn, took this kind of "seeding" even further: Clancy embedded bits of text and small images (re-photographed from other visual imagery in the issue) within the other texts, in order to create what Tamblyn called "an experimental narrative that deconstructs the inherent ideological assumptions of the entire volume [of *Cinematograph*] by highlighting the preemptive structures of language itself."[31]

Looking back now, forty years later, I can see that the Marginal Works show was not only the beginning of a series of remarkable photoscrolls, made during (and about) a transformation in Clancy's life and work, but can also be understood as a microcosm of his career. Clancy has understood that in recent decades most of us have come to make sense of our world and our lives in a manner rather different from earlier generations, and even, for some of us, from the earlier times of our own generation. We are ever more engulfed by wave after wave of obvious and subtle commercial advertising on television, on computers, on cell phones, radios, in our snail mail, on iPads—within the continually proliferating and evolving mediascape that is the context for our living and our thinking. Clancy felt, early on, that the idea of working simply in one traditionally acceptable mode of art-making and focusing on the production of saleable works had come to mean that he couldn't speak to/within the evolution of modern culture. The photoscrolls allowed him to develop a way of critiquing the commercial mediascape, especially its careful avoidance of complex thought and its obsession with the surfaces of our lives—by redirecting the language of the mediascape itself.

The fundamental irony of Clancy's career is that his resistance to seeing his work as part of the commercial wave that continually engulfs us has meant, practically speaking, that much of his work has remained under the radar for many of those who might make the most of it. One can hope that coming to grips with the methodology of Clancy's photoscroll work can provide a training ground for exploring his career as a whole, as well as for being more alert to the conceptual and physical realities of his/our/their world.

Clancy's photoscrolls, including *State Borders*; *Sandia Parallax*; *Nouvelles Impressions D'Albuquerque (Open System) Cans > Canyons / INCONCLUSIONS FOR PATRICK CLANCY*; *365/360 (The Plowed Field)*; and *Hawaii nei*, are available at Clancy's website: www.patrickclancy.org.

---

1   "Video As Attitude" took place at the Museum of Fine Arts, Museum of New Mexico, Santa Fe and at University Art Museum, University of New Mexico-Albuquerque, from May 13-June 26, 1983. The show focused on video "as a component which interacts with other media in a multi-layered, sculptural context," featuring works by Joan Jonas, Allan Kaprow, Bill Beirne, Juan Downey, Dieter Froese, Robert Gaylor, Gary Hill, Rita Myers, Bruce Nauman, Michael Smith, Francesc Torres, Steina and Woody Vasulka, and Bill Viola. Clancy is partially quoting

from *Learning from Las Vegas* (Cambridge: MIT Press, 1972), edited by Denise Scott Brown, Steven Izenour, and Robert Venturi.
2   The seven members of PULSA—Michael Cain, Clancy, William Crosby, William Duesing, Paul Fuge, Peter Kindlmann, and David Rumsey—remained anonymous during PULSA's activities, which were described in the *New York Times* as "a group effort to produce an art experience by organizing various sound and light activities in environments"; a PULSA member explains, "Our art's an experience and after it's over, it's over. There's nothing to own." See David L. Shirey, "Sound, Light and 7 Young Artists," *New York Times*, December 24, 1970, for a (patronizing) review of PULSA's activities during the previous three years. Several articles on PULSA are available online by googling "PULSA (Yale Research Associates in the Arts)."
3   In earlier years Clancy had experimented with grids, and had worked with a carpenter's chalk line on narrow strips of canvas (from an inch to a foot wide) which were mounted as friezes and rolled up for storage; the color along the chalk lines varied depending on the modulations of the string when it struck the canvas. The photoscrolls seem formally related.
4   In three instances, the Sandia range is not visible, though it seems clear from the context that we are to assume that in each image the relationship of the camera to the mountainscape is the same; that is, that the Sandias are just behind the buildings in the foreground.
5   To shoot the imagery for *Sandia Parallax*, Clancy took a walk through his new neighborhood. During the walk, he recorded ambient sound (along with the sound of the camera shutter), which during some installations of the photoscroll created an audio environment for the images.
6   The vapor trail from a plane that can be seen above the mountains in most of the images suggests that all 21 images were taken in a relatively brief period of time: there are modulations in the vapor trail, but its shape is consistent throughout the photoscroll.
7   Those of us who project 16mm prints are familiar with written indications directed to projectionists on the film leader that precedes the film proper, but, of course, cursive text on the filmstrip *within* a film, is more than unusual. A noteworthy exception is *Secondary Currents*, produced by Peter Rose in 1983, a film in which the only imagery is visual texts, seen, at least at first, as the translated subtitles of the "language" we hear Rose enunciating on the soundtrack (a nonsense language evocative at various points of Swedish, Japanese, and Italian—Rose's allusion to the European art film making its way into American theaters during the era and the subtitles these films required). Near the end of *Secondary Currents*, a set of final visual texts transitions into cursive writing directly on the filmstrip, partially readable, but only fully readable, as is the case in *Peliculas*, by reading the filmstrip unscrolled or on rewinds. See Scott MacDonald, *Screen Writings: Scripts and Texts by Independent Filmmakers* (Berkeley: University of California Press, 1995), 156-72, for Rose's text. Canyon Cinema rents the film.
8   Email to the author, July 4, 2019.
9   Email to the author, July 4, 2019. Of course, Hollis Frampton, who was Clancy's neighbor, friend, and collaborator in the 1970s and early 1980s (he had been lured to Central New York, at least in part, by Robert Huot) had been exploring, at least since *Surface Tension* (1968) and *Zorns Lemma* (1970), the cultural imbrications of text and image, as well as—in the epic *Magellan Cycle*, which was Frampton's focus during his final years (he died in 1984)—the transition from celluloid/emulsion-based cinema to digital video. Frampton was Clancy's collaborator on two parts of the Marginal Works show.
10 In fact, the purpose of the Clancys' trip west was to settle Flora and Raphael in Albuquerque (Flora had accepted a position at the University of New Mexico); Patrick would soon return to Central New York to complete his teaching and do the Marginal Works show, before rejoining his family out west.
11 The state seal of Indiana is a circular image commemorating the creation of the state in 1816. Within the image, a man is chopping a sycamore tree and a buffalo is jumping over a log, presumably to escape the domestication of the landscape that is taking place; the sun is setting over distant hills.
12 Roland Barthes, *The Pleasure of the Text*, trans. Richard Miller (New York: Hill and Wang, 1975), 7.
13 While the railroad tracks in the drawing demonstrate a vanishing point lost in the surreal West of this image, the people we see along the tracks on the left and further back at the "point" itself, are not drawn in perspective: they are the same size wherever they are along the track.
14 Email to the author, June 10, 2019.
15 Clancy, in email to author, July 14, 2019: "I have clear memories working at Xerox on a couple of series of Xerox prints and getting the idea to make rubbings by hand with 3 layers of

rubbings, using the same process pigments of yellow, magenta and cyan, in that sequence, just like the sequence of color scans that the Xerox machine made. I asked them about the pigments and they put me in touch with American Cynamide."

16 Clancy, in an email to the author, July 14, 2019.
17 I detail my interest in Akeley and the habitat diorama in the introduction to *The Sublimity of Document: Cinema As Diorama (Avant-Doc 2)* (New York: Oxford University Press, 2019).
18 Skype conversation with Clancy, August 19, 2019.
19 The seeds were both literal and conceptual. Clancy hoped that birds might visit the atrium to eat some of the seeds, that other seeds would take root in the atrium space over time, and that those visitors to the gallery who saw the seeds would be drawn into considerations of what they might mean. The conflation between natural process and performed activity was also evident in one bit of imagery devised after the performance ended: a tree dressed in a guerilla outfit! Skype conversation, August 19, 2019.
20 For details about this story, see Mike Dash, "Uncovering the Truth Behind the Myth of Pancho Villa, Movie Star": https://www.smithsonianmag.com/history/uncovering-the-truth-behind-the-myth-of-pancho-villa-movie-star-110349996/.
21 Barthes, *The Pleasure of the Text*, 29-30.
22 Frampton's "Inconclusions for Patrick Clancy" was reprinted, as a separate essay, in Bruce Jenkins, ed., *On the Camera Arts and Consecutive Matters: The Writings of Hollis Frampton* (Cambridge, MA: MIT Press, 2009), 292-95.
23 See *On the Camera Arts and Consecutive Matters*, 300, for reproductions of these images. Frampton, from "Notes: By Any Other Name": "Language and image, each trespassing in the other's house, secrete disquieting disjunctions, conundrums, circularities. We are accustomed to the poetic strategy, within language, of bracketing a noun within the genus of yet another noun which may come from an alien phylum, a foreign kingdom. Translation of that strategy into the economy of images yields artifacts—savagely grotesque, arch, silly—that seem to flee the rigors of self-reference: contradictory images, far from coalescing in a dialectical encounter, annihilate one another in a gesture that sweeps language clean of specification and seems on the point of suggesting a raw map of the preconscious work—the material *action* of language" (298).
24 Actually, these two images and a third image of Clancy's pants (and, barely visible through the glass doors, Clancy, seemingly nude), is itself interrupted by a less obviously related image of what looks to be an outdoor electric outlet.
25 James Benning would film in Chaco Canyon for his *Four Corners* (1997). During the film, visual texts that roll up through the frame tell stories that relate to imagery of four locations: Chaco Canyon, New Mexico; Milwaukee, Wisconsin; Mesa Verde, Colorado; and Farmington, New Mexico.
26 The subtitle of *365/360* was not entirely stable. When the piece was installed at the Houston Center of Photography in 1986, it was ("The Plowed Field and the City").
27 Boustrophedon, from the Greek, meaning "Ox-turning"—as in an ox turning at the end of one furrow to pull the plow in the opposite direction to make the next furrow—is a type of bi-directional text, mostly seen in ancient Greek manuscripts. Every other line of writing is flipped or reversed, using reversed letters.
28 Edward Bryant, "Patrick Clancy's *365/360*," in "The Recent Photoscrolls of Patrick Clancy," *Artspace: Southwestern Contemporary Arts Quarterly*, 10, no. 2 (Spring 1986), 13-14.
29 Clancy's use of a plowed field as a metaphor for the "furrows" of image and text in *365/360* was preceded by Larry Gottheim's use of the same image as a major motif in his *Horizons* (1973). During the years when Clancy lived in Central New York State, there was much interaction between filmmakers and media artists in the region. No doubt other filmmakers have also worked with this metaphor.
30 In a gesture typical of Clancy, the space that would follow the colon in "LIVING:Disappearing" is not used in the subtitle—dramatizing the disappearing space of the West by ignoring, and thereby drawing attention to, one of the conventional dimensions of printed language.
31 Christine Tamblyn, "Introduction" to *Cinematograph* 3 (1988), 1. *Cinematograph: A Journal of Film and Media Art*, was published by the San Francisco Cinematheque.

2020

Robert Huot: The Painter as Filmmaker

This essay was written on the occasion of a show of Robert Huot's paintings at what was then called the Munson-Williams-Proctor Arts Institute (now "Munson") in Utica, New York. The show, organized by Mary Murray, opened on October 12, 2019 and ran until January 19, 2020. "Robert Huot Paintings" focused on paintings made during the early years of Huot's career, beginning in 1963 and continuing until 1998. Huot's paintings of this period are distinctive and elegant, rigorously and inventively formalist—and, at least from our current vantage point, comparatively safe. The show didn't suggest the full panoply of his early and more recent work, much of which is not only aggressive and confrontative, but also proto-cinematic. A single diary painting was included in the show (the diary paintings are roles of canvas along which are embedded individual paintings, just as individual frames of imagery are embedded along the celluloid filmstrip), along with *Mira, Mira 13's* (1967), one of several '60s paintings organized along the horizontal that implicitly predict Huot's movement from painting into film. None of the many films Huot had made from the late 1960s into the early 1980s, sometimes in collaboration with Hollis Frampton, were shown in conjunction with the paintings. A number of Huot's 16mm diary films and *Turning Torso Drawdown* (1971) had been part of the earlier "Frames of Mind" show—see chapter 7 (the nudity in the films shown during "Frames of Mind" had caused some consternation).

The most recent work pictured in the catalogue is a pair of large-form photographs from Huot's "Red Classics Series" (2008-09) in which Huot and Carol Kinne (Huot's long-time partner, to whom he dedicated the show—Kinne died in 2016), enact Jan van Eyck's portraits of Adam and Eve at opposite ends of the Ghent altarpiece (1432). Huot and Kinne collaborated on various photographic series into the 2010s. Huot had been inspired by re-reading Kenneth Clark's *The Nude, a Study in Ideal Form*, and he and Kinne worked together (with Katy Martin) on three series of large photographs (actually pigment prints on Hahnemuhle photo rag paper): "Red Classic Series," "Red Classic/Red Figure" (2009-19), and "Death and the Maiden" (2009-21). In these startling images, Huot and Kinne posed nude, in defiance of the idea that aging means a loss of physical beauty, and in Kinne's case, in defiance of death itself. Instances of this recent work have been shown in Paris at Galerie Arnaud Lefebvre and at Alexander Heath Contemporary in Roanoke, Virginia, which Huot helped found, with Edward Hettig and Gregg Weinschreider. In 2018, Huot established the Carol Kinne Memorial in Columbus Center, New York, where Kinne's painting, sculpture, and digital work (and work by Huot and other local artists) is on view.

Meeting Huot was important for me. I had been alerted to him when I interviewed Hollis Frampton. He and Huot had been friends in New York in the late 1960s; Frampton taught Huot how to edit 16mm film, and to some extent Frampton had followed Huot to Central New York State. Huot's work helped me see that the films I was exploring were as closely related to the New York art world as to film history in general and Hollywood in particular. We have remained in regular contact.

* * *

At some point during the latter part of his childhood, Robert Huot remembers coming into possession of a strip of sepia-toned 35mm movie film, an object that became for a time a kind of talisman. Younger generations may wonder what a 35mm filmstrip is and why possessing such a thing might have mattered to a boy, but those of us who grew up before the cultural transformation into digital imaging may well empathize with young Bob. As I write this, hanging behind me in my office is a black-and-white 35mm filmstrip with the text "The End" on each frame, given to me by filmmaker Bruce Conner to commemorate the completion of *A Critical Cinema* (University of California Press, 1988), a book of my interviews with independent filmmakers, including Conner and Huot. The book's cover image is a still from Huot's film *Diary 1974-75* (1975) in which Huot is seen, in reflective/distortive mylar, filming himself filming.

So I knew Huot as a filmmaker before I knew he was a painter and while in recent years (and really for most of his life) he has been more of a painter than a filmmaker, much of his most interesting work was produced during a period when he explored both painting and film, and various intersections between them. He was not alone in this exploration. The 1960s saw a transformation in American film culture precipitated by the influx of "foreign films" coming into American theaters from France, Sweden, Japan, Italy, Germany, Mexico..., by the advent of inexpensive sync-sound rigs for shooting cinema-verite documentaries, and by an excitement among artists coming from photography, painting, sculpture, and performance into what came to be called "avant-garde cinema" or "underground film."

In the years before Huot embraced filmmaking, his movement toward film was evident in some of his paintings. Like many artists in the mid-1960s, Huot was questioning what exactly constitutes a painting or a sculpture or a film. During the early 1960s, he had begun to work subtly and creatively with grids and over the next years grew increasingly interested in modular work, in some cases making "paintings"—sometimes no actual painting was involved—that are narrow, often modular strips. The filmstrip, of course, is made up of modules, individual frames, each the same size, arranged in a continuum along the celluloid strip. In *Ins+Outs* (1966) and *Scott's Scribble* (1966), it is as if Huot's paintings are stretching toward the filmstrip. Indeed, *Ins+Outs* (at least for a film person!) evokes both the filmstrip and the take-up reel of a movie projector.[1]

During this period, artists of all kinds could hardly avoid knowing that New York City, especially Soho and the East Village before gentrification, had become the East Coast home of avant-garde filmmaking and exhibition (the Bay Area was its West Coast home). Huot—along with Jonas Mekas, Andy Warhol, Michael Snow, Yoko Ono, Ken Jacobs, Carolee Schneemann, Hollis Frampton, Yvonne Rainer, Ernie Gehr, and many others—shared a quest to create what Annette Michelson would call an "artisanal cinema" that could compete, at least aesthetically, with commercial narrative film and implicitly and sometimes explicitly critique the hierarchical Hollywood production process and product. Jonas Mekas became the leading spokesman for what he called this "New American Cinema" and the instigator of Anthology Film Archives and the Film-Makers' Cooperative—institutions that have continued to serve independent film.

Hollywood had created a tradition where the metaphysics of filmmaking were suppressed; the avant-garde was providing a critique of this tradition by focusing on the particulars of the motion picture camera and projector, the nature of the filmstrip, and the assumptions about editing and cinematic structure that had seemed virtually automatic to previous generations. These filmmakers were interested in remaking cinema from the ground up, a project that attracted Huot, whose earliest films were focused on the filmstrip, less as a means to the end of photographic illusion or narrative, than as a physical object that could be manipulated the way a painter manipulates paint and a sculptor, materials and material objects.

For his first film, *Leader* (1967), Huot edited strips of various kinds of 16mm film leader—placed at the beginnings and ends of developed film rolls to protect films from damage during handling and projection—into a montage. *Leader* was the beginning of a series of experiments during 1967, including *Scratch*, where Huot scratched into the emulsion of black-and-white film, foregrounding what had usually been damage that viewers struggled to ignore so that they could "see the movie"; *From Loops*, where Huot used a hole punch to perforate the frames on the filmstrip, creating a projected ballet of light-circles; and *Spray* (available at Huot's website), where he spray painted a strip of clear celluloid, creating animated dot patterns when the film is projected.

These experiments were followed by four films in which Huot playfully confronted Hollywood's (and soft-core pornography's) coy marketing of sexuality, while adding a cinematic dimension to the history of the nude. For *Red Stockings* (1969) Huot exposed only a single frame of film (traditional cinema projectors show films at 24 frames per second): a close-up of a woman's genitalia. This single frame is preceded and followed by a consistent eye-bending red, so that even if the viewer does "see" the single frame, it is lost in the afterimages produced by the red "stockings" that lead up to and away from this image. In *Cross Cut (a Blue Movie)* (1969) Huot intercuts, for one minute, between brief shots of the torso of a woman in a fur G-string doing a high-speed shimmy and blue film leader—at the time, pornographic films were called "blue movies."

During the period when Huot was making these first films, while simultaneously moving, in his gallery work, toward what came to be called conceptual art, he was in close contact with photographer-turned-filmmaker Hollis Frampton (1936-84), who taught Huot how to splice lengths of filmstrip together, to edit.[2] The two men were soon in a productive cinematic conversation with each other, beginning with Frampton's *Manual of Arms* (1966), a series of mini-portraits—what Frampton called "courtly dances with friends and lovers"—of Carl Andre, Rosemarie Castoro, Lucinda Childs, Lee Lozano, Larry Poons, Joyce Wieland, Michael Snow, Twyla Tharp, and Huot, who is the only subject who stands up and abruptly leaves the frame, a gesture provoked, perhaps, by his impatience with Frampton's project. Huot can also be seen in Frampton's *Prince Rupert Drops* (1969) and *Artificial Light* (1969).

In 1969, Huot completed two films—both of them related to painting, though in different ways—for which Frampton was the camera operator: *Black and White Film* (available on the Huot website) and *Nude Descending the Stairs*.[3] Both films confirm Huot's interest in the tradition of the nude. In *Black and White Film*, Sheila Raj is seen emerging from darkness as she gradually lowers a black body stocking to reveal her naked body; then, reaching out into the darkness surrounding her, she takes handfuls of what appears to be black paint and paints herself from toe to head until she is invisible except for slight reflections of the lone, off-screen film light on her body. Frampton would describe the film for the Film-Makers' Cooperative catalogue: "This film is 'about' painting. Outside of painting itself, it is the only really intense criticism I have ever seen." *Nude Descending the Stairs*, as described in an intertitle two-thirds through the film, is an "Homage to Duchamp, [Eadweard] Muybridge, and [Étienne-Jules] Marey." Huot, dressed in what appears to be a house painter's jumpsuit, goggles, and gloves, slowly descends a long staircase toward the camera in a single shot; he is followed by a young woman, nude, who slowly descends the staircase, also in a single shot; then, after the credits, again, a second time.

Frampton was impressed with Huot's early forays into filmmaking:

> Some painters and sculptors approach our art with a kind of chauvinistic arrogance. Their use of film, however interesting as documentation, is fundamentally exploitive. Robert Huot has been one of the most inventive and rigorous of the younger generation of radical painters. He brings the same attributes to film, along with an inquisitiveness that is by no means cautious. He tries not to exploit film but to find out what film *is*. Huot's films will seem "simple" to many. In fact, he is doing basic work that we filmmakers ought to have done for ourselves decades ago, work that is both an addition and a reproach to film art.[4]

During the same year he did the camerawork for *Black and White Film* and *Nude Descending the Stairs*, Frampton would finish his own *Lemon*, which includes the dedication "(for Robert Huot)." Later, in *Less* (1973), Frampton would echo *Black and White Film*.

By 1970, Huot had become disenchanted with what he felt was the obliviousness of the "art world" to troubling political realities, particularly the war in Vietnam—and decided to reboot his life. Using a grant he had received from the NEA as down-payment, he bought an old farm and moved to Central New York, just north of New Berlin; by 1971, with Huot's help, Frampton had joined him, moving to Eaton, a few miles drive to the west.[5] Frampton's transition from urbanite to rural resident is documented in his *Zorns Lemma* (1970), an hour-long, 3-part film, the middle section of which is a cinematic puzzle in which single-shots of individual words, filmed within their New York City context, are presented in alphabetic series until, letter by letter, each word is replaced by one-second bits of a continuous action. The letter K is replaced with one-second images of Huot painting a wall—an allusion, I assume, to *Two Blue Walls (Pratt and Lambert #5020 Alkyd, Sanded Floor Coated with Polyurethane)*, a conceptual painting Huot had done for Paula Cooper Gallery in March-April 1969—the gallery couldn't sell the "painting" without selling the gallery wall!

During the final section of *Zorns Lemma*, Huot and Marcia Steinbrecher, who was married to Frampton for a brief period, are filmed in four continuous 100-foot roll-long shots (about three minutes each), as they walk into the distance across Huot's farm, finally disappearing into a wooded area. I have suggested elsewhere that this was Frampton's homage to Huot as a man of action.[6]

Huot's buying a farm in Central New York transformed both his filmmaking and his painting. Filmmaking became his primary way of dealing with this new environment, as well as a continuing exploration of the nature and potentials of celluloid cinema. The new films were personal depictions of his surroundings and the new dimensions of his life—and his life with Twyla Tharp. Huot and Tharp were partners for nine years, beginning in 1963, and Tharp, with Huot's support, began her career as a dancer/choreographer at the farm. The new films were longer (several were feature length) and more elaborate than the early experiments—though Huot's interest in modular construction is still evident. For example, *One Year (1970)* (1971; 200 minutes) is divided into forty-nine sections, during which Huot first explores chiaroscuro and composition, building on *Black and White* and *Nude Descending the Stairs*, then documents the process of renovating house and barn to create a functioning farm and dance studio. *One Year (1970)* was followed in 1972 by *Rolls: 1971*, a more aggressive and structurally complex film than *One Year (1970)*. I have always assumed that *Rolls: 1971* was at least an implicit response to *Zorns Lemma*. Frampton divides his film into three separate, implicitly chronological sections, each representing a stage of life. Huot's more complex structure (based on the process of "drawdown" that he had learned while working as a pigment chemist during his early years in Manhattan) sees life as a constant juxtaposition of rural and urban, mundane and sublime, learning and learned, edited and single-shot images. *Rolls: 1971* opens with a stunning three-minute single shot of snow that was subsequently released as *Snow* (available on the Huot website) and is part of the Munson-Williams-Proctor Arts Institute collection.[7]

Rolls: 1971 was followed by *Third One-Year Movie—1972* (1973; 70 minutes); then, by what Huot was now calling "diary films": *Diary Film #4—1973* (1974) and *Diary 1974-75* (1975). For *Super-8 Diary 1979* (1980), he switched to the smaller, less expensive Super-8mm gauge, which offered the option of sync sound, and continued to make diary films along with short experimental works into the early 1980s. From 1973, Huot frequently collaborated with his partner, artist Carol Kinne (1942-2016); see, for example *Beautiful Movie* (1975, available on the Huot website).[8]

If by 1970 filmmaking had become a major interest for Huot, he did not stop painting. His early diary films were produced in counterpoint with a considerable series of "diary paintings." From 1971 to 1975 Huot painted on rolls of canvas, unrolling the canvas to paint a section, then, once the paint had dried, rolling that section up and unrolling the next section of canvas—that is, using rolls of canvas as if they were rolls of film. The finished paintings are unrolled for exhibition, just as traditional celluloid films scroll through the film projector from feed reel to take-up reel. If Huot's film diaries of this era looked toward the future—cinema being the new artistic option—the diary paintings often referenced painters and paintings (from Jackson Pollock to ancient Chinese scroll paintings) that continued to be important in Huot's thinking.

The most recent film listed on Huot's filmography is the last of a series of playful erotic films, *Doctor Faustus' Foot Fetish* (1981-82), but his fascination

Hollis Frampton in Robert Huot's *One Year: 1970* (1971).
Courtesy of Robert Huot.

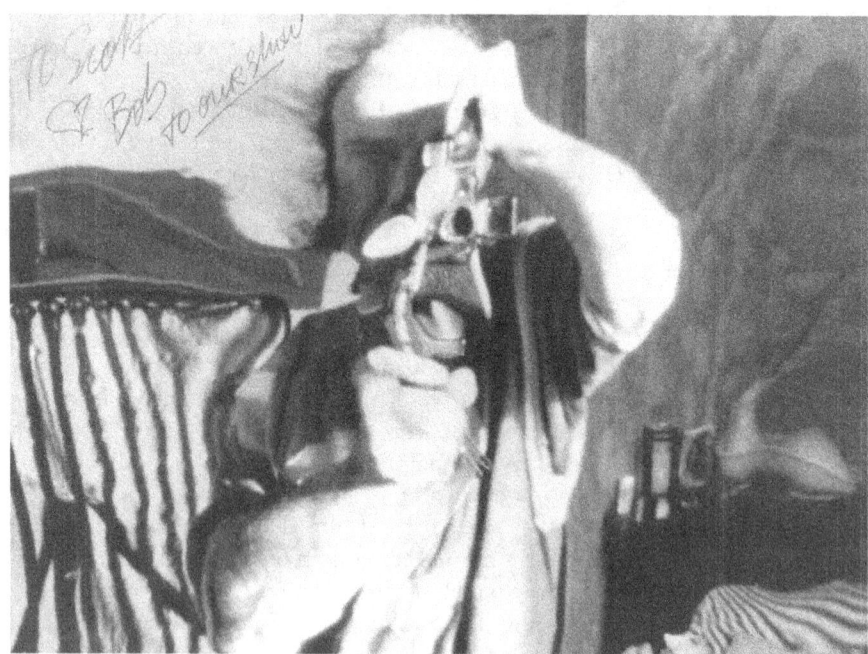

Signed still of Robert Huot filming himself in mylar,
from *Diary 1974-75* (1975). Courtesy of Robert Huot.

with the basics of cinema, including its origins, was evident in the show, "Robert Huot: Forms of Motion—An Exhibition of Pre-Cinema Devices," for which he designed and constructed zoetropes, phenakistiscopes, and other forerunners of cinematic animation, using drawings of himself and Carol Kinne as subjects to be animated.[9]

After the early 1980s, Huot was, once again, primarily a painter—though the fascination with modular structuring that had led him to film has remained obvious in the long series of equilateral-triangle paintings (presented sometimes as sets of individual paintings of identical shape and size) that dominated his attention through the 1990s. Like the diary paintings, Huot's triangles often evoke painters and paintings that had continued to be important to him—Albert Pinkham Ryder, Bradley Walker Tomlin, Hans Hoffman, de Kooning, *Venus of Willendorf*—and sometimes films. For example, in a triptych of triangles called "Icon Series" (1995, reproduced as a separate fold-out in the catalogue of a retrospective show of equilateral-triangle work at the Hunter College Art Gallery in New York in 1998), *Venus of Willendorf* and *Triskellion a.k.a. Michael* flank *Divine*, Huot's wry homage to "Divine" (the late Harris Glenn Milstead), icon and star of John Waters' *Pink Flamingos* (1972), a Huot favorite.

Huot's interest in the intersections of painting and the photographic arts remains evident in his final collaboration with Carol Kinne, the "Red Classic Series," a set of photographs that challenge the history of the nude as a paean to youth. Huot and Kinne posed nude and photographed each other, as they re-enacted artistic poses from classic painting and sculpture.

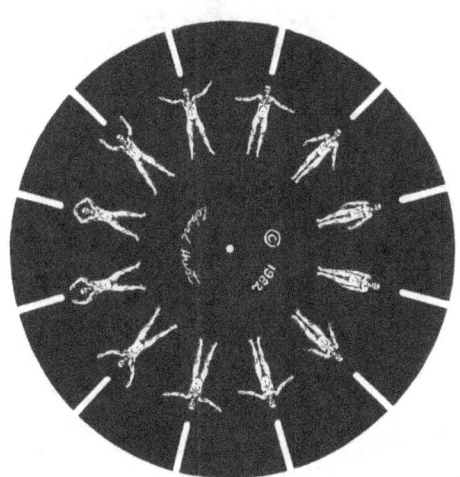

Phenakistoscope disc, designed and produced by Huot for
"Robert Huot—Forms of Motion: An Exhibition of Pre-Cinema Devices,"
a show of phenakistoscopes, zoetropes, and flipbooks at the Edith Barrett Gallery,
Utica College of Syracuse University (now Utica University),
from March 21-April 9, 1982.

Huot *Diary Painting No. 21* (1973) on floor of Munson. Photo by Richard Walker.

Huot's films are available, as 16mm prints and digital files, at Canyon Cinema (canyoncinema.com) and at Light Cone (lightcone.org). The catalogue for the "Robert Huot Paintings" show is available through Munson, 310 Genesee Street, Utica, NY 13501. Huot was interviewed for *A Critical Cinema* (University of California Press, 1988), 98-115.

1   See Huot's website (www.roberthuot.com/early-work/mid-60s) for images of many of his paintings.
2   See, for example, Scott MacDonald, interview with Annette Michelson, in *Avant-Doc: Intersections of Documentary and Avant-Garde Cinema* (New York: Oxford University Press, 2015).
3   The best sources for information about Hollis Frampton are Bruce Jenkins and Susan Krane, eds., *Hollis Frampton: Recollections/Recreations* (Buffalo: Albright-Knox Art Gallery; Cambridge: MIT Press, 1984); Bruce Jenkins, ed., *On the Camera Arts and Consecutive Matters: The Writings of Hollis Frampton* (Cambridge: MIT Press, 2009); and Michael Zryd, *Hollis Frampton: Navigating the Infinite Cinema* (New York: Columbia University Press, 2023).
4   Watch *Black and White Film* at http://www.roberthuot.com/black-white-film/.
5   Jenkins, ed., "Notes on Filmmakers," in *On the Camera Arts and Consecutive Matters: The Writings of Hollis Frampton*, 190.
6   Huot commuted to Hunter College in New York, where he had taught since 1963; Frampton, from 1973, to SUNY Buffalo.
7   MacDonald, *The Garden in the Machine* (Berkeley: University of California Press, 2001), chapter 8.
8   Watch *Snow* at http://www.roberthuot.com/snow.
9   *Beautiful Movie* evokes impressionist painting, with a feminist twist: in very soft focus, Carol Kinne, nude on a bed, brushes her hair for two minutes, slowly coming more fully into sharp focus; then there is a dissolve to Huot himself, in the same composition, also nude, brushing *his* hair, and the image slowly goes back out of focus, then fades out. Watch *Beautiful Movie* at http://www.roberthuot.com/beautiful-movie/.
10 Edith Langley Barrett Gallery, Utica College of Syracuse University, 1982.

2021

40-Year Diptych

"40th Birthday Poem"

"Going on 80"

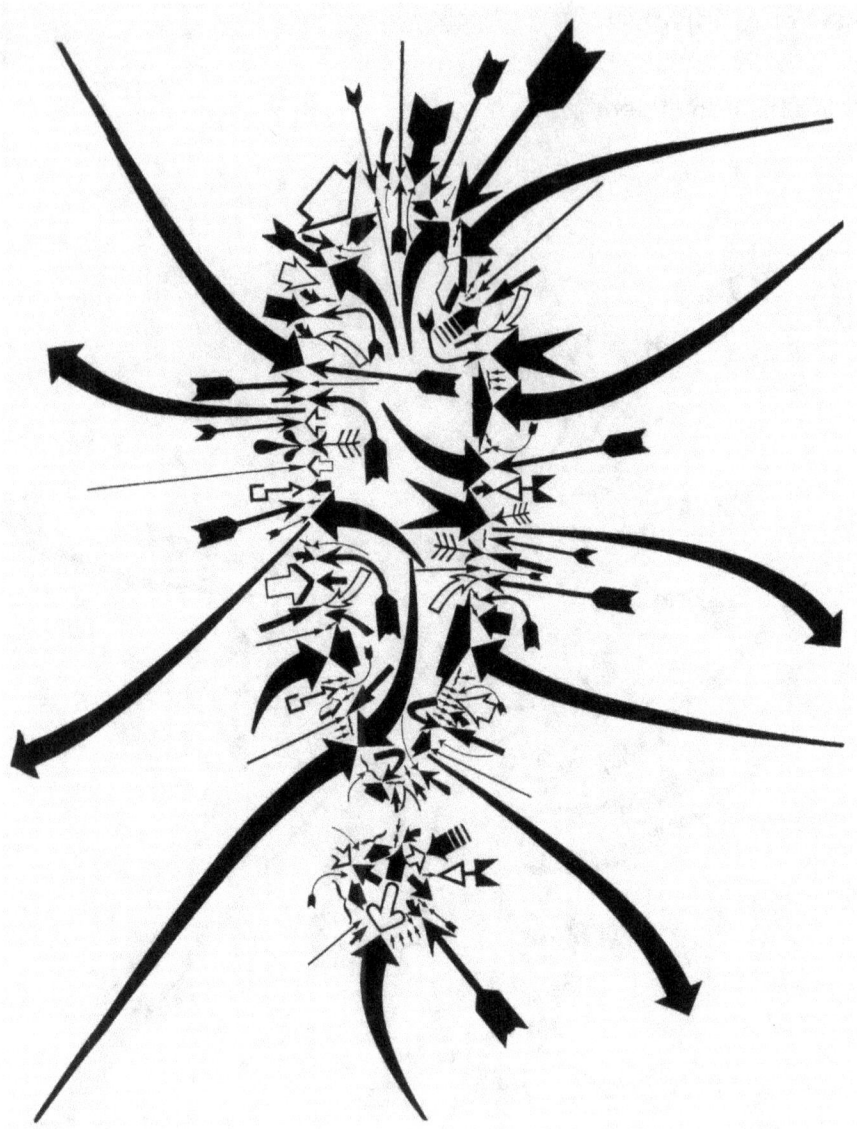

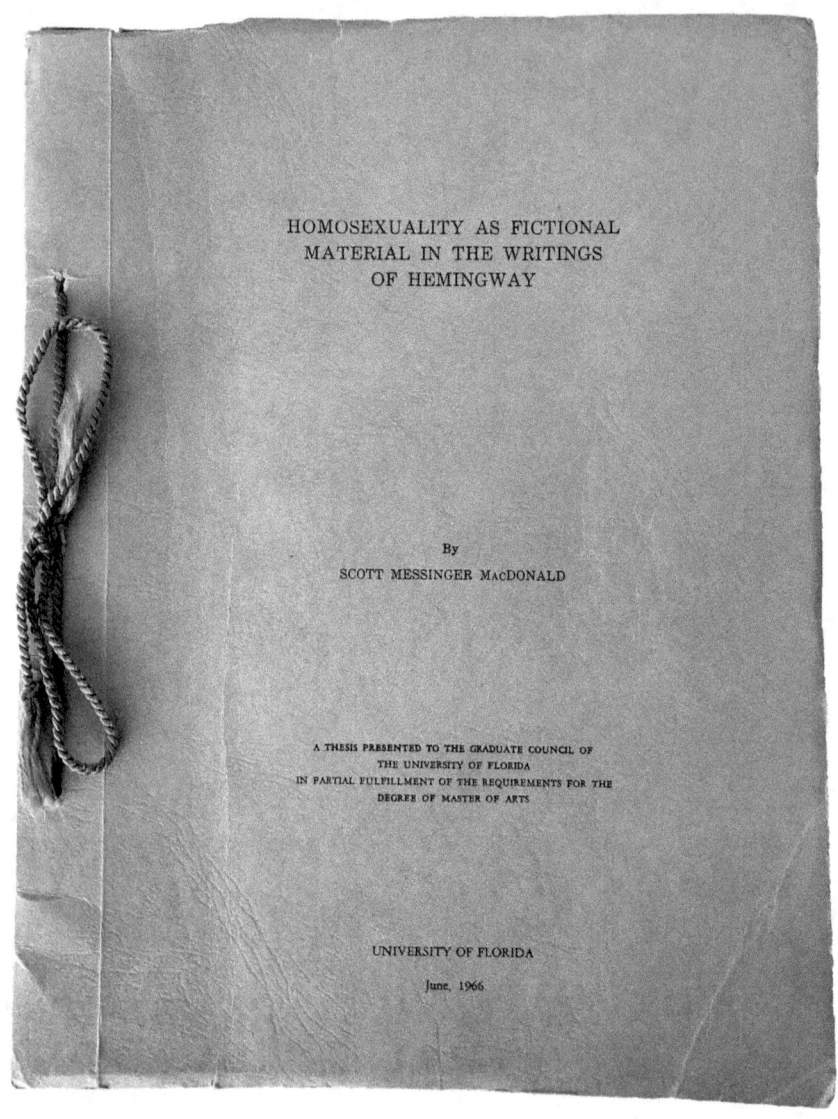

The cover of Scott MacDonald's M.A. thesis: "Homosexuality as Fictional Material in the Short Stories of Ernest Hemingway" (University of Florida, 1966).

2024

Geezer Story

One of the surprises of getting old is discovering forms of experience that are, except in very unusual situations, *only* available to those of us who are "seniors."

* * *

At some point in the early 2000s, I became aware of the fact that I could not locate the M.A. thesis I had written at the University of Florida in 1966. I knew where the thesis, which was bound by brown string in a cream-colored cover, should have been: on the top shelf of a bookcase behind where I sit in my home office.

I keep a hardcover and a paperback of each of my books there—something I learned to do when I was researching a book on the American writer Erskine Caldwell, the once mega-popular author of *Tobacco Road*, *God's Little Acre*, *Trouble in July*; as well as *North of the Danube* and *You Have Seen Their Faces*, these last two photo/text books made with photographer Margaret Bourke-White. In a bookcase in his Florida living room, Caldwell's many books—one hard cover, one paperback—were aligned chronologically.

My bookshelf, like Caldwell's, is arranged left to right, in chronological order. My thesis had, for years, rested at the far left of this shelf, next to my blue-cover-bound Ph.D. thesis, "Narrative Perspective in the Short Stories of Ernest Hemingway" (now available, amazingly, at http://ufdc.ufl.edu/UF00097727/00001/9j?search=MacDonald+%3dScott), which was completed in the spring of 1970.

I was looking for the thesis, "Homosexuality as Fictional Material in the Writings of Ernest Hemingway," because it had occurred to me, after many years, that perhaps I should have, and maybe still should, transform the thesis into a publishable essay: the idea that Hemingway, of all writers, had written nuanced narratives that focused on homosexuality might still seem a surprise (see e.g., "A Simple Inquiry," "The Mother of a Queen," and "The Sea Change").

Of course, well before 2000, I had reinvented myself, as did so many scholars of my generation, transitioning from a "literature person" into a "cinema person." My sudden re-interest in the long-ago M.A. thesis was a kind of nostalgia, as much curiosity as serious commitment. But when I could not locate the thesis, I was frustrated—where could I have put it?

Regardless of one's age or whatever transformations have taken place in one's life, an M.A. thesis, however limited it might seem or, in retrospect, be, is not something one is likely to throw away. I knew for sure that I'd not knowingly disposed of mine. Periodically over the following years, I would search for the thesis the way one searches for a particular pen or a memorable souvenir, long after one doubts of actually finding it. Had it fallen behind the books on another shelf? Had I put it in the file drawer where I still keep a few graduate-student essays?

By 2010 or so, I'd lost interest in solving the puzzle and had adjusted to the fact that sometimes in life, to paraphrase a Neil Young lyric, you let some things, even some good things, go.

Years slid by.

One afternoon, I think in the fall of 2015 (I regret not having made note of the date), I was walking back to my office at Hamilton College with a mug of coffee, when I saw a man standing in the hallway, apparently looking for something. It was early in the semester with registration still open and I asked him what I could help him find.
"Actually," he said, "I was looking for you."
"Do you need me to sign you into, or out of, a course?"
"No, sir. It's something else. Twenty-seven years ago, when I was a student at Utica College, I was thinking about doing an independent study project over the summer, focusing on some aspect of homosexuality. You agreed to meet with me to discuss possibilities and when we met, I described the project. You offered to loan me your master's thesis, which you'd brought to that meeting, and I took it with me. I have it here."
He handed me a manila folder.

I still feel a modicum of guilt that when I graduated from DePauw University in 1964 and moved back east for the summer before driving down to the University of Florida and graduate school that fall, I'd carried with me a book (I no longer have any idea what it was) that Nick Steele, my favorite professor at DePauw (he taught an amazing course in Greek and Roman mythology) had loaned me, and which I'd kept so long that I was embarrassed to admit to myself, or to Steele, that I still had the damned thing—especially since I'd never gotten around to reading it.
I assume that at some point I left that book behind with many others when I exited my first marriage and entered a new life.

It was immediately clear to me that the man handing me my thesis had been living in Central New York all these years—my final years teaching at Utica College, retiring in 1999 to become for a time a nomadic film-history professor, first at Bard College beginning in 2000 and at the University of Arizona for one semester in the spring of 2001 (driving west across Texas on New Year's Day hoping the world wouldn't shut down on Y2K), then finally in 2006, returning to Hamilton (where I'd taught as an adjunct, in addition to my classes at Utica College, from 1981 until 1999), where I've continued to teach, with occasional visiting gigs at Harvard and Colgate since the mid-2000s.
He must have been feeling enough respect for an M.A. thesis and enough embarrassment about keeping it, once he'd decided not to do the independent study, to hold on to it for all those years. I was, back then, a reasonably visible college professor in the Central New York region; I frequently weighed in on political and aesthetic issues for the *Utica Observer-Dispatch*. I expect he knew he could find me.

I guess he carried his guilt until he could no longer resist the urge to relieve it if he could, and finally found his way to my Hamilton office.

I'd only spoken to him at those two brief original meetings, then again for a moment, 27 years later. I didn't remember his name and didn't think to ask. I wouldn't recognize him if I saw him on the street.

When I took the manila envelope, I couldn't resist hugging him.

In the process of writing this piece, it occurred to me—strangely enough, for the first time—that Nick Steele might still be alive, and that, of course, even if he weren't, I could have written to him and apologized, or whatever, at any point those last 56 years. It's strange how, when we move from one life to another, we tend to erase much of what we've experienced. We immerse ourselves in the present and focus on the near future.

In the end, I decided that this piece could not be complete until I made an effort to find Steele, which, of course, was not terribly difficult: a woman named Dee at the DePauw alumni office assisted me and I wrote to Steele on March 23, 2020.

So far, I've not heard back…

The barn in Gottheim's *Barn Rushes* (1972).
Courtesy Larry Gottheim.

2024

Entanglement: Going Against the Clock— an essay intercut with a conversation*

A half-century has passed since I first became aware of Larry Gottheim. The expansion of my cine-awareness that his early films instigated continues to be as exciting fifty-plus years later as it was in 1972. Each new personal cine-fascination simultaneously leads me into new thinking and writing *and* confirms and reframes earlier work that continues to be part of my experience. Indeed, it has ceased to surprise me when I discover that a brand-new excitement references the films that originally transformed my sense of cinema. For example, as I explored Max Tohline's *A Supercut of Supercuts*, then his other work, I discovered that the central section of his seven-part series, *The Sharply Interrupted Sky* (2012-15), includes visual references to Gottheim's *Fog Line*, Frampton's *Zorns Lemma*, Bruce Conner's *Crossroads*, and Joyce Wieland's *Dripping Water*. Tohline studied avant-garde film in Ruth Bradley's graduate course at Ohio University and can still recall "the delight-at-first-sight of Harry Smith's *Numbers* series, Bruce Baillie's *All My Life*, Marie Menken's *Go! Go! Go!*, Deborah Stratman's chilling *In Order Not to Be Here*, and most of all, J. J. Murphy's *Print Generation*" (see the Tohline interview that follows this essay).

Gottheim has gone through a number of transformations. He began with music, studied clarinet with avant-garde composer Myer Kupferman, and graduated from New York's High School of Music and Art in 1953. After graduating Oberlin College in 1957, he earned a Ph.D. in Comparative Literature at Yale; then taught in the English Department at Northwestern, then SUNY Binghamton. He began working in film in 1966, established the Binghamton Cinema Department in the late 1960s and chaired the department most of the time until he retired in 1999. He then expanded Be-hold, his business in nineteenth-century photographs, ending the business in 2023. *Entanglement* (2022) was a surprise, completed during the Covid pandemic, after an extended period when Gottheim made few films.

* * *

In the opening chapter of his remarkable novel, *Stoner* (1965), John Williams' protagonist, William Stoner, has a transformative experience when his professor in an English literature class reads Shakespeare's Sonnet 73, and asks the class the meaning of its final couplet:

> This thou perceivest, which makes thy love more strong,
> To love that well which thou must leave ere long.

This moment changes the direction of Stoner's life, from prospective educated farmer to scholar and professor of literature.

Such an experience is probably not unusual. As I survey my life, two experiences come to mind that I understand as having been transformative for me. The first, which occurred when I was a junior in high school (I only understood its impact much later), was reading Carl Sandburg's semi-haiku, "Fog," first published in 1916:

---

* The conversation is based on the transcript of a Zoom meeting with Gottheim on November 21, 2022, plus several emails during the following week. The editing of these conversations was designed to work in tandem with the expository sections of this essay.

> The fog comes
> on little cat feet.
> It sits looking
> over harbor and city
> on silent haunches
> and then moves on.

For whatever set of reasons, this little poem demonstrated to me, for the first time, something of the magic of literary art. I had become an avid reader by the first years of junior high school (mostly science fiction and Classic Comics), but seeing this poem presented within a carefully designed illustration in that high school textbook triggered something new in me.

The second experience occurred during my second year as a professor at Utica College of Syracuse University. In 1971, I'd been hired to teach American literature and "film appreciation," and was looking to broaden my awareness of cinema: my Ph.D. was in American literature (Hemingway's short stories, especially his uses of point of view and his focus on conversation as action), but the fact that I'd taught one class in film appreciation at a time when universities were struggling to offer film courses had gotten me the job—despite my lack of formal training in what would soon become Cinema and Media Studies.

When the State University of New York announced a two-day university-wide symposium on film studies in the spring of 1972, I drove to SUNY Binghamton to attend. The symposium opened with a screening of five films: Ken Jacobs' *Soft Rain* (1968), Ernie Gehr's *Serene Velocity* (1970), Ricky Leacock and Joyce Chopra's *Happy Mother's Day* (1963), Larry Gottheim's *Barn Rushes* (1971), and Stan Brakhage's *The Act of Seeing with One's Own Eyes* (1972).

The screening infuriated me. I had no idea how to deal with several of the films or with the fact that, after the screening, the audience didn't seem to have negative reactions to what they had seen. At the same time, however, not only did I feel I understood *Barn Rushes* as a modern cine-version of Monet's series paintings, but I could feel immediately that *Barn Rushes* was transforming my understanding of what cinema could be and how I needed to teach it. I was soon including Gottheim's films in my courses and was writing about his early single-shot films, one of which, the cine-haiku *Fog Line* (1970), I understood as a metaphor for the development of my understanding that *Barn Rushes* had instigated.

I soon decided that the scholarship and writing I needed to do (in publish-or-perish academe)—and, for the first time, *wanted* to do—should focus on independent cinema. And it seemed clear that I should begin by interviewing the independent filmmakers I was learning about, as a kind of intellectual self-defense, given the narrowness of my understanding of cinema that the Binghamton event had made obvious to me. Surely filmmakers who were making films independent of commercial expectations could help me understand not only their own films, but something more about cinema itself. The first interview I recorded and edited, and the first of my interviews to be published, was with Gottheim.

MacDonald: *Barn Rushes* was the first so-called "avant-garde film" I ever understood and loved.
Gottheim: I've always appreciated that.
MacDonald: Seeing it and your other early films changed the direction of my life. I still show *Fog Line* on the first day of my Intro course.
Gottheim: For a long time, I resented *Fog Line*, only because everybody was like, "Oh, Larry Gottheim, *Fog Line*!" Now, after doing *Entanglement*, when I look at *Fog Line* and *Barn Rushes*, I see them anew. I love them in ways that, for a long time, I couldn't appreciate.

And watching *Fog Line* or *Barn Rushes* in the digital versions on my computer screen allows me to see things that I never focused on before.

Barn Rushes was Gottheim's first serious foray into film editing. The several films he had made earlier, beginning with *Blues* (1969) and *Fog Line*, were single-shot films, each of which allowed Gottheim to come to terms with a set of fundamental cinematic issues: control of light within a shot, perspective, camera movement, and in *Harmonica* (1971) sync sound. For *Barn Rushes*, he chose the most fundamental form of editing: splicing individual shots together without even eliminating the flares of light at the beginnings and ends of rolls of 16mm film (something he had learned from Warhol). Over a period of several weeks, Gottheim recorded, from a moving car, eight 100-foot roll-long passes by a Central New York State barn. In the finished, 34-minute film, the eight rolls are presented silent, except for the sound of the projector.

For many viewers, especially those whose film experiences have been primarily with commercial narrative, *Barn Rushes* can seem boringly repetitious, and the variety of subtle and not-so-subtle perceptual experiences available during the film are easily ignored. When I've shown the film to classes, particularly introductory classes, students have sometimes told me that the film frightened them; for these students, the auditory and visual quietness of the film presaged some shocking event, something the film would *do to them*. *Barn Rushes* works the opposite way: it challenges the viewer to slow down and be more perceptually active; it offers a kind of perceptual training.

What I understood during my first viewing of *Barn Rushes* was also conceptual; I understood Gottheim to be asking, what can a film be? What is a filmmaker allowed to do? What kinds of organization, of structure, can a filmmaker make use of? Within the film's rigorous organization, the eight segments of *Barn Rushes* offer somewhat different explorations of space and time and of light and color—even, implicitly, of image and "text": for cineastes, "rushes" are the early dailies that will provide the footage for finished films; but at the same time, the plants that pass the camera in the foreground of the image (and in one magical shot, seemingly in the background!) evoke the family of flowering plants called "rushes." And even if we think of the movements of the car driving past the barn as rushes, we have to smile, since these are some of the least rushed car chases in the history of cinema, especially since what is chased is not actually avoiding capture.

When I learned that Scott Hammen planned to publish Gottheim's book-length manuscript about his own films and about cinema in general, I wondered what I might contribute. I'd written extensively about the early films, but had been distracted from Gottheim's work for some years. I asked to see Gottheim's most recent film.

My initial viewing of *Entanglement* reminded me of that first screening at SUNY Binghamton, though, unlike *Barn Rushes*, the new film initially disappointed me. There didn't seem to be enough to explore. The images, many of them clearly recycled not only from earlier films but apparently from YouTube, had little of the sensual visual beauty of Gottheim's early work. At first, *Entanglement* seemed too mundane, the way *Barn Rushes* and *Fog Line* have seemed, at least at first, to many of my students. I wondered, can I really write about *Entanglement*?

The film itself seemed prepared for my consternation. "Watch!" it said, right at the beginning; then again a bit later "Watch," this time while showing me, just for a moment, a Mickey Mouse watch—a visual/auditory pun that seemed, if a bit silly, also good-humored. Then, as if the film were reminding me of my long history with Gottheim's work, the translation of a moment from a performance of Wagner's opera *Götterdämmerung* early in *Entanglement* confronted me with "Do you remember?" And suddenly, there was Gottheim himself, responding to the camera to say, "Where am I?"—just what I was saying to myself during that first Binghamton screening. I started over with *Entanglement* and made some discoveries, including how many aspects of *Barn Rushes* and other early films were implicitly carried over into, were entangled with, the new film.

MacDonald: I've wondered, is the imagery in *Barn Rushes* slow motion?
Gottheim: The original motivation was to minimize the bouncing of the car, so I shot it at the maximum speed of 64 fps. When I saw the first prints of the first rolls, projected at 24 fps, I saw many things that were not visible during the shooting, so I decided to slow the film down even more by projecting it at 16 fps. So much of the essential experience of the film became available at that speed. These days, most places can't project prints at 16 fps. Even at 18 fps, subtleties get lost. I was happy that the digital scan could be made at 16 fps; it preserves the true nature of the film.

Of course, one of the consequences of filming at 64 fps is that the film runs through a complete wind of the camera very quickly. So, as I was shooting *Barn Rushes*, I had to stop and rewind very often. Each pause is seen as a jerk in the image. "Watch the gap!"
MacDonald: In both *Knot/Not* (2019) and *Entanglement*, you do something you didn't do in your early films. In addition to the images and sounds you yourself shot and recorded, you borrow from other films, both your own and films available on YouTube.
Gottheim: What happened is that with Covid I tended to stay home. I don't have a TV, but I've been watching YouTube a lot. Some of the things in *Entanglement* come from a TV program on conductors conducting that I found on YouTube. Also, I'd come upon that Phil Spitalny musical with his all-girl orchestra. Originally it struck me as *so* utterly stupid and wrong in terms of race and gender—but for some reason, I said to myself, "I'm gonna use this. Something is gonna come out of it."

Out of curiosity, I started to watch lectures on quantum mechanics available on YouTube, from very rudimentary programs to graduate seminars at Princeton. I've learned a lot about quantum mechanics, and found that many of the things that years earlier had drawn me to Heidegger and phenomenology, were drawing me to quantum mechanics.

Another thing: I'd never really gotten into the last opera of Wagner's Ring Cycle, *Götterdämmerung*. I found two versions of the opera on YouTube. As I watched the prologue, I thought, "Holy Shit, the three Fates are talking about all kinds of things that relate to the quantum world!"

I even began to feel a connection between the Spitalny performance and the excerpts from the two performances of *Götterdämmerung*.

Of course, *Entanglement* also references my own films: *Horizons* (1973), *Mouches Volantes* (1976), *Four Shadows* (1978).

MacDonald: There's a shot of an elm tree in winter…

Gottheim: …from *Horizons*.

MacDonald: It evokes, for me, the shot of Bob Huot's elm, the replacement image for letter F in the central section of Frampton's *Zorns Lemma* (1970).*

Gottheim: In the winter section of *Horizons*, there's a shot of Hollis walking up a hill that was next to my house…

MacDonald: Oh, that's Hollis? I've always assumed it was you!

Gottheim: That shot was my little tribute to *Zorns*. I feel that of all the filmmakers, the two that I have the most connection with are Ernie Gehr and Hollis. I think *Zorns Lemma* was very influential for me.

That tree shot is not only a reference back to *Horizons*, but also to *Fog Line* and *Tree of Knowledge* (1980).

On one level, the structure of *Entanglement* is clear—and to some extent related to the structuring of Gottheim's earlier films. First, the number 1 appears, handwritten on graph paper (combining personal touch and formal grid) and accompanied by what is soon recognized as the sound of a commuter train. A four-minute montage follows; then, after a brief break, "2," and another four-minute montage (using imagery related to the imagery in 1); then "3" to "6." Each of the montages in 1, 2 and 3 is made up of closely related images and sounds. I needed several viewings to realize that sections 4, 5, and 6 are virtually an exact repetition of sections 1, 2, and 3—that basically I was seeing the same half-film twice.

Within the overall two-part, double-triad design of the film, the three individual sections include imagery that is diverse not only in terms of the content depicted and the imagery's original function, but also, to some extent, in its history. While the images of people waiting at a bus stop were apparently shot by Gottheim with a digital camera, the Spitalny sequences have a more complex history. Originally, the Hour of Charm Orchestra performed for live audiences as well as on radio, and made several appearances in narrative films. In 1937, Leslie M. Roush directed and edited a short about the orchestra, *Queens of Harmony*,

---

* Robert Huot is implicit in *Zorns Lemma*, not only in Frampton's filming of the elm, but also in the replacement for letter O (the hand bouncing a ball is Huot's) but also explicit: in letter K, Huot is seen painting a wall blue—a reference to his painting, *Two Blue Walls* (Pratt and Lambert #5020 Alkyd), shown at Paula Cooper Gallery in March-April 1969. See Lucy Lippard, *Six Years: The Dematerialization of the Art Object from 1969 to 1972* (London: Studio Vision, 1973), 92 (also 17). And Huot is the man walking with a dog and a woman (Marcia Steinbrecher) across a snowy field opposite his home in New Berlin, New York, during the final section of *Zorns Lemma*.

for Paramount. According to a YouTube note, the film was transferred from 16mm negative to digital, and Gottheim accessed YouTube to select bits from several distinct sections of the film.

Gottheim: The title of *Entanglement* is related to *entanglement* in quantum mechanics, which has to do with a connection between disparate things that aren't actually connected, and yet *are* connected. In quantum mechanics they talk about the spin of electrons: there's "spin up" and "spin down." If you look at one electron and see that's it's spinning up, then you know that the one next to it is spinning down. On one level, there's no connection between them, but the space between them is entangled, *both* up *and* down, and the quantum term for this both-ness is "superposition"—it sounds like "superimposition"…
MacDonald: I had to listen to that word several times to be sure it wasn't "superimposition."
Gottheim: As I was making *Entanglement,* everything—all these apparently disparate elements—seemed to be coming together, sometimes as superimpositions.

In *Four Shadows* there are four sound pieces and four image sequences. Each image sequence is synched to all four sound pieces, and vice versa, even though in three of the four cases the sync is not recorded but was created in the editing. Also, they superimpose in the mind of the viewer—as what I call ghost superimpositions.
MacDonald: Immediately I think of the images in *Entanglement* where we see one image very clearly, while in the background, another image, sometimes a soft-focus close-up of distant fireworks, seems to hover behind the clear image.
Gottheim: One that's uncanny is the woman drummer in the Spitalny footage superimposed on drumming from a voodoo ceremony, and in section 3 there's a third superimposition, a second Spitalny woman, playing the xylophone. Jammed in there is so much suggestion about ceremony.
MacDonald: Is the image of the Haitian man pulling a rope part of a ceremony?
Gottheim: That's from my *Chants and Dances for Hand* (1991, 2017). I think that rope image has something to do with pulling some kind of demon out of the other person during a voodoo ceremony —but I'm not really sure. I had the motif of rope and thread in my head and this image came back to me.
MacDonald: Am I correct that the following list names all the imagery and sound you shot or recorded specifically for *Entanglement*; that is, all the imagery you did not borrow from your own films or from films by others?

>Sound of train; sounds of you saying "Watch" and
>   "This is very powerful."
>Two photos of railroad conductors—one in a railroad
>   car, the other outside.
>Photograph of Mickey Mouse watch.
>People awaiting a bus: first a solo person, then an assembled group,
>   and finally the bus arriving and the group boarding.
>You, saying "Where am I?"
>Fireworks over Manhattan, seen from Yonkers.
>Photos of two signs naming the suburb of Valhalla
>   (one at the local train station, one along a road).

Gottheim: That seems basically right. The sound is from Metro North, the train I take into Manhattan. Yes, the fireworks were shot from my window in Yonkers (I hoped they'd suggest not only the 4th of July, but also war images from Ukraine). The bus stop is one I use; it's at the Rainbow clothing store. I also drew and shot the numbers of the six sections, and my signature at the end. The final credits, not part of the body of the film, come after the railroad sound ends.

MacDonald: What led to your repeating the three sections of montage, in the same order, twice? In *Mouches Volantes*, *Four Shadows*, *Tree of Knowledge* (1980), *Mnemosyne Mother of Muses* (1986), sequences of sound and imagery are repeated, but here we are seeing basically the same film twice.

Gottheim: Thanks for asking about this, because it is perhaps the most essential question. It's not easy to answer. Every element in the film is carefully presented and edited. There are very few elements, compared with *Knot/Not* and other earlier films. And even within the first three sections there is some repetition of closely related material. But it took a long time of intense editing to create the three sections.

Gottheim, in *Entanglement* (2024), asking "Where am I?"
Courtesy Larry Gottheim.

Once I had the idea of repeating the first sections almost exactly—the image of me saying "Where am I?" is different in all six sections; that's the only difference—this repetition seemed almost destined by the nature of the material, and it led to my numbering the second three sections 4, 5, 6, instead of repeating the original numbers 1, 2, 3. For the viewer who is seeing the film for the first time, seeing section 4 brings with it a slow realization: "Wait a minute. Isn't this the same as section 1?" Something similar happens in *Fog Line*, when the viewer first starts to realize that nothing is going to change in a way that would normally be expected, or when viewers of *Barn Rushes* realize they're going to see that one barn over and over.

Here, of course, I'm only thinking of a viewer who is experiencing *Entanglement* for the first time, as different from a viewer who is seeing the entire film more than once. *Entanglement* is like those poems or musical works—and some works of cinema—that we are happy to experience over and over.

Every element is loaded with rich, ambiguous associations: "Do you remember?"; "Watch the gap"; the idea of dreaming; the woman with the mask at the bus stop; "This is a story about time."; "Where am I?"; the line of prisoners…

MacDonald: Who are those prisoners?

Gottheim: They're in Bucha, Ukraine, marching to their death. Strangely enough, they look like they're doing some kind of strange line dance; there's something visually beautiful to me about that image—and yet, at the same time, it's the most horrifying image in *Entanglement*. It's similar to an image in *Knot/Not* of a book burning by Nazi students in Berlin: there's a fire and the students march behind it, throwing books (I synced music to that image to make it beautiful in a certain way—though, like the Ukraine image in *Entanglement*, what you're seeing is totally horrible).

All the words and diagrams in the film are important, including the word "entanglement." There is a lot about language—French, German, English; printed and written; diagrams, subtitles…

Something I love about this film is the pleasure it gives me. I look forward to the chance of seeing it again, and in fact I look at it more than any of my other films.

Within the three "stanzas" of *Entanglement*, various historical realities are evoked, some quite minimal, some epic. The several shots of one woman at the bus stop, then other people arriving, the group awaiting the bus, and their subsequent boarding is itself a minimal history—and it plays an implicit role in the much larger history of African Americans evoked in the film. Early on, we hear the Hour of Charm Orchestra performing "a song from the Deep South: 'Alabama Barbecue,'" which evokes the history of racial discrimination, not only because the lyrics suggest that the song might have been written by an African American composer or by a European American trying to evoke nostalgia for the racial history of the Deep South, but also because the song is performed by an all-white girl orchestra/chorus (in more recent years both The Ink Spots and the Svend Asmussen Quartet have recorded the song).

Gottheim confirms and expands these implications by cutting directly from the performance of the song to a photograph of an African American conductor on the Metro North train line—implicitly evoking the complex history of African Americans and trains, from the Underground Railroad to the development of Pullman railroad cars, to the frequent appearances in American commercial films of African Americans as train porters and conductors (two of few relatively prestigious positions available to African Americans during the decades of American apartheid), to Rosa Parks refusing to sit in the back of a bus, igniting the Montgomery bus boycott (that the first person we see at the bus stop is an African American young woman, followed by a larger group, several of whom are African Americans, provides a mini-allusion to this history within the history (which also includes the increasing attention to racial issues in Gottheim's films, beginning with *Mouches Volantes*). Within this context we might even see the repeated shot of several men being marched to their death in Ukraine as a modern lynching.

Another motif throughout *Entanglement* is the various implications of the term "conductor." There are the Metro North conductors, of course, but the film pays particular attention to conductors of orchestras, beginning with Spitalny emphatically conducting the girl orchestra. In the shots of the more recent *Götterdämmerung* imagery, we can see the conductor behind and/or above the three women playing the Fates. Less obviously, the narrator explaining the diagram about flow and resistance references the conducting of electric current.

On a more meta-level, it is clear that Gottheim is the conductor of *Entanglement*, in at least two senses. His use of the sound of the Metro North train as motif and as transition from one section of the film to the next, evokes—at least for those of us who have read Wolfgang Schivelbusch's *The Railroad Journey* (1977, 1986)— the entanglement of the locomotive and cinema, as technologies and histories, emblematized in the Lumière classic, *L'arrivée d'un train en gare de La Ciotat* (1895) and continually exploited throughout film history. Indeed, the phrase "Watch the gap," which explicitly refers to passengers exiting the train, also implicitly refers to the various visual/sonic gaps during *Entanglement*. That Gottheim presents the three montages twice may also suggest that we all repeat our commutes to work or home in more or less the same way, over and over, in different moods and with different levels of awareness.

Gottheim is also a conductor in the sense that he assembles a diverse set of images and sounds and arranges them into a cinematic orchestration. In *Entanglement* (and in his earlier films as well), Gottheim is not really a film *director*: he directs almost no one. And he's not really a documentarian: he documents no single subject or issue. He is an audiovisual musician who assembles individual performances—both in the theatrical sense and in the more mundane sense of performing daily activities—into an experience that is closer to music than to most cinema experiences.

I'll stop my train of thought here. *Entanglement* is fundamentally a puzzle, but a puzzle that functions differently from a picture puzzle or a *New York Times* crossword puzzle. Conventional puzzles ask us to solve them, to find the correct location for every piece or the correct answer for every crossword clue so that all the spaces are filled. Gottheim's puzzle cannot be solved. Each element of *Entanglement* interconnects with other elements, generating—if we can conquer our resistance— further entanglements, which require us to become aware of interconnections that we've overlooked or to learn about dimensions of cinema history and cultural history that we've not considered.

Early on, Gottheim (and other filmmakers working around him during the 1960s/70s) challenged us to rethink our conventional experiences with filmgoing: basically, to start over by deepening and broadening our perception of what the elements of celluloid cinema were and how they could be used. Now, half a century later, *Entanglement* is a kind of meta-haiku that challenges us to work at comprehending, as best we can, the media-saturated world of the twenty-first century.

Gottheim: I saw *Knot/Not* as the end, the finale, of all of my work—that's where my book, *The Red Thread*, ends. Now I've made *Entanglement*, which is pointing toward the future, whatever future I still have. *Entanglement* has also loosened up my ability to talk—I love to talk about it!

The film is so loaded that I can't "explain" everything. On the cognitive level "everything fits together." For me, *Entanglement* becomes more of a puzzle, rather than less, the more you experience it. I leave it to the film's viewers to see whether they can engage it in this way.

I'm trying my best to get good digital versions of all my films together, which is really very hard to do, but is happening in little ways—something I thought would only happen once I was dead.

MacDonald: How old are you?

Gottheim: In a month I'll be 86. But emotionally, I'm 30!

It's a little miracle that I was able to come up with *Entanglement*. I'm proud of it. I feel productive and want to keep working—because I know that I'm going against the clock.

Gottheim's book, *The Red Thread*, was published in 2024 by The New American Cinema Group/Film-Makers' Cooperative and Scott Hammen's Eyewash Books. *The Red Thread* is in three parts. Part 1 is Gottheim's own detailed review of his filmmaking life; Part 2, "Critical Notes," includes excerpts of my first interview with Gottheim (on *Fog Line* and *Horizons*), along with writings by Jonas Mekas, Barry Gerson, John Hanhardt, Michael Sicinski, and Owen Vince; and Part 3, "Personal Perspectives," includes this essay plus pieces by Steve Anker and Heinz Emigholz.

The Red Thread is available for purchase at The Film-Makers' Cooperative. Contact Gottheim at lgottheim@gmail.com. Gottheim's website is www.larrygottheimfilms.com.

Home page image introducing Max Tohline's *A Supercut of Supercuts* (2021) online.

2024

A New Form of Cine-Scholarship:
An interview with video-essayist Max Tohline

My most recent professional surprise was what has come to be called the "video essay": audio-visual works that use still and moving imagery, visual and auditory text, music— all the options digital creativity makes available—in order to explore individual films/ videos, particular media-makers, as well as the history of cinema and salient aspects of our current mediascape. The filmmaker J. P. Sniadecki alerted me to the work of Chloé Galibert-Laîné, whose video essays I found fascinating, and Galibert-Laîné's work led me into what has turned out to be an immense creative world, reminiscent, at least for me, of the avant-garde filmmaking scene that was so crucial for me in the early 1970s. In this case, however, I've not needed to pilgrimage to see films, as I did in earlier decades. I've been able to access, online, remarkable work by video essayists Kevin B. Lee, Kogonada, Jason Mittell, Maryam Tafakory, Catherine Grant, and Max Tohline. These artists have provided me with new forms of pleasure and insight, suggestions for other video essays worth knowing about—and new ways of gathering/"gathering" with others, both online and in theaters—to experience them. I've written about my early experiences with video essays for the online journal *The Edge*, first in "Is the Video Essay a New Avant-Garde?" (https://www.theedgemedia.org/video-essay-new-avant-garde/), and more recently, in "Finding My Way to Max Tohline's *A Supercut of Supercuts*" (https://www.theedgemedia.org/finding-my-way-max-tohlines-a-supercut-of-supercuts/). These two essays provide a useful introduction to my interview with Tohline, which concludes *Publication as Autobiography*.

* * *

Awash as we are within a flood of old and new media, remarkable scholarly accomplishments are sometimes hiding in plain sight. Some months ago, as I was googling to find a good definition of the term "supercut," I noticed the title *A Supercut of Supercuts*. I paid little attention in that moment, though the title stayed with me and, finally, out of curiosity, I accessed what turned out to be Max Tohline's 131-minute exploration and analysis of what has become a significant tradition within the burgeoning world of video essay scholarship. Suffice it to say that I found Tohline's epic astonishing—and puzzling. *A Supercut of Supercuts* was finished in 2021. I wondered how three years could have passed without my hearing a word about it or about him.

As I explored *A Supercut of Supercuts*, then Tohline's other work (virtually all of it is available at his website: maxtohline.com), I realized that one of the inspirations for Tohline's video essays was American avant-garde cinema of the 1960s-80s, including such filmmakers as Bruce Conner, Marie Menken, Hollis Frampton, Michael Snow, Joyce Wieland, Larry Gottheim, J. J. Murphy, and James Benning—filmmakers whose work I'd spent decades exploring. Tohline's obvious passion for these filmmakers confirmed what I had already come to feel: that the modern emergence of the video essay was instigating a new kind of cinematic avant-garde. If 1960s-70s avant-garde filmmakers had found exciting new ways of providing in-theater critiques of "normal," entertainment-oriented cinema and the conventional film experience, new generations of video essayists were using creative audio-visual means to reflect on the nature of particular films, as well as on aspects of modern cinema and the ever-expanding nature of the experience of moving-image media.

The more of Tohline's work I accessed, the more questions I had, about *A Supercut of Supercuts*, about his other video essays, his video "postcards," and a wide range of related media experimentation. Tohline kindly agreed to respond to my queries, and the following interview, conducted and edited online during the spring of 2024, is the result.

MacDonald: Max, I'm curious about how you came to have such a broad sense of film history. Since you got your M.A. in 2009 from Ohio University, I wonder if you studied with Ruth Bradley, who for many years championed a very wide spectrum of cinema. I believe I met her through the Robert Flaherty Film Seminars, and when she was editor of *Wide Angle* she published my book on Amos Vogel and his Cinema 16 film society, when no publisher was interested, in two giant issues of the journal (January and April 1997). I was a guest once at the Athens Film Festival, which she curated and hosted.

I was fascinated that, at least in some cases, she organized her avant-garde cinema course *alphabetically*: Anger, Baillie, Brakhage, Broughton, Conner…

Tohline: She organized it that way when I was her student in 2008! Ruth Bradley was one of the most important influences on how I turned out as a scholar; I'm so happy you know her. The Athens Film Festival was one of the best things about Ohio University, and not just because she brought James Benning, Deborah Stratman, and Barbara Hammer to town while I was there. I was born in 1983 to a conservative family in a conservative place—a suburb of Cincinnati. In our house, the media diet was closely controlled, which means that aside from animated Disney classics and PBS, I didn't see very much, even through high school. When I was five or six years old, my parents taped a bowdlerized copy of *The Blues Brothers* off TV, and I probably wore it out re-watching all the car crashes in frame-by-frame slow motion. The interest there was purely physics, but the temporality of VHS playback gave me a way to explore.

I should mention that my dad had a habit of turning on the television any time he entered a room. When I was ten or twelve, I was helping him truck a houseful of my grandma's possessions across the country—my grandfather, for whom I was named, had just passed away. We'd been on the road all day, I was hungry, and he'd promised that we'd eat dinner at Ryan's (a buffet chain that I loved at that age), but first he needed to take a shower. We walked into the motel room and of course he flipped on the TV. After channel-surfing for a moment, he landed on a PBS screening of *12 Angry Men* (1957). The film had just started, so he offered, "This is a great movie, Max. Watch it while I clean up, and then we'll go eat." So I did.

Fifteen or so minutes later, he reappeared. "Ready to go?" I looked up at him and replied, "I'm not going ANYWHERE until this movie's over." I was completely captivated. I'd never seen a movie that asked the viewer to think. I didn't know that films *could* ask viewers to think. And I wouldn't have believed that the act of thinking could be so engrossing or rewarding. If I'm an overthinker now—and I think that I am—it's traceable to that day.

A few years later, it dawned on me that I was missing out on a wider world of art and culture, and I wanted to correct that. Rather than try to catch up on the new releases that my friends were sneaking into, I turned to Turner Classic Movies—and saw the premiere of Rick Schmidlin's four-hour reconstruction of Erich von Stroheim's *Greed* (1924), with that fantastic score from Robert Israel. I'd read about the nine-hour runtime of the original cut in an introductory film history book a few months earlier, and became fascinated by what kind of story *anyone* could want to tell that would merit such a length. It was total luck that my learning about the film coincided with the release of the restoration. I watched that tape over and over.

MacDonald: Did you formally study film as a college student?

Tohline: Not at first. My interest in film hadn't been cultivated as much as other passions in my life. Since at least middle school, my simultaneous love of all things math and science had pointed me toward engineering as a career path.

I mention this because even in my earliest video essays on film topics, this "left-brain" approach shines through clearly, in the classificatory impulse in *Editing as Punctuation in Film* (2015) or the (albeit superficial) deployment of the mathematical concept of permutations to *The Art of Editing in "The Good, the Bad, and the Ugly"* (2013). But by 2004, after only a couple years of introductory engineering classes at the University of Missouri-Rolla (a haven for nerds of many stripes, but mostly science and engineering), I realized that I couldn't spend a lifetime on an engineering trajectory. And thanks to UMR's one and only film professor, a charismatic and singular mentor Jim Bogan, I picked up another scent. In the short version of the story, I changed majors and left UMR with a degree in English and a minor in math (why not?), then went back to my home state to pursue graduate degrees in film at Ohio University.

Not knowing at all what grad school was going to be like, I was worried that I'd get laughed out of school if anyone found out how little I'd seen growing up. So I made it a point to watch as much of the "canon" as fast as I could. That first year, I probably watched two feature films per day, in addition to my coursework and everything else. I didn't have any idea yet that learning the canon was not the point of film school, or that most of the original contributions to film theory then and now have little or nothing to do with studying the so-called canon. What I also didn't realize is that sticking too closely to the narrowness of the canon (as a proxy for moving image history more generally) also causes a viewer to get completely wrongheaded ideas about the real mechanisms of history and media's relationship with them.

And this, thankfully, is where Ruth Bradley entered the story. In the two years of my M.A. program, I only got to take two courses with her, but each added a huge branch to my scholarship. As a longtime film festival programmer, she was the truest omnivore of the scholars at OU, and nearly everything she screened seemed drawn from nooks of film history I hadn't known existed.

I remember having absolutely no idea what to do with Trinh T. Minh-ha's *Surname Viet Given Name Nam* [1989] or Jill Godmilow's *What Farocki Taught* [1998], but I'm glad they gradually pushed me to stop being combative toward the unfamiliar and ask better questions of myself. More importantly, I never would have had any interest in experimental or avant-garde work without Ruth Bradley's class. By that point, her courses had become an excuse for her to get the school to pay the rental prices for pristine prints from Canyon Cinema and other places, so that she could watch the films again. Her alphabetical approach forced us to make our own connections rather than just accept the Sitney account or something else like it. That was ideal for me. As I watched each film, I got to discover my own questions, my own impulses, my own corridors of research desire.

    I still recall the delight-at-first-sight of Harry Smith's *Numbers* series (c. 1939-60), Bruce Baillie's *All My Life* (1966), Marie Menken's *Go! Go! Go!* (1964) (a perfect way to grow beyond *Koyaanisqatsi* [1983]), Deborah Stratman's chilling *In Order Not to Be Here* (2002), and most of all, J. J. Murphy's *Print Generation* (1974).

MacDonald: Murphy's film has always been important to me—really, my favorite structural film. Alas, the demise of 16mm projectors (I'd never imagined the *projectors* would grow old and die, would outlive the film prints!) has kept that film out of my courses these past few years. Somehow a digital version of *Print Generation*, if there were one, would seem inappropriate.

Tohline: As a video essayist, it helps to be resourceful tracking down digital versions of films from which to extract fair-use clips. I can confirm that there *is* an (unauthorized) digital version of *Print Generation* out there if you know where to look. But you're right, it's not the same at all. *Print Generation* was created by and is in some basic sense "about" a photochemical duping process. The digital encoding and copying process removes the film from that lineage and weakens its metaphysical impact. The film is no longer "live," in several senses of the word. This raises a few of the unfortunate drawbacks of video essayism, the problem of access to certain films for starters. When will someone finally distribute Bruce Conner in any form but that 80s-era VHS tape that a few lucky libraries still have? Moreover, when the digital regime engulfs and ingests the analog, something of the presence of the light is lost.

    I'm most interested in structural questions about film—questions about how time is represented and manipulated, questions about the deployment of certain techniques across time and across disciplines, questions about how form can be philosophical. To circle back to Ruth Bradley, it's possible that none of these questions would ever have risen to the surface for me without the clarification process of her screenings.

MacDonald: By some miracle, I have two good DVDs of a number of Conner films; each DVD was produced by the Michael Kohn gallery (LA): *2000 B.C.* was produced in 2002 (eight short films made between 1964 and 1981); the other, produced in 2003, includes two Conner films with Terry Riley soundtracks (*Crossroads* [1976] and two versions of *Looking for Mushrooms* [1959-65, 1996]. With 16mm projection so rare now, these DVDs are a treasure.

    What led you out of academe? You seem to have been a very successful teacher at Missouri S&T.

Tohline: My passion for teaching often distracted me from the rigors of peer review. That's the simplest way to put it. I didn't publish enough or fast enough, so one day, they took it all away. I'd nearly completed *A Supercut of Supercuts*, but that didn't matter. The arts were not a focus at Missouri S&T, and the unspoken reality was that they needed to eliminate a tenure line for budgetary reasons. So that was that.

    I tried for two years to get back into higher ed, but most of the time I couldn't even get an interview. There just aren't enough positions. So now, by day, I work with spreadsheets, analyzing data and other recruitment-, retention-, and performance-related tasks in the Human Resources department of my local hospital. It suits me wonderfully. But my passion for film hasn't diminished a bit, and I do enjoy my new role as an independent scholar on the side. Of course, I'd come back to higher ed in a heartbeat if a space opened up.

MacDonald: You've made video essays of various kinds, some of them more or less typical (*Alfred Hitchcock's 39 Stairs* (2017) seems roughly similar to Kogonada's *Eyes of Hitchcock* (2014)…), but nothing that could predict *A Supercut of Supercuts*, a masterwork that required, I assume, enormous effort over several years. Was *Supercut* your Ph.D. thesis?

Tohline: No, my Ph.D. dissertation was a traditional 300-page written work on the history and aesthetics of reverse motion in cinema, from the 1890s to the present. I finished it in 2015. I realize now that the reverse motion project, like the supercut project, approaches film history cross-sectionally. It also embraces and analyzes any and every application of its chosen formal technique, from the avant-garde to music-video spectacle to special effects and so on.

I'd long been miffed by or suspicious of books in film studies that looked at one film per chapter and attempted to propose that a single close reading was somehow broadly applicable. That just didn't feel like enough data to me and I couldn't understand why more people hadn't modeled their work on Maureen Turim's study of flashbacks [*Flashbacks in Film: Memory & History* (Routledge, 1989)] or Will Wright's study of the Western [*Six Guns and Society: A Structural Study of the Western* (University of California, 1977)], both of which started with huge corpuses—seemingly the biggest they could assemble—and looked for patterns.

As I see it, a thorough search through the archive doesn't just deepen the foundations of one's analysis; typically, it demystifies the entire relationship between history, ideology, and art, forcing you to discard the kind of overwrought assumptions that arise from sticking too close to the canon or too close to one's comfort zone of interests—in other words, to an incomplete picture of how creativity works.

My dissertation advisor was Michael Gillespie, a scholar of Black cinema whom I deeply respect and a better writer than I'll ever be. At one point I pitched the idea of delivering at least some part of my reverse motion dissertation as a video, but there was no institutional support for that. No one had really done it yet. A decade later, that approach would get traction in some institutions, but there wasn't really a model or an appetite then.

Still, I managed to smuggle a 10-minute highlight reel of reverse motion, sorted by topic, into my defense. So already the supercut had a bit of a foothold in my work.

MacDonald: Chloé Galibert-Laîné was able to do a combined dissertation: a long textual essay plus two video essays: *Watching the Pain of Others* (2019) and *Forensickness* (2020). This is becoming less unusual. Also, just recently, Jason Mittell, Catherine Grant, and their colleagues have seen the video-essay journal, *[in] Transition*, admitted into peer-review status.

Tohline: Yet another thing for me to envy about Chloé Galibert-Laîné! It's devastating enough sometimes to just watch her work and wish I could do what she does, but I had no idea she'd done a hybrid dissertation involving TWO of her masterpieces. Maybe I should circle back to my dissertation with the aim of adapting it, now that I have almost ten years of distance on the material!

MacDonald: Do you still have that reverse-motion highlight reel? You indicate on your website that your video essay, *Re-Reading Time: The Emergence of Reverse Motion as a Narrative Technique in Post-Classical Cinema* (2021), began as a 2021 Popular Culture Association presentation, though it's available at your website. I assume that *Re-Reading Time* is an adaptation of that reel?

Also, there's the one-minute piece, "Reversible Divers Forever" in *The Essay Library Anthology, Vol. 2: TIME* (2021).

Tohline: I *do* still have that highlight reel, but it was hastily assembled on Windows Movie Maker (yikes!) and designed to play without sound. Still, many of the clips that I've been collecting since the beginning of the reverse-motion project did eventually also find their way into *Re-Reading Time*. The arguments in *Re-Reading Time* are a follow-up on the dissertation—a bonus chapter, if you will. And "Reversible Divers Forever" was just an expansion of the clips I used in the end credits of *Re-Reading Time*, with a couple stray poetic observations tossed in.

A further follow-up video paper, *The Palindrome, The Crystal Image, and Articulations of the Cinematic Code* (2022), is an attempt to give some sort of form to an abandoned chapter of my dissertation. For me, the process of making anything starts with gathering clips and other examples. Once those reach a critical mass, some sort of work necessarily results. But there are always leftover clips that perhaps find their way into later projects, if I'm lucky.

MacDonald: *Re-Reading Time* seems a transition piece between your early work and *A Supercut of Supercuts*, which feels not only more expansive, but more patient.

Tohline: I would've had the dissertation on reverse motion done a lot sooner than 2015, but I was also busy teaching and writing obsessively on Tumblr. One of the posts, from late 2013, asks "Why Not a Supercut of Supercuts?" [https://10oclockdottumblr.com/post/69270352197].

Which is to say that, long before I'd ever finalized anything on the reverse motion project, I was already getting started on what came next. I work—or, in some respects, fail to work—in the same way now. At the moment, I have at least a dozen projects running concurrently.

MacDonald: I accessed the link and looked at the Tumblr piece, *Movies in movies: A montage* (posted on December 7, 2013), which is super-dense and fun, and a valuable guide to supercutting—but I can't find your name on that project. The final credits say "edited by Clara Darko and Brutzelpretzel"—perhaps comic "pen names"? Also, the Tumblr piece is accompanied by an essay with links to many supercut creators and early predecessors; it seems a rough draft for *A Supercut of Supercuts*.

Tohline: My name isn't on *Movies in movies: A montage* because—unfortunately!—it's not my work. Clara Darko and Brutzelpretzel [Eusebio Poveda] are two of the best supercutters of the YouTube era. Darko's *Running in Movies* [2013] (on YouTube at youtu.be/GC5RPpHMOEU), which is an expansion of a Brutzelpretzel supercut from 2009, might be the most invigorating and rhythmically propulsive supercut I've ever seen. I wish I'd made it.

One of the best things about Tumblr is its hybridity. By nature, the platform doesn't by default encourage its users to create new things, but instead to collect, curate, and above all comment on existing work. You share things you like so that other people can see them too. But along the way, you also contribute commentary, explanations, marginalia, hashtags—to the point that Tumblr's most viral posts read like an endless receipt tape of different users each adding their own jokes or examples, upping the ante, or continuing a debate. In the case of my post "Why Not a Supercut of Supercuts?", I re-posted *Movies in movies: A montage* as a way of introducing the topic of the supercut with a lively contemporary example. What comes after that, a list of what a first-draft history of the supercut might include, was my own. And in that respect, you're right: it was the earliest rough draft of *A Supercut of Supercuts*.

To be honest, I'm not sure what first got me interested in supercuts. At the time (and still today), the moment I identify a "trend" in movies or art, my first impulse is to collect examples and turn them into a post. The trend could involve anything, from rotating sets (https://10oclockdot.tumblr.com/post/119190068685) [posted 2015], to artworks that are piles (https://10oclockdot.tumblr.com/post/139790553838) [posted 2016], to the use of the word "That" in movie titles (https://10oclockdot.tumblr.com/post/162978909605) [posted 2017]. I always told myself that these Tumblr posts could be first drafts of something else—that is, ways of dumping my first thoughts on something to make room for new thoughts. I could always come back later if the itch kept itching.

And sometimes I did come back. The reason I wrote a post on the supercut at all was that a few of the examples that immediately sprang to my mind seemed to be missing from all the popular lists of examples of the form. For instance, everyone who attempted a little pop history of the supercut online circa 2013 mentioned Christian Marclay, but they all left out Giuseppe Tornatore, whose *Cinema Paradiso* [1988] included a much earlier supercut-style montage. I couldn't figure out why.

After I'd made that first post, I walked away assuming that I had satisfied my own interest or irritation, at least enough to get the itch to stop. Then a few years later I stumbled across Agnès Varda's *You Have Beautiful Stairs, You Know* (1986). "Aha!" I thought. "So it was *Agnès Varda* who invented the supercut! *Now* I'm done." Shortly thereafter, somebody reminded me about *The Atomic Cafe* (1982). And after that, I couldn't put the project down.

At that early "re-ignition" stage, I imagined that the final video would run perhaps 45 minutes. Conceptually, I was stuck at the level of that Tumblr post— that is, that popular histories of the supercut had simply omitted some important examples and I would fill in the gaps. But that's the hazard of extrapolating from incomplete data. You assume that the waypoints you *are* aware of form a more-or-less neat line of development, and that any new landmarks you discover will also lie on that line. But when you research omnivorously, you cannot help but collide head-on with the fact that what you assumed was a line is not a line at all. History forms some other shape entirely, and it points in other directions, and you realize that many different forces have set it in motion.

Every bit of writing on the supercut up to that point, my own included, had introduced all sorts of incorrect assumptions based on our various incomplete understandings about how ideas travel through and manifest within a culture. Every time I thought I'd found the beginning, I'd find something earlier. Or every time I assumed that the supercut predominantly arose from one zone or another of moving-image history, examples would erupt from somewhere else—from *That's*

Entertainment! (1974) to sports documentaries to *Duck Soup* (1933) to Walter Ruttmann, and beyond. Thankfully I had help; other people in various disciplines had assembled collections to suit other projects that ended up being useful to this one. But no one had threaded all these collections together.

The subtitle of *A Supercut of Supercuts* reads, "Aesthetics, Histories, Databases." But at first, if there had been a subtitle at all, it would have just been "History"; I didn't have any sense that *many* tributaries of creativity fed into the supercut. I also didn't consider that the development of the supercut could not be understood as a phenomenon without considering its aesthetics, which is to say, how the form springs from, feeds, and fosters certain kinds of desire. And perhaps most embarrassing of all: I didn't even remotely imagine that the supercut sits within a network of broader cultural phenomena that fall under the umbrella of a database episteme.

This is all to say that I came to realize that the project had expanded far beyond a formal technique. It was about the relationship between humans and the archive (or database) of media created by the culture(s) around us. It was about the actions of search and retrieval and *within which contexts* and *to what ends* we apply those operations to what we've made.

On a more concrete level, part of the fun involved scanning through YouTube, UbuWeb, Kanopy, and other places to retrieve more examples. At one point, I had to obtain and translate "censor cards" for Oskar Kalbus' lost film *Rund um die Liebe* [1929] to determine what sort of clips Kalbus actually included in the film. Censor cards are detailed records of the scene-by-scene content of the film that were written by whatever office previewed films before they were passed for general release; my thanks to Michael Cowan for pointing me toward the German Federal Archive, which preserves them. Even with all that, I still left out major examples. After publishing *A Supercut of Supercuts*, I happened to watch Harun Farocki's *A Day in the Life of a Consumer* [2020]—and kicked myself.

Of the three years I spent on *A Supercut of Supercuts*, I estimate I spent over two years on research and maybe six months on outlining, writing, assembling visual materials, and editing. One of the hardest parts of the project was figuring out how to structure it so that I *could* include everything. If I sought to claim that this technique wasn't the reserve of a small number of inspired people, but instead that it bubbled up all over because it represents a new cultural mode of knowledge, I felt I had to "prove" that by putting so much on screen that it couldn't all be seen at once. *MacDonald: A Supercut of Supercuts* is remarkably broad-ranging, a research epic. But it's also full of subtleties easily overlooked because of its reach. To give a tiny instance from Part 1: when you're explaining that words derive their meaning from context, you focus on "green"—as a color (with "orange," "yellow," "blue," "purple"), as a slang word for "money" ("dough," "moolah," "cheddar," "scratch"), then as a metaphor for being young and inexperienced, then within the context of golf, and within the context of political parties. The sixth and seventh contexts are, at first, a bit puzzling. In the sixth, we read "Green," "Gaye," "Sledge," "Redding" and "Franklin"; it takes a moment to realize that these are all surnames of popular Soul singers during the 1950s and '60s: Al Green, Marvin Gaye, Percy Sledge, Otis Redding, and Aretha Franklin.

In the seventh and final context we read "Green," "Screen," "Scene," "Mean," and "Tohline." At first, the sequence seems to be about cinema, though "Mean" doesn't seem to fit. I finally deduced that you've probably struggled with the pronunciation of your surname; indeed, until I came across this set of "green" contexts, I'd assumed the pronunciation was "tow line"—not "te *leen*."

And as if this amusing realization weren't enough, once we do make sense of that final "green" sequence, we may remember, or are likely to notice next time we watch *A Supercut of Supercuts*, that you'd already prepared us for our discovery of the correct pronunciation of "Tohline." During your earlier discussion of syntagmatic/sequential structures and paradigmatic/associative structures, which sets the context for the "green" sequence—you mention such associative structures as "synonyms," "conceptual continua," "words formed from the same root," "or even words that sound alike."

Tohline: All I can say is *Thank You* for watching so closely. Over the years of making *A Supercut*, I slid in all sorts of details like that in the hope that an obsessively attentive viewer would find and enjoy them. You're the first person so far to mention that they stopped to solve that little "green" puzzle.

MacDonald: A more general question about your conclusion in *A Supercut* that the archival impulse is being replaced by the database impulse. At the moment, a person who runs a university archive has given me reason to think that they may house my papers—mostly letters to/from filmmakers, early drafts of essays.

Whether that means that my papers will be digitized is still an open question—indeed, I kind of doubt that the digitizing will ever happen. There will be several boxes of stuff on shelves somewhere and whatever database exists that "documents" my writing/interviewing career will not include this material. But even so, those documents will continue to be a resource for anyone crazy enough to want to see what's in the boxes.

And that's the whole point of my hoping that an archive will take my papers. You seem to see the database as a more complete and accessible record than the archive, but while the database *is* becoming much larger than the archive, it only *seems* more complete: the database will never know about much of what's in the archive. Indeed, aren't archives becoming *more* important, the more the database expands and provides an increasingly false sense of completeness and accessibility? As you suggest, the database sees everything as equally important, but isn't the abrogation of responsible scholarship a refusal to see, to understand, the full complexity of history?

Tohline: Reviewing my narration on the archive/database section in *A Supercut of Supercuts*, I have to agree that I committed a fairly serious error. I said, "the value of a database has everything to do with how *much* data is in it... like a concordance." But this is inconsistent with my claim a moment later that "the contents of a database are valued to the extent that they can be algorithmically instrumentalized to create profit models or means of social control."

I stand by that second statement, but I wonder now how I could've been so naïve as to believe that the first statement followed from it. It's as if I were watching another Saturn V liftoff in 1971 and predicted, "at this rate we'll all live on the moon in a few decades!"—extrapolating unreasonable conclusions because I failed to recognize that the Apollo program was an extension of the Cold War. Once the Cold War ended, funding disappeared.

Looking around online with the scant help of an increasingly buggy or outright broken Google search, I found writers suggesting that the U.S.'s National Archives have digitized somewhere between 4% and 10% of their holdings, though the public has access to less. Elsewhere I read an estimate that Google Books, which launched some two decades ago with a stated goal of digitizing *all* the world's books, has actually only digitized about 1% of them.

I have no way of knowing whether these estimates are too high or too low. But either way, it was never Google's goal to digitize all the world's books; their goal was to corner the market on full text search by producing a library *good enough* to muscle any competitors out of the way. And you don't have to digitize anywhere near every book to give the impression of an overwhelmingly complete collection, especially if the person searching is only trying to answer a question, rather than locate a *particular* book. The technology of the database ultimately serves a profit model, which means that when any digitizing project hits a point of diminishing returns, the promise of completeness can only survive in the form of a slogan.

I started using the Internet Archive around 2003. Before YouTube launched, my favorite place to watch videos online was the Prelinger Archives section. My entire master's thesis was made possible by Prelinger's upload of several dozen ephemeral films that Jam Handy made for Chevrolet in the 1930s. But from the very beginning, I remember their warnings about a "digital dark age," and I fear now that we might be living through a few additional overlapping dark ages. Digital records are not future-proof, especially when it comes to the short shelf lives of hard drives or file storage formats.

I'm able to view physical photo albums of ancestors who died before I was born, but if those albums had been photos on Facebook, I'd forever be unable to see them, since a dead person cannot accept a Friend request. And even when it comes to records on Facebook, Twitter, Instagram, or Tumblr that I do nominally have access to, none of these sites were designed to support information *retrieval*. Their search capabilities are, frankly, abysmal. And that's only a partial list. The point is: these sites don't care if they've built a good archive *or* a good database. They care that they can leverage your information and your patterns of behavior to keep you scrolling long enough to see one more ad, one more ad, one more ad.

Maybe I'm the one with the poor memory, but I vaguely recall reading a short essay about 20 years ago—probably on the Internet Archive or a related site—arguing that in this age of digitization of information, most young people (by now, most middle-aged people too) will inevitably adopt the false assumption that "if it hasn't been digitized, it doesn't exist." And that's another dark age: the assumed obsolescence of the archive. Because, as you say, the database never meant to ingest the entirety of the archive. Or, even if it did, it never meant to do so in the service of any public interest. I just tried to search Google for a dozen variations of that idea—if it's not digital, it's not knowledge—so that I could cite where I originally read it, and I got nothing back but junk. Proof, perhaps, that any hint of utopianism I once had was decidedly misplaced.

MacDonald: Earlier you mentioned your paper, *The Palindrome, The Crystal Image, and Articulations of the Cinematic Code* (2022). On your website you provide an abstract of the paper but also a video essay, *Sugar Water: Palindrome/Crystal Image/Articulations* (2022), which is a tour de force braiding of written and cinematic thinking. I'm confused. Are the paper and the video essay different works, or did you present the video essay as your conference "paper"?

Tohline: During the pandemic, conferences went entirely online for a little over two years. I probably shouldn't have taken that as an opportunity to commit to more work for myself, but I decided that if I was going to be presenting at conferences *over video* anyway, why fight that format with a traditional paper and awkwardly shared slides? Why not just create a video essay and present *that* during my 15-20-minute slot? It would allow me to show a lot more clips, integrate them into my presentation more gracefully, ensure that I wouldn't run out of time, and—most importantly—defeat the inherent ephemerality of a conference presentation. Eight or ten people saw that essay presented "live." Far more have been able to see it since. I wasn't the only person who had that idea, but now that most conferences are in person again, that moment seems to have passed. I miss it. Perhaps I should attempt to constitute some video essay panels going forward, where each presenter creates a new video essay to premiere at the conference.

MacDonald: Actually, in the past couple-three years I've attended numerous panels where video essays are shown instead of, or along with, written papers being read. I presented *Reading//Binging//Benning* (2018) by Chloé Galibert-Laîné and Kevin B. Lee, along with a bit of contextual information, as my "paper" at the SCMS conference this past March.

I'm especially grateful to you for making me aware of Michel Gondry's music video for the Cibo Matto song, "Sugar Water" (1996), of Bill Brand's *Moment* (1972)—and for referencing an old favorite: Martin Arnold's *Pièce Touchée* (1989).

Was your *Sugar Water* piece instigated by your enthusiasm for the Gondry video?

Tohline: Absolutely. Gondry was probably the first "structural" filmmaker I ever loved—I fell for his algorithmic playfulness in videos for "Star Guitar" [The Chemical Brothers, 2002], "Come Into My World" [Kylie Minogue, 2001] and "Sugar Water," long before I'd ever heard of people like Hollis Frampton or J. J. Murphy.

What made Gondry's video for "Sugar Water" different is that it kept coming back to me. The structure of that video, like the structure of *Print Generation*, causes a kind of productive befuddlement that can spark whole networks of ideas. I wish that more music videos received mainstream scholarly attention. For instance, the videos for Bonobo's "Kerala" [directed by Bison, 2016] and Russ Chimes' "Midnight Club EP" [directed by Saman Keshavarz, 2010] feel like notable contributions to ongoing structural investigations into how editing can alter perception or deal with images of thought.

And on a personal level—I just want to say that I'm delighted to have been able to share "Sugar Water" with you, because your work and your interviews over the years have pointed me toward so many films that I would never have otherwise encountered.

MacDonald: Thanks for saying so, Max.

You've worked in a range of ways, for different kinds of audiences. In your now four-part *Video Postcard* series, you direct each video essay to a particular friend or colleague in the video-essay world. Your "01. *About Time*" [2020, 9 minutes] is addressed to Keaton Wooden: "screenwriter, director, playwright, artist"; "02. *Drone Swarms*" [2020, 19 minutes], to Michael Baird, "monster/folklore expert, sculptor, art professor"; "03. *Better Homes through Editing*" [2021, 8 minutes], to film scholar and video essayist Ian Garwood, who invited other video essayists to quote or remix his essay/supercut *Mr. Grant's Dream House* [2020]. And "04. 'The Game You Don't Have to Play'" [2021, 8 minutes] is addressed to "fellow video essayist 'Sam,'" who was working on "a project that involved some ideas about games where you do nothing."

I see that it's silly of me not to have realized that video-essay scholar/practitioners have developed their own scholarly communities, parallel in function to the more formalized scholarly interest groups common to academic fields. Do you know Jason Mittell? Will DiGravio?

Tohline: I've been part of two online video essay communities for the last couple years, and if my varying levels of participation there have taught me anything, it's this: if you do a project collaboratively, you're guaranteed to get something good out of it, no matter how the project itself turns out.

Unless you're already an established creator, making videos for YouTube or Vimeo, all on your own, often makes you feel very lonely. You put in an incredible amount of time, and few people notice. However, if you make work within a community, the rest of the internet's reaction to what you made is nearly immaterial — the *making* connects you to other people.

Both of these video essayist communities are servers on a message board platform called Discord, and they go by the names "The Essay Library" and "Videographic Roundtable." The latter was started by Jason Mittell in early 2022 to coincide with the online symposium "Interrogating the Modes of Videographic Criticism." Twitter, which had been at best a tenuous hub for academic video essayists, was already losing steam, so it was truly fortunate that pretty much every major academic video essayist quickly joined — people like Johannes Binotto, Kevin B. Lee, Barbara Zecchi, Alan O'Leary, Katie Bird, Ariel Avissar, Catherine Grant, Ian Garwood, Evelyn Kreutzer, Cormac Donnelly, Will DiGravio, and many others who have appeared on Will's excellent Video Essay Podcast.

I can't imagine the community without the glue provided by people like Jason and Will — the work they make, the work they boost, the support they offer, the people they connect, and the opportunities and ways forward that they create.

The former Discord server, "The Essay Library," was started about a year earlier, in early 2021 I believe, by some YouTube-based video essayists who were not academics. I don't remember how I found my way there, but I'm so glad I did — for years, it's been a place to commune, share and discuss great video essays, offer feedback and ideas on developing work, and often just hang out, enjoy each other's company, and cultivate ideas on whatever topics have our attention on a given day.

I got on board early enough to be part of several collaborations they've done, like *The Essay Library Anthology Vol. 2* (2021), a collection of 60-second micro-essays on the theme of time. For that project I contributed "Reversible Divers Forever." The academic video-essay world and The Essay Library didn't have much overlap (besides me) at first, but some of the major members of "The Essay Library" have now emerged as important figures in the academic world, too — in particular Queline Meadows (aka kikikrazed) and Will Webb (aka indietrix), who just became two-thirds of the team that puts together the annual *Sight and Sound* poll of the best video essays of the year.

"The Essay Library" has also produced some great friends and a handful of my favorite video essayists in the YouTube space—folks like Will and Queline, as well as Sam Kern (a.k.a Afterthoughts, the addressee of my fourth video postcard), Josh Geist (a.k.a Dad Nuke, whose essay on *Winnie the Pooh* and Voltaire's *Candide* offers the only useful advice I've yet encountered on how to live in the twenty-first century), James DeLisio, max teeth, and quite a few others.

MacDonald: When I look at the chronology of your moving-image making, 2011 seems a crucial year. *The Mission of Art is to Reverse the Flow of Entropy* and *ICFADT*—two super-different films—seem to begin your immersion in projects that were inspired by 1960s-70s avant-garde film.

The Mission of Art is literally a test of patience. We need to pay very close attention, especially at first, to notice very subtle changes. As *The Mission* develops, movement gradually speeds up. When I was first looking at it, I was reminded of an early experience of Morgan Fisher's *Phi Phenomenon* (1968), when I drove 200 miles to Buffalo, frantically searched for the screening space, and got there just in time to watch an institutional clock with no second hand, for eleven minutes! Of course, the phi phenomenon is what allows us to see the motion in motion pictures, but here, Fisher figured he didn't have to play the usual game. He just framed the clock and turned the camera on; we can see that the clock hands *have* moved, but we can't see them move.

ICFADT ["I Can't Feel A Damn Thing"] also speeds up, but more dramatically. In your website description you explain that "A very personal, very painful event led me to make this found-footage structural film." I can't help wondering how what happened fed into the collage of borrowed images in that film—especially since *ICFADT* does seem to signal a change in your work. Forgive me, but the *film* seems to ask me to ask you what the painful event was.

Tohline: In *Circles of Confusion*, Hollis Frampton writes, "[t]here are ecstasies of restraint as well as ecstasies of abandon." That's a quote I go back to all the time. The official line on Frampton all these years has been that he was a structural filmmaker. But I've always looked up to him because he's one of the most lyrical filmmakers I know. The structure always asserts itself first, but within that structure, he deposits the most personal and beautiful memories, images, and thoughts. The film grain dancing to the grandmother's wedding bagpipes on the digital green in *Gloria!* (1979), for instance. It's as if he set up those structures precisely to overcome them— to give the lyrical something to splash out of and triumph over.

I mention this because embracing both the structural and the lyrical, both the restraint and the abandon, were of the greatest importance to me when I made *The Mission of Art* and *ICFADT*. The first one came about entirely by accident. I was rotating a jpeg in Windows Photo Viewer to try to create a desktop background when I noticed something bizarre: an encoding anomaly in that particular jpeg caused it to degrade every time I hit the rotate button. That's not supposed to happen. But the image was changing in intriguing ways, and I thought it might be fun to see just how "lossy" this process would get if I rotated it 100 or 1000 times.

So I spent a few weeks rotating the photo a complete revolution, copying it, rotating *that* copy a complete revolution, copying *it*, and so on. I eventually did this several thousand times. It became mind-numbing until it became meditative. When I was satisfied, I arranged the images in reverse order, and that's the film. Compared to the process of generating the images, the running time of 16 minutes 40 seconds (1000 seconds) is a breakneck trip through cosmic timescales. I just rewatched it for this interview, and I still love staring at it and almost spacing out. Combined with Mahler's "Symphony of a Thousand" emerging from a digital din, the restraint and the abandon both become ecstatic.

As for *ICFADT* (here: https://www.maxtohline.com/experimental-video#/icfadt/), I'm going to remain evasive, but it concerned my frustration about the limitations of my own emotional vocabulary. I struggled with empathy at the time, and I had a wake-up call regarding the gulf between the emotions that I *was* feeling and what I intellectually knew, based on everyone else around me, I *should have been* feeling. I had ignored this gulf my whole life, but suddenly I was frustrated to the point of anger, helplessness, and despair that no matter what I wanted to feel, I just couldn't feel it at that moment. So I grabbed a mix of images that were both meaningful and meaningless to me and wrote out an intentionally over-patterned, over-mathematical score as a way of, again, forcing the structural and the lyrical, restraint and abandon, into a grueling dialogue. I do not like watching *ICFADT*.

MacDonald: Your *The Sharply Interrupted Sky* series is elaborate. In each of the seven numbered sections of the piece, which were made from 2012 to 2015, you divide the frame into four quadrants, each with a different subject and kind of movement (in ".02" and ".06" you deviate a bit: in ".02" the bottom is a single image filling both quadrant spaces; in ".06" images are superimposed). On your website, you describe the series:

> A seven-part experimental video/ambient video series based on the idea of subdividing the screen into quadrants… and allowing the audience to 'edit' the video by choosing where to look. The name of the series, *The Sharply Interrupted Sky*, is meant to encapsulate both the aesthetics of the project as well as an interest in exploring the collisions or interfaces between the environment and the man-made.

I'm not sure how you mean "experimental video/ambient video."

Tohline: I was hoping to situate the series somewhere between the tradition of gallery video installation, where it's not so much expected that an art museum patron will watch the whole loop (and certainly not from the beginning), and composer Erik Satie's notion of "furniture music," at least as it was updated by Brian Eno for his Ambient series (especially "Ambient 1: Music for Airports"). That's my overly complicated way of reflecting on the fact that the interfaces between human-built things and the surrounding environment do not typically grab our attention on a day-to-day basis. Noticing the path of a railroad track next to a pond, or the geometric interaction between a hallway and the sun is, of course, the result of a human decision. But those decisions seem to sit in the background of our lives, ambient or latent features of the world around us—and we tend to treat them as givens rather than as choices.

The Sharply Interrupted Sky series was my attempt to offer a space to consider those interfaces as present *choices*, as *active* collisions. I chose the quadrant approach to reinforce the fact of abutment or collision in the organization of the frame.

MacDonald: My sense is that you shot all the imagery for parts ".01" to ".03" and from ".05" to ".07." But for the keystone section of the series, "04," you borrow from four films by canonical avant-garde filmmakers: Hollis Frampton (*Zorns Lemma*, 1970), Larry Gottheim (*Fog Line*, 1970), Peter Hutton (*Study of a River*, 1997), and Joyce Wieland (*Dripping Water*, 1969). Since I've been in touch, just this past month, with Gottheim and Bob Huot (the man walking with Marcia Steinbrecher and a dog during the final part of *Zorns Lemma*), I was especially moved to see ".04." The films of Gottheim, Frampton, Benning (and Huot), back 50-plus years, transformed my life.

Did you mean this moment in *Sky* series as an homage to filmmakers who inspired this extended moment of your evolution as a maker?

Tohline: I couldn't have put it better myself. These films changed my life, too. And they retain that power.

A small but important correction: the lower left quadrant comes not from Peter Hutton, but from Bruce Conner's *Crossroads* (1976), itself a found-footage film made up of military footage of the infamous Baker nuclear bomb test of July 25, 1946 at Bikini Atoll. It's hard to find a sharper interruption of the sky than that.

MacDonald: Ah, I'd imagined that image was from Hutton's *Study of a River* (1996).

Tohline: As you said, all the footage outside of part 4 was my own, but in the central "episode" I wanted to acknowledge that the mode of attention I just described had a profound and melancholy history. In fact, I have to think that my initial reaction to *Fog Line* inspired the whole series. I remember the first time I watched the Gottheim film, thinking, "that's an ugly framing. Why did he include power lines in the shot?" But of course, that's part of the piece. It not only provides the sly pun of the title; it gently urges us to "look" (that is, to *try* to look, to *imagine*) to the left and right of the frame, in the same way that the dissipating fog encourages us to look more deeply into the z-axis. Where are these lines coming from, who built them, where are they going?—it's an infrastructural and existential question that I also see in Wieland's *Dripping Water*, since that faucet presumably hooks up to a vast municipal water system outside the limits of the frame.

The z-axis is also a character in *Zorns Lemma*, where the walking figures (I never knew who they were!) disappear through their interaction with the environment. Is it a symbolic return to nature (whatever that means) or to home, away from the city; or is it instead a colonialist vector "into the West"? The snow obscures both readings, but that's beside the point: it's impossible to interpret this moment in the film *at all* without first engaging one's background beliefs about the relationship between humans and nature. Our interpretation, whatever it is, has the effect of pointing out those background beliefs.

As the "fog" of the bomb clears in the Conner quadrant, you might notice that it thickens in the *Fog Line* quadrant. I ran that clip backwards. In fact, there's a reverse-motion clip in every episode of *The Sharply Interrupted Sky*—and in practically every other video I've ever made, too.

MacDonald: In the mid-2010s, you seem to shift from working to contribute to the tradition of structural filmmaking into the more meta-fascinations of video essay and supercut. Of course, you don't entirely leave earlier interests behind: judging from 2020's MegaFavNumbers project: *10,112,358...*, you've continued to work with mathematics.

I wonder how *you* understand this general shift in your interests? It feels similar to what I've been going through these last few years.

Tohline: I don't think that my interests have changed. I just think that right now I don't have anything more to say in the space of "traditional" structural film. The same goes for reverse motion and supercuts, at least for now. But I still collect every example of reverse motion I see into a folder on my computer. Did you see the trailer for *The First Omen* (2024)? The entire thing plays in reverse! Cinematic temporality is a lifelong interest. If I ever realize that I have something more to say, I'll say it.

Happily, math is never going away. I have another project in the works that imposes algorithms on the movements of knights on infinite chessboards—ridiculous, I know. I was inspired by the same YouTube math community that did the MegaFavNumbers project you referred to ["*10,112,358*"]. There's another, which I hope will be more accessible, that proposes a new way of examining Oscar statistics to reveal ideological patterns in voting over time. Lots of spreadsheets have gone into making that so far. I'm also tinkering with a couple algorithmic projects that will end up resembling structural films, but which are responding to a more recent subdiscipline of videographic criticism known as parametric or deformative criticism.

The first of these projects is experimenting with removing individual frames from the ends of every shot of a feature film, one at a time, tracking how legibility progressively breaks down; the other uses Photoshop AI tools to digitally erase objects and actors according to an algorithm. Those will probably be somewhat less accessible, but I can't resist making them.

MacDonald: Last question, at least for now: in the long run, where do you see yourself headed, as a maker?

Tohline: I think I've been slowing down—not when it comes to ideas necessarily, but in terms of output. I've been trying to be more specifically intentional with what I'm making these days. I brainstorm freely, pre-write freely, research, collect, and watch freely, but when it comes to sitting down and doing the work of making, I can't get started nowadays unless I'm convinced of three things: that I'm still interested in making this contribution, that the work can connect to a given audience, and that it's worth their time to watch it. This is a high bar.

Do you also find it hard to make work that's simultaneously fascinating and gratifying to you, engaging to an audience, and useful to the world?

MacDonald: Sure. I wonder if I ever succeed!

Tohline: Exactly! Same! I've never had any difficulty finding topics, but there have been plenty of times when I absolutely ignored the audience, whether intentionally or by accident. Sometimes that's liberating, and sometimes that feeling of freedom connects with a small group of people. But most of the time, if the work is going to have any chance of making an impact, the audience must come first.

The YouTube essayists I've met on "The Essay Library" are always concerned with audience retention, because YouTube's analytics will tell you the exact second that most people stop watching your video. At a basic level I've been trying to learn from that, in terms of storytelling, pacing, and how to use music. In the YouTube space, it's all about first impressions: how a thumbnail and a title need to work together to get people to click, as well as how the first minute or so of a video needs to connect to the promise of both thumbnail and title, while deferring resolution of either and raising more ideas, questions, or mysteries for the viewer to think through with you.

Quite a few projects are sitting, not-quite-cracked, at that usefulness criterion. There's one that simultaneously explores copy-protection schemes on Blu-rays, fragmentation in editing, the history of destruction-for-profit, and (of all people) Paul Schrader. It's stalled at that usefulness checkpoint. I've got another that will take the form of a Benning film in miniature that throws a global wayfinding system called What3Words and Joyce Wieland's *Reason Over Passion* (1968, 1969) into a conversation about space, poetry, and ownership of the natural world. The list continues.

But everything still connects to my earlier interests: math, the database, structural film, found footage, editing, temporality… The trick is taking those interests out of the tinkerer's workshop and forcing them to anneal themselves to more urgent topics like politics, late capitalism, or climate change. Because without that concern with usefulness, the art world and academia alike become holding cells or distraction factories. I want to be able to look back at my future work, no matter how specific or weird it might be, and say, "I made that with empathy. I made that because I wanted to help."

A portion of this interview was published as a "web exclusive" in the Summer 2024 issue of *Cineaste*; and the entire interview, in *FFM (Found Footage Magazine)* no.10 (2024). Tohline's video essays are available at maxtohline.com.

Index

+ & – (Iimura), 74, 135

1 to 60 Seconds (Iimura), 135-36
8½ (Fellini), viii
9 Minutes (Riddle), 43
10 feet (Maciunas), 43
11 x 14 (Benning), 153
12 Angry Men (Lumet), 292
13 Lakes (Benning), 117, 152-56
24 Frames Per Second (Iimura), 135
365/360 (Clancy), 255
1000 Frames (Maciunas), 43

Abel, Richard, 208
A Critical Cinema (MacDonald), 67, 262
A Critical (Ninth) Assembling (Kostelanetz), 43
Act of Seeing With One's Own Eyes, The (Brakhage), 69-70, 280
A Dance Party in the Kingdom of Lilliput (Iimura), 135
A Day in the Life of a Consumer (Farocki), 298
Adorno, Theodor, 82
a girl & a gun (Deutsch), 218
Adventures in Perception (MacDonald), i
Agony and the Ecstasy, The (Reed), 218
Ahwesh, Peggy, 120
Akeley, Carl, 247
Akerman, Chantal, 70
Alfred Hitchcock's 39 Stairs (Tohline), 295
Allan, William, 111, 114
American Amateur Cinema League, 209
American Beauty (Mendes), 130
American Cinema, The (Sarris), ix, 69
American Dreams (Benning), 72, 113
American mystery (Clancy), 245
A Minstrel Show (San Francisco Mime Troupe), 110
Anderson, Keith, 79, 84
Anderson, Sherwood, x, 11, 169, 187, 194
André, Carl, 54, 263
Anemic Cinema (Duchamp), 72
Anger, Kenneth, 69, 120, 292
Angerame, Dominic, 213
Anker, Steve, 57
Animal Locomotion (Muybridge), 61
Ann Arbor Film Festival, 110, 113
Annenberg Cinematheque, 148
Annenberg School of Communications, 147
Anthology Film Archives, 262
Anthology of Concrete Poetry (Williams), 44
A Question of Silence (Gorris), 44

Ardolino, Emile, 169
A River Runs Through It (Redford), 198
Arnold, Martin, iii, 120
Arnulf Rainer (Kubelka), 70
Asch, Timothy, 101
Aspects of a Certain History (Knecht), 60
A Summer Place (Daves), 69, 169
A Supercut of Supercuts (Tohline), 217, 279, 290-307
Armstrong, Bess, 162
Art in Cinema, 69, 131, 147, 208-9
Arthur, Paul, 37
Artificial Light (Frampton), 262
Athens Film Festival, 292
Atomic Cafe, The (Rafferty/Loader), 71, 297
Atopia: No Man's Land (Clancy), 246-50
At Sea (Hutton), 223, 233
Aurora Picture Show, 213
Austen, Jane, viii
Automatic Moving Company, The (Bossetti), 219
Avissasr, Ariel, 302
Awful Backlash, The (Nelson), 111, 114
Ax Fight, The (Asch/Chagnon), 101

Badlands (Malick), 169
Baillie, Bruce, 211-12, 279, 292, 294
Baird, Michael, 301
Balagan, 213
Baldwin, Craig, 213
Baraka (Fricke), 224
Bard College, 109, 226, 234, 276
Barns Rushes (Gottheim), 32, 60, 62, 70, 278, 280-82, 285
Baron Franchetti, 80
Barrie, Diana, 44, 117
Barthes, Roland, 73, 241 249
Barton, Rebecca, 212
Basquiat (Schnabel), 218
Basquiat, Jean-Michel, 218
Battleship Potemkin, The (Eisenstein), 101, 128
Baur, John, 224
BBC, 87-88
Beautiful Movie (Huot), 265
Beaver Mountain Meditations (Bloom), 63
Beavers, Robert, 120
Bellavante, Ginia, 201
Belson, Jordan, 70, 120
Benning, James, 70, 72, 113, 117, 139, 152-56, 139, 152-56, 223-34, 291, 305, 307
Berliner, Alan, 57, 59, 62, 64, 71

Beverly Hills 90210 (TV), 172
Bierstadt, Albert, 224
Big "O", The (D'Avino), 72
Binghamton Babylon (MacDonald), v, 11
Bird, Katie, 302
Bechdel, Alison, 170
Binotto, Johannes, 302
Black and White Film (Huot), 263-65
Blakelock, Ralph Albert, 230
Blesk, Adam, 192
Blue, James, 57
Blood of the Beasts (Franju), 159
Bloom, Norman, 59, 63
Bleu Shut (Nelson), 109-10, 112-13
Blues (Gottheim), 33, 60, 281
Blues Brothers, The (Landis), 292
BNFS (Benning), 153
Bob's Elm (Kinne), 63
Bogan, Jim, 293
Borden, Lizzie, 72
Boswell, James, ix
Bourke-White, Margaret, 17, 275
Boyhood (Linklater), 171
Bradley, Ruth, 279, 292-94
Brakhage, Stan, 69-71, 120, 185, 214, 235, 280, 292
Brand, Bill, 59, 301
Brandon, Tom, 209
Breakfast Club, The (Hughes), 169
Breaking Bad (TV), 193, 202
Brecht, George, 43
Breer, Robert, 37, 120
Bromberg, Betsy, 222
Broughton, James, 69, 120, 292
Browning, Robert, viii
Bruegel the Elder, Pieter, 218
Bryant, Ed, 255
Budapest Portrait (Hutton), 228
Buñuel, Luis, 58
Burns, Ken, 234
Byron, viii

Cabaret (Fosse), 159
Caldwell, Erskine, iii, ix, 17-29, 159, 275
California School of the Arts, 110
California Institute of the Arts, 111, 234
Callenbach, Ernest, 212
Camper, Fred, 67-68, 71
Canadian Federation of Film Societies, 208
Canadian Film-makers' Distribution Centre, 123
Cannon, Terry, 109
Canyon Cinema, 32, 96, 108, 112, 123, 212
Canyon Cinema News, The, 112
Capote, Truman, ix
Case Research Lab, 57
Casting a Glance (Benning), 154
Castoro, Rosemarie, 263
Catcher in the Rye, The (Salinger), 169

Central New York Programmers Group, 57
Chagnon, Napoleon, 101
Chameleon (Shapiro), 60
Chan Is Missing (Wang), 44
Chants and Dances for Hand (Gottheim), 283
Chaplin, Charles, 173, 197
Chelsea Girls (Warhol), 69, 206
Chemical Brothers, The, 301
Chesterton, G. K., 3
Chicago Underground Film Festival, 210
Child, Abigail, 120
Childs, Lucinda, 262
Chimes, Russ, 301
Chodorov, Pip, 31
Chopra, Joyce, 280
Chronic (Reeves), 170
Chuck's Will's Widow (Brand), 59
Church, Frederic, 224
Cinema Paradiso (Tornatore), 297
CineCycle, 213
Cinema 16, 68, 131, 143, 146-47, 208-9, 213, 292
Cine-Matrix (Berliner), 62
Circles of Confusion (Frampton), 303
City Edition (Berliner), 71
Clancy, Flora, 240, 242-44, 250, 252-54
Clancy, Patrick, 57, 59, 62, 64, 72, 236-258
Clancy, Raphael, 240, 242-45, 250, 254
Clark, Kenneth, 261
Cleveland, David A., 230
Cloud Alphabet (Eder), 62
Clueless (Heckerling), 170, 176
Coen Brothers, 246
Cole, Thomas, 57, 63, 223-24, 226-27, 229, 233-34
Colgate University, 57, 237-38, 245, 275
Collective for Living Cinema, 57, 210
Comerio, Luca, 78-85
Conner, Bruce, iii, 70, 109, 120, 262, 279, 291-92, 294, 305
Conrad, Tony, 57, 120, 135
Corn (Gottheim), 60
Cowan, Michael, 298
Crane, Stephen, ix
Critical Essays on Erskine Caldwell (MacDonald), 17
Critical Mass (Frampton), 70
Cronin, Paul, vii, 143
Crossroads (Conner), 279, 305
Crossed Sequences (Eder), 62
Cruz, Wilson, 160
Cumming, Stephanie, 216-17
cummings, e. e., 11, 43
Curtis, David, ii

Dalí, Salvador, 58
Damned If You Don't (Friedrich), 71
Dances With Wolves (Costner), 224
Danes, Clare, 159-61, 172, 185

Dark of the Screen, The (Peterson), 37
Darko, Clara, 296
Das Lied von der Erde—Gustav Mahler (Gianikian/Lucchi), 82
Daves, Delmer, 169
D'Avino, Carmen, 72
Davis, Ron, 110
Days of Heaven (Malick), 169
Dazed and Confused (Linklater), 169
Dead Birds (Gardner), 101
de Antonio, Emile, 218
Degrassi High (TV), 173, 201-2
de Kooning, Willem, 267
DeLanda, Manuel, 118
Demeneÿ, George, 243
Demolition of a Wall (Lumière), 60
DePauw University, vii, 118, 276-77
Deren, Maya, i, 68, 120
Deseret (Benning), 154
de Sousa Dias, Susana, iii
Despotovich, Nada, 162
Deutsch, Gustav, 217-21
Diaro Africano (Gianikian/Lucchi), 79
Diary Film #4—1973 (Huot), 265
Diary 1974-75 (Huot), 265
Diary of a Young Girl, The (Frank), 162-64
Diary Painting No. 21 (Huot), 268
Dickens, Charles, 181, 193
DiGravio, Will, 302
Dirty Dancing (Ardolino), 162
Divinyls, 164, 167
Dickey, James, 17
Dickinson, Emily, ii, viii, 216-17
Doctor Faustus' Foot Fetish (Huot), 265
Donnelly, Cormac, 302
Dooley, Adam, 191
Doorway (Gottheim), 32
Dorsky, Nathaniel, 32, 130, 154, 224
Dos Passos, John, 220
Down the River (American Mutoscope), 231
Downton Abbey (TV), 193
Dripping Water (Wieland), 279, 305
Duchamp, Marcel, 58, 72, 253, 264
Duck Soup (McCarey), 298
Dulac, Germaine

Easy Rider (Hopper), 43
Eastman Kodak, 57, 232
Eder, Susan, 59, 62
Edison, Thomas, 59-61, 63, 81, 112, 225
Edvard Munch (Watkins), 87-88, 218
Eisenberg, Daniel, 57
Eisenstein, Sergei, 101, 159
Eliot, George, viii
El Valley Centro (Benning), 113, 153
Emerson, Ralph Waldo, 130
Emshwiller, Ed, 70
End After 9 (Maciunas), 43
Engler, Michael, 195

Eno, Brian, 304
Entanglement (Gottheim), x, 279-88
Entrance to Exit (Brecht), 43
Espelie, Erin, 223
Evening Land (Watkins), 88
Everson Museum, 57
Everywhere at Once (Berliner), 71
Expanded Cinema (Youngblood), 146
Experimental Television Center, 57
Exploded View, 213

Falkenberg, Paul, 218
Faller, Marion, 57, 59-62
Family Album (Berliner), 71
Farley, William, 71
Farocki, Harun, 298
Faulkner, William, 11, 28
Female Trouble (Waters), 170
Fennesz, Christian, 220
Field (Gehr), 65
Field Museum, 247
Filippo, Mary, 37
Film as a Subversive Art (Vogel), 142-150
Film Culture, 68
Film Guild, 208
Film in the Cities, 210
Film ist (Deutsch), 218-20
Fisher, Morgan, 71, 81, 109, 135, 303
Flaherty (Zimmermann/MacDonald), 87, 99
Flaherty, Robert, 101, 224
Flashbacks in Film (Turim), 295
Flicker, The (Conrad), 135, 159
Foery, Raymond, 11
Fog Line (Gottheim), 32, 60, 137, 279-83, 285, 288, 305
Foldes, Peter, 32
Forensickness (Galibert-Laîné), 295
Ford, John, 69, 224
Fort Apache (Ford), 224
Foucault, Michel, 73
Found Footage, 79, 307
Foundations of Cyclopean Perception (Julesz), 245
Four Shadows (Gottheim), 65, 282, 284-85
Frampton, Hollis, iii, 33, 27, 54, 57, 59-62, 65, 70-71, 109, 112, 120, 135, 237-38, 250-54, 261-66, 279, 283, 291, 301, 303, 305
France, Anatole, iv
Franklin, Aretha, 298
French Cinema (Abel), 208
Frensch Window (Lentini), 62
Fricke, Robert, 224
Frida (Taymor), 218
Friedrich, Su, 37, 72, 120, 170
Friends (TV), 160.
From the Pole to the Equator (Gianikian/Lucchi), 71, 79-85
Fung, Richard, 127
Fun Home (Bechdel), 170

Galibert-Laîné, Chloé, 291, 295, 301
Garden in the Machine, The (MacDonald), v, 137
Gardner, Robert, 101, 233
Garrison Films, 209
Garwood, Ian, 302
Gatten, David, 223
Gaye, Marvin, 298
Geary, David, 59
Gehman, Chris, 137
Gehr, Ernie, 54, 57, 59, 63, 65, 69-71, 120, 135, 262, 280, 282
General, The (Keaton), ii
Gently Down the Stream (Friedrich), 37, 71-72
Gerhard Richter Painting (Belz), 218
Geyrhalter, Nikolaus, 79
Gianikian, Yervant, 71, 79-85
Gibson, Michael Francis, 218
Gifford, Sanford, 224
Gill, Elizabeth, 196
Gillespie, Michael, 295
Girl with a Pearl Earring (Webber), 218
Gladiators, The (Watkins), 88
Glass, Philip, 84
Glide of Transparency (Bromberg), 223
Godmilow, Jill, 293
Go! Go! Go! (Menken), 294
Goelman, Jack, 147
Goldberg, David, 72
Gomez, Joseph A., 87
Gondry, Michel, 301
Gordon, Jill, 186, 188, 198
Gorris, Marlene, 44
Götterdämmerung (Wagner), 282-83, 287
Gottheim, Debbie, 12
Gottheim, Larry, iii, x, 11-14, 32-33, 57, 59-60, 62-63, 65, 69, 81, 120, 135, 137, 139, 224, 279-80, 291, 305
Gould, Symon, 208
Graff, Mark, 57
Grant, Catherine, 291, 295, 302
Grateful Dead, The, 174
Great Blondino, The (Nelson), 111
Greed (von Stroheim), 293
Green, Al, 298
Griffith, D. W., 54, 84
Group Theatre, 219
Gummersall, Devon, 160-1
Gunning, Tom, 211, 218, 223
Guy-Blaché, Alice, 81
Guzzetti, Alfred, 223

Hagiwara, Sakumi, 135, 137
Hagopian, John. V., 1, 6
Hapax Legomena (Frampton), 70
Halter, Ed, 233
Hamilton College, 31, 59, 117, 237, 276-77
Hammid, Alexander, 68
Hampshire College, i, 234

Hancox, Rick, 72
Handy, Jam, 300
Happy Mother's Day (Leacock/Chopra), 280
Harcourt, Peter, 130
Hardy, Thomas, viii
Harvard University, 234, 276
Harvey, Paul, 249
Hatfield, Juliana, 190
Hauling Toto Big (Nelson), 113
Haynes, Todd, iv
Heade, Martin Johnson, 224, 226, 228
Heckerling, Amy, 170
Hemingway, Ernest, iii, viii, ix, x, 1-8, 11, 17, 28, 168, 274-75
Herskowitz, Richard, 57, 87
Hettig, Edward, 261
Hicks, Timothy, 117
Hide and Seek (Friedrich), 170
Highway Landscape (Murphy), 32
Hill, Thomas, 224
Hitler, Adolf, 83
Hoberman, Jim, 57, 67-68, 71
Hocking, Ralph, 57
Hoffman, Hans, 267
Holland, Todd, 191
Holzman, Ernest, 182, 188
Holzman, Winnie, 160, 165, 182, 195, 198
Homeland (TV), 202
Honeymooners, The (TV), 159
Hopper, Edward, 216-20
Hopper, Josephine, 221
Horak, Jan-Christopher, 208
Horizons (Gottheim), 13, 62, 282
Huckleberry Finn (Twain), 168
Hughes, John, 169
Hundred Mile Radius (Niblock), 59
Hunger (Foldes), 32
Hunter College, 57, 59
Hunters, The (Marshall), 101
Huot, Jesse, 61
Huot, Robert, 54, 57, 59-62, 64-65, 91, 135, 237, 239, 261-69, 305
Hutton, Peter, 111, 117, 120, 139, 154, 222-35, 305
Hutton-De Wys, Manon, 226

IBM, 57
Ice (Murphy), 32
Idiolects, 37
Iimura, Taka, 54, 74, 120, 135-36
Images of Asian Music (Hutton), 231
Incense (Kano), 139
In Cold Blood (Capote), ix
Ink Spots, The, 286
In Marin County (Hutton), 223, 231
In Order Not to Be Here (Stratman), 294
In Progress (Small/Murphy), 32
In Titan's Goblet (Hutton), 226, 228-30
Into the Wild (Penn), 224

Intruder in the Dust (Faulkner), 17
Irwin, Tom, 162
Is/Land, The (Goldberg/Oblowitz), 72
It's a Wonderful Life (Capra), 167, 190

Jackson Pollock (Namuth/Falkenberg), 218
Jacobs, Ken, 57, 59, 65, 120, 262, 280
James Bond, 43
James, David, 37
James, Henry, ix
Jarmusch, Jim, 72
Johnson, Angelina, 11-13
Johnson, Blind Willie, 11, 13
Johnson, Samuel, ix
Jones, Bill T., 57
Joukei (Kano), 137
Journey, The (Watkins), 65, 72, 87-97
Joyce, James, viii
Julesz, Bela, 245
July '71 in San Francisco (Hutton), 231

Kahlo, Frida, 218
Kalbus, Oskar, 298
Kano, Shiho, 135, 137-41
Karagoez-Catalogo 9.5 (Gianikian/Lucchi), 71, 81-82
Katims, Jason, 177, 194
Kazan, Elia, 169
Keaton, Buster, ii, 69
Keene, Elodie, 198-99
Keller, Marjorie, 37
Kensett, John Frederick, 224
Kern, Sam, 303
Keshavarz, Saman, 301
Kid, The (Chaplin), 159, 173, 197
Kiernan, Joanna, 118
Kiesler, Friedrich, 208
King Kong (Cooper/Schoedsack), ii
Kinne, Carol, 57, 59, 63, 261, 266, 267
Kiri (Sakumi), 137
Kirkland College, 57, 59
Kirkland, Jack, 17
Knecht, John, 57, 59-60, 223
Kobori, Enshū, 138
Kogonada, 291, 295
Kolosov, Alexander, 96
Kostelanetz, Richard, 43
Koyaanisqatsi (Reggio), 72, 84, 224, 294
Kramer, Edith, 112
Kramer, Richard, 192
Kreutzer, Evelyn, 302
Kruger, Barbara, 44
Kubelka, Peter, 70, 83, 120
Kuchar, George, iii, 71, 109, 120
Kuchar, Mike, 71, 120
Kuleshov, Lev, 101
Kupferman, Myer, 279

Lacan, Jacques, 118
Lagomarsino, Ron, 186
Landau, Saul, 110
Langer, A. J., 160-61
Landscape (for Manon), 222, 226-29
Lane, Fitz Henry, 224, 226, 228
L'arrivée d'un train en gare de La Ciotat (Lumière), 287
Last of the Mohicans, The (Mann), 224
Lawrence, T. E., 80
Leacock, Ricky, 280
Leaves of Grass (Whitman), 94
Lee, Kevin B., 291, 301-2
Léger, Fernand, 58
Lemon (Frampton), 33, 264
Lentini, Lorna, 59, 62
Less (Frampton), 264
Leto, Jared, 159-60, 162
Library of Congress, 225
Lieberman, Charles, 188
Life Goes On (TV), 171-72
Life of Samuel Johnson, The (Boswell), ix
Light Cone, 123, 210
Light in August (Faulkner), 17
Light Industry, 213
Line Describing a Cone (McCall), v, 117, 135
Linklater, Richard, 169
Lippard, Lucy, 64
Living Single (TV), 160
Loader, Jayne, 71
Local Conventions (Faller), 62
Lockhart, Sharon, 139, 171, 223-24
Lodz Symphony (Hutton), 228
London Film Society, 69
Los (Benning), 113, 153
Lozano, Lee, 262
Loznitsa, Sergei, 79
Lucchi, Angela Ricci, 71, 79-85
Lubitsch, Ernst, 69
Lumière Brothers, 60-61, 63, 81, 140, 225
Lust for Life (Minnelli), 218
Lye, Len, 72

Macaulay, David, 242
Maciunas, George, 43
MacDonald, Ian, 137-38
Mad About You (TV), 160.
Mahler, Gustav, 82, 304
Magical Death (Asch/Chagnon), 101
Magnificent Seven, The (Sturges), viii
Majewski, Lech, 218
Makavejev, Dušan, 145
Making of Americans, The (Stein), 169
Malcolm X, 183
Malick, Terrence, 169
Mangolte, Babette, 70, 224
Man Ray, 58
Manual of Arms (Frampton), 263
Marclay, Christian, 297

Marey, Étienne-Jules, 243, 264
Markopoulos, Gregory, 120
Marshall, John, 70, 101
Martin (TV), 160
Martin, Katy, 261
MA: Space/Time in the Garden of Ryoan-Ji (Iimura), 136
Masters of Sex (TV), 202
Materialaktionsfilme (Muehl), 144
May, Charles E., 11
Mayakovsky, Vladimir, 244
McCall, Anthony, v, 116, 135
McElhatten, Mark, 57, 128
McElwee, Ross, 72
McKeller, Danica, 173
Meadows, Queline, 302-3
Mekas, Jonas, 62, 67, 70, 81, 120, 262
Méliès, Georges, 44, 54, 81, 84, 140
Mendes, Sam, 130
Menken, Marie, 279, 291, 294
Metzker, Ray K., 54
Michelangelo, 218
Michelson, Annette, 37, 262
Microscope Gallery, 213
Mierzwa, Adam, 59, 63
Mill and the Cross, The (Majewski), 218
Millennium Film Workshop, 210
Miller, Angela, 224
Mills College, 110
Milstead, Harris Glenn (Divine), 267
Milton, John, viii
Mineo, Sal, 169
Minogue, Kylie, 301
Mira, Mira 13's (Huot), 261
Mittell, Jason, 291, 295, 302
Mnemosyne Mother of Muses (Gottheim), 285
Models (Iimura), 54
Moment (Brand), 301
Monkey Dream (Geary), 59
Montaigne, Michel de, i
Moran, Thomas, 224
Moses, Senta, 192
Moss, Robb, 223
Mouches Volantes (Gottheim), iv, 11-14, 282, 285-86
Movie Stills (Murphy), 60, 63
Muehl, Otto, 144
Mulroney, Brian, 95
Mulvey, Laura, 70, 73, 120
Munson-Williams-Proctor Art Institute, 57-58
Murphy, J. J., iii, 31-35, 54, 59-60, 63, 81, 109, 135, 279, 291, 294, 301
Museum of Modern Art, 123
Musical Poster No. 1 (Lye), 72
Mussolini, Benito, 82
Muybridge, Eadweard, 54, 60-63, 264
My So-Called Life, 158-204
Myth in the Electric Age (Berliner), 71

Naaman, Dorit, 127
Naked Spaces (Trinh), 83, 101-5
Namuth, Hans, 218
Nanook of the North (Flaherty), 101, 224
National Film Board of Canada, 65, 87, 212
Natural History (Berliner), 71
Nature and Culture (Novak), 224
Near the Big Chakra (Severson), 112
Nelson, Gunvor, 110, 113, 120
Nelson, Oona, 113
Nelson, Robert, 81, 109-14, 118, 120
Neshat, Shirin, iii
New American Cinema, 69, 117, 262
New York Film Festival, 143, 147, 210
New York Film-Makers' Cooperative, 123, 262, 264
New York, Near Sleep, for Saskia (Hutton), 228
New York Portrait, Part I (Hutton), 226, 228-29
New York Portrait, Part II (Hutton), 222, 226, 228
New York Portrait, Part II (Hutton), 228
New York University, 76
Niblock, Phil, 59-60
Nichols, Mike, 187
No Country for Old Men (Coen Brothers), 246
Norman, Ellen, 197
Norris, Patrick R., 197
North on Evers (Benning), 154
Northwest Film Forum, 210
Nouvelles Impressions D'Albuquerque (Clancy), 250
Novak, Barbara, 224
Nova Scotia College of Art and Design, 44
Nude, The (Clark), 261
Nu Descendant Un Escalier (Duchamp), 46
Nude Descending the Stairs (Huot), 263-65

Oberlin College, 279
Oblowitz, Michael, 72
O'Connor, Patricia, 223
O Dem Watermelons (Nelson), 109-11
Odessa, Devon, 160-1
O'Grady, Gerald, 57
Oh China Oh (Thornton), 72
Oh! Uomo (Gianikian/Lucchi), 79
O'Leary, Alan, 302
Olmsted, Frederic Law, 139
Ondine, 206
One Way Boogie Woogie (Benning), 153
One Year (Huot), 60, 265
Ono, Yoko, 120, 262
Orff, Carl, 161
Other Cinema, 213
Our African Journey (Kubelka), 83
Our Town (Wilder), 198

Painters Painting (de Antonio), 218
Pakula, Alan J., 65

Palacz, Jerzy, 217-18
Paper Film (Berliner), 64
Parks, Rosa, 286
Pasadena Filmforum, 109
Pea Conception (Lentini), 62
Peliculas (Clancy), 64, 72, 236, 238-40
Perry, Jeff, 195-96
Peterson, Sidney, 37, 69, 120
Peter Watkins (Gomez), 87
Phi Phenomenon (Fisher), 303
Photo-Film-Strip (Berliner), 62
Picking Oranges (Edison), 113
Pierce, Leighton, 120, 137, 224
Pink Flamingos (Waters), 267
Pink Flat (Lockhart), 171
Pink Panther, 43
Pitt, Brad, 198
Piznarski, Mark, 188, 194, 198
Place, Mary Kay, 174
Plastic Haircut (Nelson), 110
Pleasure of the Text, The (Barthes), 241 249
Poetic Justice (Frampton), 70
Pollock (Harris), 218
Pollock, Jackson, 218, 265
Poons, Larry, 262
Porter, Edwin, 54, 81
Porter, John, 207, 213-14
Portrait of the Young Man (Rodakiewicz), 225
Potter, Sally, 70, 217
Poveda, Eusebio, 296
Powell, Earl A., 226
Prelude (Wordsworth), 94
Pressman, Adele, 223
Pressman, Ellen, 177
Pretty in Pink (Hughes), 169
Prelinger, Rick, 300
Prigionieri della Guerra (Gianikian/Lucchi), 79
Prince Rupert Drops (Frampton), 262
Print Generation (Murphy), 30-31, 33-34, 54, 135, 279, 294, 301
Privilege (Watkins), 88-89
Projections Instructions (Fisher), 135
Psycho (Hitchcock), 43
PULSA, 238
Punishment Park (Watkins), 87-88

Radul, Judy, 123
Rafferty, Kevin, 71
Rafferty, Pierce, 71
Railroad Journey, The (Schivelbusch), 287
Rainer, Yvonne, 70, 118, 120, 262
Random House, 144, 146
Ray, Nicholas, 57, 169
Raynal, Jackie, 70, 118
Reagan, Ronald, 95
Reason Over Passion (Wieland), 307
Reassemblages (Trinh), 99-102, 104-6
Rebel Without a Cause (Ray), 169
Redding, Otis, 298

Rees, Roger, 177
Reeves, Jennifer Todd, 170
Reich, Steve, 84, 110
Reggio, Godfrey, 72, 224
Reilly, Terry, 84
R.E.M., 166-67
Reinert, Otto, 7
Renan, Sheldon, 70
Re-Reading Time (Tohline), 295
Rice, Ron, 68
Richie, Donald, 135-37
Richter, Hans, 58
Riddle, James, 43
Riddles of the Sphinx (Mulve/Woolen), 159
Riefenstahl, Leni, 83
Riley, Terry, 294
Ringwald, Molly, 169
River in the Catskills (Wallach), 227
Robert Flaherty Film Seminar, 57, 87, 99, 292
Rocambole (Comiero), 81
Rocking Chair (Kano), 137-40
Rodakiewicz, Henwar, 225
Rodowick, David, 223
Rogers, Will, 113
Rolls: 1971 (Huot), 54, 60, 62, 265
Roosevelt, Theodore, 254
Rose, Peter, 72
Rosecolored Flower (Kano), 139, 141
Ross, Ken, 57
Roush, Leslie M., 283
Roud, Richard, 143, 147
Rowsome Jr., Frank, 43
Rund um die Liebe (Kalbus), 298
Ruttmann, Walter, 298
Ryder, Albert Pinkham, 267

Samsara (Fricke), 224
Sandberg, Carl, 279
Sandia Parallax (Clancy), 239
San Francisco Art Institute, 111, 226
San Francisco Cinematheque, 112
San Francisco Mime Troupe, 110
San Francisco Museum of Art, 69, 209
Sarris, Andrew, ii, ix, 69
Satie, Erik, 304
Savage, Fred, 172
Schemes and Variations (Williams), 44
Schivelbusch, Wolfgang, 287
Schimek, Hanna, 217, 219-21
Schmidlin, Rick, 293
Schneemann, Carolee, 120, 135, 262
Schrader, Paul, 307
Schweizer, Paul, D., 63
Scratch (Huot), 239
Screen Writings (MacDonald), 43
Scribner Jr., Charles, 7-8
Sculpture Space, 57,59
Searchers, The (Ford), 224
Secondary Currents (Rose), 72

Selected Shorter Poems 1950-1970 (Williams), 44
Serene Velocity (Gehr), 54, 63, 69, 135, 280
Seventies People, The (Watkins), 88
Seven Walls for Dziga Vertov (Clancy), 238
Severson, Anne, 111
Shadow of a Doubt (Hitchcock), 159
Shakespeare, William, viii
Shapiro, Owen, 57, 59-60
Sharply Interrupted Sky, The (Tohline), 279, 304-5
Sharits, Paul, 43, 57, 120
Sheeler, Charles, 235
Sherman, David, 212
Sherman's March (McElwee), 72
Shiki Soku Ze Kū (Toshio), 137
Shirley—Visions of Reality (Deutsch), 217-21
Shoot for the Contents (Trinh), 104-5
Sight and Sound, 302
Sink or Swim (Friedrich), 71
Sitney, P. Adams, ii, 70, 112, 135, 146, 294
Six Guns and Society (Wright), 295
Sixteen Candles (Hughes), 169
Sixteen Studies from Vegetable Locomotion (Faller/Frampton), 61
Skagafjördur (Hutton), 223, 228
Skin of Our Teeth, The (Wilder), 220
Sky Calendar (Eder), 62
Sky Blue Water Light Sign (Murphy), 33
Sky on Location, The (Mangolte), 224
Slap Shot (Hill), 65
Sledge, Percy, 298
Small, Ed, 32
Smillie, Sam, 96
Smith, Gavin, 128
Smith, Harry, 279, 294
Smith, Jack, 120
Smithson, Robert, 154
Sniadecki, J.P., 291
Snow, Michael, 70-72, 118, 120, 141, 262-63, 291
Soft Rain (Jacobs), 280
SOGOBI (Benning), 113, 153
So Is This (Snow), 72
Solomon, Phil, 57, 120
Sonbert, Warren, 120
Sopranos, The (TV), 185, 202
Southwest Arts Media Project, 109
Spacy (Takashi), 137
Spelling, Aaron, 172
Spenser, Edmund, viii
Spiral Jetty (Smithson), 154
Spiritmatters (Rose), 72
Spitalny, Phil, 282-83
Splendor in the Grass (Kazan), 169, 220
Spray (Huot), 239
Squeaky Wheel, 210
Stagecoach (Ford), 224
Standard Gauge (Fisher), 71

Stanford, Leland, 241
Star, Darren, 172
State Borders (Clancy), 240-46
Stauffacher, Frank, 147, 208-9
Steele, Lisa, 127
Steele, Nick, 276-77
Stein, Gertrude, ix, 11, 18, 28, 169
Steinbrecher, Marcia, 60, 264, 305
Steiner, Ralph, 225
Stella, Frank, 54
Sterile Cuckoo, The (Pakula), 65
Stern, Daniel, 172
Still (Kano), 137
Straits of Magellan (Huot), 60
Strand, Chick, 212
Stranger Than Paradise (Jarmusch), 72
Stratman, Deborah, 279, 294
Study of a River (Hutton), 226, 231, 305
Swarthmore, 32
Suite California, Stops and Passes (Nelson), 112-13
Summerwind (Dorsky), 32
Sundays and Cybele (Bourguignon), 69
SUNY Binghamton, i, v, 58, 65, 69, 279
SUNY Buffalo, 59
SUNY Purchase, 234
Super-8 Diary—1979 (Huot), 65, 265
Surname Viet Given Name Nam (Trinh), 103-5, 293
Suspended Animation (Mierzwa), 59, 63
Su Tutte le vetta è pace (Gianikian/Lucchi), 79
Svend Asmussen Quartet, 286
Syracuse University, 59, 65

Tafakory, Maryam, 291
Tamblyn, Christine, 256
Ten Hundred Inch Radii (Niblock), 60
Ten Skies (Benning), 153
Tharp, Twyla, 61, 262, 265
That's Entertainment! (Haley Jr.), 297-98
Third One-Year Movie—1972 (Huot), 60, 265
Thoreau, Henry David, iv, 119, 154
Thornton, Leslie, 37, 72
Ties That Bind, The (Friedrich), 71-72
Thelma & Louise (Scott), 198
Three Landscapes (Hutton), 228, 232-33
Three Lives (Stein), 169
Thursday, August 28th, 1952 6 a.m., New York (Deutsch), 218
Time and Tide (Hutton), 223, 226, 231-32
Tohline, Max, v, x, 217, 279, 290-307
Time (Sakumi), 137
Tomiyama, Katsue, 135
Tomlin, Bradler Walker, 267
Tom, Tom, the Piper's Son (Jacobs), 81
Tornatore, Giuseppe, 297
Toronto Film Festival, 79
Tree of Knowledge (Gottheim), 282, 285
Trap, The (Watkins), 87-88

Tribute (Farley), 71
Trinh T. Minh-ha, 83, 98-106, 120, 293
Triskellion a.k.a. Michael flank *Divine* (Huot), 267
True Detective (TV), 202
Tulare Road (Benning), 233
Turim, Maureen, 295
Turning Torso Drawdown (Huot), 62, 261
Twain, Mark, 168
Two Rivers (Hutton), 231

Ullrich, Keith, 79, 84
UnionDocs, 210
University of Florida, viii, 69, 275
University of Wisconsin-Milwaukee, 111, 117
U.S.A. (Dos Passos), 220
Ustarroz, César, 79
Utica University, viii, 32, 135, 237, 245, 247, 276, 280

Vancouver Film Society, 131, 209
van Eyck, Jan, 261
Van Gogh, Vincent, 218
Varda, Agnès, 298
Varela, Willie, 109
Vassar College, 57
Vasulka, Steina, 57
Vasulka, Woody, 57
Vermeer, Johannes, 218
View from 'Comealot', The (Lentini), 62
Venice Film Festival, 82
Venus of Willendorf, 267
Verse by the Side of the Road, The (Rowsome), 43
Vertov, Dziga, 101, 244
Villa, Pancho, 249
Village Voice, The, 68
Vincent, E. Duke, 172
Visionary Cinema (Sitney), 146
Vogel, Amos, ii, 37, 69, 142-150, 208, 291
Vogel, Marcia, 143, 147, 208
Voluptuous Sleep (Bromberg), 223
von Helmholtz, Hermann, 11
von Stroheim, Erich, 293

Wagner, Richard, 282-83
Walden (Mekas), 81
Walden, W. G. Snuffy, 161-62, 172, 181-82, 185-86
Wallach, Alan, 227
Wang, Wayne, 44
War Game, The (Watkins), 87-89
Warhol, Andy, 120, 206, 253, 262
Watching the Pain of Others (Galibert-Laîné), 295
Waters, John, iii, 71, 170, 267
Waterworx (Hancox), 72
Wavelength (Snow), 135, 141
Weidenfeld, George, 143-44, 148

Walden (Thoreau), 154
Watkins, Peter, iii, 65, 87-97
Webb, Will, 302-3
Wednesday, 28 August 1957, 6 p.m., Pacific Palisades (Deutsch), 218
Weill, Claudia, 192
Weinschreider, Gregg, 261
Weisman, Phil, 57
Welch, Lew, 111
Wells College, 57
Western Motel and *Morning Sun* (Deutsch), 218
What Dreams May Come (Ward), 224
What Farocki Taught (Godmilow), 293
White Caligraphy (Iimura), 135
White Tablecloth (Kano), 139-40
Whitman, Walt, 94
Whitney Brothers, 68-69, 120
Widmer, Gwen, 255-56
Wieland, Joyce, 120, 262, 279, 291, 305, 307
Wilder, Thornton, 198, 220
Wiley, Chuck, 111-12
Wiley, William T., 111
Wilhodt, Lisa, 162
Williams, Clem, viii
Williams, Emmett, 43-54, 237, 240
Williams, John, 279
Winant, Scott, 161, 179, 182
Window Water Baby Moving (Brakhage), 159
Winesburg, Ohio (Anderson), x, 169, 187, 194
Wire, The (TV), 202
Wolfe, Thomas, 17
Wollen, Peter, 70, 118, 120
Women Make Movies, 123
Wonder Years, The (TV), 172-73
Wooden, Keaton, 301
Wordsworth, William, viii, 94
WordMovieFluxFilm (Sharits), 43
Working Girl (Nichols), 187
Working Girls (Borden), 72
World of Suzie Wong, The, 69
Wright, Richard, ix, 11
Wright, Will, 295
Wuthering Heights (Brontë), 46

Xerox works (Lentini), 62

Yale University, 238, 279
You Have Beautiful Stairs, You Know (Varda), 297
Young, Neil, 276
Youngblood, Gene, 146

Zecchi, Barbara, 302
Zimmermann, Patricia, 57, 99, 209, 223
Zorns Lemma (Frampton), 54, 60, 62, 109, 112, 257, 264-66, 279, 283, 305

www.ingramcontent.com/pod-product-compliance
Lightning Source LLC
Chambersburg PA
CBHW070127080526
44586CB00015B/1591